Plunderphonics, 'Pataphysics & Pop Mechanics

an introduction to
musique actuelle

by
Andrew Jones

First published in 1995 by SAF Publishing Ltd.
SAF Publishing Ltd.
12 Conway Gardens,
Wembley, Middx. HA9 8TR
ENGLAND
TEL/FAX: 0181 904 6263

The right of Andrew Jones to be identified as the author of this work has been asserted by him in accordance with the Copyright, Design and Patents Act, 1988.

ISBN 0 946719 152

This book was written with the assistance of the Canada Council For the Arts.

Printed in England by Redwood Books, Trowbridge, Wiltshire.

Wholesale and Book Trade Distribution:
UK & Europe: Airlift Book Co, 26-28 Eden Grove, London. N7 8EF
Tel: 0171-607 5792 Fax: 0171-607 6714
USA: Last Gasp, 777 Florida Street, San Francisco, CA 94110. USA.
Tel: 415 824 6636 Fax: 415 824 1836
Canada: Marginal Distribution, Unit 103, 277 George Street North, Peterborough, Ontario, Canada K9J 3G9. Tel/Fax: 705 745 2326

For Marisa
(Docendo discimus)

ACKNOWLEDGEMENTS

The first book of any new field is bound to take a while. Six years, to be precise. Six years from the initial idea to do a book on an exhilarating new music I discovered taking shape in small-town Québec, five from the day my wife – who always believed I had a book in me – exhorted me to go for the brass ring and write it, and four from the first interview. Along the way I have gathered quite a few people to thank.

The writing of this book would not have been possible without the support of The Canada Council of the Arts, and I am indebted to Sylvie Bernier of the Explorations Program, the jury that selected the work, and the three individuals who championed my work: Alan Conter, Ken Druker and Gina Brown. Many of the chapters herein were drawn from work previously published in *Option* magazine. For their kind permission to use them [as well as the keen interest in running features on the likes of After Dinner, Amy Denio and Fat in the first place], I would like to thank Scott Becker, Mark Kemp and Richie Unterberger. And for enthusiastically backing my manuscript and bringing it to publication, I would like to thank my editors at SAF Publishing, Mick Fish and Dave Hallbery.

For acquiring recorded and print materials, I would like to acknowledge the help of Jean-Pierre Leduc at Fusion III in Montréal, Masanori Akashi at Wave/Eva in Tokyo, Elisabeth Schuler at RecRec in Zürich, Joyce Nalewijk at Cuneiform in Washington, Michael Dorf at Knitting Factory Works in New York, The British Sound Archive in London, David Ryan at the CBC's *Brave New Waves* in Montréal, Fabrizio Gilardino of *Musiche*, as well as fellow *mélomanes* Marc Chénard and Ken Doolittle. For setting up interviews, Michel Levasseur of Les Productions Plateforme in Victoriaville and Marie Marais in Montréal have been invaluable. Thanks as well go to Patrick Darby of Traquen'Art, Barbara Scales of Latitude 45, Jean Piché and René Girardin of Montréal Musiques Actuelles/New Music America 1990, Maryse Métevier, Erich Keefe and Nod Knowles.

For spiritual guidance, constructive criticism and London accommodations, Chris Cutler. For the bandage and cup of tea, Lesley Hayward. For the grammar lesson, Paul Haines. For the best food in Victoriaville, Village Mynokos. For inspiring the nifty title, Oswald, Raymond Queneau, and Sergei Kuryokhin. For a very timely suggestion, Steve Feigenbaum. [Dinner is on me the next time I'm in Washington.] And for patience and unconditional support throughout the project, my wife Marisa and our two sons, Giancarlo and Luca.

Finally, I would like to extend heartfelt thanks to all the musicians I spoke with in preparing *Plunderphonics, 'Pataphysics & Pop Mechanics*. Your music is the true reason why this book is here, and you deserve both a wider audience and a place in the history books. *A luta continua.*

CONTENTS

About the Author

Andrew Jones is a 31-year old lapsed cellist, music writer and freelance journalist based in Montréal, Québec. Musique actuelle has been his "beat" since the early '80s, after seeing Skeleton Crew live, hearing Robert Wyatt's *Rock Bottom* and buying *The Recommended Records Sampler*, he began writing features for *Option*, *Jazziz*, *Connoisseur* and *Coda* magazines. He has been a contributing editor to *Option* since 1988. During his three year tenure as the music editor for Montreal's leading English newsweekly, *The Mirror*, he built considerable experience and knowledge in the fields of jazz, classical and new improvised music; which he now covers for the Montréal *Gazette*. He currently works as an editor for the Montréal-based book packager St-Remy Press, and lives in Westmount, Quebec with his wife, Marisa and their two boys, Giancarlo and Luca. *Plunderphonics, 'Pataphysics & Pop Mechanics* is his first book.

Photographic Acknowledgments

Chris Cutler ....Unknown
Fred Frith..Sylvain Lafleur
Ferdinand Richard ....Unknown
Heiner Goebbels..Erika Fernschild
Willem Breuker ....Evelien Schoondergang
Henry Threadgill..Jules Allen
Sergei Kuryokhin ....Andrey V. Ussov
Rova Saxophone Quartet ....Peeter Vilms
Amy Denio ....Helena Rogers
Lindsay Cooper ....Val Wilmer
Zeena Parkins ....Sylvain Lafleur
Tenko..Nobuyoshi Araki
John Oswald ....Michael Reinhardt
John Zorn..Sylvain Lafleur
Charles Hayward ....Jean-Elie Battista
Roberto Musci & Giovanni Venosta.. Alexander Laurenzo
Les Granules..Pierre Crépõ
Fat ....Jiry Volek
Bruire..Yves Dubé
Justine..Suzanne Girard
The Residents ....Henrik Kam
Kalahari Surfers..Craig Mathew
After Dinner ....Unknown
Tom Zé ....Luiz Luppi

Qu'est-ce que c'est, la musique actuelle?

A brazen new music driven by the headlong speed of the late 20th Century. Fueled by the art of *bricolage, musique actuelle* is a quicksilver appropriation and reassembly of the sonically familiar – television, pop tunes, film noir, free jazz, modern art, cultural icons, folk songs, the classical repertory and the dope vernacular of the street – into a new and surrealistic whole, evoking Lautréamont's infamous phrase "Beautiful, like the chance meeting of an umbrella and a sewing machine on a dissecting table." Like the automatic writing of André Breton and Philippe Soupault, the pioneering cut-ups of William S. Burroughs and Brion Gysin or the hallucinatory blues collages of Captain Beefheart's *Trout Mask Replica, musique actuelle* lets the future leak through when musical worlds collide.

Freely partaking of all musical sources – the chord changes in *Boplicity*, Martin Denny's 1950s Exotica, Puccini's *Turandot*, heavy metal thunder, ritual Gamelan music, fiery Brazilian sambas, New Orleans funeral marches, folk songs our grandparents taught us, dance instruction records – *musique actuelle* is music about music, a metamusic that sounds like your parents' copy of *The Readers' Digest Collection of Music Of The World* put through a Ronco Veg-o-matic. The short attention span of works like John Zorn's gaming piece *Cobra* or MFC's *Bruire La Barman A Tort de Sourire* could only be the product of the information age and its saturated media landscape, bombarding us with bite-sized infotainment as we change the channels of our culture. By building exhaustive record collections and embracing the flotsam and jetsam of musical history that lies littered around us, John Zorn and Michel F. Côté have a head start that Mozart, Charlie Parker or even Pierre Boulez never even dreamed of.

To paraphrase Public Enemy's Chuck D, *musique actuelle* is politically "cold," that is to say, hip, informed, dangerous and intended to provoke. White South African dissidents The Kalahari Surfers cut up the Lord's Prayer and saw their LP *Bigger Than Jesus* promptly banned, underground Japanese groups like After Dinner and Mizutama Shobodan [The Polka Dot Fire Brigade] turned Tokyo's repressive pop music industry on its ear by refusing to conform to its sexist imagery and slick production values, and Russian jazz pianist Sergei Kuryokhin once disdained the "Russian Piano School" typified by Rachmaninoff by sawing a piano in half on stage. This quixotic, subversive attitude often places *musique actuelle* at the eye of the geopolitical storm: British composer Lindsay Cooper's 1989 *Oh Moscow* was a jazzy bit of musical providence that foreshadowed the fall of the Berlin Wall and the Soviet Union.

If *musique actuelle* is a homemade, guerrilla music, then its arsenal lies all around us. There are Cagean musical possibilities in a broken harp, a boiling kettle, or a talking Captain America doll. American avant-garde theoretician and hobo Harry Partch's duffel bag of handmade instruments included chromolodeon, surrogate zither and cloud chamber bowls. German luthier and improviser Hans Reichel builds his eerily vocal "daxophones" from thin slabs of exotic hardwood, each with its own shape, timbre and resonance. New York musician Christian Marclay "plays" several turntables at once, scratching, skipping, and abusing other people's vinyl. Montreal power trio Fat uses hijacked cassette recordings, clothespins, digital delays, and vibrators in addition to guitars, bass and drums. And Montréal's René Lussier has explored the singsong musical sonorities of language itself. [*Musique actuelle* demands consummate musicianship as well; in 1968, when asked about the technical skill and sheer audacity required to perform idiosyncratic works like *And On The 7th Day Petals Fell In Petaluma*, Partch declared, "I believe in musicians who are total constituents of the moment, irreplaceable, who may sing, shout, whistle, stamp their feet; in costume always, or perhaps half naked, and I do not care which half."]

This handmade aesthetic also extends to the manipulation of sound. Whether you have an Akai S9000 sampler or an editing block and a few sharp razor blades, the possibilities for manipulating isolated sound say a gospel choir forever caught in amber are literally endless. The quantum leap in the index of compositional possibilities offered by the recording studio and the broadcast medium of radio have forever changed our perception of music and blurred the line between sound recorders and sound reproducers. Its roots in the "contrapuntal radio" of pianist Glenn Gould's 1967 CBC documentary *The Idea of North*, the wireless in particular has become a talisman for *musique actuelle*; the psychic space of vacuumland is today inhabited by Heiner Goebbels' prize-winning Hörstücke and Bruire's *Muss Muss Hic*. Yet music copyright laws have yet to catch up to the blatant channel surfing of *musique actuelle*; plunderphonics experts at The Mystery Tape Laboratory in Toronto diced and spliced the Beatles and shortwave crosstalk late into the night, and were forced to scrap all copies of their *free* CD in early 1990 under threat of litigation from CBS records. As Canadian poet Paul Haines once said, "All sounds are immigrants. None are intent on creating a past, in fact for a sound to be considered curative, it must be capable of being forgotten."

Its earliest incarnation was "downtown music," a rather geographical term that can be traced back to the fertile new music scene that thrived in the lofts of Manhattan's Lower East Side on the cusp of the 1980s, where improvisation, ensemble playing, avant garde jazz, performance art and stylistic cross-pollination were the order of the day. The last word in hip at the time, the alias became a little too site-specific when musicians, composers and performers with the same leanings and aesthetics yet hailing from Colorado, Frankfurt, Toronto, Amsterdam, San Francisco, Chicago, Osaka, Milan, Sao Paolo, Montréal, Johannesburg, Leningrad, London, and Seattle began popping up throughout the 1980s. Leave it to a small town in Québec with a burgeoning new music festival to borrow the title of an obscure avant garde happening in the 1960s to tell the world that a new musical genre had arrived: *musique actuelle.*

It's as good a handle as any. Chicago jazz critic Art Lange has called it "Third Stream," noticing a number of striking parallels between *musique actuelle* and the theory of a hybrid jazz/classical music first proposed by Gunther Schuller in the 1960s, while the acerbic and eminently readable New York jazz scribe Kevin Whitehead isn't sure that *musique actuelle* is a brand new bag at all: "It sure sounds like a recipe for post-modernism to me," Whitehead cracked at a *musique actuelle* symposium held at Montréal in 1989. The closest anyone else has come to an elegant and succinct nomenclature may have been California new music writer Josef Woodard, who inventively proclaimed it to be the antithesis of minimalism, "totalism."

Musique actuelle has no single source; its headwaters are many and its timeline meanders, refusing to follow a straight path in the same way that polyphony gave way to the harmonies and cadences of the Baroque Era, or modal jazz grew out of bebop's fast changes. Because it is such an overwhelmingly omnivorous genre, parsing *musique actuelle* is a little like trying to decipher the Rosetta Stone. Each musician, each ensemble, each work leads to a different set of musical vocabularies, techniques and influences [and not always musical ones at that]; a new set of teleological possibilities.

While it would be futile to try and place the music of the composers and performers and musicians herein under a single theoretical umbrella [there is simply too much stylistic and methodological contradiction] certain salient characteristics are shared by all the composers, musicians and ensembles covered in this book: an encyclopedic knowledge of music, including a deep appreciation of folk forms; a willingness to juxtapose musical schools and mix improvisation with structure; a desire to experiment with new technology and new media; a healthy irreverence for authority and conformity; and a stubborn resolve to work outside the corporate music system. This is not to mention a post-modern upbringing, an attention span weaned by TV, a weakness for subversive pop songs and a stint in a rock group somewhere along the way. In this regard, *musique actuelle*'s family tree can be seen as a fractal one, a multiplicity of discrete, parallel branches with common aesthetic roots.

Plunderphonics, 'Pataphysics and Pop Mechanics, then, traces the fractal tree of *musique actuelle*, from the formation of left-leaning European movements like Rock In Opposition and the Berlin-based Sogennantes Linksradikales Blasorchester through the radical brass of Chicago's Association for the Advancement of Creative Musicians [AACM] and European cool schools like the Dutch International Composers' Pool [ICP]. From there it explores the trailblazing work of women composers and musicians in the field, the hothouse improv scene of New York during the 1980s, the cutting edge of sonic manipulation and reappropriation, and the subversion of the innocuous pop song. The summit of both the book and the genre itself is at the Festival International de Musique Actuelle de Victoriaville, an annual pilgrimage of fans, journalists and musicians alike to a small town in Québec's *bois francs* that's unparalleled in new music circles.

Like a runaway Trojan Horse virus infecting computer software, *musique actuelle* is changing fast, constantly mutating and breeding newer and more sophisticated strains of itself to tackle our fragmented world. It is their music – the music of Chris Cutler, Fred Frith, Ferdinand Richard, Heiner Goebbels, Willem Breuker, Henry Threadgill, Sergei Kuryokhin, The Rova Saxophone Quartet, Amy Denio, Lindsay Cooper, Tenko, Zeena Parkins, John Oswald, John Zorn, Charles Hayward, Roberto Musci & Giovanni Venosta, Les Granules, Fat, Bruire, Justine, The Residents, Kalahari Surfers, After Dinner and Tom Zé – that is the physical graffiti heralding the coming of the next musical generation.

Rock In Opposition

Henry Cow was formed ten years ago. Founded as a rock group, it grew out of the most experimental tendencies in that tradition. Our growth coincided with a period in which rock music was largely reappropriated and disarmed by the music industry. At least in the UK, this music lost its radical, critical, experimental function and by the early Seventies became just another depressing sector of show business...

It seems to us that our music must challenge not only in its conception but in its execution...There must always be unknowns and hazards, a tension between written and unwritten, discipline and interpretation. To this end we do not hesitate to draw on all the elements we identify as progressive or useful, whatever the original context. [Both our instrumentation and our playing seem to belong variously to jazz, modern classical and rock music.] We are surrounded by music and we must choose what to accept and develop and what to reject or attack, because nothing that communicates can avoid the consequences of its own language.[1]

With this note, Henry Cow wrote their epitaph. Ten years on, the socialist "dada blues" band founded in Cambridge, England in 1968 by guitarist Fred Frith and pianist Tim Hodgkinson found themselves at the crossroads. From the beginning, Henry Cow were committed to forging a contemporary rock music, rock that eschewed the vacuous commercialism and ubiquitous Anglo-American influence of the music industry, rock that was revolutionary in form as well as in content. Against the turbulent backdrop of wide-spread student riots, the Vietnam War, Prague Spring, Situationism and the unraveling social fabric of the late 1960s, Henry Cow caught the comet of confrontation and counterculture experimentation that flared through the skies after the summer of love died. New compositional possibilities were being explored by progressive rock ensembles like The Soft Machine, Faust, Magma, AMM and Pink Floyd, groups that rejected the cul-de-sac of the Serialists and radically reappraised both rock and contemporary composition through new vocabularies of playing and recording technique.

Henry Cow joined the ranks of this rock avant garde with a triptych of successively breathtaking LPs for Virgin.[2] What Frith, Hodgkinson, bassist John Greaves, reed player Lindsay Cooper, and drummer Chris Cutler[3] did was not so much preach a radical, revolutionary message as they lived and played it: Despite being signed to Virgin – then a struggling young independent label – they worked resolutely outside the system, organized their own gigs and tours, and steadfastly refused to be co-opted. According to Henry Cow, the revolution was coming, but it wasn't the same revolution prophesied by The Beatles nor Gil

Scott-Heron, rather it was a revolution of form where music was the tool for social awareness and change: "Art is not a mirror, it is a hammer," read the sleeve notes of their third LP, *In Praise Of Learning*.

In 1975, Henry Cow began tours of Europe, where they encountered other grassroots rock radicals who shared their ideals and goals. Italy's Stormy Six started out in 1965 as a bar band with little more than an Italian translation of The Small Faces' "All Or Nothing," yet Umberto Fiori and Franco Fabbri quickly set their sights on folk-rock stars, Tin Pan Alley, and what they saw as the institutionalisation and ossification of the political song. In a country where it was chic to be left, Stormy Six stuck out like bloody tourists. The musical and political situation was much the same in Sweden, where most popular music was either traditional folk or leftist folk-rock. Led by accordionist Lars Hollmer, the quixotic Samla Mammas Manna cut a path through the middle, drawing from both camps and refusing to take any sort of political stand. France had Etron Fou Leloublan, whose wild mix of improvisation and garage pop was shunned by the French press, and Belgium had the mysterious Univers Zero, an obscure chamber rock ensemble who favored Orff and Stravinsky rather than Clapton and Hendrix.

After having successfully booked Henry Cow on a 1975 tour throughout Italy and having brought Etron Fou to play England the following year, their tour manager, Nick Hobbs, booked a festival at London's Drury Lane Theatre for March 12, 1978 with these five groups on the bill. Four hundred and fifty people showed up, and Rock In Opposition was born. Hobbs took on the administrative and organizational duties of the ad hoc coalition and urged the Group of Five to think collectively, internationally. As Rock In Opposition, they resolved to uphold musical excellence, to work outside the system, and to have a social commitment to rock. Rock In Opposition thus became Henry Cow writ large: an attempt to forge a new compositional form balancing virtuosic playing and improvisation, folklore and new music, medium and message.

Yet a tour of British universities before the London festival received lackluster press and lost money for all involved. Also by that time the subtle fissures in Henry Cow, brought on by changes in the band's lineup, had widened. The note of resignation between the lines of the above press release was a reflection of the difficulty the group had in reaching a consensus when recording what was to become their first independent release, *Western Culture,*[4] in January of 1978. On December 8 of that year, the Group of Five met at Sunrise Studios in Kirchberg, Switzerland. Despite tabling the compilation of a European source book and proposing another festival in Milan for April of 1979, they could not reconcile deep differences in how their music and cause should proceed. There may have been strong threads binding the groups together, but the resulting quilt was far too crazy to work. As with Henry Cow, this was to be Rock In Opposition's undoing: squabbling in the face of indifference, RIO disbanded two years later.

Rock In Opposition may have failed to find a larger audience, but its posthumous influence has been undeniable. For one, it revealed that progressive rock ensembles were by far the most open to new polystylistic forms and recording techniques, and that there was a shared sense that folk music is an important codex of musical and social history. These ideas have been further developed by drummer Chris Cutler, an eloquent and keen pop theoretician and perhaps the best proponent of the original RIO ideology. Through his record label, ReR Megacorp, Cutler has assiduously researched the strong pull of folk music [particularly in Eastern Europe] and recording technology on compositional form and choice. Likewise, German composer, multi-instrumentalist and one-time student activist with a "radical brass band," Heiner Goebbels, has applied RIO's tenets and outlook to theater, radio and multimedia.

Rock In Opposition also proved that a small yet worldwide community of musicians and listeners with a social commitment to rock was out there. Several key RIO members have since been instrumental in networking and knitting this community together: Etron Fou Leloublan bassist Ferdinand Richard now runs an annual RIO-style festival, Mouvement Internationale des Musiques Innovatrices, in St-Rémy-de-Provence, and guitarist Fred Frith, the "Patron Saint of Victoriaville," continues to be a strong supporter and producer of independent, new and improvised music, working extensively in Canada, Japan, Europe and America. As a revolution, Rock In Opposition may have been a noble failure, but without its sense of community and stubborn dedication to a music that must go forward, *musique actuelle* would not exist.

1. Biographical press release prepared for The British Arts Council for the 1978 Rock In Opposition tour, and reprinted on the sleeve notes for *The Virgin Years*; ReR Megacorp, 1991
2. *Legend, Unrest* and *In Praise Of Learning*; 1973, 1974 and 1975, respectively
3. For two stunning LPs in 1975 [both on Virgin], *Desperate Straights* and *In Praise Of Learning*, Henry Cow merged with the members of Slapp Happy: vocalist Dagmar Krause, guitarist Peter Blegvad and pianist Anthony Moore
4. Broadcast, 1978

Chris Cutler

"Certain phenomena of 'mass dissent' [hippies, beatniks, new Bohemias, student movements] today seem to us negative replies to the industrial society: The society of Technological Communication is rejected in order to look for alternative forms, using the means of the technological society [television, press, record companies...]. So there is no leaving the circle; you are trapped in it willy-nilly. Revolutions are often resolved in more picturesque forms of integration.

"But it could be that these non-industrial forms of communication [from the love-in to the rally of students seated on the grass of the campus] can become the forms of a future communications guerilla warfare – a manifestation complementary to the manifestations of Technological Communication, the constant correction of perspectives, the checking of codes, the ever renewed interpretations of mass messages. The universe of Technological Communication would then be patrolled by groups of communications guerillas, who would restore a critical dimension to passive reception. The threat that 'the medium is the message' could then become, for both medium and message, the return to individual responsibility. To the anonymous divinity of Technological Communication our answer could be: 'Not Thy, but our will be done.'"

Umberto Eco, "Towards a Semiological Guerrilla Warfare," 1967[1]

In the summer of 1991, irony has come home to roost in St Saviour's Road. It has come to the study of drummer Chris Cutler's sprawling Brixton flat in the form of a promotional CD of Pere Ubu's *Worlds In Collision.*[2] For those who came in late, Pere Ubu were a cult group from Cleveland named after Alfred Jarry's corpulent surrealist monarch, an impossibly grotesque Tin Jesus who ruled over a theater of the absurd. Just as Captain Beefheart kicked the blues forward,[3] Ubu took the dislocation and alienation of the pop song and gave them a frightening new urban spin on LPs like *Dub Housing*[4] and songs like "30 Seconds Over Tokyo." They were fronted by one David Thomas, a singer whose hurtling bulk was only surpassed by his high-pitched, quavering warble.

Cutler had written the first review on Ubu to appear in England, for *Sounds*, and a correspondence was begun. After the group imploded in 1982, David Thomas moved to London to pursue a solo career, playing improvised gigs with Cutler and Lindsay Cooper. They soon added bass player Tony Maimone, and the group evolved into The Wooden Birds, which counted in their ranks Ubu alumni Jim Jones on guitar and Allan Ravenstine on synthesizers. "We were one spit being away from Pere Ubu, with one difference: as The Wooden Birds we could hardly command a reasonable fee to do a gig," Cutler explains. After The Birds enjoyed a modest success with a quirky collection of short stories, *Blame The Messenger,*[5] a mutual decision was made to rename the group. Original Ubu drummer Scott Krauss came on board, they were signed by Phonogram, and released a critically acclaimed "comeback" album, *The Tenement Year.*[6] After touring the U.S. and Europe in 1988 to glowing press, the problems started.

"With Ubu we were on a kind of success-or-else treadmill," says Cutler. "No overt pressure from Phonogram, but when we finished the first album and took it to Dave Bates at Phonogram, he said, 'Remix it.' We asked, 'Well what do you want different?' and he said 'It's not good enough.' So we had to guess. So we remixed it. And it wasn't good enough again, so it was remixed again. The second time, they didn't take any chances and they got other people to remix a lot of the tracks, Stephen Hague being one of them. The Wooden Birds record was made in about five days start to finish, and the last Ubu took a year and a half. It got more and more out of our hands. On one hand the group was trying hard to write more commercial songs, but on the other hand, our production values were being consigned to third party pleasers. By the next album,[7] it was already pretty much clear the way things were going."

After writing some of the third album, Cutler made his exeunt, followed by a disgruntled Allan Ravenstine, perhaps the most misunderstood member of the ensemble. Listening to *Worlds In Collision* was almost a foregone conclusion; morning coffee under the headsets at Virgin's Oxford Street Megastore earlier that day had confirmed my fears: stripped of Cutler's intricate, muscular drumming and Ravenstine's quasar-burst EML synthesizers, and retooled with slick production values courtesy of Pixies producer Gil Norton, Ubu was no different than a hundred other eccentric college-rock combos. Even Thomas' vocals had all but the necessary trademark idiosyncrasies ironed out. *Ubu Roi* had abdicated the throne.

"Truth be told, Phonogram didn't care about anybody in the group except David," Cutler admits. "They could have replaced any one of us. I had long conversations with Allan, whom I got on with and get on with extremely well. He said – and it's exactly how I feel – that it was really fun working with The Wooden Birds. There was a lot of workspace, freedom; there was no pressure to do this or that. And I could hear it. After that it stopped being fun."

Chris Cutler's fleeting fame with Pere Ubu and his brush with the star-making machinery at Phonogram makes an ironic footnote to a lifetime's work as a communications guerilla. For the past two decades, the wiry, energetic drummer has been popular music criticism's *eminence grise*, working within the system to provide a forum for enlightened discourse on popular music forms past, present and future, all the while casting a sharp analytical eye at musical "progress." His company, ReR Megacorp – which he cheerfully describes as "always on the brink of insolvency" – is the economic concept of vertical integration at work: Cutler handles every aspect of the music, from writing the score to booking the studio time, from editing the tape to silkscreening the record jackets, even stocking the local record shops.[8] To top it all, he is a gifted critic and theoretician, having published a series of essays, *File Under Popular*,[9] on topics as diverse as Phil Ochs, Sun Ra, The Residents and progressive music, regularly giving papers and lectures, and editing an LP/magazine package, The *Ré Records Quarterly*, dedicated to new theoretical writing in the field of popular music.

The Ubu anecdote is an illustrative example of Cutler's ethos, which is at the heart of his work and can be summed up in a simple equation: skill, knowledge and expertise = instrumental, compositional and expressive possibilities. Cutler is a drummer of rare grace and detail, a musician who has built up his craft the hard way. His personal and driven style goes beyond a trap set and infuses whatever musical projects he is involved in, be it the chilling, austere beauty of The Art Bears pop, the Brechtian *sprechstimme* of News From Babel, or the apocalyptic free jazz fury of Cassiber. The fact that Phonogram's remix of Pere Ubu's *Cloudland* could be done from existing rhythm tracks merely underscores Cutler's argument that without skill, music cannot possibly hope to go forward:

"Music exists in time and space; it has a history and was made by work. Commodities, as we have seen, always conceal and render *invisible* the work that went into their creation – they dehumanise. To humanise we need, among other things, to demystify music making and all the mechanics of composing and performing – to become *informed*. We have not only to reinsert music into time and space but into a communicative space, and into the world of *work*. In other words, to engage with it rather than consume it – and for this we need skill, knowledge and expertise.

"Commodities hide behind ignorance and personal property. A *social* music will belong to all who participate in it: but like the practise of democracy itself, this can only happen when all are 'skilled' in the culture – informed, *living* through an expertise rather than simply operating a consumer taste."[10]

Chris Cutler was born in Washington, DC in 1947, the son of a British foreign correspondent and his Austrian wife. The Cutlers moved to England the following year, where Cutler has lived ever since. "Grammar school education. No university education," says Cutler tersely. "Played in psychedelic rock bands...Nobody that anybody's ever heard of. You can scour the gig pages of the *Melody Maker* for 1967 for names like..." Pause. "Nothing stuck. There you go. The first thing of any significance was forming a 26-piece rock composers' orchestra with Dave Stewart, the Ottowa Music Company, and listening to *Nuits de la Fondation Maeght* by Sun Ra."

The banality of personal historical data may not interest Cutler, yet tracing the family tree of music, with its roots in polyphony and tonality and its blossoming into the multiplicity of musics we face today, has been a lifelong passion. "Loudest of all we hear the voice of History," he once wrote.[11] "Appearing as a totality of questions, problems, attitudes, choices, possibilities – which, like a magnetic field, exercises a unifying influence over every apparent individual alignment." His telling mention of Sun Ra reveals the key to his advanced musical thinking; Ra's cosmic consciousness, while deep in the tradition, was also plugged into the future, as evidenced by his embracing the first generation of Moogs.

"I would have to agree with McLuhan on his basic proposition of the nature of communicative need," says Cutler. "The clue to all these questions lies in electronic media." Marshall McLuhan is just one of the authors represented in Cutler's well-stocked library; there are books on philosophy, literary criticism, unfinished papers, scores of scores, periodicals on music, and, of course, a vast and comprehensive record collection. Pere Ubu has been removed from the CD player; as London's afternoon sun streams through the windows, a gentle, shimmering Keith Rowe guitar piece suffuses the air as tea is poured. "That's why the last 30 or 40 years has seen this confluence of elements from what before were different genres. In the crudest possible way, music became universally available when it was encoded by the gramophone for broadcast on the radio. Whereas you had to be rich to go to the opera in the early 1800s, today you can copy it onto a cassette. Once it has entered into its electronic existence, it's interchangeable as electronic information. *Musique concrète*, all the stuff that came after it, quintessentially all the stuff that's done in sampling, recognizes this fact above all others. It's all plunderphonics;[12] it's all there to be plundered.

"Now the question of whether plunderphonics is an expression of a post-modern sensibility is a big question. I gave a lecture on this in Holland a year ago, and argued – or tried to argue – that on the contrary, it wasn't. It's not good enough to say that this is just pastiche, jamming stuff together. The fact that this music brings together elements from different musical genres is based on some overriding sense of music as a whole, and how to deal with problems raised by musical history as it crashed into the 20th century. At the end of the last century, the question on the table was a question of tonality. This raised the question of structure and the question of by what criteria could you make decisions about organizing the material. Big questions on the table.

"Because it was a crisis in composing, a lot of different composers tried to deal with these problems in different ways. You can't compare Harry Partch, Edgar Varèse and Arnold Schoenberg – to take three people at random – in the way that they try and deal with this question. They all take very different tacks. Partch was a composer with a highly developed theory about composition, and he made extraordinary demands on his performers when it came to performing his music. If you were to follow one or the other of them, it's not at all sure that you'd end up anywhere very interesting. But people did follow them. People followed Schoenberg; serial composition became very highly developed. In fact, it crossed over into electronic music, which is far better than they realized; the Americans were able to apply tone rows to timbre and dynamics. I think these kinds of concerns affect people who actually are making music."

For Cutler, the questions on the table have to do with much more than simple tone rows, they have to do with where our music is headed in the late 20th Century. The holy grail that Cutler is seeking is nothing less than the next evolutionary step in music. After the groundbreaking possibilities raised by *musique concrète* in the 1950s, what's next? In attempting to quantify the music being represented in this book, Cutler expressed an admiration for the concept but a wariness that it could actually be done. "If you do," he joked, "you'll be up there with Beethoven and the big boys." It's not that Cutler dismisses *musique actuelle*, he is merely wary of waterproof theoretical umbrellas. He is equally uneasy with classifying the work of modernist visionaries like John Cage or Karlheinz Stockhausen – who definitely opened up the listening experience with their ideas – as music: "The importance of Cage seems to me to have been that he clarified and verbalised this particular aspect of twentieth century music's 'crisis' and proposed, as a counterbalance, the *creativity* of the listener."[13]

"Stockhausen was a media hound," Cutler says tartly. "A great composer, and a great non-composer. When Stockhausen wrote a piece that says 'Play this note until it turns golden,' or any of the other instruction pieces he gave in the '60s where there is no notation, it was basically an exhortation to the musicians to improvise under certain very mysterious conditions imposed by the presence of Stockhausen giving the instruction. What is he doing? He may have been an *enfant terrible*, but he surely was always supported by Deutsche Grammophon. John Cage, after a very short time of being looked at with one eyebrow slightly raised, was welcomed into the bosom of the musical establishment. Nobody could be more established in American music than John Cage. Is that a good thing, a bad thing, or does it mean anything at all?"

No, according to Cutler, the future of musical thought is not to be found in Cage's mesostics nor Stockhausen's electronic *zyklus*. No, it comes from the most unlikely of sources: early European progressive rock. "Generally speaking, I would say the most liberal sector of the divided genres of the music world is the rock music model," says Cutler. "They are much more ready listen to other stuff, and therefore it was in that field that you get the most input. It's still a big number when somebody like Glenn Branca brings a few very boring rock ideas into the classical music world. It's all new to them, it's old hat to everybody else. The jazz world is not as narrow as it used to be, but it's still fairly insular because of the grip of improvising; the ethics of expression, virtuoso and individuality doesn't help. Especially the virtuoso ethic, which is not at all prevalent in rock groups.

"The great proportion of groups on our label are first and foremost rock groups; that's where they started, that's their generation. They grew up learning about music by playing electric instruments, listening to goodness knows what, then getting more towards the edges precisely because all of these different kinds of music are available. You'll read interviews that Pete Townshend did in 1967 where he said he listened to Stockhausen a lot at the same time he was bashing his guitar about and making a lot of abstract noise. There was a brief moment in the late 1960s when a lot people tried to do a lot of things which were quite short lived, but they left strong tracks, because the most influential groups of the 1970s – Faust, Magma, and Henry Cow – picked up on that moment.

"In all three cases, you have kind of a proposition on the table for a way to do music that's drawn from all three previously separate genres: improvised jazz, 20th century music, and rock. In all three cases, you get very different results. You can play Faust, Henry Cow, and Magma next to each other and they will sound completely different, as different as Varèse, Partch and Schoenberg. But all in a way exemplify the same consciousness of the same kind of problems, or sharing a similar aesthetic, sharing a similar appreciation and grasp of a broader musical palette than any one genre would allow. Listen to the music of these groups: It's composed, there's virtuoso playing, it's profoundly expressive in a jazz kind of way. It has brought these things together, but not in a pastiche, but a new form, a real form that's convincing and very satisfying to be in front of, therefore very influential to other musicians. This way you become part of music history, in a way that if you're Bobby Vee you're part of a kind of sociological history of music, but sure to hell you're not part of the history of music *qua* music."

The term "progressive rock" only came into currency long after Yes, Genesis and Gentle Giant had triumphed and the progressive elements had long been leached out of the music. However, the triptych of "progressive" groups – Henry Cow, Faust and Magma – were forging a new compositional and improvisational alloy, equal parts East European folk music, Carl Orff, Stravinsky, Coltrane, the Cologne/Darmstadt school of electronic music, Frank Zappa, Beefheart, The Velvet Underground, Stockhausen, Bartók, *musique concrète*. Also seminal progressive groups like The Soft Machine, who were already were a hybrid, bringing elements of song music, rock, and jazz together in a very strong and unique way. "Until the fourth album, which doesn't count," ripostes Cutler. "In the same way Frank Zappa doesn't count after the seventh album. He comes and goes, but basically he's given up his original focus, which occasionally he now dips back into with his culture hat on. With the Mothers of Invention, because *he* wrote the stuff and *he* got the group together and *he* taught them how to do all that stuff, Zappa lived under an illusion – and the demise of the Mothers was concrete proof – that he created the group, and he could do the same stuff with another group or on his own. He didn't understand that the dynamic of the Mothers as a whole came from the dynamic of that group of people as a whole and their history of working together, and the ideas that he thought were his ideas were ideas that were merged in the course of their working together. I think this is critical in this whole story of the influence working in a group had on the development of the music.

"Take for instance, a group like Henry Cow. You have Tim, whose background is free jazz like Coltrane and Ornette; Fred, who had a classically trained education abandoned and replaced by an interest in folk music and the blues; John Greaves, whose background was playing dance bands; Lindsay, who was completely classically trained, and me, I played in psychedelic rock bands. So you can imagine what happens when a group of people like this gets together to play. They bring not only in the form of their own playing things that they suggest about doing, but they also discuss the music: I didn't listen to Sun Ra nor AMM before I was in Henry Cow; It was Fred who suggested I listen to AMM. You realize quite quickly as soon as you get out of your ghetto that the same kinds of problems and same aesthetic background inhabits other genres than the one you know about."

During the 1970s, Henry Cow were virtual exiles from their homeland, finding more respectability and gigs in Europe, where they met a handful of other committed, like-minded groups who lived outside the commercial rock circuit's ideals and goals, groups who were not aping popular British and American styles: France's Etron Fou Leloublan, Italy's Stormy Six, Sweden's Samlas Mammas Manna, and Belgium's Univers Zero. A movement began to coalesce around this quintet of progressive groups. Nine months later, the groups met at Sunrise Studios in Kirchberg, Switzerland, the name Rock In Opposition was formally adopted, a constitution was hammered out, a blueprint laid for a network of gig bookings and record distribution, and three more groups – France's Art Zoyd, Holland's Aksak Maboul, and The Art Bears – were invited to join. While the aims were organizationally feasible and coherent, the ideologies were poles apart; in particular, Stormy Six and Univers Zero were diametrically opposed to each other on political grounds. The cultural differences and the character of each group's struggle in their respective homelands were, as Cutler put it, "profound and existential," and RIO disbanded by effluxion in 1980.

"Rock In Opposition was quite short lived, but it obviously had an effect well beyond its material festivals that we ran," says Cutler. "The term stuck, so lots of groups who wanted to identify themselves with that area of work called themselves 'Rock In Opposition' groups. Now the same kind of selection, the same kind of unwritten manifesto exists in the program of ReR. At the time, there was no kind of distribution that dealt with this kind of music and that was selective. There was some distributions that handled certain kinds of this music or one strand of it in a blanket sort of way, but none that put them together and none at all that were selective. At ReR, it's completely autocratic. It's my taste. I like it or don't like it, or I think it's worth recommending to people. That's why the original title was Recommended Records. It was like a punk shop list, where you go into a shop and you pin up your top 10 favorite records to recommend them to other people. It got into a lot of trouble in the early days, and still do because I don't take certain things via certain people who think I should. Some of my friends records' I didn't stock, for instance, that I didn't think were terribly good. [Fred Frith's] *Cheap At Half The Price*[14] was one of them. The whole point about Recommended and ReR is to get to people stuff that they otherwise wouldn't listen to, or wouldn't get or wouldn't find. If I start including stuff that I don't think is really good, all the people who buy things that they don't know on the strength of being recommended won't trust the recommendation anymore. It has to be reliable."

At the time when Cutler set up Recommended Records with Nick Hobbs in 1978, the manifesto was unwritten, although Cutler later formulated that the groups and composers must share an engagement with "[i] *instrumental possibilities* [new techniques and treatments]; [ii] *compositional possibilities* [iii]; and the *expressive possibilities* [*engaged content*] of the above."[15] Launched with a double LP,[16] Recommended's roster included groups that Cutler "recommended" – Sun Ra, Faust, South Africa's Kalahari Surfers, France's ZNR, and Québec's Les 4 Guitaristes de L'Apocalypso Bar – as well as groups that he was actively involved in as a drummer and composer – News From Babel, Cassiber, and The Art Bears. These last three groups show the breadth of Cutler's approach as a collaborator. News From Babel was a chamber project with unusual instrumentation drawing on the traditions of Brecht and Weill, featuring Lindsay Cooper and Zeena Parkins, Dagmar Krause, Robert Wyatt and Phil Minton; Cassiber was an ambitious, white-hot fusion of spontaneous improvisation and prepared text with Heiner Goebbels and Christoph Anders, while The Art Bears wrote diamond-cut, classical maxims for modern existence.

Inspired by the satirical sketches of Lucian, the first Art Bears album, *Hopes And Fears*,[17] was written while Frith, Krause and Cutler were still in Henry Cow, and was ultimately rejected by the group as being more "pop" than populist. "Fred and I both wanted to do a record of pop songs, as it were, and that's something that Henry Cow hadn't done," Cutler explains. "Short songs in a pop form, and I think that's what they are. Very minimal, austere, absolutely nothing extra on them except what's absolutely necessary. Very stripped-down arrangements, sometimes only one thing on a tune. That's what we aimed for, and I'm perfectly satisfied with the results. It was a good group."

Many of Recommended's acts have a subtle political undercurrent if not an explicit, overt one; they are after all, in opposition to the hegemony of consumer-driven American and British pop. Yet for Cutler, progressive *music* must to go hand-in-hand with progressive politics; content *and* form must progress together, otherwise the result is merely banal agit-prop:

> "What of the progressive text? Suppose we look at the Form of this Content, especially where it has ended up – constrained by the blunting nature of the Music into which it has had to fit – as cliché, jargon, slogans or doggerel. Here we find, typically, only another form of commodity – a 'political' commodity. After all, anything can be consumed; in the marketplace, anything can be stripped of its Human content. Suffice it that when life itself can be hollowed out of meaning, a rhyming text doesn't stand much chance."[18]

This marriage of form and content provides the rationale behind Recommended's focus over the years on Eastern Europe: Czechoslovakians Iva

Bittovà and Pavel Fajt brilliantly deconstruct Eastern European folk forms with violin, voice and prepared metals; Latvia's ZGA plunder the junkyard, limning a electroacoustic landscape with homemade instruments; Yugoslavia's Stevan Kovacs Tickmayer is a formidable young composer who hotwires Satie, Stravinsky and ragtime in his *Wilhelm Dances MCMXCII*,[19] and Czech composer Jaroslav Krcek sculpts an electroacoustic psychodrama based on the fall of Jericho on *Raab*.[20]

Yet western market forces being what they are, promoting this bold new music to an increasingly fractured listening public proved to be an uphill task, even during the salad days of the 1980s when adventurous independent labels like Rough Trade, Factory and Postcard popped up all over Britain like mushrooms. Recommended was particularly plagued with problems at the distribution end; three major crises in 1980, 1983, and 1986 forced Cutler to drop everything else and put the label back on its feet. "In the end, I got sick to death of it, since I wasn't actually running it and not really responsible," he says. "It was me who had to pick up the pieces when everything went horribly wrong and the bailiffs came around and wanted to take away my flat." In 1986, Cutler washed his hands of the distribution of Recommended and gave it to the people who were running it as a gift.

Cutler then formed Ré Records independent of Recommended distribution, which had become a workers' co-op, giving them the exclusive rights to distribute Ré releases. This arrangement worked for two years, until Cutler discovered that Recommended owed his label in the vicinity of £17,000 sterling for stock they had sold. "At this point, I said enough was enough. I had to sit down and think about what I really wanted to do. I decided that if I really wanted to run the label, I had to run the distribution. Anyway, I had to do something fast, because I had such enormous debts. I did what I always do in these situations, which is to run up more debts in order to produce stuff in order to sell the stuff you produce to get the money back in order to pay the debts off. You've got to spend your way out." So Cutler established the ironically-titled ReR Megacorp in 1989. Despite having to move house twice in as many years – once to Sutton in 1992 and back to Tulse Hill in Brixton the following year – ReR Megacorp is still up and running. He must be doing something right; ReR has become a prototype model for similar distribution outposts around the world: there are independent Recommended branches in France, Switzerland, Germany, Italy, Czechoslovakia, and Brazil.

In its formative years, Chris Cutler had been involved with an organization called The International Association for the Study of Popular Music, an academic project at Cambridge University Press which produced conference proceedings, newsletters, and a journal, *Popular Music*. By the mid-1980s,

Cutler found their ideas to be stale and out of date, but not the thinking behind the questions, and established the *Ré Records Quarterly* to fill the vacuum of informed writing on popular music. "I think that it is necessary to think seriously about these questions and about this music, and not just say what people had for breakfast," he explains. "There are no record reviews in the Quarterlies, and no interviews. There's very little that's academic. I like to have musicians themselves think and write about what they do, and about the field of music in general, and I want it to be of liberal intelligent interest. As editor, I do a lot of work to try to make sure that everything's written clearly and is completely comprehensible. At the time – this was 1984 – the idea to have a sound magazine hadn't really been done to my knowledge. This meant that I could commission smaller things from composers, not whole albums. It seemed to kill a lot of birds with one stone."

Over the years, Cutler has published incisive analyses of the blurred no-man's-land between sound and music in the wake of Cage and *musique concrète* in Philip Tagg's "Reading Sounds [Music, Knowledge, Rock & Society],"[21] Eddie Prévost's "AMM: A Few Memories & Reflections,"[22] and Tim Hodgkinson's interview with Pierre Schaefer.[23] He has kept pace with new technologies as they relate to composition in Michael Gerzon's "Creative Possibilities of Compact Disc"[24] and John Oswald's "Plunderphonics, or Audio Piracy as a Compositional Prerogative,"[25] and has kept us entertained with whimsical dispatches like Peter Blegvad's "On Numinous Objects & Their Manufacture"[26] and Jean Derome's "Matter/Manner."[27] The Quarterlies manage to sell about 1000 copies each, many of them going to universities and music libraries.

In May of 1994, with the fourth volume of the Quarterly, Cutler made the switch from LP to CD. While not a quantum shift in emphasis, it reflects the ongoing development of the recording studio, digital technology, and the music being mapped out by AMM, Biota, After Dinner, Kalahari Surfers, David Myers, Fat, Lutz Glandien, and the duo of Roberto Musci and Giovanni Venosta. With this music, Cutler and ReR have delved deeper and deeper into the studio, tapping into the current of electrification and exploring the compositional, improvisational and expressive possibilities locked deep inside magnetic tape and the recording process. "Musicians just don't go into the studio and lay down their stuff and record it anymore. They mess with it afterwards," says Cutler. "You'll notice that the ReR programme more and more includes concrete music techniques and contemporary music, because I think it a very fruitful area. Actually it is *the* area because it develops the actual medium in which the music is played. The recording medium is a qualitatively different thing from written notation and interpretation of notation, or improvisation.[28]

Recording is the opposite of notation. It has all kinds of qualities that are hard to explain. There's biological memory, written memory and electronic memory. You think about Marshall McLuhan, and you see that they're all opposites. You can see that the recording studio and recording has certain properties. And if you investigate and develop these properties, in the same way that investigating and developing the electrification of the instruments, then you're working in a really fruitful medium, a medium in which there are discoveries to me made, and a new language to be evolved.

"On the one hand, electricity and recording as a medium are central to these forms of music, without which *they would not exist.*[29] Even groups who don't use these facilities nevertheless possess an aesthetic, a judgement about what kinds of sounds are interesting, that comes from this medium. John Zorn doesn't cut tape together; all that stuff is done in real time, like doing music for a cartoon, which is I'm sure where the inspiration came from. But without cutting tape, without editing, you would never have that perfection. It would be impossible, unthinkable. You can reproduce this aesthetic in a number of different ways. I can play you pieces by especially Romanian contemporary composers that sound like *musique concrète*. The aesthetic of the sound is very much like that; you can't tell what the hell it is that's making that sound.[30] Which comes not from manipulation, but the recording technique of close miking something. Basically it's played on real instruments by real people, but the aesthetic comes from electronics, concrete sound. These things enter the imagination, the musical consciousness, the decision-making process, which is ultimately what the aesthetic process is, and there's no going back. Studio and electricity is the *sine qua non* of this stuff. If Carl Orff could have done what Magma did, he probably would have. Magma had the facilities to produce certain kinds of effects that Carl Orff would have liked to produce. And tried to: I mean, there's a piece where he used seven grand pianos, where you get this really big bass note, and they all played it together. You don't need seven grand pianos to achieve that effect anymore. You don't need fifty violins to make the violin line audible. You need the volume."

Although Cutler flirted with this compositional aesthetic in Cassiber, particularly on their last album *A Face We All Know*,[31] it would come to full bloom on his work with East German tuba player and studio visionary Lutz Glandien. During 1991 and 1992 Cutler and Glandien collaborated on several works for live electronics, tuba and drums – "Strange Drums," "Turbo Mortale," and "Trompose" – at various Berlin festivals. Their album together, *Domestic Stories*,[32] was born out of texts initially written together, texts inspired by three women from the Bible – Lilith, Salome and Magdalene. "Lilith was Adam's first wife according to Hebrew tradition," explains Cutler. "She was the mother of night and didn't like lying underneath Adam and generally being submissive, so she took off back home, where she bred a horde of monsters. Salome danced the seven veils for Herod, who was gobsmacked and offered her anything she chose as a reward. At the prompt of her mother she asked for John the Baptist's head on a platter. Magdalene is a reformed whore, and appears in the Bible washing Christ's feet. Apocryphal writings have her as a mirror to Christ, with twelve followers of her own who support Christ financially. Some wild stories have her escaping and setting up an order in Marseille, but she's best known as a whore. These are all women who are generally reviled and rejected." Cutler pauses, then quotes from Luke Chapter 20 for good measure. "'The stone the builders rejected has become the cornerstone.'"

Cutler and Glandien then built this suite of Biblical portraits into songs from the vocals up, painstakingly assembled from disparate studio sessions where the players – Dagmar Krause, Fred Frith, Alfred 23 Harth – never even met. With its lush attention to sonic detail, *Domestic Stories* takes *concrète*, sampling and computer editing techniques to a highly advanced level, and is the most forward-looking pop project that Cutler has released; it has the same feel as *Winter Songs*-period Art Bears, only now Cutler and Glandien finally have the skill and technology to fully realize their ideas.

As the stone the builders rejected, Chris Cutler soldiers on, the cornerstone of progressive musical thought. His current work has him preparing a slate of new ReR releases, including *Ritual Nova 1 & 2*,[33] a layered and extraordinary exploration of East European folk roots by Yugoslavian composer Boris Kovacs, and *Brainweather*,[34] Australian cellist Jon Rose's latest *opera pervers* starring Shelley Hirsch and Phil Minton; as well, he is mixing projects further down the pipe by Peter Blegvad, California's modern chamber ensemble The 5UUs, and a trio with Jean Derome and René Lussier. In his *spare* time he has been crisscrossing Europe playing exhilarating, noisy pop in The [EC] Nudes, his new trio with Seattle vocalist Amy Denio and Swiss free guitarist Wädi Gysi.[35] In the meantime, Cutler continues to listen, ear to the ground, for the music of the future.

"This need for, and absence of, belief in the future is one of the central problems of all the civilised arts today. What hope have we? How could it be expressed, what could it be made of, what language could it speak?...I have no answer, but I am one of those who is convinced that a music for our own times, a music that might have a chance to find hope, give pleasure, bring meaning to consciousness of the present, must be made from the new means and through new relations that make the present what it is. It is the present we want to transform and live in. This stuff now. And Musical values, like linguistic values, must always be in a state of change and of becoming."[36]

A luta continua.

Chris Cutler
Henry Cow: Legend (Virgin, 1973), Unrest (Virgin, 1974), In Praise of Learning [with Slapp Happy] (Virgin, 1975), Desperate Straights [with Slapp Happy] (Virgin, 1975), Western Culture (Broadcast, 1979), The Virgin Years (ReR Megacorp, 1991)
Art Bears: Hopes And Fears (Ré, 1978), Winter Songs (Ré, 1979), The World As It Is Today (Ré, 1980),
News From Babel: Work Resumed On The Tower (Ré, 1984), Letters Home (Ré, 1986)
Cassiber: Man Or Monkey (Ré, 1982), Beauty And The Beast (Ré, 1984), Perfect Worlds (Ré, 1986), A Face We All Know (ReR Megacorp, 1991)
The [EC] Nudes: Vanishing Point (ReR Megacorp, 1994)
with **David Thomas And The Pedestrians**: Winter Comes Home (Ré, 1983), More Places Forever (Ré, 1985)
with **Les 4 Guitaristes De L'apocalypso Bar**: Tournée Mondiale Été 1989 (Ambiances Magnétiques, 1987), Fin de Siecle (Ambiances Magnétiques, 1989)
with **The Wooden Birds**: Blame The Messenger (Rough Trade, 1987)
with **Pere Ubu**: The Tenement Year (Phonogram, 1988), Cloudland (Phonogram, 1989)
with **Fred Frith**: Live in Prague and Washington (Ré, 1979), Live in Prague, Moscow and Washington (ReR Megacorp, 1992)
with **Lutz Glandien**: Domestic Stories (ReR Megacorp, 1992)
as **editor**
Ré Records Quarterly Vol.1 N1 - Vol.4 N1 (ReR Megacorp, 1984-1994)

Footnotes:
1. Reprinted in *Travels In Hyperreality*, Harcourt Brace Jovanovich: London, 1986: p.143
2. Phonogram, 1991, 3. I am indebted to Chris for this phrase.
4. Rough Trade, 1977, 5. Rough Trade, 1987, 6. Phonogram, 1988, 7. *Cloudland*; Phonogram, 1989
8. The care and dedication with which Cutler carries out his work is seen in the unique nature of all ReR releases, from the curious items subscribers receive to the actual records themselves. For example, an exquisitely packaged 7th anniversary boxed set of "hit" singles featured 15 45s with silkscreened covers, colored and engraved pressings, a generous booklet of art and texts, even a tea cloth!
9. November Books: London, 1984; revised 1992
10. Editorial Afterward, *Ré Records Quarterly* Vol.1 N2, 1986: p.4
11. Editorial Afterward, *Ré Records Quarterly* Vol.2 N3, 1988: p.46
12. Composer John Oswald's term for music crafted from existing musical and sonic sources; see *John Oswald*, p.132, 13. Editorial Afterward, *Ré Records Quarterly* Vol.2 N3, 1988: p.46
14. Ralph, 1983, 15. ReR manifesto, 1991, 16. *Recommended Records Sampler*, 1982, 17. Ré, 1980
18. "Necessity and Choice In Musical Forms," in *File Under Popular* [2nd Edition], pp.147-148
19. ReR Megacorp, 1993, 20. Recommended, 1986, 21. Vol.3 N2, 1992, 22. Vol.2 N2, 1987,
23. Vol.2 N1, 1987, 24. Vol.2 N4, 1989, 25. Vol.2 N1, 1987, 26. Vol.1 N2, 1985, 27. Vol.2 N4, 1989
28. This is explored in luminous detail in "Necessity and Choice In Musical Forms," *File Under Popular* [2nd Edition], pp.19-38
29. Italics mine. 30. Cutler is referring to Iancu Dumitrescu, a Romanian electroacoustic composer who specializes in dense, hallucinatory and intense recordings of prepared piano, wind instruments, percussion and amplified sound
31. ReR Megacorp, 1991, 32. ReR Megacorp, 1992, 33. ReR Megacorp, 1993, 34. ReR Megacorp, 1994.
35. See *Amy Denio* p.98, 36. Editorial Afterword, *Ré Records Quarterly* Vol.2 N1, 1987: p.51

Fred Frith

Which is more musical, a truck passing by a factory or a truck passing by a music school? Are the people inside the school musical and the ones outside unmusical? What is the ones inside can't hear very well, would that change my question? Are sounds just sounds or are they Beethoven?

John Cage, "Composition As Process"[1]

The sound of *silence*

On a cold and drizzly Thanksgiving Friday in early October of 1992, Fred Frith finds himself onstage at the Grand Café in downtown Victoriaville, Québec, soundchecking his new work, *Stone, Brick, Glass, Wood, Wire*, as the ghost of John Cage waits in the wings.[2] "I've been thinking a lot about Cage since he died," Frith admits in an aside. "More and more I come to understand that one of the things that was most important to me about reading Cage when I was young was that he had a sense of humor. And so much of what I was reading about music in those days was very academic. To read somebody talking about music in such a fresh way, with a lot of warmth and humor, was very touching to me, and obviously it left a deep impression, and continues to do so. The strange thing is, I never listened to his music for years. When I read *Silence* it would be another six or seven years before I heard one piece of Cage's. Since then, of course, I've begun to look at things, and I find his prepared piano pieces very interesting. But I still find him eminently readable. His idea that sound itself could be a parameter just like any other musical parameter left a very deep impression. You know, if you're alert to that and hear it as that, then sound can become what you want it to become."

Frith first read Cage's writings as a 17-year old blues purist and nurse stationed in a mental hospital, and he has had his ears cocked ever since. At Cambridge in 1968, the British-born guitarist first applied the teachings of Cage and Cornelius Cardew to the blues of Alexis Korner and the jazz of Wes Montgomery alongside Chris Cutler, Tim Hodgkinson, Lindsay Cooper, and Dagmar Krause in the seminal, socialist, "dada blues" band Henry Cow. From there, a keen aleatory awareness has informed all of Frith's subsequent projects: the sonic brilliance of his guitars on the table approach, his intuitive and visceral duet work with maverick guitarists like Henry Kaiser, René Lussier and Hans Reichel, his admired, open-minded production and soundtrack work, and his infamous improvised solo performances, where his guitar can be a fluid conduit between between the audience and performer. And that's just the short list. At 43, Frith is perhaps the most forward-looking, restless guitarist on the planet.

The Festival Internationale de Musique Actuelle de Victoriaville's 10th anniversary would be unthinkable without Frith, who has become the festival's patron saint after numerous appearances there, so *Stone, Brick, Glass, Wood, Wire* is receiving its North American premiere here in Victoriaville.[3] Onstage, clad in black jeans, a red flannel shirt, a chocolate-colored leather vest and the ever-present black beret, Frith rubs his face, the venerable, weathered face of a *sympathique* farmer from the Midi. It's a tricky soundcheck, taking most of the afternoon, not only because the ensemble is a nonet, but because there's an acoustic harp amidst the fray, an instrument notoriously difficult to mike properly. As he directs the proceedings, a buried laugh threatens to break through into a guffaw, and the humming he does as he walks about the stage in between setups is infected with the same *bonhomie* as his music.

It's a scene that would have easily fit in with any of those Werner Penzel and Nicolas Humbert shot in Tokyo, Osaka, Verona, St-Rémy-de-Provence, Leipzig, London, New York, Zurich and Bern for their 1989 *verité* documentary/celluloid jam *Step Across The Border*. Like Robert Frank's 1987 road movie to end all road movies, *Candy Mountain*, *Step Across The Border* reveals more about its "have guitar, will travel" protagonist by focusing the camera on the world around him: In between the images of snaking, dadaesque typography, eerily rustling cornfields, and an industrial candy machine chewing over an impossibly huge wad of gum, we see a rumpled Frith singing "Spring Any Day Now,"[4] staring down a flock of sheep somewhere in Yorkshire, and engaging in a lively discussion of Art, Tarkovsky, and Communion at a Tokyo noodle stall.

In conversation after the soundcheck, Frith reveals himself to be a sharply articulate, honest and humble musician, one with a knowledge of several languages and a witty, Cagean sense of humor: later that evening, to a predominantly francophone audience, he greets the crowd wryly with "Buona sera, tutti." In fact, in our conversation, many of the double-edged rapiers Cage first explored are echoed: improvisation versus structure, freedom versus form, the use and abuse of technology, found objects as instruments, chance and itinerary, revolution and reckoning.

"Cage's whole philosophy was based on leaving things alone, and letting the sounds be themselves with as little interference from him as possible," Frith explains. "Hence the random composing approach and so on. And I was influenced by him to the extent that I also adopted certain chance methods of generating material, but what I did with them afterwards was *not* leave them alone, so from this point of view we're probably philosophically contrary to one another. I use playing cards rather than the *I Ching* to generate tone rows or melodies, just to bring something in that doesn't have my habits. As an instrumentalist and a composer, you have all sorts of habits, and anything you can do to contradict them is probably quite useful even if you decide not to go with it. That was the same reason I very much liked those cards that Brian Eno produced, the *Oblique Strategies*.[5] Always useful.

"But I think anyone can generate their own oblique strategies. In many cases people who used the cards found that they became a block to their own creativity, because they could always go to the cards. It's much better, as you gain experience, to codify it for yourself. Brian keeps notebooks, and he inspired me to do the same. Whenever I was hanging around with him, he would be always writing things down in his notebooks. Since then, I've kept notebooks handy, either a music book or a non-music book. If I think of something, I'll write it down. You never know whether it will be useful or not, but you'll forget it either way. The more you live, the more information comes in, the more information that you'll forget. And you'll usually forget your own ideas."

Graphic scores, handmade music

Author Cole Gagne once described Fred Frith's work as porous.[6] The adjective is a felicitous one, as Frith soaks up a world of influences, ideas, music, instruments and everyday sounds like a sponge. His wonderful solo album of ethnological forgery, *Gravity*,[7] was the result of two years' worth of reading and traveling through Greece, listening to dance music in odd meters. He has long carried with him a portable cassette machine, recording rain pattering on the roof of his van, improv gigs, Native American tribal dances, assorted birdsong, street musicians, political demonstrations and playgrounds. Frith believes musical ideas surround us in the air, and the tools of capturing them are varied, be they a notebook, walkman, or camera. Which brings us to the photographs.

"I started taking photographs of things about, oh 10 or 15 years ago, and I've accumulated masses and masses of them. At a certain point recently I started using them as inspiration for when I was in the recording studio. So, in the last few years, whenever I've gone in to mix a record, I've selected a handful of pictures, usually log piles on trucks, rocks, and that sort of thing, and put them on the wall when I was mixing. I find them every interesting in the same way that I guess someone like Bartók used to have fir cones on his desk to remind him of the Fibonacci series. I like having these photographs of strange pattern phenomena because they throw up ideas."

Opening up his photo album, Frith displays the photographs: geometric studies of striped brick walls, cobblestones, skylights, a blanket of mottled snow over gravel, stacks of logs in a lumberyard, grass poking through patio stones, and telegraph wires strung across the sky. "From there," he continues, "I thought this could be interpreted a music in a way. So I then started thinking about how that could be realized. When I was a student in the 1960s, I was quite interested in then current trends in modern music, one of which was graphic scores, which were quite fashionable in the late '60s even though they go back to the 1950s. Cornelius Cardew wrote in a way what is considered the definitive graphic score which was *Treatise*,[8] a very long work that's usually performed in pages. I was curious about what it meant, a graphic score, and I performed a couple of pages of it. But then I kind of lost interest in it and went into other directions."

The object of *Stone, Brick, Glass, Wood, Wire* is for the individual musicians to interpret the photographs as they see fit, using their contours, textures, and patterns as guides. [In performance, the photographs aren't projected; Frith feels it would look too much like a geological lecture.] Frith, meanwhile, modulates time and structure in an approach similar to John Zorn's game pieces,[9] yet leaves what a brick or glass should sound like up to the musicians. "Zorn's game pieces are much more to do with getting at the bottom of what makes improvisers tick, and then formulating it in such a way as to create structures using those parameters," Frith says. "In most of the game pieces I think I'm right in saying the musicians are giving the cues themselves. Whereas I'm much more a non-musical participant in this work, I'm directing time structure more than anything else. I'm not dictating what people actually play at all. I'm more or less a traditional conductor inasmuch that I'm dealing with tempo and dynamics, just like the conductor of an orchestra."

In concert, *Stone, Brick, Glass, Wood, Wire* is much like the color xeroxes of the photographs placed on the music stands: static, yet subtly shifting, with a wealth of harmonic and timbral variety. It begins with a series of impeccably timed orchestral slashes, broken by Ikue Mori's odd drum machine fumbling, a blush of keys from pianist Myra Melford, reedist Jean Derome's inventive mouth percussion, or the earnest, broken waltz of Guy Klucevsek's squeezebox. Things open up from there as drummer Han Bennink kicks it over in a busy drum solo. With his beret at a jaunty angle and a stopwatch in hand, Frith "conducts" *à la* Butch Morris.

The photographs bear only a passing resemblance to the finished musical product, and as such are merely ciphers for the players' imaginations. But when the musicians happen to be world-class improvisors like Mori, Klucevsek, Melford, Bennink, Derome, guitarist René Lussier, trumpeter Leslie Dalaba, and harpist Zeena Parkins, the result is a suite packed with finely honed and fertile duets, trios, and quartets. In terms of texture and dynamics, *Stone, Brick, Glass, Wood, Wire* offers an aural experience akin to consuming an eight course meal of cuisine from around the world in one sitting. The composition is never the same twice, and its unpredictability can be quite funny: with his battery of duck calls, Derome made Frith crack up more than once. It's typically Frithian: hands-on, homemade, and continually fostering new accidents to happen.

Frith plays two handmade instruments in *Stone, Brick, Glass, Wood, Wire*, and their origins stem from a luthier's fascination with the inner workings of guitars and his stunning 1981 solo improv performances in Japan, collected on the double LP *Live In Japan*.[11] On works like "Fukoka I" and "Maeabashi I" Frith lays his guitars flat on the tabletop and brutalizes the strings and pickups with – among other *objets trouvés* – paintbrushes, scarves, E-bows,[10] alligator clips, and eggbeaters. One of *Step Across The Border*'s most intriguing sequences follows Frith through a Tokyo grocery shop, as he buys noodles, rice, chopsticks and octopus chips – only to go home and drop them on his guitar to see what they sound like.

"It was a long evolution," says Frith. "I started playing guitars, then I started laying the guitars flat, then I started playing two guitars flat, then gradually I became aware that the fact that it was a guitar was becoming increasingly irrelevant to what I wanted to do with it, and I was damaging the guitars in the bargain, so I thought rather than do that, maybe I should build something really crude that I won't worry so much if it gets knocked about." So Frith took a couple of planks of wood and strung them. One of the resulting paradoxes was that he was expecting to produce instruments which would be very crude, but as plucked instruments, they were actually more delicate than a guitar. "They're like little kotos in a way," he says. "There are even tuning possibilities. Now, I never considered myself a very serious homemade instrument builder because I'm not very good on a craft level, and I've got other fish to fry. Besides, there is an enormous interest in homemade instruments now, and since Partch, there have been all kinds of great instruments and builders out there. Someone like Hans Reichel[12] kind of reinvented the guitar. He's a wonderful craftsman.

"But for a long time, I improvised only on these handmades. When I played with Derek Bailey's Company for example, I wasn't playing guitar at that time, I was playing only homemade instruments. Maybe that's why he invited me. [*Frith chuckles*] At a certain period, I guess it was about 1987 or so, I kind of decided to go back to the guitar again, and found that I had learned a lot of things from playing these homemades." In 1991, Frith encouraged the concept of homemades to a group of 16 unemployed young rock musicians from Marseilles, who were being paid by the French government to be "taught" by Frith for six months. The group, who called themselves Que d'la Gueule, had wildly disparate skills at the beginning, which is exactly what Frith was looking for in scoring a theater/opera project called *Helter Skelter*.

"It was very difficult to make a coherent group out of such an enormous range of style, taste and ability," Frith explains. "But that was one of the things that was most successful, actually. Somehow all their personalities infected the kind of music we ended up making together. I wrote the music very much for them and what they could do and how they could do it. So it's a music of a kind that I wouldn't normally write, which made it fresh and exciting. But because there were so many guitarists and drummers and so few other instruments it was kind of frustrating to kind of get a good balance of instruments out of it. There were three musicians I really liked, but who weren't particularly good on their instruments, which were guitars and drums. So I told them if you want to be in the group, and I would like you to be in the group, you have to invent your own instruments and make them, and I gave them lots of material like books to read and exhibitions to go and see and ideas where they could find junk to make stuff out of, and they basically produced their own instruments for the ensemble."

While billed as an operatic tragedy, featuring a "libretto" by François-Michel Pesenti, *Helter Skelter* is as far from *Nixon In China*[13] as it is from *Tannhauser*. Que d'la Gueule show themselves to be a powerful ensemble bristling with talent and volatile contradictions, and in *Helter Skelter*[14] they sketch a broad canvas of despair and hope, an urban maelstrom with moments of pure beauty peering through the shards of electroacoustic reality. Listening to it is like a ride on the subway and a stroll through a bustling market while listening to music on a walkman: striated fragments upon fragments leak through, from Eastern European jigs and dances [the ones that fascinated Frith so much on *Gravity*], samples of street life, radio broadcasts, plaintive chords arising from the horns, a soprano singer launching into Catalani's *La Romance*, all layered in an astonishingly dense, chaotic mix and anchored by two airtight drummers.

The music of Que d'la Gueule is far removed from Frith's usual fare; the dank, Brechtian mood, soprano vocals, and operatic nomenclature recalls the work of The Art Bears – the group he formed after Henry Cow with Chris Cutler and Dagmar Krause – but charged with the fierce guitar aggression of Massacre and armed with the technology of today. It's as if George Fewkoomby and the gang of unionized beggars from *Threepenny Opera* were alive and walking the streets of Marseilles with digital samplers next to their pencil tins.

are you loaded?
Since his days with The Art Bears, Frith's work shows a quixotic ambivalence to the tyranny of studio technology, and, like Eno, he is often guilty of throwing out the instruction manual in the quest for the hidden intention, the random code, the broken fragments from before. He has an ongoing passion for the poetry of malfunction, taking razor blades to tape, and physically abusing the Revox, techniques which he explored to full fruition in *Speechless*[15] and in the cutup television ads he spliced into live performances with Skeleton Crew. It is an aesthetic he took to its logical conclusion with digital sampling in Keep The Dog, where Bob Ostertag brought along the sound bites and their attendant technical problems; at a 1989 performance of Keep The Dog in Victoriaville, Frith would often ask Bob Ostertag "Are you loaded?" before each number.

"I've never wanted to pursue technology to keep up with what's new and always try to learn how to use the stuff as it gets more and more complicated," Frith insists. "Instead I've always very much appreciated going to work with engineers who are keeping abreast of things; I can say 'Is it possible to do *this* now?' and they say yes. Seriously, I like working with computer editing and sound tools and so on, they're great. I even think sampling has all kinds of potential possibilities. In point of fact most people use it very cosmetically, which is why I like Bob's work, because he understands it in a much more profound way. His solo work and the stuff he wrote for The Kronos Quartet is really hard-hitting stuff that uses sampling in a very deep way. He's interested in something more than [*Frith mimics scratching a turntable and the rapid-fire, duck-like sample often heard in hiphop*]. On the other hand, I don't want to reject all the qualities of analog recording that I like. So I tend to be always mixing things, which in a way is what *The Technology of Tears* was all about."

A powerful electronic collage/suite for dance that brilliantly subverts the modern tools of sampling and editing, *The Technology Of Tears*[16] was sparked by a chance meeting with Henry Kaiser's newly-purchased synclavier guitar. Frith pits the cybernetic, staccato pulse of the synclavier against Christian

Marclay's dusty, disembodied turntables, Tenko's fierce, controlled vocals, John Zorn's high-octane alto sax, and his own joyous violin. While the quote by author Zbigniew Herbert on the jacket speaks of tears, *Technology* has a lot to do with breath as a metaphor for life, and how our voices can become lost amidst the cluttered soundtrack and noise pollution of jump-cut modern existence.

"We were using completely parallel music technology, some of which was comparatively crude," Frith recalls. "I mean I was cutting up tape and doing all those old things that one doesn't do anymore, because it actually produces a sound quality that you can't get with digital sound editing. What I liked about that record was that we were cutting up tape on the one hand, and digital editing on the other, and juxtaposing the technologies. There's a part of Tenko's voice where she sang the line directly, and we sampled the line, then had the one transform into the other, so you get the feeling of like the mechanization of something living, and it gradually starts to become mechanical. It's very subtle, and very interesting to hear things like that."

Just as Frith has employed the medium of magnetic tape in a manner intrinsic to it, as a producer, he has used the multi-track recording studio as a means to achieve musics not possible in traditional live performance,[17] something that *musique concrète* expounded as far back as the 1950s, yet which rock never cottoned on to, with Frank Zappa, Captain Beefheart and The Beatles being honorable mentions. A quick survey of the bands Frith has produced confirms this: The Muffins, Orthotonics, Mizutama Shobodan, V-Effect, Tenko, Etron Fou, and Dr Nerve are all artists who would rather leave the perfect, clean snare sounds to the session men and Steely Dan fanatics, and inject unorthodox ideas into the recording process.[18] Take, for example, Yasushi Utsonomiya, the sound engineer for the Japanese pop ensemble After Dinner, whom Frith worked with on the 1985 Celluloid compilation of Tokyo pop, *Welcome to Dreamland.*[19]

"Working with Utsonomiya was very important because he had such a left-field way of looking at things," Frith says. "He was always very refreshing to be around. I was telling the story today about the time when he came to record a quartet that I was doing and his manner of placing the microphones was completely eccentric; you couldn't understand it at all. He'd go and put his ear to a wall, and muck around a little bit, ostensibly putting a microphone on you, he'd point it away from you, down into a corner somewhere, and you couldn't figure out what on earth he was doing. You'd hear the recording afterward, and he would have calculated every angle of reflection in the room, and the density of every surface, and you'd have something that sounded like a studio digital recording. It was really something."

From the first recordings of Henry Cow, which he saw as a crash course in production as well as musical politics and economics, to his ambient yet multi-layered soundtrack work on art films like *The Top Of His Head*,[20] Frith has strongly believed that production work is key to understanding dynamics, both personal *and* musical. "Inevitably, studio work has taught me an awful lot about structure, and especially about time," Frith says. "When you're composing, you tend to write things rather long and drawn out, and when you get into a studio you rather quickly find out what's redundant. In this way studio work *is* composing, that's what it comes down to; it's just another kind of process. But it's a good discipline. Like the first time you do a multi-track recording and then play back your one track solo: Terror, knees knocking. Then you find out how good you really are. That's very educational. There's nobody who goes through that process without being better off for it afterwards, because it really shows you what your weaknesses are."

Speechless

Given his recent mute work in film and dance, it seems that the days of Fred Frith singing joyous, cheeky ditties like "Norrgården Nyvla," "Absent Friends," and "Same Old Me" are a thing of the past; we will have to content ourselves with reissues of his classic Ralph records from the early 1980s: *Gravity*, *Speechless*, and *Cheap At Half The Price*.[21] From the beginning, Frith has admired distinctive, offbeat vocalists with a human purity rather than a tonal one; during Henry Cow he was under the spell of The Soft Machine's Robert Wyatt. By the time he had heard vocalists such as Phil Minton, David Moss, Pere Ubu's David Thomas and Cassiber's Christoph Anders, his interest in lyrics as pop verse had waned; the underlying theme of *Speechless* is ultimately about being unable to articulate the words that once flowed freely. What was left was the polemic and joyous shouting of Skeleton Crew, a response to the heyday of the punk movement; today, Frith admits more influenced by Inuit throat singers these days than any vocalists. Even his recent collaboration with Ferdinand Richard, *Dropera*,[22] a folksy fable about the ghosts of an Arab diplomat and a Scots whiskey salesman marooned on an Aegean isle with only a miracle food to keep them alive, featured only Frith's guitars and distinctive violin playing, leaving the whimsical lyrics to Richard.

"I write words all the time," Frith says. "I've been writing a lot of I suppose you would have to call poems lately, but they're not things I would like to sing. Lyric writing is a very special and peculiar discipline. I think when Tom [*Cora*] and I were writing together we had a very good effect on each other; most of the lyrics we wrote together absolutely. Since I've stopped collaborating with Tom for the time being, they're not so easy for me. And I'm not so interested, because I'm not doing that at the moment anyway. There are also people whose words I really like. When I did *In Memory* at New Music America in New York, I worked with a poet from San Francisco called Sarah Miles, and her work is wonderful. Given that, there's no need for me to write lyrics."

The words also kept getting in the way of Keep The Dog, the supergroup Frith assembled to play his "hits" from The Art Bears, Massacre, his solo pop albums, and his recent collaborations with John French, Henry Kaiser, and Richard Thompson.[23] Featuring René Lussier on guitar, Jean Derome on winds, Zeena Parkins on harp, Bob Ostertag on samples, Frith himself on bass and Charles Hayward behind the traps, Keep The Dog was an surprising success, bringing Frith critical acclaim and booking offers from many quarters, particularly in Europe. Yet Frith's own reaction was mixed, and the group disbanded last year. "I'm glad I did it, and the good gigs that we did were wonderful," he says forthrightly. "But somehow the idea was flawed somewhere along the line, and I think because it was that I couldn't relinquish the material enough. When I formed the group I wanted to see what would happen when musicians other than me or the ones I used on the record played the material; to see what new contexts would arise. At the same time, the records themselves and the material we were doing were somehow monumental. I don't mean in a qualitative sense necessarily, but what they *are*. It was very hard to go to that material and do it a different way once you knew what that material is. On one hand, I was saying 'Okay, here's the material, let's see what happens to it.' On the other, when something *did* happen to it, I'd say, 'No, it should be like this.'

"So on the last tour, more and more I'd very often say 'We're not going to do this song or that song. Instead we're going to a trio: Zeena, René and Charles, you're going to play song form A and we're going to play song form B without any preordained material at all.' And Claudia [Engelhart], the sound engineer, would also be involved, and would sometimes get to do duets with one of the musicians in which she would change all the sound parameters on the board. She was delighted because she got to tweak all the equipment and do all the kinds of things that musicians tell you not to do. But the more we did it, the more it sounded suspiciously like Henry Cow to me. So on the last tour, we did some very good gigs, but I didn't feel that anything new was happening compared to what I did before, and I didn't want to fall back into a group because we were successful and people wanted to book us and so on. That's kind of what happened to Henry Cow, we got so popular in a certain way that we kept on doing gigs when we didn't really have anything to do anymore. So I felt we should stop the group now while we're ahead. I've got at least 30 DAT tapes that Claudia recorded. So when I get a little distance, I will listen to them."

a step across the border

Distance is something Frith has covered a lot of in his day. Going where his music takes him, be it Moscow, Tokyo, New York, Leipzig, or Victoriaville, his life is a seeming blur of trains, hotels, and soundchecks. In fact, one of the most memorable images we have of Frith is found in *Step Across The Border*: Frith asleep on a train as it hurtles through a European landscape, cradling his guitar in his arms.

First was the move to New York in the early 1980s after the dissolution of The Art Bears. Lured by the energy of the burgeoning downtown scene there, Frith took an apartment on the then-hip Lower East Side, and gigs in Massacre and Skeleton Crew. Then an invitation to play brought Frith to Japan in 1981, and he brought his guitars to their tables. "I had such a wonderful time there, it was not difficult to imagine going back again," he says. "I used to go there at least once a year. Some years I would go back two or three times, in fact. But Japan is a strange country. It's very welcoming when you first go there, and rather hostile the longer you stay there. They're very protective of their own insular cultural habits, so as long as you're definitely not in the culture, they can accept you completely. But if you're kind of burrowing your way into it, you've got some problems. Which is why Westerners tend not to rise very far in Japanese companies."

Most of 1992, Frith has lived in Europe, touring with Keep The Dog, and working with Que d'la Gueule in Marseilles. "I moved back to Europe because it made no sense for me to be in America if I was going to be spending all my time traveling to Europe, which I was. Most of the economical structure for musicians of all kinds, but including Americans, is European. Particularly Swiss, German and Austrian. That's where the money is. We do a couple of hours a day, and we're getting three times as much money as you do in America, and you're getting a full house every night; it's very gratifying. So it doesn't make much sense to be spending all your time traveling back and forth in airplanes; you might as well be there all the time. But now I'm thinking of taking a year's sabbatical just for composing. If that were the case, I can think of nicer places to be than Munich."

Despite his ever-changing address, Frith doesn't think of himself as a restless soul, a musical nomad. "It's not true," he protests. "I lived in New York for 13 years. That's a long time. Although I was traveling a lot in that time, I was always coming back to my home, and that was my home. Since I moved away from New York, and I kind of did make the break and take my stuff away and not have an apartment anymore, so the umbilical cord to New York was broken. And since then, that was earlier this year, I have been a bit not quite sure where I want to be or where I'd like to end up. Right now I'm not so interested in traveling anywhere; everything's a little fluid at the moment."

Yet casting back, Frith feels that he wouldn't pursue any other path. "That's not the kind of question you can really answer," he says. "I don't particularly have any great regrets about what I've done. There are sometimes I think I've been *blind* to things, or caught up to things a bit later than I should. I'm always amused when I think about the time when people were saying that I was influenced by Keith Rowe, who is a guitarist I like very much. But when I first heard Keith Rowe,[24] and until not very long ago, and certainly long after I was playing guitars on the table, I didn't even know Keith Rowe played the guitar." Frith laughs.

It's an ironic laugh, because more than any other instrument, Fred Frith has been identified with the guitar, from his days in the mid-1960s as a young guitarist playing in Ventures knockoff bands in London pubs, his imagination fired by John Cage, Frank Zappa, Howlin' Wolf, and just about any guitar vinyl he could get his hands on. Yet many overlook the fact that Frith's first instrument was the violin, as part of a classical education that started at age 6. Indeed, in addition to *Stone, Brick, Glass, Wood, Wire*, this weekend at Victo Frith is playing violin in Lars Hollmer's Looping Home Orchestra. "In the beginning, I loved guitar music, but I loved other kinds of music, too," he says. "I was pretty eclectic. These days I play just as much bass as I play guitar, and violin, too.

"And sometimes I don't play at all."

Fred Frith: Guitar Solos (Caroline, 1974), Gravity (Ralph, 1980) Speechless (Ralph, 1980), Live In Japan (Recommended Japan, 1982), Cheap At Half The Price (Ralph, 1983), The Technology Of Tears (RecRec, 1988), The Top Of His Head (Crammed/Made To Measure, 1990), Step Across The Border (RecRec, 1990), Quartets (RecRec, 1994)
with **Henry Cow**: Legend (Virgin, 1973), Unrest (Virgin, 1974), In Praise of Learning [with Slapp Happy] (Virgin, 1975), Desperate Straights [with Slapp Happy] (Virgin, 1975), Western Culture (Broadcast, 1979), The Virgin Years (ReR Megacorp, 1991)
with **The Art Bears**: Hopes And Fears (Ré, 1978), Winter Songs (Ré, 1979), The World As It Is Today (Ré, 1980),
with **Massacre**: Killing Time (Celluloid, 1981)
with **Skeleton Crew**: Learn To Talk (Rift, 1984), The Country of Blinds (Rift, 1987)
with **Chris Cutler**: Live in Prague and Washington (Ré, 1979), Live in Prague, Moscow and Washington (ReR Megacorp, 1992)
with **French/Frith/Kaiser/Thompson**: Live, Love, Larf And Loaf (Rhino, 1987), Invisible Means (Demon, 1990)
with **Henry Kaiser**: With Friends Like These (Metalanguage, 1979), Who Needs Enemies (Metalanguage, 1982)
with **René Lussier**: Nous Autres (Victo, 1987)
with **Que D'la Gueule**: Helter Skelter (RecRec, 1992)
with **Hans Reichel**: Sundown (FMP, 1990)

with **Ferdinand Richard**: Dropera (RecRec, 1991)

Productions
The Muffins - 185 (Random Radar, 1981), Etron Fou Leloublan - Les Poumons Gonflés (Turbo, 1983), Mizutama Shobodan - Sky Full Of Red Petals (Kinniku Bijo, 1984), Orthotonics - Wake Up You Must Remember (Artefacts, 1984), V-Effect - Stop Those Songs (Rift, 1984), Curlew - North America (Moers, 1985), Etron Fou Leloublan - Face Aux Elements Déchainés (RecRec, 1985), David Moss - Dense Band (Moers, 1985), Various - Welcome to Dreamland (Celluloid, 1985), Orthotonics - Luminous Bipeds (RecRec, 1986), Dr Nerve – Armed Observation (Cuneiform, 1987), Tenko - Slope/Gradual Disappearance (RecRec, 1987)

Footnotes:
1. Reprinted in *Silence*, Marion Boyars: London, 1968: p.41
2. An earlier version of this chapter originally appeared as "Elements Of Style: Fred Frith's Constructive Approach," the author; *Option* Magazine N49, March 1993: pp.38-81
3. It had been previously staged in Wels, Austria and Bologna, Italy in 1991
4. From *Speechless*; Ralph, 1980
5. Subtitled "Over 100 Worthwhile Dilemmas," the oblique strategies were a series of cards created by Brian Eno and artist Peter Schmidt as a sort of private oracle to navigate creative impasses in the studio; messages were printed on the cards such as *Discover the recipes you are using and abandon them* and *Honor they error as hidden intention*
6. In *Sonic Transports: New Frontiers In Our Music*; de Falco Press, New York: 1990
7. Ralph, 1980
8. 120 pages, to be exact. *Treatise* [1966-8] was written for the peerless British improvisation collective AMM, and went far beyond the simple graphic scores of Cage, Morton Feldman, and Christian Wolff. Its complex and enigmatic geometry has rarely been performed since
9. See *John Zorn*, p.147,
10. Recommended Japan, 1982
11. A small electromagnetic pickup which generates a constant sustain when held near a guitar's strings
12. A German luthier and improvisor who specializes in unusual, hand-crafted guitar hybrids; see *René Lussier*, p.180. Frith also duets with Reichel on *Sundown*; FMP, 1990
13. John Adams' 1987 modern opera about geopolitics, the landmark summit between Richard Nixon and Mao Tse Tung, and the opening of China to the world
14. RecRec, 1992
15. Ralph, 1980
16. RecRec, 1988
17 See *Chris Cutler*, p.25
18. Many of the bands Frith produced returned the favor by collaborating with him on his solo projects; Washington's Muffins and Sweden's Samlas Mammas Manna provided the backing tracks for *Gravity*, while Massacre & Etron Fou Leloublan did the honors for *Speechless*
19. See *After Dinner*, p.243
20. Crammed/Made To Measure, 1990
21. Ralph, 1983
22. RecRec, 1991
23 *Live, Love, Larf and Loaf*, Rhino, 1987; and *Invisible Means*, Demon, 1990
24. Guitarist for the seminal British new music ensemble AMM

Ferdinand Richard

"Like drums, the bass is exhausting to carry when you go somewhere to play, and then you are persecuted by the other musicians who neither hear nor respect you. On the other hand, you can hide ten kilos of chocolate in it when you come back across the border from Belgium."

Boris Vian, "He Who Wants To Can"[1]

"With music, you have to be a specialist in terms of handicraft," says Ferdinand Richard. "You have to *touch* it very well. In terms of opening your mind, you also have to be flexible. This is the power of Miles Davis, for example. Miles integrated hard rock guitarists and drummers; no-one else did it. I am not a fan of Miles but I can clearly see that he came to his position because of this openness. Miles said once that he was interested in Fred Frith as a percussionist. I find that a little extreme, but it clearly shows that Miles was listening."[2]

In a nondescript greasy spoon at the crossroads in Victoriaville, over quintessentially American fare – a hamburger and a shake – bassist Ferdinand Richard is reflecting about technique, apropos of the gut-wrenching gig by one-time journalist and sampler Bob Ostertag that opened the 1991 edition of The Festival de Musique Actuelle de Victoriaville. Built up from three samples – a buzzing fly, a sobbing child whose father has just been murdered by

Nicaraguan contra soldiers, and the sound of shovels sinking into the ground – Ostertag's *Sooner Or Later*[3] was riveting, horrifying, and difficult to shake off; neither of us are much interested in the anemic fast food before us. "The harmony between the person and the instrument is very seducing for me," Richard continues. "When I like a musician, I like him because of his music, but most of the time it's no surprise that I like his face, his physical appearance, and the way he handles his instrument. All this is bound together, I think. It may sound a little mystical, but I'm not a mystical person. If you feel good with your music, you feel good with your instrument, and you can see that. It's like a living sculpture. It was very clear with Bob Ostertag; nobody was moving, his body was not moving, the instrument was flat, he was not moving. But a lot happened."

Following in the footsteps of the great Boris Vian, Richard believes that this empathy and passion does not stop with the instrument. French author, playwright, trumpet player, jazz critic, and 'pataphysician who headed up the Fontana jazz division at Phillips for a while, Vian [1920-1959] was a true *bricoleur* who perceived a certain immediate and prophetic resonance in what then was considered trash: science fiction, jazz, hard-boiled American detective novels. It is precisely these 'pataphysical qualities – his foresight, impudence, cynical wit, and good taste in jazz – that Richard brings to his *metier*. Few know, for instance, of his passion for literature and medieval poetry; he carries a thick notebook filled with neatly written verse and prose which eventually find their way into his solo projects. Or that for the past seven years he has been running Mouvement International des Musiques Innovatrices [MIMI], a spring festival in the south of France dedicated to showcasing new and unknown *musique actuelle* acts from Europe, North America, and around the world.

No, Richard is best known as the bass player of French cult group Etron Fou Leloublan, whose satirical, non-conformist rock in opposition spree lasted for six albums and 13 years of obscurity before disbanding in 1986. To be fair, Richard liberated his instrument from its traditional metronomic role in Etron Fou to explore more textural and melodic areas, using double stops, chords, harmonics and onomatopoeic sound effects. Richard's bass carried many a melody of their songs; typically tuned up a minor third to bring it closer to his voice.

Yet his subsequent collaborations and solo projects since Etron Fou are no less passionately driven, whether it's the zen poetry of Bruniferd, his intimate duo with saxophonist Bruno Meillier, or the post-modern "instant composition" of Gestalt Et Jive, his trio with saxophonist Alfred 23 Harth and drummer Peter Hollinger. His latest group – which he has brought to Victoriaville this year – is Ferdinand Et Les Philosophes, a power trio with guitarist Alain Rocher and drummer Dominique Lentin that retraces Richard's steps back to the woodshedding days of his adolescence. "Like any French youngster, I started playing in a garage band when I was 17, playing covers," Richard explains. "These are my roots. I am not a classical musician, I am self-taught. All these notions of avant garde, popular, and middle of the road; I don't really know what all these mean. I think these labels make less and less sense. You can see in the music industry today that all these genres are becoming more and more mixed; you have people crossing very easily from baroque music to rock groups and back again.

"The audience is not so stupid, either. Statistics show there is a range of people, growing every year, who do not want to be part of this big, uniform, gray mass of consumerism. I think the biggest mistake economists have made in recent years is that they thought they could easily define a 'common' consumer. But young people don't want to follow that schedule. I don't know if it is enough for a market to survive and a professional musician to make his living; but it's getting better. The beginning of the '80s was very dark for musicians like us; people saw us as old hippies with no ideas, and that we should get lost."

Hervé Richard was born on June 25, 1950, in Meknès, Morocco. After a childhood spent in Saint-Malo and Paris, he studied Medieval Literature and Law at Grenoble between 1969 and 1973, although music became more and more important in his life, and his studies suffered. So despite an attempt at music school [one and a half years], and a stint as bassist for the Conservatoire Régional de Musique de Grenoble [two years], he decided to adopt the pseudonym Ferdinand, and dropped out to join a local underground rock group that went by the name of Etron Fou Leloublan.

Etron Fou Leloublan were non-conformist from the outset. Their *nom de guerre* defies translation; the closest English comes is "mad shit the white wolf."[4] The coarse pun is indicative of the group's irreverence and delightfully vulgar wit; the Etrons sported an absurdist, scatological humor in their lyrics that tipped the bowler to the black tradition of great French surrealists Alfred Jarry and Benjamin Péret. A riotously funny, self-penned biographical release they wrote for publicity purposes when touring with Rock In Opposition during the 1970s features wonky spelling and fractured syntax that are very much in keeping with their cheeky spirit and fierce independence:

"In Grenoble they prowled at night about cultural centers, one with a very small saxophone, the other with a ridiculous 'pocket handkerchief' drumset. Sometimes under the name Grace-Molle [soft grace], Grosse Malle [big trunk], Grasse-Mole [fat mole], even Graisse Moelle [grease marrow], they act again and again in the shadow of sordid places. However, during 73, looking for a steadyer situation [the tripode], they desperately look in the local newspaper for Ratledge-or-MacCoy Tyner-like pianist. And this is the irrefutable proof that Hazrd makes [objectively] well the things for a pianist, they take Ferdinand out of a stern boarding-school class-room. Ferdinand is a bit for the electric bass what Louison Bobet was in France for the bicycle: in a word, a 'killer.'"[5]

On December 27, 1973, Richard, drummer Guigou "Samba Scout" Chenevier, and reedist Chris Eulalie Ruyat set up their instruments on a rectangular mat of astro-turf – complete with matching parasol and assorted summertime paraphernalia – and played their first gig, opening for Magma. Like Magma,[6] Etron Fou offered a viable, musical alternative to both French rock'n'roll and French free jazz, both of which had ossified into styles that canonized the attributes of their influences: French underground pop closely apes American garage rock, hiphop and punk, while French jazz remains an exercise in idol worship, in much the same way seminal French cinema can be seen as an elaborate *hommage* to the films of American *auteurs* like Clint Eastwood, Sam Fuller, and John Cassavettes.

"I have big problems with jazz people in France," Richard says testily. "You have so many assholes in the French jazz scene who believe they are Gods and don't know anything about what's going on. They have no spirit and they keep on copying the Anglo-American stuff. They don't want anything else except having all the signs and symbols of jazz nobility. The jazz scene in France lost its soul because of this. Jazz started in basements with illegal alcohol in Saint-Germain-des-Près. Forty years later they are all looking like doctors. They have no place in history unless they change their minds." Raw and strangely seductive, Etron Fou play with a surfeit of this passion and intensity. On both *Les Poumons Gonflés*[7] and *Face Aux Eléments Déchainés*[8] they employ a traditional jazz ensemble's instruments – drums, bass, organ and sax – to play lean, scrappy rock. [For most of their career, the band's lineup was essentially Chenevier, Richard and orbiting saxophonists, an approach which honed them into a flexible and gifted rhythm section.] The absurdist anecdotes are driven both melodically and percussively in fine Beefheartian style, with the instruments playing repeated lines that mesh in a rhythmic counterpoint. Producer Fred Frith balances all these elements, preserving the band's essential rawness and jazzy swing.

Living under the soot-filled skies of Avignon in the industrial south of France also helped to foster an irascible self-reliance, both in the trio's individual and eccentric approaches to their instruments and in their collective survival skills as an independent band afloat in a sea of record industry sharks. In an interview for *Impetus* magazine, Richard told writer Kenneth Ansell of the wariness he has always had for major label dealings: "I don't think they have any consideration of 'serious' or 'not serious,' 'political' or 'non-political,' they just don't worry about it. The only reason they exist is to make money. You can be ultra-left wing, but if you sell records, you are always interesting for them... If you don't sell records, they are not interested."[9]

From the beginning, Etron Fou channeled their politics into the managerial and administrative duties of the group, rather than the songs. Around the time they met Henry Cow, in the mid-1970s, they helped establish a regional cooperative, Dupon Et Ses Fantômes, dedicated to promoting new French music. "We are reserved...about taking a direct political position and we are not very interested in doing very concrete lyrics," Richard has said. "I think our system and organization of our work speaks for itself. For the stage, we prefer madness to speaking seriously; it is dangerous to be very serious...In France they laugh at free jazz groups for being very serious."[10] This madness was what kept Etron Fou striving in the face of obscurity. On April 19, 1984, they played the first of three concerts on the first floor of the Eiffel Tower in Paris; a historic enough occasion seeing as no band had ever done so. *France Soir* covered the event with the pithy acknowledgement: "A la recherche de nouvelles harmoniques, cet ensemble est beaucoup plus célèbres aux Etats-Unis."[11] *Quel prestige...*

"For 13 years, it was like five people at our gigs in France," Richard recalls ruefully. "We were totally unknown and marginalized. Since we've split, of course, we've become somewhat of a legend. It's ridiculous. The group has been dead since 1986, and you still read articles about this famous cult group Etron Fou. But if I remember well at the time, nobody wanted us to play. It's always the same story. Now, we have been propositioned to reunite for some anniversary concert. Of course, my answer is no. That's the past. I am not a veteran, you know. There's this guy in Paris who is overseeing the printing of the *intégrale*. It's very nice; I thank him, I will make some money out of it, but I feel strange, really. It's like a military decoration or something."

Richard pauses to light an unfiltered Gauloise. "I think the split of Etron Fou was a big mistake, though, and I regret it very much. We had a program of material that was never recorded. You know, you stop a group like Gestalt because you run out of ideas. That was not the case with Etron Fou. I think the old members have begun to realize it was a mistake, particularly Guigou. But it's over and done with now. I am from West France, and people there are supposed to have stone heads."

After the dissolution of Etron Fou, Richard focused his energies on Alfred 23 Harth's ensemble Gestalt Et Jive. Richard had been the bassist for Gestalt Et Jive since 1984, when Harth formed the group as an antidote to the atrophy of improvisation pervasive in free jazz during the 1970s. Originally the group's name was a clever rebus of their multinationality and direction – West German saxophonist Harth, French bassist Richard, British keyboardist Steve Beresford, and assorted musical hangers-on set out to harness structure [gestalt] to improvisation [jive]. After four years and two records, the trio of Harth, Richard and percussionist Peter Hollinger reached a creative peak with their "instant composition" technique. Delivering on vinyl and on stage an exciting racket of structured free playing that defied proper description, Gestalt Et Jive had clearly breathed life into something new in post-modern music.

Their farewell concert in Victoriaville in October of 1988 bristled with a taut, keening energy. The music was dark, gripping, and visceral. Keith Richards on a bad day looked better than Hollinger [he was actually down with the flu], who brutalized his drum kit and assorted metal objects with eggbeaters, smashed crockery, and kept precise time in an empty Pepsi cup. Hollinger managed to hold together Richard's power chords and Harth's split-toned squalls in an incredible display of controlled tension. With its grim humor, physicality, and fluidity of blending genres, it was thrilling spectacleand sheet music for the future.[12] At the encore, Hollinger walked onstage looking disgusted. After all, what else was there?

Richard also devoted more time to his ongoing duo project with saxophonist Bruno Meillier, Bruniferd. With two albums to their credit and a Japanese tour under their belt, Bruniferd is, according to Richard, dedicated to precise and condensed musical poetry. "If a note is there, it is because it has to be there," he says. "Our music is very concentrated. As such it is not a spectacle, it's not a show. Bruniferd is very powerful as it is trying to give a maximum of things with a minimum of element. Just one bass, no effects, one saxophone, no effects, and some *poesie*. We could eventually play with no PA; we could play in your bathroom. Many people do not see the importance of Bruniferd in light of Etron Fou, but they will in a couple of years."

Richard found another fertile duo collaboration with his old friend Fred Frith, who had produced the last two Etron Fou LPs; Etron Fou returned the favor by playing on Frith's *Speechless*.[13] Fred and Ferd's latest outing is *Dropera*, a strange little "opera" about the ghosts of a Scots whisky salesman and an Arab diplomat, a shipwreck, and a recipe for manna. "Our relationship is very peculiar," Richard says of his friendship with Frith. "We are very close friends, and we've work on projects together, but never as musicians. After all these years, we found playing together was very special. We wanted to more or less do something together. I came to this idea of text/opera. The story of *Dropera* is a very simple story in the picturesque tradition of 18th Century France. You could go on with such a story for albums and albums. The musical idea of the story was to work in a continuum, not like song form, but with acts and intermezzi, like an opera. This was the proposition. I wrote the texts, Fred liked it, and we exchanged musical ideas."

The whimsy of *Dropera* and the poignant classical simplicity of Bruniferd's latest album, *Un Putch Kitsch*,[14] reveals the bard in Richard, an unselfconscious narrator whose arresting images and glimpses of life passing by dominate Richard's solo albums. Richard's most personal solo effort, *En Avant*,[15] also betrays his passion for languages; the eight songs are written and sung in French, English, Vietnamese, German, Arabic, Polish, Dioula, and Spanish. Whether it's the life of "Victoria," telescoped onto a postcard and sung in Arabic, the meditations of a childhood in Saint Malo, or the surrealist fable of "Mr White Goes Hunting" in Dioula, the texts show a deft juxtaposition of culture and tongue, and a poetic heart at work.

Richard's most recent project delved even deeper into ancient tongues and linguistics. His chief collaborator was Michael Montanaro, a specialist in Occidental medieval music from South France and globe-trotting flautist and percussionist who could play the *galoubet* and tambourine simultaneously. The resulting work, only performed once in a small village outside Marseilles, was bound between modernity and polyphonic music and texts from the 12th to the 14th Centuries; the musicians called upon to breathe life into this past are bassist Barre Philips, saxophonist Charles Tyler, and Fred Frith. Since the untimely passing of Tyler in 1993, however, the work will remain unrecorded, consigned to history from whence it came. "It's a very sad story," laments Richard.

Montanaro approached Richard with the idea for the project after attending the Mouvement International des Musiques Innovatrices festival one May. Running MIMI is the task that takes up all of Ferdinand Richard's spare time. He founded the annual spring festival in May of 1986, and it has been uphill work ever since. Nestled in the Provence countryside, the towns of St-Rémy-de-Provence and St-Martin-de-Crau have proved to be idyllic locations where musicians from Europe, North America, and points east could gather and exchange ideas in the summer air. A spring companion to Victoriaville, the festival has an intimate feel; particularly successful are its workshops and open stage, where musicians could hold impromptu jams. Over the years, MIMI has showcased groups like After Dinner, Les Quatre Guitaristes de L'Apocalypso Bar, E, Fish & Roses, and Que d'la Gueule.[16] The umbrella organization that runs MIMI, Aide Aux Musiques Innovatrices, now has eight people on staff and has expanded to include a record shop/label, Stupeur Et Trompette. In 1992 Richard acquired a disused factory in Marseille, Friche Belle de Mai, to stage year round concerts, theater productions, art installations and dance events.

MIMI has been free since 1991. He modeled his new *gratis* MIMI on a highly successful Belgian festival, the Saint Jacob Festival in Ghent, which annually draws 25,000 people and shuts the city down to cars. Saint Jacob's program is extraordinarily eclectic, featuring everything from pop stars to avant garde, and is paid entirely by concessions and record sales, with zero grant money. Richard had brought the Japanese group After Dinner there in 1990, and thereafter decided to make MIMI free, something which pleased his government cultural sponsors greatly.

"Since our philosophy is to defend and present mostly unknown and creative people, our target is not to make money," says Richard. "We are a non-profit organization. So we thought 'Why don't we keep on presenting unknown people, but instead of doing a commercial "selling" act, make it free?' We paid less taxes since there were no ticket sales, we raised the price of the beer and the drinks, and we sold much more records at the records shop. Because of this, most of the people also stayed for the four days. The audiences for this kind of music are not rich people, and I know in past they had to make choices in past. As soon it was free, they stayed for the whole festival."

Held from the 8th to the 11th of July 1993, the Eighth Annual MIMI fest featured a weekend of audacious programming that mixed cultures, timelines, and pop styles. Breton singer Erik Marchand opened the proceedings with a stunning trio that featured Pakistani musician Hameed Khan and oud player Thierry Robin, while a *Nuit des Têtes Dures* ["Night Of The Hardheads"] featured the hardscrabble improvisation of The Ex and Tom Cora paired with Guigou Chenevier's propulsive new ensemble, Octavo. Permutations on pop, jazz, and fusion were offered by Americans Zero Pop and German guitarist Hans Reichel, who premièred his ensemble for daxophone, The All Dax Band. The festival closed with Phillipe Loli and Christiane Bonnay – a classical guitar/accordion duo from Monaco who specialize in concise, thorny modern classics – and the otherworldly, spine-tingling voice of Mongolian singer Sainkho Namtchylak.[17]

Even as musical director of a festival dedicated to new and challenging music, Richard is often faced with the same conformism that haunts the larger worlds of pop, rock and jazz. "When you travel in Europe from jazz festival to jazz festival, and you're in a hall listening to a group, you suddenly don't know whether you're in Stockholm or Barcelona," he explains. "Or whether the group is Dutch or German, it all looks the same. I received over 500 proposals for the MIMI Festival last year, and I received a lot of tapes which were *à la* Fred Frith. It's weird; you have to look on the envelope to see where it comes from. There's somebody banging a metallic plate with contact microphones, somebody sawing an electric guitar plugged into a double marshall, and a singer singing in Serbo-Croat. They tell me 'This is avant-garde music, you should like it. Why don't we play MIMI?' It's not as easy as that. It's not cleverness to escape those traps. It's your heart."

Ferdinand Richard: En Forme (Celluloid, 1979), En Avant (RecRec, 1983)
with **Etron Fou Leloublan**: Batelages (Gratte-Ciel, 1976), Les Trois Fou's Perdégagnent (9h17 Records, 1977), En Public Aux Etats-Unis (Celluloid, 1979), Les Sillons De La Terre (Turbo, 1979), Les Poumons Gonflés (Turbo, 1983), Face Aux Eléments Déchainés (RecRec, 1986)
with **Bruniferd**: Bruniferd (RecRec, 1986), Un Putch Kitsch (Les Disques NM, 1992)
with **Gestalt Et Jive**: Nouvelle Cuisine (Moers, 1985), Gestalt Et Jive (Creative Works, 1987)
with **Fred Frith**: Speechless (Ralph, 1981), Dropera (RecRec,1991),
with **Ferdinand Et Les Philosophes**: ...enclume (RecRec, 1991)

Footnotes:
1. First published in *Combat* Magazine, January 14, 1949; translated by Mike Zwerin and reprinted in *Round About Close to Midnight: The Jazz Writings of Boris Vian*, Quartet Books: London, 1988: p.74
2. Portions of this section were originally published as "Where The Hell Is Victoriaville?," the author, *Option* Magazine N24, January 1989: pp.52-57
3. Released on RecRec, 1991
4. In France, the expression "Connus comme leloublanc" ["as well known as the white wolf"] is often used in instances of such infamy
5. Self-penned biographical release of Etron Fou Leloublan, mid-1970s, reprinted in "Etron Fou Leloublan," Kenneth Ansell, *Impetus* Magazine, issue N9, 1979: p.390
6. And the French experimental bands which cropped up in their wake such as Art Zoyd and Albert Marcoeur
7. "Filled Lungs," Turbo, 1983
8. "Against The Fury of the Elements," RecRec, 1986
9. Ansell, "Etron Fou Leloublan," p.390
10. ibid., p.391
11. "In search of new harmonies, this group is critically acclaimed in the United States;" "Du rock à la tour Eiffel," *Paris Soir*, April 18, 1984
12. Not everyone in the audience appreciated it, however. It brought hisses from saxophonist Evan Parker and dark mutterings of "Scheisse" ["shit'] from saxophonist Peter Brötzmann.
13. Ralph, 1981; see *Fred Frith*, p.35
14. Les Disques NM, 1992
15. "In Front;" RecRec, 1983
16. See *Fred Frith*, p.33
17. See Fleurs Carnivores, p.95

Heiner Goebbels

When music is a commodity it is consumed as a commodity. As a thing to use, not as a form of human interaction. Typically, it is swallowed whole, in sealed packages – habitual to the point of marginal consciousness. Listening to music in this way is like smoking a cigarette: gratifying, familiar, reinforcing, reflexive. Certainly the mass of consumers no longer expects [or looks for] *communication*.

> *Chris Cutler, "'Progressive' Music, 'Progressive' Politics?"*[1]

Pop life/Everybody wants a thrill/Pop life/We've all got a space 2 fill

> *Prince, "Pop Life"*[2]

As a marketing tool wielded by Madison Avenue, the pop song has infiltrated just about every avenue of our daily existence.[3] We live in an age where toothpaste jingles and whatever video clip is on medium rotation on MTV are indistinguishable. Indeed, entire back catalogs of once-famous record labels have been hijacked by baby boomer advertising executives for Muzak canonization and ubiquitous commercial beds: The Beatles shill for Nike, Marvin Gaye's voice croons for Post, Carly Simon sings the 57 varieties of Heinz, Gary Numan quaffs Ice beer. Now more than ever, today's pop wunderkind [new, improved, disposable], is tomorrow's cut-out king, pushing Pontiacs between the canned laughter of American sitcoms.

If pop music can be seen as a mirror reflecting social reality, however, its position and attitude as a sign 'o' the times must be constantly reassessed and redefined. While theoreticians such as Chris Cutler may be right about the inherent commodification of pop, Heiner Goebbels goes out on a limb to defend the inherent innovation of the disposable pop song.[4] He even wrote a 1988 treatise in German on Prince. "I like pop music a lot," he protests. "Last night I went to a Wendy & Lisa concert. I think that most musical progress made in the last ten years was *not* made in theory or the academic field of music; it was made in the experimental and subcultural scenes. Post-modern music doesn't have to be restorative. There are possibilities using the musical experiences from which we are made as language, and speak with them, and that's what I think Prince does. He's able to work with a lot of different types of music, and keep his own language in the different mixes of music. "I think a lot of innovative things happened in disco, too."

Heiner Goebbels defies the neat archetype of the intense, youthful German composer we're led to believe roosts in what used to be the German Democratic Republic: Heiner K, stoking the fires of past glories and trying to rebuild his shattered culture and uplift the national psyche through tortuous, neoclassical dirges that run rings around Wagner. No, Goebbels is closer in spirit to filmmaker Wim Wenders, part of a young generation of apolitical German artists struggling with the legacy left them by two world wars, trying to make sense of their country's difficult past with the art and technology of today. He even has a degree in Sociology to prove it. His dissertation? "The Question of the Progressiveness of Musical Material. The Social Relationship Between Compositions Produced During the Pre-Classical Period and by Hanns Eisler."

As a composer, Goebbels dips his quill into many inkwells – radio, film, ballet, theater – so praising "Burn Baby Burn" is as good a place to start as any. His specialty is retrofitting avant garde techniques, such as montage and *musique concrète*, with strategies pilfered from popular music, such as the plunderphonics of sampling or the semiotics of hiphop. Beneath the surface tension of his music lies the spoken word, a deep lattice of hidden meanings, coincidence and significance, creating compellingly dense and complex collages of text that approach the sublime technique of Kurt Schwitters' *Merz* period.

With his striking manipulation of voice and text and grasp of pop visuals, Goebbels' "aural drama" has injected new life into the moribund contemporary German theater, effectively creating a new form of Romantic art. His tireless energy and Teutonic devotion to work is quietly inscribed, half-hidden, in a maxim at the end of his 1989 multi-media adaptation of Heiner Müller's *The*

Man In The Elevator: Our anti-hero, resigned never to make his appointment with The Boss, observes two kids trying to jump-start a dead car engine in the Peruvian outback. Saddened at the apparent futility of their actions, he silently concludes "to work is to hope."

"I think that's a very ambiguous remark because the context in which it is made is a little cynical, but in a deeper sense, I think it's a very serious remark," Goebbels explains. "Heiner is usually blamed for having a nihilistic perspective and overseeing the collapse of social things. I don't think that's true at all. Heiner always creates a new perspective on destruction. I think if somebody tries so hard to find pictures of the destructive society and the landscape around us that we destroy so much, if somebody tries so hard there must be a big...*hope* underneath, and a big desire to change it."

Born in Neustadt in August of 1952, Heiner Goebbels was a budding tenor sax player drawn to the West German student movement of the late sixties, a movement that brought many of Frankfurt's disaffected youth together but didn't exactly incite them to change the world. "All political activity on the left – the student movement included – didn't have any relationship to culture whatsoever, sad to say," recalls Goebbels. "Nothing really grew out of it which somehow expressed the political needs, wishes, and fantasies of our future in a cultural way. If you were a musician, there was already something odd about you. I knew a lot of people who were good cellists or violinists, but they hid it. In the strong times of the student movement, culture was always seen as bourgeois."

So, in April of 1976, Goebbels and 16 others formed a musical-cum-cultural collective, calling themselves Sogennantes Linksradikales Blasorchester, or "The So-Called Left Radical Brass Band." Equal parts Sun Ra, Count Basie, and Zappa, the Blasorchester was a non-dogmatic, political big band fueled by an acidic wit, who performed in the streets, at demos, blowing summits, and jazz fests. They were not afraid to call things as they saw them; appropriating key phrases from a 1978 speech by a faceless National Socialist Party zealot, the Blasorchester penned "Ohne dass sich sagen wurde, ich bin der neue Führer,"[5] an absurdist romp that gets progressively darker and totalitarian as it goes on.

"Politically, we had an important edge," says Goebbels. "We had a strong connection to the streets. In the middle of the seventies, it became possible to develop a new cultural and musical expression of what was happening politically. Everybody seemed to have a very strong opinion about the bourgeois, yet nobody used music as a political illustration except for shouting or singing simplistic songs. We tried not to use words, but to address various fantasies and various political discussions in a spontaneous musical language."

In concert the Blasorchester explored new definitions of deft arrangement and pastiche. Goebbels and company blurted their neopolitical tarantellas and funeral marches like a Liberation Orchestra with a very pregnant horn section, shifting gears from a tango to "In The Mood" at the drop of a hat. "Trozalledem," from their second LP, the half live/half studio *Mit Gelben Birnen* ["With Yellow Heads"] is a Scots reel that ends up sounding like Benny Carter in a blender. The greasy trombone fighting for supremacy of "Zirkus," from the same album, even approaches the controlled anarchy of Willem Breuker's Kollektief. "The orchestra was quite wild," Goebbels admits candidly. "Amateurs were welcome, and we didn't care to play perfectly or exactly. We were influenced by jazz orchestras as well, but we weren't 'jazzy' in the strict sense of the word. It was a funny institution, actually."

In July of 1980, the Blasorchester played the "Rock Gegen Rechts" ["Rock Against The Right"] festival, an anti-fascist rally that drew a crowd of over 500,000 to Frankfurt. Shortly afterwards, Goebbels went into the studio with a Blasorchester comrade, tenor saxophonist Alfred 23 Harth. Neither knew the Blasorchester would stutter to a stop a year later, or that they were about to begin a fruitful exchange of ideas and a musical partnership that would last to this day. Goebbels' alter ego, Harth has an austere, coppery tone that was finely balanced against Goebbels' blustery, muscular piano work on albums like *Vom Sprengen Des Gartens*,[6] their second LP together. Their duets range from "The Crow Song," a lyrical children's song peppered with growling saxophone squeals, to an ode to sorrow and resistance from the Spanish Civil War, "Los Campesinos."

Yet both Goebbels and Harth were looking to do more than just pollute Erik Satie with the ugly sounds of today – they were looking for a new muse. It eventually presented itself in the guise of the German theater. *Zeit Wird Knapp*[7] features German actor Ernst Stötzner and singer Dagmar Krause interpreting the work of the great Bertold Brecht. Stötzner, whom Goebbels has known for a long time, has a deep, sonorous voice that would be well-suited to radio ["It's funny," Goebbels mentions, "a lot of people say that, but he has never done radio"], while Krause surprised one and all by graduating from the avant-garde whimsies of Slapp Happy to become, in the words of producer Hal Willner, "our Lotte Lenya." The two read such vintage Brecht vignettes as "Tagesanbruch" ["Dawn"], "Liebeslied" ["Love Song"], and "Apfelbock or The Lilies of The Field" [with the memorable line "In the mild light of dawn Jakob Apfelbock bludgeoned his mother and father to death"] in a kaleidoscope of musical settings – rich, swelling orchestras, decadent, shell-shocked rock arrangements, soulless Kraftwerk landscapes.

Goebbels and Harth further enhanced Brecht's dank world by choosing accordions, calliopes, and circus instruments as their weapons of irony, spinning elliptical, Kafkaesque carnivals of madness. They also employed unusual recording methods. The sessions for *Zeit Wird Knapp* began to open Goebbels' ears to the studio's potential as a recording instrument – and its Burroughsian potential for interrupting linear thought. The idea of overdubbing voices in particular would recur to Goebbels years later in a much more important context.

"I think a lot came out in the facility and use of the studio as an instrument for recording," says Goebbels. "All the noise artists in New York – Glenn Branca, Rhys Chatham, Sonic Youth – they've invented a lot. I think there's a lot going on in pop music today that's really interesting and new, provided it's used in the right context. Not in the sense of content, mind you, but in the progress of the facilities." Goebbels worked closely with Harth in applying these ideas to both composition and live situations, and the full-blown results can be heard on *Live A Victoriaville*.[8] Not only do they belt out a passionate take of Chic's "At Last I Am Free," but they offer retooled renditions of their hits like "Peking Opera" – a wonderful populist collage with some *out* blowing and piano work built on looped traditional eastern motifs from the Peking opera *Shachiapang* – and stunning pieces like "Lightning Over Moscow," a circular synthesizer saw that's triggered by a Thomas Dolby sample. Blinded by science, indeed.

Like Glenn Gould, radio proved to be the perfect medium for Heiner Goebbels. The wireless offered Goebbels an unparalleled psychic space to work in, the absence of visual stimuli allowing him to combine the textural physicality of found sound, the phonic topology of text, and the natural dramatism inherent in the medium. His *hörstücke*, or radio works, have won the Karl-Sczuka-Hörspielpreis des SWF Baden Baden three times: in 1984 for *Verkommenes Ufer*, in 1990 for *Wolokolamsker Chaussee I-V*, and in 1992 for *Schliemann's Radio*.[9]

"I do want my music to be heard in a conscious way, like seeing a film or listening to a radio piece," he explains. "I don't know if I want to or I'm able to change listening habits, but I always notice after I've done something musically that it *needs* to be heard in all its detail. Radio gives me the space to concentrate on the richness of the picture just on the acoustic side. Also, in Germany, you have great studios and sympathetic funding for radio, but not a huge audience. On the other hand, you can create your own audiences; for a long time, instead of playing concerts, I took my radio works to concert halls and cinemas and just turned down the lights. Three, four hundred people came to the cinema, not to look but to listen. When I came to Boston to do that, everyone said 'Nobody will come to something like that in America. Americans are so visually related, can you show some slides?' But we had two, wonderful, crowded shows in Boston, with long discussions afterwards."

The wireless work Goebbels that brought to Boston was *Shadow/Landscape With Argonauts*.[10] After being commissioned to create a new radio work by the Massachusetts Cultural Council, Goebbels hit the streets of Boston in February of 1990. Canvassing passersby, he asked them to read fragments of "Landscape With Argonauts," an abstract modern poem by East German playwright Heiner Müller set in an apocalyptic, science-fiction-now world where "forests burn in Eastman color, populated by zombies perforated by TV spots in the uniforms of yesterday morning's fashion."

"On one hand I was looking for the roughness of speech, situations where the reader is clearly not more intelligent than the text," Goebbels says. "Usually, when actors interpret a text they show that they understand it. Most of the time they're wrong, but they always try to show this. What I was trying to get was a reading of the text which was on the same level of understanding as the listener, including mistakes. Also, I was looking for as many accents as I could find. In Boston you have a perfect mix or confrontation between different accents; it's very hard to find a voice which is not Irish, Russian, Italian, Jewish, Black or whatever. I was looking for accents in the voices which tell the listener about more than just the text, but about the social class, age, sex, and origin of the voice, the forgotten biography or history of this person, who may never have seen Europe, but somehow came from there three or five generations ago."

The text is declaimed, stuttered, whispered, mumbled, shouted, and sang by the puzzled and unsuspecting readers, who gamely struggle with lines like *A shred of Shakespeare in the paradise of bacteria*, *This engine is what my grandmothers used to call God* and *Between the rubble and the ruins it's growing/New fuckcells with district heating*. Goebbels cuts, splices, overlaps, and refracts the vocal samples rhythmically, punctuating them with traffic noises, firecrackers, Zoviet France samples, and – in one sublime piece of synchronicity – places them atop a musical bed crafted from syrupy TV movie strings and a 1-900 sex line tease Goebbels taped in his hotel room.

The eclectic nature of the voices gives rise to some hip musical recombinations. "2 Dollar" has a homeboy hustling a fee for reading the text, then discovering he has trouble getting his mouth around the words. [When he gets to the line *My grandfather was an idiot in Boeotia*, he proclaims "That's it. I can't go *no* further. I *love* my grandfather."] Goebbels uses the natural rhythms of his voice to at once comment on the pervasive influence of rap in pop music and also drop some def breaks. "I think the way that hiphop musicians think about music is for me the most exciting influence to have come out of pop music in years," Goebbels enthuses. "Of course I don't agree with a lot of the words and attitude, and I don't pretend to be a poor black suburban youth or a gang member or whatever. But the gift they have, the way they treat several musics into the rhythm and the sharpness and strength of cutting things together is much more exciting for me than any influence from contemporary music in the last four or five years."

To contrast the outdoor ambience of *Landscape With Argonauts*, Goebbels alternates the poem with *Shadow*, a dark, gothic tale by Edgar Allan Poe suffused with a cloistered, fetid atmosphere of decay. As a foil to the verse of *Landscape*, Goebbels made *Shadow* more musical, yet mirrored the ethnic mix by hiring Iranian-born singer Sussan Deihim, Québécois guitarist René Lussier, British drummer Charles Hayward, and Christos Govetas, a Boston-based Greek clarinet player. Deihim's soaring vocals are chilling, floating atop the whirling dervishes and investing the harrowing text with the appropriate sense of dread and finality.

"For me it was a very exciting mixture of three or four levels of working," Goebbels says. "On one level, it was musical, contrasting the music and the sound of the words. On still another it was literary, analyzing words and interpreting the structure of the text, and on another level it was a sociological work where I was going to these neighborhoods and learning all about these people's lives. Finally it was sightseeing as well, as I learned about Boston in two weeks. And these aspects influenced each other in making decisions."

Heiner Müller is perhaps the greatest living proponent of 20th century experimental theater in East Germany. Heavily indebted to Brecht and Eisler, Müller's thinly-disguised Greek tragedies and impersonal, concrete futures [it's no accident one of his plays was entitled *Zement*] were often suppressed or altered in the 1940s and 1950s due to their pessimistic or critical points of view. "You could say he's traditional in that he's continuing the stories of Bertold Brecht," says Goebbels of Müller. "But he rewrites Brecht and other playwrights in an entirely new language." In 1985, Goebbels helmed a German radio production of *The Liberation of Prometheus*, Müller's 1968 play which recast Prometheus in a contemporary, East German sociopolitical perspective.

"Heiner has a strong and ambivalent connection to the DDR," Goebbels continues. "He makes a lot of criticisms. I think he leans very much to the fire of confrontation rather than the silence of common sense, and I think you can see the fun he has with this confrontation. The way that he mistrusts discussion and confrontation is more creative to the social process than the 'global harmony' way of official German thinking. If somebody said to me that Heiner was nihilistic or cynical, I would have to disagree very strongly. I'm not interested in straight cynicism. It's an edge for me. Sometimes, in theater adaptations of Heiner's plays, I can see the director's going over the edge into darkness."

Goebbels can relate to Müller's calling. Between 1978 and 1980, Goebbels cut his teeth on modernist adaptations of Goethe, Shakespeare, Sophocles as musical director of the Frankfurt Shauspiel for plays such as *Othello*, *Antigone*, and *Iphigenie*. It was natural that he would invest his interest in the Germany's tradition as the seat of European theater with his desire for increased studio sophistication, and in 1987, he did. *Der Mann Im Fahrstuhl*[11] is a musical adaption of a play by Müller, and but a small part of *The Mission*, a protracted theater work written in 1983 which actually has a lot more to do with the French Revolution and its consequences than lifts. "In Heiner's pieces, he throws stones into a landscape," explains Goebbels. "He likes to put other elements there which seem to be totally different and seem to be from another age. But in the deeper sense there's a lot of connections. So while this story about the man in the elevator is a story by itself, there's a lot of consequences and deep relationships throughout the entire play."

The man in the elevator is a nervous office clerk toiling somewhere in the concrete bowels of an anonymous office building. He has been summoned to see The Boss, and during the elevator ride to the 20th Floor, he becomes unsure of his reason for being called, and fears The Boss [who he calls Number One in this thoughts] will kill him if he's late. The elevator door opens, and he finds himself in Peru, lost in a no-man's land he believes to be a simulacra his company has constructed to fool him. The events follow a humid, dreamy logic, and the story reverberates with a distant, blackened humor. "On one hand, the story itself can be somehow translated to a couple of specific personal and political situations," Goebbels reveals. "On the other hand, it's easy to talk about the story because it's such an obvious one. More important for me is the incredible power of [Müller's] language. As a composer I don't have to interpret the content again, because the content is already there in the words. And the more I look into his words, the more I always get from their structure and syntax, not their semantics. So what I do is somehow look for the structure the words and written in and discover other levels of meaning, other aspects of what he wanted to tell or describe. I put a big trust in the value of his words, and I'm sure there's never a word too much."

The Man In The Elevator gives Goebbels three languages to play with, and he delightfully overlaps all three texts. Ernst Stötzner handles the *basso profundo* German, and guitarist Arto Lindsay alternates between nervous English and beatific Portuguese. Time is suspended as the text overlaps, folds back on itself, and shifts back and forth, revealing hidden sonorities in and alternate interpretations of an essentially simple story. The backdrop is also a shifting musical shorthand, a series of vignettes seemingly shuffled and dealt at random like a deck of cards. A downtown New York groove set up by Charles Hayward's tight, peculiar skiffle of percussive metals and drums and Fred Frith's sturdy bass segues into an incongruous, lovely Brazilian samba number. There's some German no wave, propelled by Lindsay's trademark guitar skronk and brass courtesy of George Lewis and Ned Rothenberg. Clanking, oppressive atmospheres yield to breathtaking silences populated by Don Cherry's lone pocket trumpet. *The Man In The Elevator* is one of those rare birds – an "art rock" record that rocks.

Since *The Man In The Elevator*'s successful run in Frankfurt and its presentation at Victoriaville and New York,[12] Goebbels has produced several such large-scale *muskitheatreprojektes*, works that feature very autonomous relationships between sets, music, performance, character, and text. *Newton's Casino* [1990] and *Römische Hunde* ["Roman Hounds," 1991] were both staged in Frankfurt in collaboration with stage designer Michael Simon, and were wildly successful multi-media productions that had more to do with music, video, and film than greasepaint and summer stock. Staged in Paris, *Ou Bien Les Débarquements Désastreux* [1993] is a stylistic cross-pollination/collision for one actor, two African musicians, and three Western musicians.

"There's quite a strong link between words, music, light, sound, and stage," Goebbels explains. "They do not rely on one of the common hierarchies you commonly have in theater, that is to say, the most important thing is the text, and then the actor, and then the costume, and then the stage and so on. It's rather a strong struggle between these elements. *Ou Bien Les Débarquements Désastreux*[13] is not a world music concept integrating everything, but rather a confrontation between Boubacar Diabate and René Lussier, the languages of a Senegalese kora player and Western guitar player. In *Newton's Casino*, it's between mezzo-soprano Gail Gilmore and experimental vocalist Catherine Jauniaux. It's not like being center stage and trying to teach people the classics or a strong dramatic story. It's a whole theater evening where each instrument, actor, singer has meaning with their voice."

Offstage, Goebbels still finds time to compose modern chamber music and rock the opposition in the peripatetic trio Cassiber as well. Goebbels, Alfred Harth, and Christoph Anders – the three tenor saxophonists of the Sogennantes Linksradikales Blasorchester – started Cassiber with drummer Chris Cutler in 1982. "We conceived Cassiber because we thought the Blasorchester was not a good solution for the questions that were raised a decade earlier. We found it funny in its sound and vivid quality, but we didn't find it strong enough. We found it a little too harmless. So we founded Cassiber as a way of finding a new aesthetic for the eighties." Cassiber can certainly flex a bit more muscle now that they're down to a [sort of] power trio.[14] Like a piece of carbon under pressure, Cassiber yielded hard diamonds on albums like *Perfect Worlds*,[15] which flirted with musical collapse, and treaded close to the edge of an imagined future that meshes James White, free jazz and ecological disaster. Their strongest album, *A Face We All Know*,[16] is a devastating memoir of Big Brother, synchronicity, and conspiracy theory inspired by Thomas Pynchon's 1966 cult novel about a world-wide postal underground, *The Crying Of Lot 49.*

As a tonic to the bracing freedom of Cassiber, Goebbels has been composing modern classical chamber works for Ensemble Moderne, a chamber orchestra based in Frankfurt, since 1986. The works – collected on *Ensemble Moderne*[17] – range from ballet scores to graphic polemic pieces to a filmic *hommage* to French author Alain-Robbe Grillet called *La Jalousie*. "The title plays with both meanings of the word," Goebbels says. "On one hand you have the window blinds as you call them in French, and you have jealousy. In the book he's mostly talking about the blinds, but he's actually describing jealousy. It's a wonderful book with an empty center: The thing he is looking for is never expressed, but by reading it will be created in the head of the reader. This is what interests me most about writing composition, writing music which gives more the essentials for the feeling, the sound a paper in a letter, like the footsteps of a woman, but not the feeling itself. Music is more the architecture for the feeling which can come up when you listen carefully."

Heiner Goebbels: Es Herrscht Uhu Im Land (ECM, 1981), Der Mann Im Fahrstuhl (ECM, 1988), Shadow/Landscape With Argonauts (ECM, 1993), Ensemble Moderne (ECM, 1993), Hörstücke (ECM, 1994)
with **Alfred 23 Harth**: Hommage/Vier Fauste Für Hanns Eisler (FMP, 1976) Vom Sprengen des Gartens (FMP, 1980), Zeit Wird Knapp (Tonstudio Zuckerfabrik, 1981), Indianer Für Morgn (Riskant, 1981), Frankfurt/Peking (Riskant, 1984), Live A Victoriaville (Victo, 1987), Goebbels Heart (Eva, 1992)
with **Sogennantes Linksradikales Blasorchester**: Sogennantes Linksradikales Blasorchester (Trikont Verlag, 1976), Mit Gelben Birnen (Trikont Verlag, 1980),
with **Cassiber**: Man Or Monkey (Ré, 1982), Beauty And The Beast (Ré, 1984), Perfect Worlds (Ré, 1986), A Face We All Know (ReR Megacorp, 1991)

1. In *File Under Popular* [2nd Edition], November Books: London, 1992: pp.154-155
2. From *Around The World In A Day*; Paisley Park, 1985
3. Portions of this chapter were originally published as "Enter Stage Left: Heiner Goebbels' New Directions In Political Theater," the author, *Option* Magazine N29, November 1989: pp. 42-45
4. This theoretical disagreement provides some of the psychic friction in Cassiber, the group Cutler and Goebbels both play in
5. "Needless To Say, I Am Your New Leader," from *Mit Gelben Birnen*; Trikont Verlag, 1980
6. "What Springs From The Gardens," FMP, 1979
7. "Time Will Be Short," Tonstudio Zuckerfabrik, 1981
8. Victo, 1988
9. *Verkommenes Ufer* and *Wolokolamsker Chaussee I-V* can be found on *Hörstücke*; ECM, 1995
10. ECM, 1993
11. "The Man In The Elevator;" ECM, 1989
12. At the fifth annual FIMAV in 1987 and at New Music America, 1989
13. "The Hapless Landing," a phrase which occurs in *Landscape With Argonauts*
14. Harth left after the second album
15. Ré, 1986, 16. ReR Megacorp, 1991
17. ECM, 1993

Radical Brass

In the autumn of 1959, at the tempest at the Five Spot that was the debut of the Ornette Coleman Quartet, the world was shocked by a bold new music. Fakebooks were thrown to the wind as Coleman took to the New York nightclub's stage with his plastic alto saxophone. Unfettered by the changes that had up to then been the unquestioned foundation of jazz, Coleman nevertheless swung hard, soaring in astonishing, near-telepathic free interplay with his bandmatespocket trumpet player Don Cherry, bassist Charlie Haden and drummer Billy Higgins. Free jazz was born.

Free jazz broke all the rules. Instead of the usual head-solos-trade fours-head, free jazz hit from the word go. For Coleman and a few other bold souls of the day, bebop's chord changes and fast runs had become confining; "vertical prisons," as clarinet player Jimmy Giuffre once called them. The focus in free jazz was on collective rather than solo improvisation, and it got its message across through an unbridled energy and intensity. It also emphasized a growing awareness of social and cultural issues, not the least of which were the adverse living and working conditions many of its musicians had to deal with on a daily basis. Coming to the cultural vanguard along with the rise of the civil rights movement in America, free jazz meant self-empowerment for many struggling Black jazz musicians; fierce and uncompromised, it took no prisoners.

To paraphrase Coleman, it was the change of the century.[1]

Yet while free jazz was undeniably liberating, by rejecting all metrical, harmonic and melodic structures it would eventually dead-end in a creative cul-de-sac. Free jazz could only grow if it began to incorporate other musics into its potent maelstrom: blues, third world music, classical and contemporary music, the European avant garde. Pianist Cecil Taylor and reedist Anthony Braxton produced a unique and enduring form of free jazz by casting improvisers in large orchestral contexts; radical brass, if you will. Taylor's "Unit Structures" crossed the shamanistic with the secular; the music of 20th century European composers with the very roots of jazz. Braxton, fascinated with the graphic scores of Cage and Stockhausen, worked within complex time-space structures and often used algebraic titles for his compositions. To them, free jazz was not about abandoning structure, rather its inherent freedom was to be found in the decisions made *within* those structures. And in the hands of a quick-thinking ensemble like The Rova Saxophone Quartet, these decisions can be complex indeed: the San Francisco-based quartet have worked with interactive computer programs and played improv games using labyrinthine rules and bizarre stage props.

The most popular example of this radical brass remains the music that emerged from the South Side of Chicago in the 1960s, where the jazz community contrasted sharply with the cut-throat competitive scene in New York. Led by the enigmatic pianist Muhal Richard Abrams, The Experimental Band was an drop-in jazz orchestra that functioned like a workshop for new avant garde writing. If The Experimental Band was the heart of a new jazz solar system, Sun Ra was orbiting around its outer reaches with his Intergalactic Arkestra. Claiming to be from Saturn, Ra believed that "space is the place," and that free jazz was the ticket. His cosmic big band was a curious microcosm within Chicago jazz circles, an idiosyncratic family of devoted players who preached a futuristic message of peace and freedom, complete with their own poetry, record label – El Saturn – and literature. Afrocentric decades before the term was coined, Ra was a true visionary, and a vital link between jazz in America and Europe. Two years after his passing in 1993, his influence remains undeniable.

The Experimental Band evolved into The Association for the Advancement of Creative Musicians, a hothouse collective that produced an organic, new free jazz that explored new tone colors, drew upon the idiom's rich history of styles, sported a sense of humor and used unorthodox instrumentation, particularly "little instruments:" percussive gewgaws like cowbells, log drums, sirens and bird whistles. Along with the Art Ensemble Of Chicago, Henry Threadgill is one of the best-known AACM graduates. A saxophonist, bandleader and composer who has gathered the divergent musical paths of the African Diaspora into a rich new Black music, Threadgill fuses New Orleans rags and electric-period Miles Davis at the helm of ensembles like Air and Very Very Circus.

While Europe generally followed America's lead in the development of jazz from ragtime up through bebop, something soured in the 1960s, and the latest trend in the States was no longer guaranteed to be emulated by European musicians, let alone the subject of a fervent write-up in *Le Jazz Hot*. Part of this was due to the anti-authoritarian stance taken in the student uprisings of 1968 in France and Germany and the anti-Americanism that rippled through Europe as the Vietnam War dragged on. Their cultural impact can be felt in caustic and edgy large ensembles that skewed orchestral jazz with a tart, contemporary atonality, spiking Hans Eisler with Albert Ayler: German pianist Alexander von Schlippenbach's Globe Unity Orchestra, The Sogennantes Linksradikales Blasorchester, or even Russian dissident pianist Sergei Kuryokhin, whose massive music/theater ensemble Pop Mechanics often resembled anarchy onstage. In Holland, irascible pianist Misha Mengelberg and irreverent Dutch bandleader and composer Willem Breuker gave the big band a perverse twist with their improvisers collective, The International Composers Pool, and The

ICP Orchestra. Unlike their American counterparts, the populist music of these European players has gone a long way towards erasing the barriers between jazz and new music there.

Of course, bassist Charles Mingus had blazed these trails in the early 1960s with compositions like *The Black Saint And The Sinner Lady*. In his famed Jazz Workshop, Mingus pushed his intrepid collective way past hard bop into abstract improvisation, but never lost the pulse of gospel and blues. Just as Mingus acknowledged and built upon Duke Ellington in his arrangements, New York cornetist and composer Lawrence "Butch" Morris built upon Mingus in his "conductions." As heard on LPs like *Current Trends In Racism In America [A Work In Progress]*,[2] these conductions feature Morris conducting a large ensemble of crack improvisers. The artists in this section explore the legacy of Mingus and how the role of jazzfree, big band, and orchestralhas influenced the development of *musique actuelle*, with particular emphasis on the differences between American and European innovators and how the cult of the improviser fits in to larger-scale work where 20th century classical, avant garde jazz and free improvisation collide.

1. The title of a 1959 Atlantic LP by the Quartet
2. Sound Aspects, 1986

Willem Breuker

It was twenty years ago today/ That Sgt. Pepper taught the band to play/
They've been going in and out of style/ But they're guaranteed to raise a smile

The Beatles, Sgt Pepper's Lonely Hearts Club Band[1]

The French have a whimsical phrase to describe those who chuckle to
themselves at nothing in particular: "rire dans sa barbe." After first jolting
audiences in the mid-1960s with a decidedly European *mélange* of theater,
political satire, and big band jazz improvisation, Dutch composer and bandleader
Willem Breuker has been laughing into his beard for years. After all, this is a
man who shines the shoes of audience members, named his record label
BVHaast [roughly, "do-it-fast"], and is given to funny, tactile packaging jokes,
like releasing compact discs in round cheese boxes.[2] "Why should a record come
every time in the same plastic box?" Breuker says, with a mischievous twinkle in
his eyes. "The idea of putting a CD in a record sleeve is so simple, but nobody
did it. I thought, some fool must have. But nobody did.[3] Now a lot of record
shops don't want to have *Heibel*, because they don't know where to put it."

Unless you have seen the Willem Breuker Kollektief live, you may not get the
joke either, nor know where to put it. The joy and laughter is infectious on

Breuker's cheese box, *Heibel* ["Bickering"], recorded live in Stockholm and Amsterdam. During a pregnant, waddling version of "Bolero," mutes are plunged into horns and we can only imagine what antics the Kollektief are up to onstage. Live, this rambunctious ensemble of ten post-free jazz musicians are the closest any genre has come to recapturing *Sgt Pepper's Lonely Hearts Club Band*'s celebratory feel of Hyde Park on a Sunday afternoon, and garner standing ovations and rave reviews whenever they play North America. While Breuker doesn't share the psychedelic taste for studio experimentation The Beatles did during the 129 days of the landmark 1966 sessions for *Sgt Pepper's*, he does share their wide-eyed appetite for polystylism. The fab four tipped their hats to Karlheinz Stockhausen, George Bernard Shaw, Aleister Crowley, Terry Southern, Lenny Bruce, and Bob Dylan; during the long workouts typical at a Kollektief gig, eras of musical history hurtle by at the speed of an alto solo: Irish jigs, blues vamps, Dixieland, Russian folk songs, Tin Pan Alley schmaltz, hiccuping Calypso and ardent tangos, all punctuated by surreal skits, mean parodies of sweating-brow, self-absorbed free jazz, shameless mugging, and their traditional show-stopper, "Besame Mucho." George Grosz, meet George Gershwin.

"Our whole life is filled with music every day," says Breuker, fiddling with his spectacles. Casually rumpled, in sock feet, Breuker sits in a tiny Montréal hotel room, relaxed amidst the hurlyburly of preparation for tonight's show at Maison de la Culture Frontenac. "This band had been together for 17 years and I have written for every formation you can think of. I wrote for symphony orchestra, for amateur orchestra, for big films, for church bells, for mandolin orchestras and accordion orchestras. I even wrote pieces for bell organ, too." He stops to laugh. "People in the street were looking into the organs and asking, 'What's happening? Is there a bomb in there?'"

The floor, couch and bed of the hotel room are littered with refugees from an orchestral wind section: a selection of vintage Selmer saxophones [alto, soprano and tenor], B-flat, E-flat, and bass clarinets, and a flute or two. Elsewhere there are metronomes, effects pedals, cases, a package of Rico reeds. A musical score fights for space on a small table top. The names André Goudbeek, Andreas Altenfelder, and Henk de Jonge are jotted down instead of the more traditional front line designations of saxophone, trumpet and piano; this is Breuker's homage to Duke Ellington, who used to write the names of his players on the score instead of instruments.

"In the beginning, people scoffed, but after a while, they understood that we were doing something no other orchestra was doing: having some fun. Now, most times it is strictly forbidden to have fun with music, because you have to be so terribly serious. Of course you have to take your music seriously, but this whole attitude to the music can be changed and nobody knows how because everybody is dressed very well and sitting there in an official way.

"This is all nonsense. What's official? When we played free concerts in the street in France and Italy, and we saw different kinds of people, young people and old people, from different social classes. They either liked the music or they didn't. We've done a lot of concerts for small children. How great it is to play in front of them. The more you play, the more they laugh, the more they like it. But when they become 11 or 12, they put the names of pop stars on their backs, and then the whole thing's over. Then it's 'I belong to a certain scene.' And also, the musical training in schools is very bad because the teachers themselves don't know what to do with music. Even they are hanging in a certain scene." Breuker's voice drops to a quiet whisper. "I've known this for 50 years. But it's not my way."

Born in 1944, Willem Breuker grew up during the reconstruction years following the Second World War in working class East Amsterdam. Not quite the card-carrying anti-romantic yet, young Willem was nonetheless mad about dissonance, if a little lackadaisical in learning how to play it properly: when Breuker was 11, so the story goes, he'd improvise on his clarinet because he was too lazy to the turn the page on the printed score. A neighborhood paper route netted him 15 guilders a week, which he promptly spent on records, the first of which was the Julliard String Quartet tackling Schoenberg. "I was very shocked by the music of Schoenberg and Varèse," Breuker remembers. "I often went down to the open library after school to listen to them. You could make an appointment there and listen to music; they would put on records for you. Afterwards, when I got the paper route, it was my chance to buy records, a tape recorder and things like that. Then the collection started."

The streets of Amsterdam was Breuker's school. He joined a marching band, served time in brass orchestras and glockenspiel orchestras, even mastered the barrel organ, that ubiquitous hurdygurdy whose valves are found parked on countless Dutch streets.[4] "I tried to get classical training but they kicked me out of the conservatory," Breuker recalls. "They told me I had no talent, and it would be a real mess if I continued in music. They were completely right." A deadpan pause. "I basically came to the conservatory when I was about 17 or 18 years old, and I came there unprepared. I couldn't convince them of what I wanted to do. I was interested in a completely different music, not the dead music that they wanted to teach me. But I was too lazy to even do that."

During the late 1950s, Breuker was a regular at Amsterdam's night owl jazz haunts, where he saw Louis Armstrong, Art Blakey's Modern Jazz Quartet, and perhaps the two acts most influential to his blooming compositional sense, the Duke Ellington and Count Basie bands. A decade later, however, Breuker was baptized by the fires of free jazz, hearing Eric Dolphy, Albert Ayler and Ornette Coleman for the first time. In 1968, he fell into the motley gang of Peter Brötzmann's infamous Octet, which counted among its firebrand soloists pianist Fred Van Hove and saxophonist Evan Parker and later ejaculated the free jazz masterpiece *Machine Gun*.[5] The same year, Gunter Hampel, the German fife player and flutist, asked Breuker to join his band with drummer Steve McCall, reedist Anthony Braxton, and guitarist John McLaughlin.

"From Holland one day I was dragged off to Hollywood, and I met everybody," says Breuker. "When I came back to Holland I saw how narrow-minded everybody actually was. There were always big fights between the new musicians and the popular musicians. To make a living, the new musicians had to play in the radio orchestras and the dance bands, and they hated to do that. The popular musicians hated to go to a jazz club and play until three in the morning, and then be back in the morning to do a radio broadcast. So for many, it was easier to make your money with radio than go to a jazz club."

Then came Misha Mengelberg. Breuker had known and worked with the enigmatic, eccentric Dutch pianist for years, and decided to form a jazz performer's collective with him and their mutual drumming acquaintance, Han Bennink. The trio inaugurated the International Composers Pool in 1967. "It was an incorporation of talents and ideas," Breuker explains. "You make a bigger first with more fingers. When we formed, we decided we would never go down to the level of a radio orchestra, we would do just what we want, and I think there is place enough for our kind of music in our community. If you always hassle it up, mix it up with being there for security, and doing what you want in your spare time, your free time, that's nonsense."

Having said that, Breuker quit the ICP seven years later. The creative differences cited had to do with the class of player the ICP was after: Bennink and Mengelberg wanted top-drawer improvisors, while Breuker was fascinated at the results gained from placing amateurs alongside professionals. He founded his record label, BVHaast, and formed the Kollektief to this end, and started looking for a few good men. "He has to be a nice person, a good musician, and he has to take himself very seriously," Breuker says, describing the ideal Kollektief member. "But not in the way most people take things seriously. In the Kollektief, it's forbidden to have competition. Nobody thinks he is better than the other. You just play in the band or you don't. That's all. Ten years ago, people came to us who thought they could earn a lot of money and play in a band that was relatively famous, but they didn't fit at all. If you don't have that mentality, forget it."

In the beginning, instruments played little part in the ensemble's lineup; a washboard player even drifted in and out. "When we started in the mid-1970s, we had a lot of nice players, but they couldn't read that well; they weren't good instrumentalists," says Breuker. "I write 95% of the music, and it's important to hit the notes. A lot of them stopped playing, and the others developed their training. So now we have classically trained guys, who have played for a long time in the symphony orchestra, and we have guys who have just come in from the street, just like me. That's a strange combination, but it's worked for a long time, so I haven't changed it."

Like the bands of Duke Ellington and Sun Ra, Breuker's Kollektief commands a high degree of member loyalty. Bassist Arjen Gorter [who gigged with Breuker in Hampel's group] has known Breuker since the early 1960s. Trumpeter Boy Raaymakers, who was active on the improv music scene in Nijmegen, Holland, joined at the outset as well. The other two life members of the Kollektief are trombonist Bernard Hunnekink and drummer/percussionist Rob Verdurmen, also a veteran of the Dutch improv scene. Gifted with safecracker's hands – check his *noirish*, elliptical riff on the title cut of *Heibel* – pianist Henk de Jonge hails from the world of greasepaint and footlights. After sitting in the orchestra pit in scores of Dutch theater productions from *Fiddler On The Roof* to *Man of La Mancha*, De Jonge signed up in 1979. The next decade saw the remainder of the Kollektief come on board: alto saxophonist André Goudbeek, who has recorded with John Tchicai and Chris MacGregor's Brotherhood of Breath [and is the hidden treasure of the Kollektief, much like John Gilmore in Sun Ra's Arkestra], German trumpeter Andreas Altenfelder, tenor saxophonist Peter Barkema [who boasts a fascination with ethnic musics and cultures], and the youngest Kollektief member, American trombonist Gregg Moore. To this rich cast Breuker often adds the robust elegance of either Vera Beths' String Quartet or the Mondriaan Strings ensemble.

Whether they're called on to read chamber music or nail the changes and blow, Breuker puts his charges through the paces on albums like *Bob's Gallery* and *To Remain*.[6] The former album is a treasury of the Kollektief's talents, containing a 1940s Cole Porteresque hit parade tune, "Remarkable Girl;" a bittersweet snapshot dedicated to Ennio Morricone, "Morribreuk;" a lilting cover of Kurt Weill's "I Don't Love You;" a pulse piece, "Minimal," which betrays his 1970s collaborations with Dutch modernist composer Louis Andriessen; and the traditional South American march "La Santa Espina." The title cut is a 23' suite of Mingus proportions with frenzied solos for Goudbeek, Raaymakers, and Breuker [he screams and shouts through the reed] that shifts stylistic gears effortlessly thanks to Verdurmen's busy, propulsive drumming.

Live, all ten sport the requisite sense of humor. Their slapstick clowning can verge on the sublime; more frequently, however, it verges on the ridiculous: The everyone-try-and-stop-the-drum-solo gag has been part of their act for years, yet never fails to elicit helpless laughter. Altenfelder and Raaymakers always impersonate an audience member or two. During the concert staple, "Sahara Sack," the band often squats about in burnooses as Breuker upends a sack of percussion instruments. A clarinet is then disassembled, passed around during a trumpet solo, then furiously reassembled before it's time for the clarinet solo.

Despite the vaudevillian anarchy, the Kollektief can musically stop on a dime anywhere during their lunatic performances, thanks to years of honing the routines to run with cuckoo-clock precision. "Most of the things are structured because we play pieces," Breuker admits. "We don't have the freedom we did years ago. There are always places in the music where people can do what they want, and we change that all the time. But I think what we're actually doing is giving more a kind of story about the music than playing jazz the way most jazz players do: you know, play a head, improvise, and at the end repeat the head and it's over. They chat, and then play the next piece. Then there's a ballad, a quick piece, then a ballad, and so on.

"We don't do that. The form we have has a kind of psychological musical meaning, and what that is very hard to explain. Often it's just what's in my mind and what I think that will really work out. I am my own listener at the same time. When we're playing, I can cut pieces if I think they're overlong or not interesting anymore, or if we lose contact with the people or each other. That's very important. A lot of music is boring because it takes too long to get started. I always try to come up with a form so that nobody falls asleep. There always must be a surprise for the audience and for us."

First heard on record in early orchestral works such as *Baal Brecht Breuker Handke*,[7] Breuker's trenchant fusion of music and theater has had its predecessors, most notably in the seminal and legendary works of Brecht and Weill. Like Weill, Breuker has also drawn inspiration from the silver screen. He has done straight soundtracks to Dutch thrillers like *Doodzonde* and *Drums In The Night*, and many of his own compositions have a kinetic, associative quality that embraces everything from the 1920s German impressionistic cinema of Fritz Lang to Sergio Leone's hip spaghetti westerns of the late 1960s. Breuker has arranged and recorded the film scores that made both genres famous, *Metropolis* and *The Good, The Bad, and the Ugly*,[8] using strings to augment the cinematic musical shorthand Ennio Morricone and Ferde Grofé had used to explain the vast arid stretches of speechless action.

"I think popular music has always come from the theater," Breuker reasons. "You can see that in history, and you can see it in my work for sure. In the end of the 1960s and the beginning of the 1970s. I wrote a lot of theater plays myself, text and music. We were also the performers and the actors, we did everything. I needed to do that because I had to find the music. Music has to come from somewhere; in my case the theater was very important. And also film. Because in film, you have to react to images. Your music may come from yourself; but you have to base your reactions on the things you see. The film and its structure must remain upright and in a good condition. You cannot disturb the film. Also, the film pressures you to make different types of music, or a music you have never played before. Say you have two dogs walking in the street. You have to give your interpretation of that. Looking back in history, you can pick what you want. You can pick a classical piece, you can pick out a contemporary piece, you can make your arrangements of pieces you like, you can even do a big fanfare, but what's important is what's fitting to the film. It's an everyday problem actually. My whole life. I have nothing else to do," he says, with a slight revelation. "But for me, that's what makes it interesting to go on with music. That's what keeps it fresh."

Breuker's predilection for surprise has traditionally placed him at arms' length of the authorities. Nobody fell asleep in the Dutch town of Loodsrecht in 1966, when Breuker shocked the Low Countries by commemorating an ongoing strike; a bastard orchestra culled from classical and jazz players played a *Litany* in memoriam to a protestor who died after riots with police.[9] 1980's *Dirty Laundry* was a savage critique of Dutch governmental propensity to fund traditional, conservative classical ensembles who travel abroad [the plot had the Kollektief travelling the world in a shipwreck and eventually being rubbed out by Dutch marines for refusing to play in South Africa].[10] His most recent theatrical production, *Deze Kant Op, Dames!*,[11] has a timely plot following the peccadilloes, lost heirs, and skeletons in the closet of a morally bankrupt European royal family. This Kafkaesque sense of the absurd in dealing with the government is not surprising, given that Breuker tirelessly campaigned the government between 1970 and 1986 as chair of the Dutch Foundation of Jazz and Improvised Music. Yet it becomes ironic when one learns that the Kollektief survives in part by being funded by – you guessed it – the Dutch government.

"When we first came up to the government and told them we were professional jazz musicians, professional improvisors, they said '*What*? What's that? That's only what you do on your weekends. That's not a serious profession,'" Breuker explains. "They seriously thought that way. They only knew a bit about jazz from their schooltime dixieland. On the other hand, there is no school or study for being a jazz musician. If you want to be a classical musician, then you get a diploma afterwards, and you show it to everybody and they have to give you work. A lot of institutions are there to help you immediately: you can be a teacher or play in an orchestra. Never mind that when contemporary Dutch composers, who were not so often played on the radio, were played, the announcer would always make an excuse for them. But if you say I'm a jazz musician, what's that? They don't exist. In the beginning of the '70s, we had to change that mentality completely."

Breuker's subsequent career shows all the earmarks of success in doing just that: in 1988 he was voted the "Bird" award for best Dutch jazz musician. When he returns to Holland on Tuesday, he will premiere a fanfare commissioned by Queen Beatrix for her visit to the Arts Council in Holland. "It's very strange that they've asked me," he muses, gesturing to the score lying on the table. "Maybe they want to prove that they're hip to new movements or they want to do an extra special thing. Maybe they're knocking holes in the old conservative way, like so many things happening today. A lot of young people are working in the Arts Council, maybe that will change things a little bit. But you cannot wait for that. Just go on, do you thing, play. You have one life; make something of it."

Willem Breuker
Willem Breuker Kollektief: In Berlin (BVHaast, 1976), In Holland (BVHaast, 1981), Collective (About Time, 1984), Bob's Gallery (BVHaast, 1988), To Remain (BVHaast, 1990), Heibel (BVHaast, 1992), Deze Kant Op, Dames! (BVHaast, 1993)
with **Vera Beths String Quartet**: Rhapsody In Blue (BVHaast, 1983), George Gershwin [1898-1937] (BVHaast, 1988)
with **Mondriaan Strings**: Metropolis (BVHaast, 1990), Parade (BVHaast, 1991)
solo: Baal Brecht Breuker Handke (BVHaast, 1975), Drums In The Night (BVHaast, 1977), Doodzonde (BVHaast, 1979), Music For The Samuel Falkland Show/The Resistable Rise of Arturo Ui (BVHaast, 1990)
with **Misha Mengelberg, Louis Andriessen et al**: The Busy Drone (BVHaast, 1981)
with **Peter Brötzmann Octet**: Machine Gun (FMP, 1968)

Footnotes:
1. Parlophone/EMI, 1967
2. *Heibel*; BVHaast, 1992
3. Breuker eventually did, for his album *To Remain*; BVHaast, 1989
4. See the 1981 BVHaast release *The Busy Drone*, a collection of works scored for the organ by Breuker, Misha Mengelberg, Louis Andriessen, and several classical composers
5. FMP, 1968
6. BVHaast, 1988 and BVHaast, 1989, respectively
7. BVHaast, 1975
8. On *Metropolis*, BVHaast; 1990, and *Rhapsody In Blue*; BVHaast, 1983
9. See Ben Watson, "Kollektief Calls," in *Wire* Magazine N68, November 1989: p.44
10. See Michael Bourne, "Willem Breuker & Kompany: Euro-bop With A Twist," in *downbeat* Magazine, May 1989: p.28, 11. "This Way, Ladies!," BVHaast, 1993

Henry Threadgill

Make a habit of your history. Be knowledgeable and you shall be free.

Molefi Kete Asante, Njia – The Way 9:3[1]

As the golden anniversary of Jelly Roll Morton's death came and went with little fanfare, trying to predict where jazz is headed is getting tougher all the time.[2] The revolutionary schools that launched a frontal assault on bebop's hegemony in the 1960s have made little headway in the two decades since – the Third Stream has trickled into a brook that only a few composers still dangle their hooks in, the cacophonic free school is largely a thundering memory save for FMP diehards like Peter Brötzmann, Ornette's harmolodics never really successfully crossed over, and the current vogue among British jazz artists like Steve Williamson, Courtney Pine and Andy Sheppard shows a holy reverence for the changes one could hear at any of the dozens of smoky *boîtes* lining 52nd Street in New York on July 10, 1941, the night Jelly Roll Morton died.

Perhaps the most trusty weathervane we can use to forecast the future directions of everything that's currently blowing in jazz is the music of graduates of Chicago's Association for the Advancement of Creative Musicians, and the work of the saxophonist and composer Muhal Richard Abrams called "The

Magician," Henry Threadgill. "Last year I found that my ideas were changing. I was starting to hear something different musically. Not so much the music scene. Just the reality of the music and the reality of the world scene. I think the reality of the world has changed. It's in a really critical state of change, going toward 2000, this last dec*ade*. So much stuff has changed so radically in the last year. Political systems, social things, I was getting a little kind of whisper in my ear: 'Give it a chance man, we're approaching the turn of the century.'"

Along with fellow AACM alumni Muhal Richard Abrams, Roscoe Mitchell, and Joseph Jarman, Henry Threadgill first heard these whispers when he followed the lead of '60s conceptual movers and shakers like Cecil Taylor and Anthony Braxton, postulating worthy if thorny musical dilemmas as the AACM wrestled with both the roots of traditional ragtime jazz and rigorous post-modern aesthetics; exploring the sound of Jelly Roll Morton jamming with Sun Ra. Like Jelly Roll, Threadgill insists that his music has to *swing*. And, like Herman "Sonny" Blount, he is deeply empathic to the importance of jazz as a continuing tradition, with wisdom passed on from generation to generation; in the words of The AACM's flagship group, The Art Ensemble Of Chicago: "Great Black music – ancient to the future." Yet jazz as a naïve and faithful reiteration of the wisdom is just a shell game to Threadgill. When chosen for a Dewar's Scotch Profile in 1988, his quote on the subject raised a few eyebrows among jazz puritans: "Tradition is a background of ingredients; in and of itself it's nothing. If you can't make something out of it, the world can do without it. "I come out of Black culture, and Black culture is full of oral tradition."

His tall, loose-limbed frame decked out this morning in pale orange overalls, pilot's cap and sunglasses, Henry Threadgill is digging into his soft cheese omelette at a Victoriaville café and putting last night's U.S. debut of his new ensemble Very Very Circus into perspective. "It's funny you brought it up," he continues. "We were discussing symphonic players yesterday. They don't come from an oral tradition, which is part of the reason why they have trouble dealing with an improvisation. Improvisation is irrevocably connected to oral tradition. In other parts of the world, wherever you find more improvisation, you find more of an oral tradition. People are taught more music than say, read music publications. They talk about it, and most important, they *play* it."

The 51-year-old Threadgill has been honing his musical heritage on reeds ever since his salad days in Muhal Richard Abrams' Experimental Band, a group of Wilson Junior College Students who started meeting informally at a South Side Chicago tavern in 1962. Then, as now, Threadgill's phrasing on alto sax was highly vocalized, and reminded more than one critic of a preacher's passionate fire-and-brimstone cadences. Possessed of the most wicked sense of humor of the lot, his subsequent ensembles – Air, The Henry Threadgill Sextett, and now Very Very Circus – explore classical, ragtime, and folk music traditions, traffic in sly puns and mordant humor, offer robust dialogue between players at the peak of their form, and are often earmarked by plenty of bold brass, a refreshing insouciance and a dry, vinegary wit that would turn Carla Bley green with envy. His work has captured the Best Composer honors in *Downbeat*'s International Jazz Critics' Poll for 1989 and 1990, the critics taking their cue from the magazine's readers, who had voted Threadgill the same honors the two previous years.

When reading about Henry Threadgill, the word "alchemist" keeps cropping up. And just as he has transmuted the base metals of the jazz tradition into something infinitely more precious and valuable, Threadgill has also deftly woven a unique personal mythology to accompany his music, a deliciously morbid cloak of ideas as enigmatic as the Shroud of Turin. While not as out there as the cosmologies of Lee "Scratch" Perry or Sun Ra, Threadgill's personal beliefs in life and the afterlife are essential to his compositions, and just as mysterious, as British journalist Graham Lock discovered in a 1989 interview.[3] For example, asked about the personnel who have graced his ensembles, Threadgill waxes, "I don't think that I was seeking them out; I just think that they were in my path." Asked if he agrees with Pharoah Sanders that playing brings one closer to the Creator, he admits "I think I'm tapped into a part of something. Something that gets into me, comes into me, adds to where I'm at and surprises me in some kind of way. I see myself as part of something, a larger life form." Ask him when he was born, and he may well echo Abrams' oft-quoted epistle, "of course the real answer is I've been born many times."

The pulpit vocalisms and cosmic trappings can be traced back to family and church life in Chicago, where Threadgill was born in 1944. "I come from a real vocal tradition," he says. "As a kid I was always around a lot of singing. Now, I really love singing, but I'm not a singer. But the first horn players in jazz were totally connected to and inspired by the vocal tradition – Bessie Smith, Ma Rainey and Ethel Waters. And my two grandmothers were always going to church. Church was always really strong in my community. Churches seem to have a real ritualistic type of religious ceremony. There's theater there; there's a lot happening there. It's more than just music. There's music, movement and theater, all exists there simultaneously. As a kid I was always totally impressed by it. We used to play church. It was a game my little sisters and cousins would play. One Sunday or one night at seven, we would set up, get dressed up, and play church. [*laughs*] It was funny."

Add to this Threadgill's tutelage under Abrams, the years he spent crisscrossing the States in New Orleans marching bands, R&B ensembles, church revival groups and army rock outfits [he did a short tour of duty in

Vietnam in 1967], a stint in St. Louis' Black Artists Group, plus his deep space baptizum by The AACM, and you have a timeless, Afrocentric recipe for a group like Air, the bold trio Threadgill formed in Chicago with bassist Fred Hopkins and drummer Steve McCall in 1972. "The reality of playing music is that first you have to come through a door, and given my background, jazz was the only style that made any kind of sense to me in the beginning," Threadgill explains in his 1991 biographical notes. "I was surrounded by so many important elements of the music while growing up – improvisation and ritual and going to church – that jazz was just easier to identify with than anything else. Of course, in time I realized I was interested in and could be influenced by all types of music, whether it was created by classical composers like Verdi, Ravel, and Mahler, free jazz pioneers like Ornette, Cecil Taylor and Albert Ayler, or by Anthony Braxton, Roscoe Mitchell and Leroy Jenkins."

While Air's popular *Air Lore*[4] fondly tipped the hat to the rags of Jelly Roll Morton and Scott Joplin, their albums recorded for the Japanese Why Not label in the mid-'70s like *Air Song* and *Air Raid* revealed Threadgill to have a more ambitious and fiery approach to the tradition in mind. Fluent on a parade of reeds [he wields flute, baritone, tenor and alto saxes with equal aplomb] Threadgill introduced new timbral possibilities with found instruments like his "hubkaphone," a gamelanesque, percussive readymade he built from automobile hubcaps he saw glimmering in a junkyard while driving along Chicago's Dan Ryan Expressway.[5] His ragtime-into-Bartók compositions also gave Hopkins and McCall room to navigate, blow *and* exchange ideas, bestowing Air with a deeply-felt, intimate and telepathic interplay. "I write music for people, I'm of the human species," Threadgill insists. "I don't write music for anything other than people. That's the strata of life that I'm a part of. I deal with that head-on. I'm not involved in any kind of intellectual trip. I mean, it's theoretically clear to me what I do. I don't play down, because I have a high respect for that strata of life. I'm a part of it; if I disrespect you, I disrespect myself."

Air made the move to New York in 1975, where Henry Threadgill the composer successfully tried his hand at writing for flute quartet, his WindString Quintet, chamber ensembles, even full orchestras with strings, percussion, brass, and woodwinds. He worked with artists, poets and filmmakers and premièred his works at performance spaces as diverse as La MaMa and CBGBs. After Air disbanded in 1985, he recast some of the personnel who shared his desire for exploring the music of unorthodox, recombinant instrumental jazz lineups in his seven-member Sextett [the seventh member was another drummer; the extra 't' a pun], the ensemble that would occupy much of his attention during the 1980s. Alongside David Murray's acclaimed Octet – in which he played as well, contributing some gorgeous bass flute work – Threadgill's Sextett was admired as a forum for some of the freshest writing in jazz in the last decade as much as it was for the stripe of player Threadgill enlisted: cornetist Olu Dara, cellist Deidre Murray, bassist Fred Hopkins, trombonists Craig Harris and Frank Lacy, and drummers Reggie Nicholson and Pheeroan akLaff.

The Sextett reached a sublime peak early on with three albums recorded for the About Time Label – *When Was That?*, *Just the Facts and Pass the Bucket*, and *Subject To Change*.[6] In this trilogy Threadgill draws a turbulent, brass-heavy orchestral sound from a palette of just seven players, deftly dovetails the diaspora of traditional Black musics, and recodified the New Orleans funeral band to play *Escalator Over the Hill*. The middle album is a standout. The players smoulder as they focus their energies on one spot, smoking until they explode, as in "Black Blues," where Threadgill, Dara and Harris trade fierce gospel hallelujahs over the dual drums of akLaff and Nicholson going full bore, or the shattering climax to "Gateway," which wouldn't sound out of place in Puccini's *Turandot*. The morbid iconography of the album covers – fish skeletons, a snapshot of the band in a cemetery, a sinister character named Trinity Deliverance – obliquely reveal Threadgill's fascination with death, a subject whose myths and taboos he explores with wit, innocence, and style.

As Trinity Deliverance was a symbol of simultaneous death and rebirth, Threadgill began anew on a second triptych of albums with The Sextett, applying the principles of scoring post-Mingus big band jazz for a chamber ensemble that he learned from gigging with David Murray's Octet. Fittingly, many pieces on *You Know the Number*, *Easily Slip Into Another World*, and *Rag, Bush and All*[7] unfurl slowly, with felicitous shifts in time and texture that signal one player to pick up another's ideas, develop them, and pass them along, in settings from a joyous calypso vamp ["Black Hands Bejewelled"[8]] to rags revisited ["The Devil is on the Loose and Dancin' With a Monkey"[9]]. The latter offers a jaw-dropping sequence of solos – after Threadgill drops his bomb, Deidre Murray's astringent cello spirals push against *Peter Gunn*-isms, bowing out to a laconic dialogue between Fred Hopkins and the empathic percussion team of Newman Baker and Reggie Nicholson, followed by Ted Daniels' skittish, tart trumpet blasting off to charts unknown. Threadgill balances the three-ring circus with modal ballads like "Paille Street" and "Gift," a gentle and meditative piece for brass, splashes of cymbal, wind chimes, and curious trumpet cries that can only be described as dawn breaking over New York.

Rag, Bush and All signaled an end to The Sextet. The '90s were upon Threadgill, and he was hearing voices again, voices that spoke of particle physics, the chaos theory, and a second alto. "I see it as a brand new situation," Threadgill told Mitch Goldman of Columbia University's WKCR-FM in March of 1991.[10] "I feel the Sextett didn't need any further work. It reached a satisfying conclusion. This is a new perspective I've placed myself in. On a theoretical basis, when one organizes and composes the type of let's say systems and ideas that are at the disposal of a composer, it's a form of musical logic. You might not avail yourself to some particular systems that exist or ideas that are outside of the realm of the systems you are using, because you might be trapped by the understanding of the nature of life, if that makes sense to you. When there's a change in the expansion of our knowledge of the entrapment of thinking, we can move over into newer creative areas."

Threadgill had also been hearing the same things that Miles heard when he went electric and what Ornette heard when he formed Prime Time. When riding a train in Europe in 1989 listening to Wagner's *Ring* cycle, it all fell into place. "I had been thinking about another group for a while," he says. "I started being concerned with what was happening around me. Eastern Europe has collapsed. Things have started to change in Africa. Social problems, exploration of space, technology, all kinds of critical arguments in that field. A lot of stuff. Those things kind of put me on another whole vibration, and it made me think about what I was doing with the Sextet, for one, and I kind of felt that I had done what I was going to do writing-wise with that. At that point I don't know what day or when it occurred, but I started hearing something different in the music. In late spring of last year, it really came together."

"It" was Very Very Circus, another seven-member sextet featuring Threadgill and trombonist Curtis Fowlkes, two guitar players [Masujaa and Brandon Ross] and two tuba players [Edwin Rodriguez and Marcus Rohas], and drummer Gene Lake bringing up the rear. Fowlkes and Ross are best known for their hip improvisational forays at New York's Knitting Factory, Fowlkes for blowing with The Jazz Passengers and Ross helming his own group, The Overflow. Rohas has worked with Threadgill in the WindString quintet, and a Venezuelan friend of Threadgill's recommended Rodriguez to him, lamenting that his horn was lying tarnished. "In Puerto Rico they use tuba players in salsa bands, here they don't," Threadgill explains, looking slightly bemused.

Live, Very Very Circus is all about chaos. The tunes – juju workouts and piano rags with heads that surface *after* the solos – are packed with explosive statements for alto and trombone, and a sense of dynamics that Stravinsky would envy. Against Lake's rolling thunder, the two tubas lay out a fantastically fat bottom end, while Masujaa and Jerome Harris [subbing for a sick Brandon Ross] peal off phosphorescent solos and layer harmonic overtones. Curtis crabwalks over the furious arrangements, alternating between split-toned slithers and a voicing game of hop skip & jump, and Threadgill follows a mid-tempo New Orleans-style march with a syncopated salsa number, complete with the theme passed around behind bawdy, barrelhouse solos. "The bigger the circus, the more rings there are," Threadgill told Goldman.[11] "And the big feat is to have all the rings operating simultaneously. That creates a real spectacle."

More than any of his AACM contemporaries, Threadgill has taken his original teachings and concepts and made them sound fresh, particularly on his through-composed works. On *Song From Out Of My Trees*,[12] Threadgill the composer evokes Verdi, Ravel and Mahler as much as he does Ornette Coleman, Cecil Taylor and Albert Ayler, fusing their styles in unusual arrangements such as a rondo for four guitars. In Very Very Circus, Threadgill the bandleader has bridged the gap between populism and art, creating a jazz classicism steeped in dark funk and world rhythms. On their debut *Spirit of Nuff...Nuff*,[13] Threadgill is a formidable ringmaster, brewing a more complex tension than he had with the Sextett and nurturing a playful sense of humor dark as blackstrap molasses. After a trip to India in 1992, Threadgill began to hear the electric guitar differently, spiced Very Very Circus' mix with extended writing for the guitar, then folded in violinist Leroy Jenkins, Venezuelan vocalists/percussionists Johnny Rudas and Miguel Urvina, Brazilian vocalists Mossa Bildner and Arenæ and Moroccan *oud* master Simon Shaheen on their stunning followup *Too Much Sugar For A Dime*.[14] [The title is an aphorism Threadgill's father was fond of; it means that "someone is getting more than they deserve for a change, after getting shorted all the time."] The turbulence of the world circa the early '90s *can* be heard in Very Very Circus. But, donning the mask of Trinity Deliverance, Threadgill stops short of ascending the soap box. "I don't use music to confront issues head-on," he says. "It's a much more complicated. I'm not really prepared to explain how I deal with that. I'm sure a lot of artists find themselves being really confrontational with their art. I'm not. I do deal with issues, but I can't say I deal with them in a way that I can even explain. It's a little bit too complicated."

These days Threadgill is dividing his time between Very Very Circus and The Society Situation Dance Band, a 15-strong live outfit he hopes to never get near a recording studio with. "I'm not in any hurry to record with that band, because I'm interested in a live situation, and people's response," Threadgill reasons. "It could easily become a very commercial item; but I don't want to get tied up in a recording studio. You have to see people moving in large numbers." Helping to get the crowd moving in The Society Situation Dance Band are Fowlkes, Ross, Harris, Murray, Leroy Jenkins, Billy Bang, Akbar Ali, Terry Jenoure, John Stubblefield, among others. "I hadn't been at a dance since I was a kid," says Threadgill. "Back then it was all kinds of music. Dance music today is one-dimensional. You go to a dance now; it's the same kind of music being played all night long. *If* there's a live band – more often than not, there isn't. And you're not gonna hear all kinds of rhythms. You'd probably never hear a damn waltz. We're about movement, social and dance. It's really different –

Polka, pasa doble, two-step, there's just so many things. At times when we play I think it overwhelms people. They stand there listening rather than move. It's intimidating in a way, kind of embarrassing. You hear this music, and you don't move to it. 'I don't know how do that dance.' Well, you don't have to do that particular dance; you move the way you feel."

At the silver anniversary of the AACM in September through October of 1990, Threadgill, Roscoe Mitchell, Leroy Jenkins, Amina Claudia Myers, and Muhal Richard Abrams led ensembles in New York and Chicago that featured three generations of AACM players who have reached formidable creative maturity. Twenty-five years on, is Threadgill finally getting too much sugar for his dime? "I think as we've changed, the goals have gotten broader," he says, reflecting back on his tenure with Abrams' Experimental Band. It's taken all of us a long way. All those individuals I played with back in Chicago are now institutions in themselves; little AACMs. Everybody has grown so much in their own direction. Yet I think the principles are the things we started out with are still very strong and have proven very real. To me, music is an open door, a wide open door. I don't have too many limitations in terms of what I like. I have tastes like everybody else; some things I enjoy more than others, and some things I don't enjoy at all. I think it's very important that musicians actually don't have too much of a right to be closed to sound. They're human, like everyone else, but I think they should fight it. Everything don't come easy."

Henry Threadgill
Solo: Song From Out of My Trees (Black Saint, 1994)
Air: Air Song (Why Not, 1975), Air Raid (Why Not, 1976), Air Time (Nessa, 1977), Air Lore (Arista, 1979)
Henry Threadgill Sextett: When Was That? (About Time, 1982), Just the Facts and Pass the Bucket (About Time, 1984), Subject To Change (About Time, 1986), You Know The Number (Novus, 1987), Easily Slip Into Another World (Novus, 1988), Rag, Bush and All (Novus, 1989)
Very Very Circus: Spirit of Nuff...Nuff (Black Saint, 1991), Too Much Sugar For A Dime (Axiom, 1993)
with **The David Murray Octet**: Ming (Black Saint, 1980), Home (Black Saint, 1982), Murray's Steps (Black Saint, 1983)

Footnotes:
1. From *Afrocentricity*, Africa World Press: Trenton, 1988: p.21, 2. An earlier version of this chapter was originally published as "Spirituals to Swing...and Way, Way Beyond," the author, *Option* Magazine N37, March 1991: pp.66-72, 3. Graham Lock, "Riddles of a Chicago Alchemist," *Wire* Magazine N61, April 1989: pp.25-27, 4. Arista, 1979, 5. See John Litweiler, *The Freedom Principle: Jazz After 1958*, William Morrow & Co.: New York, 1984: p.193, 6. About Time; 1982, 1984 & 1986 respectively, 7. Novus; 1986, 1987 & 1988 respectively, 8. From *You Know The Number*, 9. From *Rag, Bush and All*, 10. Interview conducted by Mitch Goldman for WKCR-FM; March 25, 1991, 11. ibid, 12. Black Saint, 1994, 13. Black Saint, 1991, 14. Axiom, 1993

Sergei Kuryokhin

"[A] roll on the kettledrums as much as Romeo's soliloquy, the cricket on the hearth no less than the cannon fired over the heads of the audience. For all, in their individual ways, bring us to a single idea – from their individual laws to their common quality of attraction...every element that can be verified and mathematically calculated to produce certain emotional shocks."

Sergei Eisenstein, 1923[1]

In the seventy-odd years Vladimir Ilyich Lenin presided over Red Square at the heart of what used to be the old Soviet Union, Communism's ideological gulf between culture and commerce fostered the growth of art that was at once unofficial, trail-blazing and dangerous, a mixture of subversive non-conformism, lip service to the establishment, and good old Russian romanticism, a package tidily appropriated and retrofitted in the 1960s as the "avant garde." The proof is in the painters and the poets, the filmmakers and the composers. Just ask Vassily Kandinsky, Vladimir Mayakovsky, Sergeis Eisenstein and Prokofiev, or Lev Termen, pioneer of electronic music and inventor of the *termenvox*[2] Indeed, when we were watching *Forbidden Planet* [or listening to "Good Vibrations"] and marveling over the sound of Termen's brave new world, or grooving in the lofts to the art "happenings" of the '60s, we were actually celebrating a rich

Soviet heritage which embraced the dada movement, the Armoury Show, the surrealists, and the Russian futurists, brilliant studies all in contradiction and paradox, art that reflected the tempest of its time.

So it comes as no surprise that Sergei Kuryokhin's piano bench sits squarely in the middle of this bold, polarized tradition. Indeed, the 30-year old Russian pianist is seemingly fond of sweeping contradiction. He will profess to liking the pianistic greatness of Cecil Taylor, then recant and say that his *oeuvre* represents the ultimate cul-de-sac of piano technique: "God gave him strong physical prowess and strength and not bad brains, and he looks great onstage, but he's done nothing new for the last 30 years." He admires Taylor, Monk, Muhal Richard Abrams, and Alexander von Schlippenbach as pianists, but believes jazz to be "dead," with all the radical black musicians – David Murray, the Art Ensemble of Chicago, Sun Ra and Pharoah Sanders – looking backward.[3]

As the latest envoy of the shock troops of Soviet artists, Kuryokhin also has a brilliant affinity for theatrical jolt: he has, in past, sawn a piano in half, and placed goats at peril amidst the quixotic "happenings" of his Pop Mechanics performances. "The concept is total madness," Kuryokhin once told Walter Rovere about Pop Mechanics.[4] "This is very important, because it's the Russian style of Art. Most people ask me what is Russian Art, what is Russian jazz, what is Russian rock, what is Russian culture? I believe that Russian culture is total madness. If you play many styles of diverse music and bring to it elements of this madness, you have Russian music." Yet flamboyant and grotesque stage behavior for Kuryokhin is merely an extension of the music, graphic punctuation to what's being played. As he told Leo Feigin in *Russian Jazz: New Identity*, "For me there is a definite contradiction between art and creative work. Creativity is a spirit, a liberation from the burden of matter, and when the spirit leaves, what is left is a dead work of art, a museum exhibit, an object of worship. That's why I think that the real essence of art is to be found outside art, but is contained within the creative process. A real artist is always a nonconformist."[5]

Western listeners first got a taste of Kuryokhin's pianistic dissidence in 1981, when *The Ways of Freedom*[6] was covertly smuggled out of the Soviet Union. Kuryokhin's meta-passionate playing on the album fell somewhere between the percussive atonality of Cecil Taylor and the orgasmic romanticism of Keith Jarrett's *Köln Concert*; his tempos clocked in at blinding velocities. Several stunned critics could only decide that Kuryokhin had a little help at the mixing board. "When I released *The Ways of Freedom*, nine out of ten critics said that it was impossible, that the tapes were electronically fiddled with," says Kuryokhin's "producer," Leo Feigin, who released five of Kuryokhin's albums in England before ever meeting the Russian musician. "I've never heard such nonsense. Who would electronically remaster the tape? Who would be doing this in the Soviet Union when it was recorded on a broken Revox? Because the guy played so fast, so well, they thought it was impossible."

Kuryokhin's speed, agility and passion were on hand at a rare Western recital in May of 1991 at the hip Jazz Café, located in the Dickensian squalor and crush of London's Camden Town. Playing like a petulant Brahms at first, Kuryokhin then segued into a barrelhouse boogie silent film score, hitting imaginary visual filmic cues, only to let the tempo of his ragtime slowly decay. Kuryokhin's fingers are astonishingly and deadly accurate. So is his contempt: from a trickle to a torrent of notes, he built up a Jarrett-like cloudburst, only to spike it by sourly hitting the black keys. A synthesizer was used sparingly to deploy some 1950s cool organ sounds while he played walking blues lines with his right hand. At the end, Kuryokhin took us to – where else – Las Vegas, winding up with a self-parodic bombast of Stephen Sondheim schmaltz.

"I'm not interested in playing one kind of music, even if it's great," Kuryokhin says the following day, over chicken and black bean sauce in a noisy Szechuan eatery in London's Soho district. "The most important thing and the most interesting thing is for me to build bridges between different kinds of music. It is a higher music, like Tchaikovsky." Tall and handsome, with short, jet-black hair and the mesmerizing stare of a silent film star, Kuryokhin can be as equally flippant in conversation as he is in concert. When asked about future projects, he quips, "I'm preparing for my death. I don't know when it's coming, and I think I should be prepared." Describing the manner in which master tapes of his records made it to the West in the early 1980s before *perestroika*, he deadpans that friends in scuba diving gear smuggled them out diving under the Black Sea, and that sometimes British spies visiting Russia brought them back. Then he goes on to say he's really keen about the establishment of a cosmic center in Leningrad, if he can get any money from the Soviet government. "You may be smiling, but I'm dead serious. It's a completely new way of preparing astronauts for space travel. That's all I'm allowed to say at the moment."

When the conversation turns to discussing technique, Kuryokhin's responses become less cryptic. "I don't need to practise anymore," he states bluntly. "I've played the piano for 33 years, every day for 15 of those years. It's enough to listen to the music. It needs the right kind of atmosphere. Yesterday there was no preconceived structure to begin with, just two simple melodies, and lots of improvisation. And I wasn't playing at full speed. The more music that is inside my head, the easier it is to play. It's like free movements through all cultures, different times, different people, different places, the more the better." [Indeed, a high point of Kuryokhin's visit to London was spending hours browsing through the Tower Records store in Piccadilly Circus, searching for '20s and '30s blues and Hawaiian music.]

This fanatical stylistic catholicism can be heard on his latest album *Some Combinations of Fingers and Passion,*[7] and his score for *Buster's Bedroom,* Rebecca Horne's 1990 cinematic paean to the genius of Buster Keaton, the silents, and the inhabitants of an eccentric nuthouse in sunny Southern California. On the former, Chopin, Satie, Fats Waller, Jerry Lee Lewis and Dave Brubeck are all grist for the mill as Kuryokhin spins simple motivic material into fantastic, extended solo piano improvisations [Brubeck's bland style in particular is hilariously distended and deformed like silly putty on "Blue Rondo a la Russe"]. On the latter,[8] Kuryokhin matches Horn's tightly controlled anarchy with a score that crams doo-wop, Monkish criss-crosses, hothouse R&B, and silent movie piano music. "I like Charlie Chaplin, his films, and the music of his films," Kuryokhin once confessed.[9] "Each time Chaplin's movies come to mind, their music echoes in my ears and there's no way I can get it out of my head." A remarkable set piece at the end of the film has two of the principles careening around the hairpin turns of seaside mountain pass in an ambulance as a stuck gramophone in the back stutters a scratchy march; a remarkable visual analogue to Kuryokhin's high-wire improvising at the 88s and his approach to composition as well. "It is like scoring a movie," Kuryokhin agrees. "I like taking several film projects on at once. One movie score is rock, the other movie score is set in St. Petersburg in the 19th century. Different places, different times. I like to think about all of these places and times simultaneously, and I like to write the music for all of them simultaneously. I listen to all kinds of music. And by all, I mean all."

Sergei Kuryokhin was born in Murmansk in 1964. His father, an officer in the Soviet Army, was transferred to Moscow when young Sergei was three, and he was raised there until 1971, when he moved to Leningrad, home base to Sergei Eisenstein and the Eccentrics in the 1920s. As a youth, Kuryokhin would rely on friends in the West to bring in records. "Good music was always available, and a lot of the trash you have in the West wouldn't reach the Soviet Union, so we listened only to the great groups like the Stones and the Beatles. It was the same with jazz, only a different circle of people. But the good thing about *perestroika* was that these circles overlapped. If people listened to rock, they'd also get to know some great jazz records."

Kuryokhin listened to Little Richard in the second grade, but he hadn't the faintest idea what he looked like. "No one did," he says of his first major musical influence. "There were murky pictures of Little Richard with The Beatles that circulated in the black market. You couldn't distinguish who was who. You see, we had no information, only the BBC world service. The Voice Of America was jammed, we had no foreign journals, so it was mostly though word of mouth that information was spread at the time. We only knew The

Beatles because of their long hair. Lots of Soviet kids used The Beatles as a common name for any group of four guys with long hair."

Kuryokhin's second big musical impression – not counting the abbreviated, aforementioned infatuation with Cecil Taylor – was the duo of John Coltrane with McCoy Tyner, whose records he discovered while attending The Leningrad Conservatory. Kuryokhin went straight into the third year of conducting and choral departments of the Conservatory, a school with a proud history in piano, and whose pupils included Dmitri Shostakovich. Historically, the Russians were always rooted in *a capella* church services and traditional folk music forms, yet they embraced the well-tempered keyboard with a passion. By emphasizing a vocal approach to piano rather than an orchestral one, The Leningrad Conservatory has become recognized around the world for the technical sophistication and emotional power of its pianism.

"In the Soviet Union, people are taught the sum, the quantity of knowledge. Here in the West we teach how to *get* this knowledge," says Leo Feigin. "People in the Soviet Union are incapable of personal search or research. They don't have the instrument, they are not give the instrument. They are given the sum of knowledge and that's it, you must have it. In the West they teach you how to get this knowledge. Individuality in the West is so much more important. Musicians who make it to the top, they have such incredible command of their instruments, it's scary. It's like that in jazz, too."

Yet Kuryokhin calls the virtuosity of the Russian piano school style exemplified by Rachmaninov "Russian piano disease,"[10] and was expelled from Leningrad Conservatory after just six months for refusing to conform to their curriculum. Kuryokhin says the state music schools train students one way. "Badly. They pay a lot of attention to practise; its very rigid. But they don't give you enough material to think about musically. In school they will teach you how to play. The teaching is just great, but all the teachers are just stupid." Three months later, he was also kicked out of The Institute of Soviet Culture, where he was studying piano, flute, and conducting, for similar treasons.

The nadir of Kuryokhin's bitter contempt for the Russian piano school and authority in general can be found in the mad rhapsodies of his ambitious collective, Pop Mechanics. A shotgun wedding between the *Modern Times* of Charlie Chaplin and the corruscating avant garde theater of Mauricio Kagel, Pop Mechanics offers an onstage anarchy not seen since the days of the Cabaret Voltaire. Kuryokhin's piano is pitched into a maelstrom of up to 60 improvisors at a time – including Boris Grebenschikov [leader of the Russian rock band Aquarium], saxophonist Vladimir Chekasin and singer Valentina Ponomovera – not to mention sequencers, goats and other assorted animals. "I lack the facilities," Kuryokhin has said of his sprawling ensemble. "I need a choir, I need a symphony orchestra, I need a circus with all its characters, I need a zoo and a gypsy camp."[11]

Kuryokhin's notation systems for Pop Mechanics are flexible, ranging from traditional to graphic. In a typical Pop Mechanics performance, about 20% of the music is notated, the rest is improvised within the structure. "It's important that the structure is very rigid," he says. "There is lots of improvisation, there are also melodies that are simple and very recognizable which I use as bridges; melodies the musicians learn beforehand. But in Pop Mechanics, it's important that the melodies are not just music, but they serve as a *symbol* of music. If we play tango, I want it to be a symbol of tango. It's not real tango. Just like this strange dish." Kuryokhin pokes his chicken in black bean sauce with his fork. "The chicken doesn't taste like chicken, the mushroom doesn't taste like mushroom. Besides, I usually want these melodies to obscure the place where I go. If a person knows what is going to follow, it's not interesting to follow, is it? Sometimes you can make a well-rounded guess, but surprises are better."

The surprises on albums like *Introduction In Popular Mechanics*[12] would delight even Tristan Tzara. Yet no matter how anarchic the proceedings get at this 1986 gig in Leningrad – and with six guitarists and three poets quoting from everyone from Pink Floyd to Pushkin, things are bound to – Kuryokhin has a way of sidestepping dada's nihilism and avoiding irony's hip quotation marks. There is a palpable tension in the audience, which feeds on the anger seething below the music's surface. "I've had this feeling of anger for a very long time, since my school days when I was being taught by very stupid teachers who ordered me to do this and that, though I knew even then that they understood absolutely nothing," Kuryokhin once explained to journalist Bob Doerschuk.[13] "Still, you had to obey them, or you were kicked out; that is where my anger comes from. It was a logical development from there to get angry at musicians who don't want to understand you. You find that the people who do understand you are not musicians, but rather your friends: artists, writers, and so on. Therefore your compositional and performing methods are dictated not so much by purely musical values, but by the general intellectual atmosphere. This doesn't mean that I want to express my anger directly, however. Very often I find that the best way to express it is in the opposite way. My anger comes out as irony, but it's a very joyful irony."

With *perestroika* and the sweeping changes in Soviet political structures and cultural ideology at the end of the 1980s, Kuryokhin has been able to quit his day job and make a living both at home and abroad as an "official" musician. When he landed in Tuscon, Arizona on October 8, 1988, setting foot in America for the first time, Kuryokhin opened the door for what may be the most fertile exchange of artistic ideas between nations since the 1920s. On his visit to

America, Kuryokhin worked and recorded with everyone from John Zorn to musicians from the Soundings Of The Planet label, and played a solo performance at New Music America in Miami that left them standing in the aisles. He even spent a week in LA meeting with counterculture überlord Frank Zappa. "Everybody keeps asking me about my meeting with Frank Zappa," he grumbles, "but Zappa just called me up and I went to his studio and we just talked and played music. It was fun, it wasn't work."

In San Francisco, he sat in one night with Boz Scaggs, and recorded a duet CD at the Oakland home of maverick guitarist Henry Kaiser, who introduced Kuryokhin to Synclavier technology. While Kaiser has been using the sophisticated Synclavier as a diving board into new improvisational territory for years, driving it from his guitar via a MIDI hookup, sitting in front of it for the first time Kuryokhin intuitively plays the instrument's index of possibilities like a virtuoso on their duet together, *Popular Science*.[14] "Music is not born in a logical way," Kuryokhin once said.[15] "At first comes inspiration, which is worked out afterwards in a logical manner. It's characteristic of inspiration that it is born in an impulsive moment. This is one of the major complexities in improvised music. Because during a concert where the musicians don't know what they'll be playing, if it doesn't match the inspiration, the concert won't succeed. We need to learn to work so that inspiration always happens."

In Kuryokhin's hands, the Synclavier rattles like a *faux*, *Perils of Pauline* harpsichord in "Sales Pitch," peppers the modern "Seeing Red" with Balinese gamelan, birdsong and steel drum accents, and sifts lush Nino Rota vocals into a demented Zappaesque mix on "My Amazing Rat." At its best, *Popular Science* recalls Kaiser's chameleonic guitar duets with Fred Frith:[16] when Kaiser's knife-edge blues improvisation howls across Kuryokhin's rock solid left hand work in the Mike Hammer stripper music of "Rattlesnake Roundup," or when Kuryokhin conjures a melismatic, Middle Eastern bed for Kaiser's dry, dusty oud samples on "Foreign Accents." At its worst, the session meanders like even the best of free jazz records, squeezing out sparks only sporadically. Curiously enough, Kuryokhin doesn't put this down to his relative digital primitivism, but rather the language barrier between the two players. "At the time I recorded with Henry I couldn't speak two words," Kuryokhin says. "The communication was entirely musical. I can speak a little English now, so the next time I meet Henry I want to be locked up with him and *really* play the thing."

In typical Kuryokhin fashion, he's let two American record contracts, with Ryko and Elektra Nonesuch, languish. "I get lots of offers from different companies, and I'm in a position to choose to do what I want to do," he says. "But now, American projects are not all that important to me. For example, Nonesuch offered to underwrite a new record, but I refused. Not because I didn't want to, but because some projects were more important at this time." In the good old USSR, if you didn't sign with Melodiya, Russia's one and only legal label, you risked house arrest by putting out a bootleg LP. Needless to say, Melodiya considered Kuryokhin about as suitable for release as The Rolling Stones. The irony of it all is that after the final dismantling of the Soviet Union at the end of the 1980s, Kuryokhin was signed by Melodiya after all, and recorded for the label in 1989.[17]

"I guess it was only a matter of time. And talent [*laughs*]. Any concert hall is open to me now. This changed when I became known abroad. Since we are moving to a market economy, market economy laws are starting to operate in the Soviet Union. The musicians who are doing a lot of experimentation can only do it for a very limited audience. Before *perestroika*, the audience was limited for ideological reasons, now it's limited for economic reasons. It's the same everywhere. if you're not middle of the road, your audience is by definition limited. So nothing's changed, really."

Sergei Kuryokhin: The Ways Of Freedom (Leo, 1981), Popular Zoological Elements (Leo, 1987), Morning Exercises In The Nuthouse (Soundings Of The Planet cassette, 1988), Polynesia: Introduction To The History (Melodiya, 1989), Some Combinations of Freedom and Passion (Leo, 1992), Sparrow Oratorium (Sparrow International, 1993)
with **Pop Mechanics**: Introduction In Popular Mechanics (Leo, 1987), Insect Culture (Ark, 1987), Pop Mechanics N17 (Leo, 1989), Buster's Bedroom (Pocket, 1991)
with **Boris Grebenschikov**: Subway Culture (Leo, 1986), Mad Nightingales In The Russian Forest (Leo, 1989)
with **Henry Kaiser**: Popular Science (Ryko, 1990)

Footnotes:
1. Quoted in Cook, David A., *A History of Narrative Film* [2nd ed.], W.W. Norton & Co.,: New York, 1990: p.152
2. The theremin, an oscillating device popularized in the Beach Boys' *Good Vibrations* and the forerunner of the Moog family of synthesizers
3. "The Ways of Freedom," in *Russian Jazz: New Identity*, Leo Feigin, ed., Quartet Press: London, 1985: p.106
4. Quoted in Rovere, "Sergei Kuryokhin," *Musiche* N8, Inverno 1990: p.12
5. "The Ways of Freedom," p.111
6. Leo, 1981, 7. Leo, 1992, 8. Released on Pocket, 1991, 9. Rovere, "Sergei Kuryokhin," p.15
10. "The Ways of Freedom," p.101, 11. "The Ways of Freedom," p.103, 12. Leo, 1987
13. Bob Doerschuk, "Sergei Kuryokhin: A Controversial Improvisor Thrives Despite Soviet Bureaucracy," *Keyboard* Magazine, July 1987: p.124
14. Ryko, 1990, 15. Rovere, "Sergei Kuryokhin," p.15
16. *With Friends Like These* and *Who Needs Enemies*; Metalanguage 1979 and 1982 respectively
17. *Polynesia: Introduction To The History*; Melodiya, 1989

Rova Saxophone Quartet

"Wind is invisible, but the movement it imparts to clouds and waves, leaves and grasses, makes its multiplicity apparent...The age-old identification of wind and breath is proof of its invisibility, on the other hand, enables it to stand for invisible crowds, and thus for spirits. They come roaring like a storm, a wild host; or they are spirits in flight, as in the vision of the Eskimo shaman."

Elias Canetti, Crowds and Power[1]

I "We weren't officially there, we were just not officially not there." Larry Ochs October, 1989. After a transcendent, high-wire gig at the hip altar of Victoriaville's Église St-Victoire, The Rova Saxophone Quartet pack their bags for the Soviet Union, and leave behind a sleepy Québec town famed for its hockey sticks for the chilly shores of the Baltic. Rova find things changed since the last time they got back in the USSR, in 1983, when they unofficially played to packed union halls, cutting the wild, exuberant and subversive *Saxophone Diplomacy*.[2] Rova's second dispatch from Russia with love, the brilliant live set *This Time We Are Both*,[3] again reveals them at the peak of their playing, yet is just as important between the notes. Recorded in Moscow, Leningrad and three Baltic capitals when the Berlin Wall was coming down, *This Time We Are Both* is useful in gauging the changes in Soviet attitudes to jazz since perestroika: This time, Rova played Moscow's Palace of Culture instead of the basement of the Dostoïevsky Museum, although the crowds were decidedly cool at the 12th Annual Leningrad Jazz Festival. It had to happen eventually – when they returned as official guests, Rova were old hat.

"1983 really felt like the flipside of western society in the sense that everybody there knew they had no say in what their government did, so they just didn't pay any attention," says the 'O' in Rova, tenor Larry Ochs [b.1949, New York City, former student radical and founder of Metalanguage Records, produced an album by Diamanda Galás, bears a passing resemblance to Muppet saxophonist Zoot]. "They had these games they had to do to get through. Other than that, they were just 100% into art. They really thought of art as a countercultural thing that had impact. This time, it was just like the West. Half of the artists we met the first time we out of town, out in the West trying to make money. People were kind of despondent, because all of a sudden this Pandora's Box of music and information had been opened. A lot of it was probably jive, or just pure panic, but it gets you to watch TV. Last time we were there, the man in the grey suit was reading the news, and of course there was no information. This time, they had a 35 or 40-year old guy in a black leather jacket sitting behind a desk smoking a cigarette reading the news. Media was great this time."

II "Harmony rests primarily on the principle of antithesis." Vassily Kandinsky[4]

In keeping with good old Vassily's dictum that a powerful work of art must reflect the characteristic tone of its time, The San Francisco-based Rova Saxophone Quartet can be seen as children of the information age. Like Kandinsky's search for rhythm in contemporary painting, Rova have been ferreting out and disseminating kernels of truth from a world of contrasting musical information since 1977. Their heads in the ivory towers of the European avant garde, their feet in the muddy waters of American gospel, blues and R&B, John Raskin, Larry Ochs, Bruce Ackley and Steve Adams are saxophone daredevils, perched precariously, to quote altoist Adams, "between precision and wildness." Superb albums such as *Beat Kennel*[5] walk this tightrope smashingly, shifting from the four-way hot potato of "Sportspeak" to the twin heads driving the Monkish "What Was Lost Regained" to the corruscating, through-composed Anthony Braxton composition of 1974[6] that blueprinted the possibilities for the modern saxophone quartet long before the World Saxophone Quartet made it fashionable: "Composition —^{30}—EGN-KBM—$_{78}$."

"When we first got together, the idea was 'Let's have a group that doesn't have a rhythm section and see what we can do,'" says soprano Bruce Ackley [b.1948, Detroit, architecture major and former disc jockey, co-founder of the celebrated Blue Dolphin artists' space in San Francisco]. "We had the broadest range of possibilities in front of us. As time goes on, I think the focus had gotten specific. I hate to say that it's narrowed, because I don't think that's the case. I think we've targeted areas that are interesting to us, and we've been working to refine them."

"It's easy to say that when we first started out, we were heavily influenced by people like Lacy, Braxton, Mitchell, The Art Ensemble," says Ochs. "That was obvious. We were interested in layering information and having a voice for the group; just like individual saxophonists look for a voice. At this point, I'm so far into this music I hear world music influences in there, and I hear Scelsi, Ligeti and Xenakis' concept of mass sound as opposed to notated music or counterpoint. It's definitely more than the sum of its parts."

One of the most crucial elements in this noble equation is the altoist who scuttled Rova's acronym, Steve Adams [b.1952, New York, bearded multi-instrumentalist, once performed with Sam Rivers and Jaki Byard]. Rova hijacked Adams from Boston's Neighborhood Saxophone Quartet in September of 1988 to replace outgoing member Andrew Voigt on a tour that had already been booked. Adams brings a flair for the fiery, microtonal spice and modal improvisation of Indian music and a journeyman's background in playing with rock'n'roll bands, which comes in handy negotiating the hairpin turns of rhythmically knotted works like guitarist Henry Kaiser's "Sugaki For Conlon," which crops up on their recent Sound Aspects platter, *Long On Logic*. "Henry took a piece he had written for guitar and had it transcribed for saxophone and written out in, like, 132nd notes," explains Ochs. "He wanted rock'n'roll saxophones – skewed, of course."

Adams is also a Kandinsky fanatic, and "K/24" is a piquant attempt at transcribing the spatial dislocation and dissonant hues of a Kandinsky watercolor into a jazz suite. "I've always felt looking at his stuff there's all sorts of inspiring elements that can be perceived in musical terms," Adams says. "In 'K/24,' there are a lot of V shapes, so there are a lot of opposing lines that are moving in vees in the writing. And then there's the emotional quality of the painting. The last section of the piece is this long chorale-like part; in one corner of the painting there's a large series of concentric arcs that are red. It had a warmth and feeling to me that I tried to capture."

"Since Steve joined I feel as if the group has taken a quantum leap in a new direction," says Keep The Dog's musical gypsy, Fred Frith, who contributes a triptych of pieces to *Long On Logic*,[7] including a nifty history of the saxophone condensed into the title cut. "I used to find them very dry, actually. I feel they're much warmer now, and much more open to a lot of different kinds of things that they weren't able to do before."

III "It's hard as hell to write for the saxophone and not make it sound like Glenn Miller or the World Saxophone Quartet." Alvin Curran

The CD jacket of *Electric Rags II*[8] depicts a slice of German baloney stamped with a laughing clown's face. The cold cut, reveals composer Alvin Curran, was designed to encourage the future leaders of Germany to eat their lunch. The work it's wrapped around was designed to encourage Rova to swallow whole the history of music according to Alvin Curran. *Electric Rags II* is just thata populist set of 30 three-minute, post-modern rags with titles like "scusami, I walk alone," "corny island" and "continental shelf dance" that encompasses hard bop, one-tone studies, free jazz tussles, ragtime, Nino Rota quotes, and Michael Nyman triads. "It's a challenging piece from a technical point of view," says Curran. "In some cases it brings them to the edge of their own technical abilities, and I must say they meet the challenge."

In fine '90s pay-attention fashion, the miniatures are shuffled every time the piece is played, and every three minutes a Cuban band, John Cage's voice, or a rapper dropping rhymes on drums says time's up. "Those little time bombs let Rova know where they are in the piece, because even with a stopwatch and a clock going from the beginning to the end they couldn't keep a focus on the time and the notes," Curran explains. "So these signals – sometimes a foghorn, sometimes Groucho Marks telling a joke – would blurt into the music [*he snaps his fingers*] and tell them, 'Stop what you're doing and go on to the next piece.'"

"It was a real challenge to focus on what we're doing with all this insanity flying all over the place," says Ochs. "A lot of the time we're playing these quiet chords and we have train wrecks coming across." Each saxophonist pilots a synthesizer through a MIDI hookup that gives Curran a mulligatawny stew of electronics and samples to stir and throw back at Rova in real time, imbuing *Electric Rags II* with a structural unpredictability despite the fact that it's 85% notated. "It is, but that's elusive," counters Ackley, the soprano of the quartet. "Because there's a wide variety of notation that's used. Some of the pieces you're reading off the page, note for note. It goes from that to structured improvisations, and Alvin has touched on many of the grey areas between. He has really interesting ways of graphically notating areas he wants to get at, and giving us just enough room to run with it." And run with it Rova does. *Electric Rags II* is a stylistic funhouse for the saxophone family, a musical kaleidoscope that's different each time its shaken. "I can say this, because none of us wrote it," ventures Ochs. "I think it might be an American classic some day."

Raising the spontaneity stakes even higher is *Maintaining The Web Under Less Than Obvious Circumstances,*[9] a random games piece issued as a limited edition EP on virgin vinyl. *Maintaining The Web* grew out of Rova's affinity for John Zorn's gaming works like *Lacrosse, Archery* and *Cobra,*[10] but unlike

Downtown's resident speed demon, Rova found mere hand signals as cueing devices too limiting, and began to pick up unusual props, like a plastic Tyrannosaurus Rex. "If you picked it up by the tail it indicated that the piece would go one way, if you picked it up by the head, it went another," says Ochs dryly. Yet explaining inflatable dinosaurs to customs officials proved to be too daunting a task, so they settled for chinese fans painted with pictures – cactus, shoe, spider, saxophonist, hand, checkerboard – serving as cues for elaborate improvisational manoeuvres. Add some hats, balls, and a set of instructions and playing strategies more complicated than the rules to fizzbin, and you have a piece that takes Rova's gamesmanship, chops, and their ability to think on their feet to the stratosphere. "There's a sense of play in that piece which is great," says Adams. "It feels so free because we're not dealing with any notated music. We've done it enough that all the structures are automatic, yet we're always finding new ways to combine things. You never know where the piece is going to go. It's always dictated by the moment."

IV "Rova is always looking for people." Fred Frith

"I hadn't been pining to write a saxophone quartet for years," says Fred Frith. "When they asked me, it was the first time I ever thought about it. It was intriguing to try and do something that Rova hadn't done before, because when you're writing for a group like that who've been playing for a long time, you're kind of aware of what they've tackled, and they've tackled everything imaginable." Frith, like Kaiser and Curran, came to Rova through PreEchoes, a series of commissioned works by composers Rova initiated both to heighten their profile in the Bay Area and give the repertoire of the saxophone quartet a much-needed infusion of new blood. Inaugurated in 1986 with a concert from Russia's Ganelin Trio,[11] the plasma is still pouring through. To their repertoire Rova have added a new work by Jack De Johnette that Ackley wickedly dubs "the closest thing we've ever done to the World Saxophone Quartet;" Terry Riley's shamanistic, oriental retelling of the 8th Century Irish epic "The Tain;"[12] Robin Holcomb's lyrical "Laredo;" and the late John Carter's sweeping, rigorous "Colors."

"John Carter has a very personal style of writing which is concerned with the virtuosic use of the instrument," says Adams. "He tends to write things that are just about as difficult for other people as what he writes for himself." Just ask Ackley. "Carter plays very high into the altissimo register. Well, he's got me doing that on the soprano, too. Luckily, I'm ready for him. I think it's important to realize that we had a body of work that was happening when Steve joined that we had to realize before we moved on," Ackley continues. "Now I think we're at a point where everything's documented that Andrew had anything to do with.

The work that happens from here out will have the character of the new Rova. And I don't know that it's gonna be necessarily the tight focus we've seen in the last couple of records. There are definitely some things on the plate that are very tight and refined and strictly ordered, but we're fooling around with some things that are kind of fuzzy, that are more improvisational, radical, and not as sure-fire."

The newly-minted Rova made its studio debut on *From The Bureau of Both.*[13] Adams has two pieces on the album, the inquisitive yet flint-hard open piece "Cage – For John Cage" and a gutbucket Albert Ayler tribute, "What's The Frequency, Kenneth?" Amongst the other gems are a roaring games piece drawn from 1940s *film noir* motifs, "Swapmeet! Swapmeet!!," and a stunning example of through-composed classical *gravitas*, "Pinnacle," from baritone Raskin [b.1954, Heppner, Oregon, contemporary classical education, dance and theater background, Lennie Tristano buff]. This wig-hat six-step through the fields of improvised jazz and modern composition makes for eclectic albums and stunning concerts, yet all too often sends journalists riffing through thesauri to get a handle on Rova's music. "Rova is more often discussed in the synthetic language employed in the service of post-serialism and other forms of avant-garde classical music, than in the jive talk that has traditionally set the tone for jazz," journalist Francis Davis once observed.[14] "Critics have appointed terms such as *pointillism* from the vocabularies of arts and the optic sciences, and *discontinuity* from the lexicons of mathematics and geology in the futile attempt to convey a sense of Rova's converging lines and pebbly textures." It is precisely this prickly perception that keeps Rova bouncing back and forth between the jazz and new music departments of the National Endowment of the Arts as well. "Rova has received a number of grants that were either from the NEA or that were sponsored in part by the NEA, so I can't really complain about that," says Ochs. "But as a group that isn't a jazz group in the traditional sense of the word and isn't a new music group in the sense that we improvise. But the point is that we write a lot of our own music and most contemporary new music groups don't. That's radical for the NEA, which is an institution, and institutions are always 10 or 15 years behind. The jazz component of the NEA is more concerned with maintaining the jazz tradition of jazz, and frankly I don't see anything wrong with that. I'd like to find a nice for *all* these individuals."[15]

The mention of the seven-letter word that starts with R and ends with L rouses Ochs briefly. "I have to say that after doing this for 12 years, I don't really feel radical anymore. I feel like this is what I do." A thoughtful pause.

"But given the current climate of culture, I guess we're still out there."

Rova Saxophone Quartet: Cinema Rovaté (Metalanguage, 1978), The Removal Of Secrecy (Metalanguage, 1979), Daredevils (Metalanguage, 1979), As Was (Metalanguage, 1981), Favorite Street (Black Saint, 1984), Saxophone Diplomacy (Hat Art, 1985), The Crowd (Hat Art, 1986), Beat Kennel (Black Saint, 1988), Long On Logic (Sound Aspects, 1990), Maintaining The Web Under Less Than Obvious Circumstances (Extraplatte, 1990), This Time We Are Both (New Albion, 1991), From The Bureau Of Both (Black Saint, 1993)
with **Anthony Braxton**: The Aggregate (Sound Aspects, 1987)
with **Alvin Curran**: Electric Rags II (New Albion, 1990)
with **The Ganelin Trio**: San Francisco Holidays (Leo, 1993)
with **Terry Riley**: Chanting The Light Of Foresight (New Albion, 1994)

Footnotes:
1. Victor Gollancz, London, 1962: pp.100-101
2. Hat Art, 1985, 3. New Albion, 1991
4. *On The Spiritual In Art and Painting In Particular*, Wittenborn & Schultz: New York, 1947: pp.52-53, 5. Black Saint, 1988
6. The original can be found on Braxton's *New York, Fall 1974* [Arista, 1974], with three quarters of the World Saxophone Quartet: Julius Hemphill, Hamiett Bluet, and Oliver Lake
7. Sound Aspects, 1990
8. New Albion, 1990
9. Extraplatte, 1990
10. See *John Zorn,* p.147
11. The concerts were recorded for posterity on *San Francisco Days*; Leo, 1993
12. Recorded as *Chanting The Light Of Foresight*; New Albion, 1994
13. Black Saint, 1993
14. Francis Davis, "Jazz Quartet's New Work Owes a Debt to Charles Ives," Philadelphia *Inquirer*, October 10, 1987
15. In fact, the 1993 *Meet The Composer* Awards earmarked Rova with $24,000 to commission compositions from Muhal Richard Abrams, Steve Adams and Fred Frith

Fleurs Carnivores

The history of women in new music would be slim volume indeed. It's unfortunate, but the ivory tower of new music has long had an Old Boy's Club ensconced at the very top floor. The alumni of new music's various departments – Serialism [Karlheinz Stockhausen, Pierre Boulez, Milton Babbitt], Minimalism [La Monte Young, Terry Riley, Philip Glass, Steve Reich], and the New York campus of Indeterminacy [John Cage, Morton Feldman, Christian Wolff] nabbed all the fellowships and grants, were the subject of countless books, dissertations, monographs and historical analysis, and became the movers and shakers of 20th Century music.

Yet where were the women? Outside of Meredith Monk, Marian Zazeela, Yoko Ono, Carla Bley and Pauline Oliveros, they barely made it into print. And even these women rarely saw their artistic achievements elevated to the same lofty academic and artistic plateaux. The marginalization of Yoko Ono is a good case in point. Aesthetics aside, Ono's music on LPs like *Approximately Infinite Universe*[1] was no more radical or shocking than that produced by Schoenberg's *Pierrot Lunaire* [1912], any number of her fellow Fluxus alumni, or even Captain Beefheart. Yet it was ridiculed and never taken as seriously as the work of her male contemporaries. Even as late as 1992, when a long-overdue Ono renaissance was touted upon the release of the 5-CD retrospective *Onobox*,[2] it quickly fizzled and cognoscenti went back to the influence of John Cage.

To borrow a phrase from Cole Porter, one need only look at improvised jazz to see that it ain't necessarily so. In the eyes of many myopic jazz critics, improvisation is still the domain of firebrand players like British soprano saxophonist Evan Parker, and always will be. Yet improvising vocalists like England's Maggie Nicols and France's Catherine Jauniaux have creatively pushed the vocal envelope as much if not further than American vocalist Joan La Barbara did in her entire career of singing the works of John Cage. French bassist Joëlle Leandre has devoted her career to creating a new, extended improvising language for her instrument and performing the work of modern composers like Scelsi, Ligeti and, yes, Cage. The scintillating and muscular pianism of Germany's Irene Schweizer on albums like *Wilde Senoritas* and Storming *The Winter Palace*[3] has made her a key figure in the European free jazz movement. Sparring with Evan Parker, Gunter Sommer and Louis Moholo, Schweizer became accepted as a musical equal, and a bandleader of considerable force.

When it comes to composition, the emphasis among women composers in Europe leans toward ensemble work, as in the groups of British composer

Lindsay Cooper. A classically-trained bassoon player, soprano saxophonist, feminist and quintessential European, Cooper gigged with Henry Cow before going on to score independent films and conceptual works like her 1988 meditation on the Cold War, *Oh Moscow*, or 1993's *Sahara Dust*, a lyrical paean to existentialism. Where a fierce individualism was the order of the day among American female composers, in Europe composition grew from a dynamic, improvised and collective standpoint in outfits like England's Feminist Improvising Group and the series of Canaille festivals held across Europe during the 1980s,[4] both of which Cooper, Schweizer, and Nicols participated in.

Free improvisation unlocked doors for women performers in America during the 1980s as well. Yet paradoxically it came to the attention of the media through the back door of performance art, when Laurie Anderson's self-deprecating little ditty about New York social life and her trusty answering machine, "O Superman," became an underground hit in 1980. By the time Anderson unleashed her sprawling song cycle/postmodern raree show about America, *United States I-IV*,[5] at The Brooklyn Academy of Music in 1984, new music was firmly entrenched downtown, roosting in the lofts and performance spaces of Loisaida, on Manhattan's Lower East Side. During the 1980s "downtown" scene in New York, women more than proved that they could hold their own improvising and composing with men. In an given week circa 1988, one could take in the microtonal rapture of Iranian-born singer Sussan Deihim; the sharp, witty peregrinations of improv vocalist Shelley Hirsch; the Zen-like austerity of electronic drummer Ikue Mori; the rugged Ivesian purity of composer and pianist Robin Holcomb; the avant-garde hoedown of violinist La Donna Smith; the harrowing performance art of Diamanda Galás. In this milieu there was no distinction between masculine and feminine, between improvisation and composition. This open borders policy is vividly underscored in the work of Zeena Parkins, an impulsive New York harpist and accordionist who brought her electric harp to a variety of mixed ensembles.

Today the ranks of intrepid women in new music have grown around the world to include Czechoslovakia's Iva Bittová, a traditional folk singer with a stunningly avant-garde sensibility; Québec's Justine, a womens' collective who have programmed bold festivals of new music by women;[6] Tuva's Sainkho Namtchylak, a spine-tingling vocalist who can charge even a large free orchestra with her plaintive, split-toned Mongolian cry; Russia's electrifying Valentina Ponomoreva, one of the few vocalists with the guts and technique to match John Zorn's visceral saxophone eye for eye; and Tenko, a Japanese vocalist and improviser deeply involved in Butoh and pitched between ancient and modern Japan. Decidedly outside the new music loop, these women are fierce, determined and take chances live like no other performer.

It would be both right and wrong to state that women hear, compose and perform music different than men. It would be right because there *are* qualitative differences between the two; just compare the ways Carla Bley and Henry Threadgill pilot big bands, for example. But to generalize that women are better at improvising than men would be inferring a case for determinism and sexism where there are simply no sufficient grounds to do so. After all, pianist Marilyn Crispell can tear up Trane with the best of the boys, and Seattle-based vocalist, multi-instrumentalist and stylistic haberdasher Amy Denio often seems like one, whereas the quirky ditties of New York songwriter and performer David Garland sport a whimsical and decidedly unmasculine outlook on modern life. *Musique actuelle* remains one of the few new music fields where women are vital and they participate on an equal level with men, and not just as the singer or bassist. It's high time that women composers received their due as well. As the once-entrenched boundaries between composition and improvisation become increasingly tenuous, it's more important than ever.

1. Apple, 1972
2. Ryko, 1992
3. FMP, 1976 and Intakt, 1987; respectively
4. See *Lindsay Cooper*, p.113
5. Warner Brothers, 1984
6. See *Justine*, p.209

Amy Denio

A bim beri glassala gladride/ E glassala tuffm/ I Zimbra

Talking Heads, "I Zimbra"[1]

"Every language has an inherent musicality that is beautiful and only expressible in that language, and it reflects the culture along with it," reasons Seattle-based vocalist, improviser and multi-instrumentalist Amy Denio.[2] "Like *fado*, the national pop song of Portugal, reflects the *soledad* of the Portuguese. All these different musical styles reflect a different emotional state for me, and I really love to sing them. As this woman said to me in Vienna, 'Thank you for the bath of feelings.' I cried 'That's perfect! That's really what I'm driving at with this music.' Broken English really is the best sometimes."

Broken English is merely one of the musical vocabularies Amy Denio [rhymes with Ohio] has been gifted with. The 33-year old vocalist loves to sing, whether fronting the off-kilter funk pop of Seattle's Tone Dogs, the cut-up jazz of Curlew, or transposing it to the blowing alto of The Billy Tipton Memorial Saxophone Quartet. In these ensembles, her uninhibited voice draws on a plethora of tongues, both real and invented; in the parlance of the street, Denio's work is all about the phonetics of phat. "It's fun. I have to say, I do like to sing,"

Denio admits. "And not just three notes, why not go for four? Really, I guess I'm influenced by everything that I hear whether I like it or not. There are elements in all kinds of music that are really interesting to me."

Denio is relaxing in the Bern kitchen of Swiss guitarist Wädi Gysi. Gysi [rhymes with icy] lives just down the road from Müri, a posh enclave where the ambassadors live. His flat is one of a series of parallel low-rise, modern apartments lining the Mürinenstrasse, all painted radically different shades [Gysi's is the color of bright mustard]. Spring has come to Switzerland this sunny April Sunday, and today Denio has been visiting such Bern attractions as the World Post Office and the Bärengraben, or The Bear Pit, where several of the city's namesake and mascots live in a huge sunken cage. "It's really sad," Denio says. "They have a real zoo as well, but this is like a bear torture area."

For the past month, Denio has been on tour with Gysi and British drummer Chris Cutler as The [EC] Nudes, an immensely satisfying and fun avant garage band that rips through sets of punk and tangos live ["Wädi was born in a garage," Denio jokes] and grinds gears between Portuguese rock and electroacoustic radio works on their debut CD *Vanishing Point*.[3] The "EC" stands for European Community, and was hastily added to avoid – you guessed it – litigation from another American group of the same name. "There is an American band called The Nudes, which I didn't know; none of us knew," Denio confesses. "I was on tour this fall in a small town on North Carolina, I stopped in a bookstore and there was this CD of a band called The Nudes. I thought, 'That's interesting,' so I copied down their address and called them up, and they said [*Denio puts on a brusque, officious voice*] 'You can't be The Nudes; this is a registered trademark Nudes.' All right. So at the last minute we added 'EC,' which is probably not the best choice, but we really wanted to get the CD out so we made some rash decisions quickly."

Quick and dirty has since become The [EC] Nudes modus operandi. The trio has been zipping about the European countryside in a tiny Renault Espace – passing all the East European Trabants which owners have desperately taken to painting wild colors to compete with the new automotive affluence on the open highways – and playing gigs at a breakneck pace in Czechoslovakia, Italy, Austria, Switzerland, Eastern Germany, France, and Holland. Shortly before their tour they cut *Vanishing Point* in a matter of days. "We glued everything together in a pretty darn short time last May," says Denio. "For the first session, we had four days of rehearsal and fewer than ten concerts under our belts. We'd been together for a total of 14 days when we started recording. Not premature, but at least fresh."

Like the music of The [EC] Nudes, Amy Denio is a freewheeling spirit, an enthusiastic vocal magpie whose eclectic choice of music carries is matched only by her eclectic life. Much like the DIY women's groups that came out of the British kitchen in 1980s – like Delta 5 and The Raincoats – Denio plays a cornucopia of musical instruments, including bass, saxophone, recorder, bass mbira, organ, slide guitar and dishwasher, all of which she taught herself after piano lessons as a kid that were an unqualified disaster. "There's always some possibility in playing, say...this skin therapy lotion bottle sitting in front of me!" Denio laughs. "Instruments just come to me. For instance, in Budapest I had all this Hungarian money which, currency-wise, was useless everywhere else, so I marched into a music store and asked them to sell me an accordion." [She just bought a new one in Prague last week, a candy-apple red Delicia.]

Denio is the Peppermint Patty we all knew as kids: smart, funny, able to make music from paper clips, rubber bands and blades of grass. All grown up, she is a down to earth improviser, a West Coast boho sporting the requisite haberdashery yet without any threads of pretentiousness; Joni Mitchell minus the airs. As our afternoon conversation free-associated between Seattle, kids, muzak, scat and Italian national radio, she even gamely owned up to a skeleton rattling about in the closet of her *curriculum vitae*: playing bass for and starring in a 1990 B-grade mythology/skateboard epic entitled *Shredder Orpheus*.

"Oh, it's really bad," she groans. "It's filmed beautifully, but the text is *so* bad. Orpheus, he was in a band called The Shredders, see. And so they played in this club, and that's where he met Eurydice, because she was a go-go dancer at this club, see. And later he visits the river Styx, where there's a paper shredder that shreds your memory when you go to Hades." Denio collapses in laughter that quickly mutates into a coughing fit. "Anyway," she continues, regaining her breath, "this guy named Roland Barker wrote the music. Barker used to be in the infamous Seattle band The Blackouts, who were really big in 1981-1982, when the new wave was really fresh and raw. So he needed a quartet of musicians to play The Shredders, and I made my film debut. I even got a line: I got to say, 'Probably needs batteries.' Well, it needed a lot more than batteries."

Born on June 9, 1961 in Boston, Amy Denio grew up in Detroit. The youngest of three sisters, Amy was the most musically inclined, and was heartily encouraged by her parents, bassists both. Her mother played her upright in classical ensembles and jammed with The Depression Derelicts, a Detroit-area jazz band devoted to music from the '30s and '40s and whose ranks included trumpet player Al Matisse, son of the famous painter. "I was pretty tomboyish and extremely musical from a very early age," she says. "My two older sisters are nine and ten years older than I am, so as a kid I struck out on my own a lot. When I was growing up, my father was headmaster at a Detroit elementary school that was part of an educational community, so I had a 300-acre estate to go romping around on. When I started playing music, both parents were extremely supportive. My older sisters, on the other hand, were like "You're going to support yourself with *music*? That's *insane!*' But my parents were both cheering for me: 'Yay! You're following your dreams.'"

Denio's dreams eventually took her to Seattle in 1985. Land of espresso, Muzak and grunge, Seattle was a sleepy bohemian mecca with an open attitude, a place where post-hardcore musicians could rub elbows with the avant garde. Now that the entire nation is flying the flannel and making Pearl Jam rich, Seattle has become a tad overcrowded. "Seattle has tripled in size since I've moved there, and the air is really bad because there are far too many cars," Denio says. "It's a lot more violent and a lot more random. When I moved there it was really provincial and really open. That feeling has completely evaporated. The whole grunge thing made the demographics swell. There are thousands and thousands of 20-year-old lanky, long-haired white guys there now."

At night, Denio played in an experimental jazz ensemble, The Entropics. As a day gig, she toiled in the spotless, sterile halls of Muzak, where she was in charge of the "administrivia," as she so poetically puts it, of elevator music. "I didn't actually have to listen to Muzak, which was great," Denio says. "I was the programming office supervisor. I was in charge of custom programming, so I talked to these very bizarre people all over the nation who would have these weird requests: 'Yeah could we have a combination of John Philip Sousa and The Dead Kennedys?' Then I'd dole that out to some bewildered programmer."

In 1987, Denio met Portland multi-instrumentalist Fred Chalenor, and they formed a loose studio partnership, calling themselves The Tone Dogs. A pop band that dipped its quill into the avant garde inkwell yet painted in a far funkier fashion than Mondriaan, The Tone Dogs went on to become regional celebrities and tour Europe to wild acclaim before disbanding in 1992. Albums like *Early Middle Years*[4] zeroed in on the locus of their appeal: polyrhythmic, polytonal, and polystylistic jam sessions brimming with fresh ideas and nimble improv playing. Smart, hip and way funky, The Tone Dogs occupied that rare middle ground between art and rock, and could attract both Soundgarden drummer Matt Cameron and new music guitar gypsy Fred Frith.

Denio's saxophone work also caught the attention of other women sax players in Seattle like soprano saxophonist Marjorie de Muynck, who were tired of sitting around waiting for gigs only to nail the changes. "I really love hearing other styles of music played by saxophone quartet," Denio says. "I'm a huge fan of WSQ. There's so much music that can turn the saxophone quartet into this living breathing organism. Marjorie and I thought 'Wouldn't it be great if we could play sax all the time? And it wouldn't it be really great if we could start a quartet that included just women?'"

So De Muynck and Denio formed the Billy Tipton Memorial Saxophone Quartet in October of 1988 with Babs Helle and Stacy Loebs. The spirit of the Tiptons' playing is qualitatively different from that of The Rova, WSQ, or 29th Street saxophone quartets. A spin of their debut CD, *Saxhouse*,[5] confirms Sir Henry Threadgill's theorem that time spent in defining jazz is time spent killing it: these four gals swing like mad through a funhouse set that touches on traditional Bulgarian folk song, klezmer, drone/tone poems, some nimble four-way improvising and a transcription of Czech singer Iva Bittova's "Big Beat." For their followup CD, they have waxed some Tex-Mex and Appalachian fiddle tunes, and Denio's arrangement of "Do You Know The Way To San Jose?" with "Kashmir."

"We have a heart and spirit that says a lot of different music can be made with a saxophone," De Muynck has said. "We try to do innovative things with the sax and break the stereotype of what it can or can't do. It's a very versatile instrument, so it's not that hard. We're also a bunch of crazy nuts, with five extremely definite musical personalities.[6] Beauty and humor; that's our motto." "Bus Horn Concerto," on *Saxhouse*, combines these two virtues in equal parts, and came as a result of Seattle's gridlock in crosstown traffic. "Seattle is growing too fast," says De Muynck. "We're still in the Old West, with everybody on their own horse out here. It's really hard for people to let go of their cars. Yet we have a wonderful, efficient transportation system. So in 1992 the metro bus system here put a call out to artists to come up with ways to encourage people to take the bus." So De Muynck and Lurie wrote an interactive concerto that rivals Rova for its daredevil playing and conceptual fun. In it, the Quartet jam on top of buses driven by musicians who "play" their horns, breaks, starters, and wheelchair lifts, while opera singers sing the bus schedule. "It really blended well with the bus sounds, as you could imagine," says De Muynck. "We can make so many weird sounds with the sax while being very melodic. People now come up to me in the grocery store and say every time they ride the bus they hear it differently."

The Tiptons' puckish, trailblazing spirit was inspired by their namesake, a Spokane booking agent who had lived her life as a man ever since she took her brother's name at 18 to play saxophone in Kansas City. "Billy was a really, really kind soul," says Denio. "I don't really know why she chose to live her life as a man; we just felt it to be a really courageous act. Follow your own path no matter what society's expectations are, or no matter what the cost." In 1989, a year after they started gigging together, Tipton died of a bleeding ulcer; he was 74. The Quartet decided to carry on in his name, setting their sights on both saxophone and gender stereotypes. "When I was a youngster, my father was a jazz saxophonist, and to be able to play the saxophone as a young girl was impossible," De Muynck says. "It just wasn't allowed then. Ever since I have felt very strongly about women instrumentalists. Even now, we get asked 'Do you sing too?' They never ask guys that."

When she wasn't gigging with Tone Dogs or the Tiptons, Denio became heavily involved in promoting new music in Seattle, working on the board for Soundwork Northwest, tirelessly scheduling gigs and generally trying to bring San Francisco's Pacific Rim-style arts culture up north. Recently, Soundwork Northwest declared bankruptcy, although Denio had long since left the promoting circus. "I used to set up a lot of shows, but I stopped doing it because it was too stressful. I would feel so bad if nobody comes." Through her booking activities, Denio got to play in some pretty hip company: guitarists Frith, Henry Kaiser and Hans Reichel, cellist Tom Cora, all of whom were drawn to Denio's pure, homegrown voice and her devastating way with the poetry of nonsense.

Many of Denio's songs are infused with a Babel of nonsense tongues: glossolalia, nursery rhymes, dada, and scat. The odd title of her publishing company, Spoot, as well as the title of the first Tone Dogs LP, *Ankety Low Day*,[7] were the result of spontaneous vocal improvisations. She has written a great neo-garage tarantella built up from Italian non-sequiturs ["Salvatore"], and a giddy canon ["Nostrilc Mittening"] from the couplets: *Mirthful birth night/Girth of searchlight/Eartha Kitt's fight/Dearth of right height*. "My favorite language is ur," she chuckles.

The name of Denio's publishing company came in an improvisational, epiglottal epiphany one evening. "The etymology of the word spoot comes from the side of a band-aid box," Denio says. "Years ago in Colorado Springs a group of us were all improvising at Bob Tudor's house. Now Bob was one of the biggest influences in my life; he's an improviser, instrument inventor and all-around amazing guy. He basically introduced me to improvised music. We were all getting louder and louder, and I was working with this band-aid box. I was saying 'Absorbs wound fluids! Absorbs wound fluids! Wound fluids! Wound fluids!' Then there was this huge vacuum of silence and another guy just sat there looking disgusted and said...'Spoot.' I said 'That's the word!.' It's exactly the word for empathetic listening in musical spheres."

The pinnacle of Denio's sublime vocal art can be found on two projects. The first is Curlew's *A Beautiful Western Saddle*,[8] a tribute to the surreal sonnets of Canadian poet Paul Haines, best known for his work with multimedia artist Michael Snow,[9] his Mystery Tapes[10] and the libretto for Carla Bley's 1972 "chronotransduction" *Escalator Over The Hill*.[11] With his musical verse and vivid juxtaposing of meter and image, Haines is a kindred cut-up spirit, and Denio has a ball with lines like *To the amazement of even secret carnival workers/The Prince continued to shit three days past death/Little bay scallops*. "I had heard *Escalator* once years ago in my early college years, and I was absolutely amazed by it," Denio says. "So when George [*Cartwright, Curlew's saxophonist*] called up and said 'What would you think of singing this stuff?' I was really honored. Curlew is only one of my very favorite bands in the universe."

The other is her sophomore solo CD *Tongues*,[12] which is sung in several tongues, both real and onomatopoeic. In addition to revisiting "Salvatore," there's "Gymnosalyagi," a traditional Greek ode to slugs; "Czechered Pyjamas," a list of hotel requests for fresh razors and room service in broken Czech; and "Gdye Damaskaya Parikmakirskaya," which is useful if you ever have to find a Russian beauty salon. Oddly enough, *Tongues* has become Denio's most accessible release, and speaks across the generations unlike anything she's ever done. "*Tongues* received really great responses in the two-and-a-half to sixteen year old range, for some reason," Denio says, bemused. "I had a friend who was two-and-a-half and he would only listen to rap at first; he would get terrible temper tantrums otherwise. I gave his mother a copy of *Tongues* and then he would refuse to listen to anything else except for that. I was shocked. That same day I came home and heard a message from a four-year old on my machine going [*she switches to a tiny Elmer Fudd voice*] 'I wike your cee-dee!' Then I heard a room full of teenagers in Chicago endorsed it. All of this within two days. In fact, I hear Martin Scorcese wants to use something from it in a new movie he's executive producing. I guess I have universal appeal."

Amy Denio: Birthing Chair Blues (Knitting Factory Works, 1991), Tongues (Fot, 1993)
The Tone Dogs: Ankety Low Day (C/Z, 1990), Early Middle Years (Soleilmoon, 1991)
The [EC] Nudes: Vanishing Point (ReR Megacorp, 1994)
The Billy Tipton Memorial Saxophone Quartet: Saxhouse (Knitting Factory Works, 1991), Make It Funky God (Horn Hut, 1994)
with **Curlew**: A Beautiful Western Saddle (Cuneiform, 1993)

Footnotes:
1. From *Fear Of Music* [Sire, 1979] and freely adapted from dada artist Hugo Ball's 1917 phonetic poem "O Gadji Beri Bimba"
2. An earlier version of this chapter was originally published as "Sing The Body Electric: Amy Denio's Works In Progress," the author, *Option* Magazine N59, November 1994: pp.66-69
3. ReR Megacorp, 1994, 4. Soleilmoon, 1991, 5. Knitting Factory Works, 1993
6. Tenor Jessica Lurie and baritone Barbara Marino have since replaced Helle and Loebs; drummer Pam Barger is the fifth Tipton
7. C/Z, 1990, 8. Cuneiform, 1993, 9. See *Vive Le Québec Libre*, p.171
10. See *John Oswald*, p.134
11. Watt, 1972, 12. Fot, 1992

Lindsay Cooper

High above the desert/ River patterns on the floor/ There's a story on the front page/ On the front there's a bitter war/ There's a monsoon blew them one way/ There's a monsoon blew them back/ It's the vein in the leaf/ or the breath in the smile/ or the mark of my own sand-tracks

Robyn Archer, Sahara Dust

"The songs tonight are about the cold war, a silent war that cuts deep." With these quiet words, British composer Lindsay Cooper unveiled *Oh Moscow* to the seventh Festival Internationale de Musique Actuelle de Victoriaville.[1] An eerily prescient song cycle about a Europe embittered and divided after the Second World War, *Oh Moscow* sports a bold and unconventional septet of musical gypsies – Cooper, vocalist Sally Potter, vocalist/trumpeter Phil Minton, saxophonist Alfred 23 Harth, pianist Elvira Plenar, bassist Hugh Hopper and drummer Marilyn Mazur – blowing for a united Europe.

Oh Moscow[2] is a musical quilt whose rugged weave sews together the many strong, disparate threads Lindsay Cooper has been busy spinning from the fringes of the European progressive scene for the last decade. Her work with the Feminist Improvising Group in at the turn of the '80s resulted in the groundbreaking series of Canaille festivals showcasing the work of vocalist

Maggie Nicols, pianist Irene Schweizer, bassist Joëlle Leandre, and drummer Anne-Marie Roelofs. She has also gigged in Mike Westbrook's vaudevillian orchestras, collaborated in Chris Cutler's dark, Aeschulean ensemble News From Babel, and sparred with Derek Bailey, Lol Coxhill, and Evan Parker at Company Week. With *Oh Moscow*, Cooper – socialist, feminist, multi-instrumentalist, historian and improviser – has created a work that signals the arrival of a first-rank European composer.

Barely a month after *Oh Moscow* triumphantly brought the house down in Victoriaville, a riding tide of *perestroika* and protest triumphantly brought down the Berlin Wall after 44 years of post-war oppression and psychological intimidation. In the months that followed, the entire Iron Curtain quickly rusted away as Czechoslovakia, Hungary, Romania and Bulgaria embraced free-market economies and political reform, while the Balkan republics of Latvia, Lithuania and Estonia loosened their fetters and boldly declared their political autonomy. In Romania it took a bloody battle, but Europe's final lone dictator was brought down. In 1992, the Maastricht Treaty dismantled the trade borders of the EEC nations in Western Europe. Lindsay Cooper may well find herself out of work before long.

"My eyes get opened all the time. When I was a kid, my father worked doing publicity at the Royal Festival Hall in London. All that theatrical spectacle was an unbelievable eye-opener for a suburban kid. Orchestras, ballet, vaudeville, it was enchantment, really. I think that even though in later years, when you learn how things work behind the scenes and put up with high ticket prices at Covent Garden, it doesn't alter the fact that the spectacle is magic." Visibly happy with last night's performance, Lindsay Cooper's eyes are unusually alive and warm despite the short kip she called a night's sleep. Quick-witted, genial, with short, peppery, close-cropped hair and owlish features, she gladly traces her past with a fork as we chat over lunch.

Born in Hornsey, North London, in March of 1951, Lindsay Cooper had childhood of eye-openers, like the time she went on a school trip to West Africa when she was 16. "Adventurous little school I attended. Meeting African musicians and seeing them play, I suddenly realized there was another way of making music." Cooper's adventurous little school was The Dartington College of Arts in Devon, where she studied piano, violin, and bassoon, and played with National Youth Orchestra of Great Britain from 1966 to 1968, before spending two stifling terms at the Royal Academy of Music. "After I left The Academy, joining Henry Cow was perhaps my biggest eye-opener. I had been involved in the women's movement for some time, so Henry Cow and the world of new political thinking was not entirely a whole different planet, but it did take me to a different level of, shall we say, political engagement."

Cooper's stint in the Cow was her introduction to both the commercial mechanics of pop culture, and to the guerilla tactics that the Rock in Opposition movement designed to circumvent them.[3] The four years between 1974 and 1978 were a whirlwind course in political awareness and underground finance, especially when it came to the star-making machinery at Virgin records. Working with Fred Frith, Chris Cutler, and Tim Hodgkinson also necessitated a certain measure of unorthodoxy. By luck, Cooper's instrument of choice was the noble woodwind of the orchestra, the bassoon. Five feet of polished burnt rosewood and glistening brass, the bassoon is certainly a striking thing to wield onstage, yet Cooper – barely taller than her instrument – manages to make blowing a bassoon look cool, in the came way Ray Anderson can make a trombone look drop-dead sexy. "I took it up when I was about 14 or 15, and just loved it from the moment I first heard it," recalls Cooper enthusiastically. "I really loved the sound. In many ways it's a promising kind of instrument, but it *is* limited – it would be very stupid to hint otherwise. It can't do the same things a saxophone can do, or a string instrument. It does have limitations. On the other hand, within those limitations, it can do some interesting things."

Like the bassoon, Cooper's other elective instrument was also chosen by chance. After the breakup of Henry Cow, Cooper wanted to pick up an instrument which had nothing whatsoever to do with classical music. She sold her flute – which she hates deeply to this day – and left her oboe lying fallow for years. "The last time I played it, I swore I'd never play it again," she says. "It's quite a nice instrument, but it's ever so hard. I think that unless you're passionately devoted to the instrument, somehow life's too short to put in the hours that it takes to maintain the technique." Technique be damned, Cooper was inspired by 'Trane, Bird, Lol Coxhill, and Evan Parker, and opted for the soprano sax before fate stepped on a taxi ride home one evening. "I saw a sopranino saxophone in a music shop on Charing Cross Road. I said, 'That's for me. That instrument has my name on it.' I found that it occupied the same ground as a soprano and oboe. I'm often surprised at what I can do with it. I used it extensively in Westbrook Rossini;[4] I thought it was a courageous move of Mike's to have sopranino rather than trumpet. That band lasted a few years, and it was great fun playing just one instrument."

Totally dedicated to her craft, Cooper recently visited the Stuttgart factory where her bassoon was made for a spot of tea with the owner. "He had some new Brazilian wood that he was terribly excited about. There were these huge lumps of Brazilian wood sitting up on the shelf, and they have to sit there for ten years to mature. He's already terribly excited about the prospect of making bassoons with them. That was kind of nice, seeing something that was much closer to being a tree than it was a bassoon, and seeing the whole process of it evolving, like music. Being a musician *is* quite organic. I do get vague images in my mind, images that may take years to come out. Music is a plant that grows."

Lindsay Cooper's first major project, *Rags*, blossomed from some seeds planted long ago in her English History class. In 1979, she was offered to score *The Song of the Shirt*, a documentary by filmmakers Sue Clayton and Jonathan Curling that examined the London needlewomen whose sweat and labor built the metropolitan garment industry in the late 19th century. "It was a fabulous first project to work on because I was so interested in that period," remembers Cooper. "I just loved doing that research into 19th century English history, which I studied in school, and it just fit in with all of my most passionate interests at the time. But at that time, I hardly wrote music at all. I had written a few really rather insubstantial pieces for Henry Cow which appear on the second side of *Western Culture*. But I was not even remotely an experienced composer, just really in the foothills of composition, if even there. So I started having to learn as I went along as I did that score."

For a first score, *Rags*[5] is extensively and impressively researched, attesting to the long hours Cooper spent in the British library, poring over pages of sheet music and history books. Sporting more literary references than your average Mekons album, the scope of *Rags* encompasses more than just the seamstresses' struggle, soaking in the odors of London in the 1830s and 1840s. Vocalist Phil Minton's characters of the union organizer in "General Strike" and the commoner in "Lots of Larks" throw light on the social functions music had at the time, whether the street singing of popular ballads, theatrical accompaniment, piano hall music, or brass bands designed to keep workers from joining unions.

At the British Library, Cooper had stumbled across a vast collection of original broadside ballads and used these as the basis for many lyrics, cleverly brushing the dust off of them and setting her modern feminist songs within them. "The Song of the Shirt" is an effective, haunting example. A sad song redolent of dreamy depression movies, it features a sad Sally Potter passively singing *Stitch! Stitch! Stitch!/In poverty hunger and dirt/and still with a voice of dolorous pitch/she sang this song of the shirt*, while in the background a clattering chorus of disorder is provided courtesy of Cooper, Fred Frith and Chris Cutler. Even across the gulf of generations, the bitter tone of the song rings true. "They had to sell broadsides quickly because they were so current," Cooper explains. "An event would happen; they'd have to have a song on the streets the next day, because after that another event would happen and the people would want a song about something else. They were comparable to today's gutter press newspapers, but had a certain kind of integrity the gutter press lacks entirely."

Strains of vaudeville and the music hall echo strongly throughout *Rags*. To the opera house what today's downtown lofts are to the "serious" ivory tower world of Lincoln Center, the turn-of-the-century Music Hall boasted popular fare that would give rise over the years to Ray Davies and some of England's most enduring pop music styles, not to mention its counterparts in Germany and America, the cabaret and Tin Pan Alley. "A lot of people relate both *Rags* and *Oh Moscow* to the Weimar Republic stuff," which in some ways I like, because I have enormous respect for that tradition," says Cooper. "In other ways it makes me feel slightly uneasy, because there *are differences*. I think its because of this syndrome that people have to put a label on something, so Kurt Weill/Hans Eisler/Bertold Brecht is an easy reference point. I do actually see what I'm doing is in some ways as a continuation; I see in my work an equivalent response to the kind of response they were having to what was going on in the '30s. But it's also an irrelevant reference point; I draw on a lot of other things as well."

In the liner notes of *Rags*, Cooper notes that the function and mass appeal of the Music Hall was eventually replaced by that of the cinema, which demanded an entirely different sheet of music. This was something Cooper explored firsthand after scoring *Rags*. *Music For Other Occasions*[6] is a collection of Cooper's cinematic curlicues; two-minute soundtracks for various British experimental theater productions and films for BBC's Channel 4. Nimbly supported by the strings and vocal cords of her progressive [and mostly British] sisters – violinist Vicky Aspinall, cellist Georgie Born, harpist Zeena Parkins, and vocalists Dagmar Krause, Kate Westbrook, Maggie Nicols, and Sally Potter – Cooper shows a swift grasp of mood and structure, even in miniature settings. Potter's elliptical haiku on "As She Breathes" and "Speed of Light" intuitively steers Cooper's approach: the former is a minimalist lullaby, the latter an atonal nightmare. Pieces like "Plate Dance" and "Assassination Waltz" show a successful assimilation of more traditional music idioms, and the tango and Eastern European waltzes are remembered in evocative silent film scores reminiscent of *Rags*.

"Certainly working in cinema and dance has been a huge influence," Cooper admits. "It's really shaped my compositional style in a big way. It's actually very interesting now to have a bit more room to maneuver, and to let things develop, and let the music and lyrics create their own dynamic momentum, and expand into structures that are being determined by the ideas of the piece rather than being determined by its time frame." Cooper studied her craft under the lens of filmmaker Potter, who would go on to direct the 1993 art-house hit of Virginia Woolf's *Orlando*. Cooper met Potter with Nicols and Born ten years ago in the then-fledgeling Feminist Improvising Group, a collective of European women whose mandate was seizing the moment with an exceptional measure of wit and flair. Their first gig, at the Almost Free Theatre in November of 1977, had the members of FIG – Cooper, Potter, Nicols, Born, pianist Irene Schweizer, and drummer Anne-Marie Roelofs – singing, tap-dancing, improvising, smashing plates, and doing the wash. In *Melody Maker*, Hannah Charlton observed that "Improvised music gives [them] the joy of being utterly flexible and therefore able to accommodate their need to make music as women and for women."[7]

"I must say that in Henry Cow, it became a source of considerable aggravation that I would look out to the audience and I'd see maybe a couple of women with their boyfriends," says Cooper. "I'd think 'Why am I doing this? Who am I doing this for?' With FIG I think it took off more when there was a lot of women just going with us and really enjoying the show." The varied backgrounds of the ensemble's members, as well as their individual humor, experience and politics, helped to push the improv in new directions. "There was all kinds of things in improvisation that wouldn't have happened otherwise," says Cooper. "One of the obvious differences was that apart from Georgie's bass, it was all acoustic instruments. Henry Cow was very electric. The other thing that was radically different from what any other improvising group was doing at the time was that we brought in a lot of other elements: We could veer off into theater, tap-dancing, or whatever, we just went with it. That at the time seemed to be a kind of feminist statement, bringing our whole lives into what we were doing in a way that in that time was quite hard to do in a mixed context." Paving the way for the critically acclaimed Canaille festivals held in Zurich, Frankfurt, Vienna, and Amsterdam, FIG enjoyed an unusual creative camaraderie, and continue to do so, even though FIG dissolved in 1982. "When I do gigs with the various women in FIG, I get very excited," says Cooper, "because now there's quite a long history behind us. We're talking 10 or 12 years we've been working together. We found a lot of ideas, and the ideas have carried on, and it's very exciting to see how we've developed."

In particular, the bond between Cooper and Potter has been a lasting one. "It's not that we have very similar backgrounds, but rather that we've arrived in a very similar place in the way that we think," says Cooper. "There's a real common language; we don't have to map out the grounds for hours in order to be able to work together. It's really been a complementary relationship: she's a singer, I write songs, she's a filmmaker, I write film scores, she's a choreographer, I write dance music." The two spent the whole of one summer researching a new project and mulling over their curious "European" identities. "For, I don't know, the last ten years, I've identified very much as a European person rather than an English person," says Cooper. "I work so little in England that a lot of the musicians I work closely with are actually Europeans. Irene

Schweizer" – Cooper leans across the restaurant aisle – "when were you last in England, Irene?" Schweizer looks up distractedly from her eggs. "1984?"

"There you are. This is how it is. I've played in London once in the last two years. It's very tight, really hard. I talked a little bit with Sally about this, and then Sally made several trips to the Soviet Union in her capacity as a filmmaker, and bit by bit the idea of the piece evolved, and took shape." The fruit of of Cooper and Potter's collaboration, *Oh Moscow*, is a jazzy bit of musical and theatrical providence. It was first performed in 1986, before the advent of *glasnost* and *perestroika*. The eight songs, which have been played in Vienna, Zurich, East and West Berlin, Boston, Hartford, Toronto and Victoriaville, illuminate the bittersweet loss of innocence of a continent cleft in two. Once allies against Germany in the Second World War, Britain, France, America and the Soviet Union partitioned the continent in 1945, erecting the Berlin Wall to cement the deal.

"What turned it from idea into reality," Cooper continues, "was that the Zurich Jazz Festival called up and said, what have you got that you can bring this year? It was then that I thought I should go for it and do this piece, finally." With that in mind, Cooper scored *Oh Moscow* for an international ensemble consisting of herself, Potter, vocalist Phil Minton, German saxophonist Alfred 23 Harth, ex-Soft Machine bassist Hugh Hopper, drummer Marilyn Mazur, and Czechoslovakian keyboardist Elvira Plenar. I can't remember what came first, the musicians or the instruments," Cooper recalls. "Phil and Sally were obvious. I had just been doing some film music in Frankfurt with Alfred and Elvira, so they were pretty obvious as well. Marilyn I straightway asked. But I got really stuck when it came to the bass player. I just didn't know what to do. After my mind had gone totally blank, I finally decided just to go through my record collection. There must be someone I hadn't thought of. The first record I pulled out was [Robert Wyatt's] *Rock Bottom*.[8] I thought of course! Why didn't I think about him before?"

If the ensemble brazenly trespasses across borders of both age and nationality, the music of *Oh Moscow* virtually defects and demands stylistic asylum. The opener has brassy *Mission Impossible* horn charts and veers between cool '50s jazz and a Soft Machine roll, spiked with Alfred Harth's squeals, while "The Allies" is a vaudeville showstopper about the "special relationship" between the United Kingdom and America during the Cold War: *We bought your culture/we bought yours cars/we bought your dreams/we lost ours.* Yet the most exhilarating aspect of these songs is the room they leave for soloing. Cooper lets her work *breathe*, knowing full well she has an ensemble with lungfuls of air and no shortage of personal statements to make. Improv motormouth Minton is in fine formhe parodies Les Voix Bulgares, cuts loose on come jazzy glossolalia, and comes close to Donald Duck in bebop hell. Drummer Mazur [late of Wayne Shorter's and Miles Davis' recent groups] offers the solo of the evening, making her drums talk like Max Roach. Hugh Hopper demonstrates his title as noble king of the fuzz bass, and Cooper talks to her bassoon through a delay, pensively dropping notes into the audience and listening as they wash away.

All this blowing smells of a recent collaboration somewhere. "I think you're right," Cooper concurs. "A lot of people have seen me as a jazz musician, which I find quite surprising, because I don't really see myself that way. I think that's Mike Westbrook's influence. I really like Mike's approach to composition, and I like the musicians he chooses to work with. He has a very good nose for a good band, Mike does. Writing with Mike has meant that through him I have worked a good deal in 'jazz' ensembles."[9] Westbrook's influence can be heard in Cooper's touching lament of the immigrant, "Prayer," a stirring anthem that could pass for an olde English hymn if it weren't for the deft flamenco touches and gypsy overtones. "That song was first written for the waves of immigrants that came from mainly Eastern Europe to the United States," explains Cooper, "carrying with them all of these hopes for a new life, and also the kind of trauma of having to leave their past lives. It can also now be dedicated to all those who will come out from behind the Iron Curtain. It's all about the contradictions of being uprooted from your past and hoping for your future."

A dry summer breeze wafts up from the courtyard in a set of apartment blocks just south of the midday bustle of King's Cross in London. It is almost two years after the 1989 Victoriaville performance of *Oh Moscow*, and the world outside Lindsay Cooper's flat is a different place indeed. For starters, the Soviet Union is no more; Mikhail Gorbachev was ousted, reinstated, voted out, and became a speaker on the American college circuit. The giant trading blocs of Southeast Asia, North America and Europe have altered the economic map of the world radically, while cartographers the world over have been scrambling to revise maps of what used to be Czechoslovakia and Yugoslavia. The former nation at least had an amicable split; its president conceding to a fevered, absurdist nationalism straight out of one of his plays. Yugoslavia on the other hand, remains a crucible of the bloodiest civil war Europe has ever seen as Muslims, Serbs, and Croats raze each others' cities and towns and destroy centuries of history for the right to a homeland.

But the subtle ironies of *perestroika* and the political reform that swept across Eastern Europe in the winter of 1988 are not lost on Cooper. In April of the following year, the *Oh Moscow* troupe was at the Vienna airport, waiting for a connecting flight. "I was in a little shop where they get people to buy things they don't really want or need," recalls Cooper, "And they were selling these watches that had engraved faces. The faces had a hammer and sickle, and 'perestroika' written in Cyrillic letters round the watch face as numbers. It came in this little package with a picture of Gorbachev on the back. It's all happened so quickly. Gorbachev came, did this sort of radical sweep, and in a matter of moments the West had turned it into a product."

When the Berlin Wall fell, Cooper found herself in Berlin rehearsing with keyboard player Ulrike Haage. "It was an amazingly charged atmosphere," she recalls. "I could really feel it, in the way that one can feel these things, and I really didn't want to leave Berlin at all, yet we had to get in a plane and go to Säarbrucken to do a gig. That night, the Wall opened. Touring Germany the following week was phenomenal; people were in shock. It was a cross between a trauma and a party. We played Gottingen, near the border on one Saturday morning and I have never seen so many people. The whole downtown was filled with East German people coming over, looking at the West and spending money. You know, when we first performed *Oh Moscow*, people said, 'Why are you doing something on the Cold War? No-one is interested in that anymore.' Nobody thought that things would really change."

In the intervening months, Lindsay Cooper has changed as well. There was a time when she found playing in an orchestra difficult because of the rigidity of the score. Now she is writing a new piece for a group called Lontano, a contemporary chamber group based in London. The commission, "The Road Is Wider Than Long,"[10] is based on an "image diary" written by British Surrealist Sir Roland Penrose while he trekked through the Balkans in 1938. with its intimate, Elgar-meets-Smetana score. Inspired by the random kinetic relationships of quantum physics and the Tao of Eastern mysticism, *Schrödinger's Cat*[11] is an instrumental suite written for dance, with Cooper's bassoon leading an eclectic ensemble of clarinets, keyboards, accordions, cello, bass and trumpet. *An Angel On The Bridge*[12] is primarily a bassoon project that sounds like elliptical Aboriginal songlines augmented by a baroque ensemble of harp, percussion and vocals.

Then there's Cooper's new ensemble, Sahara Dust, with Phil Minton, Elvira Plenar, accordionist Dean Brodrick, percussionist Robin Shulkowsky, and trumpeter/cellist Paul Jayasinha. Written during the Gulf War in 1991, *Sahara Dust*[13] is a breathtaking, polystylistic and ultimately rootless work drawn from poetry by Australian singer/writer/filmmaker Robin Archer that observes the geopolitics and seismic social shifts of a contracting world as refracted through the minutæ of our everyday existence, and is characterized by Cooper as "cosmos, excess baggage, despair, and infinite hope." Turning inwards from the "big message" of her tale of the continent that came in from the cold, Lindsay Cooper asks herself *Bags and baggage/Bags and baggage/Can't you ever learn to travel light?*

"I have this reputation as being a sort of experimental or jazz musician or whatever, and I've always found this very odd, because I've always seen myself as a kind of accessible composer," Cooper muses, smiling thoughtfully. "It's just that in any given situation there's many more levels than the literal, and I'm always much more excited by exploring those kind of levels rather than going for a kind of literate portrayal of things or a kind of agitprop political song. I like to go about it a bit more obliquely these days. Art has that wonderful quality of being able to marry the heart and mind together, without which life is worth very, very little. Any kind of art addresses those areas of the human spirit that don't get addressed by run of the mill economic activities that we are engaged in, often to the exclusion of everything else. It's been said before, but it's still a truly shocking comment on society that artists are valued so little, and art is accorded such a low place, and treated as a luxury and an indulgence. I would say it's a total necessity for everybody."

Lindsay Cooper: The Gold Diggers (Ré, 1980), Rags (Recommended, 1983), Music For Other Occasions (no man's land, 1986), Oh Moscow (Victo, 1991), An Angel On The Bridge (ABC/Phonogram, 1991), Schrödinger's Cat (Line, 1991), Sahara Dust (Intakt, 1993)
with **Henry Cow**: Unrest (Virgin, 1974), In Praise of Learning [with Slapp Happy] (Virgin, 1975), Desperate Straights [with Slapp Happy] (Virgin, 1975), Western Culture (Broadcast, 1979), The Virgin Years (ReR Megacorp, 1991)
with **News From Babel**: Work Resumed On The Tower (Ré, 1984), Letters Home (Ré, 1986),
with **David Thomas & The Pedestrians**: Winter Comes Home (Ré, 1983), More Places Forever (Ré, 1985),
with **Trio Trabant A Roma**: State Of Volgograd (FMP, 1994)

Footnotes:
1. Portions of this chapter were originally published as "You're Right, I'm Left, She's Gone: The Musically Correct Lindsay Cooper," the author, *Option* Magazine N32, May 1990: pp.43-45
2. Victo, 1991, 3. See *Rock In Opposition*, p.11
4. Mike Westbrook's jazz ensemble devoted to the overtures and arias of Rossini; Westbrook Rossini has recorded both live and studio sessions for Hat ART
5. Recommended Records, 1983, 6. no man's land, 1986
7. "No Apologies," *Melody Maker* Magazine, December 8, 1979: p.41, 8. Virgin, 1973
9. Cooper also has a nose for a good band as well. She was so pleased with how the jazz elements of *Oh Moscow* turned out she formed an intriguing, polyphonic improvising jazz trio with Harth and Minton for Berlin's Total Music Meeting in 1993. The concert, by Trio Trabant A Roma, can be heard on *State of Volgograd*; FMP, 1994.
10. Available on Lontano's CD *British Women Composers Volume 1*, 1991
11. Line, 1991, 12. ABC/Phonogram, 1991, 13. Intakt, 1993

Zeena Parkins

"The '90s are going to be the decade of women composers. There are too many brilliant ones, they've been shamelessly ignored, and they've got a huge body of work you haven't heard yet. Those floodgates can't stay shut much longer. BAM, Serious Fun! and other series organizers, take note: Laurie Anderson, Meredith Monk, and Pauline Oliveros no longer count as women. You've been using the same three people as your token women for over a decade, and nobody buys it anymore. If you want to prove that you aren't systematically excluding females, you're going to have to come up with new names, and I've got a long list if you need it."

Kyle Gann, "Rock Rules"[1]

Pop music may have lost its innocence when Dick Clark pleaded guilty to payola charges in the 1950s. Yet when Nirvana's major label debut *Nevermind*[2] shot through the roof in the winter of 1992 [helped by an aggressive marketing campaign blueprinted after some serious market research into the lifestyles of students in Seattle], few expected pop music criticism to roll over and follow suit. David Geffen's gamble worked; as major record labels engaged in bidding wars over indie bands, the pop music press enthusiastically coined a new term, "grunge," and was midwife to the birth of a new marketing niche. If, as Elvis Costello once said, writing about music was akin to dancing about architecture, pop sages across the dancefloor were tripping over each other to praise the new skyline. When Nirvana's Kurt Cobain committed suicide in April of 1994, the media wasted no time in proclaiming him the patron saint of grunge; martyr to Generation X. Yet Nirvana's hometown is merely the latest pop mecca to be discovered courtesy of the keen myopia of the music press. Before Seattle there was Liverpool, Detroit, Nashville, Athens, Austin and Manchester. Zeena Parkins remembers the hip place to be in the mid-1980s was in the lofts of Loisaida, in downtown Manhattan. Moving to the Big Apple in 1984, Parkins found herself the Holly Golightly of the electric harp, one of a dedicated and creative posse of improvising musicians from the Lower East Side – John Zorn, Butch Morris, David Weinstein, Elliott Sharp, Shelley Hirsch, Christian Marclay, Arto Lindsay, Eugene Chadbourne, Tom Cora, Fred Frith – who jammed regularly in each other's ensembles, musicians who espoused an openness of form, a freedom of ideas, and a plurality of influences. "In the mid '80s, New York Noise, the downtown scene was 'the thing.'" says Parkins.

Parkins is in Montréal for a gig and to book the recording sessions with Justine for their multimedia work *La Légende de la Pluie*[3] in June. We have just paid a visit to Tau, an upscale, boho health food outlet on Rue St-Denis where Parkins satisfied her macrobiotic cravings with a couple of bags of blue corn chips, and have settled down with two cups of espresso in a dusty coffeeshop next door. "Part of the reason that the Knitting Factory opened was because there were music writers in the press who were excited and giving musicians a lot of support," Parkins continues. "Everyone thinks it doesn't exist anymore, but no-one has written about the transformation that has happened. Now, in a way, it's more interesting; everyone has developed. Some people who started out only improvising are now composing more structured or more specific works. Others, like Jim Staley,[4] are still improvisors. Some people, like David Shea, are doing collages with records and live players, while others are combining improvisors and readers, or using material processed or not in some way.

"So it's not this hot new thing in New York anymore. But when you go out of New York– and there's more to the United States than just New York – you can see how this scene has filtered out and what influences it has had on other cities. In San Francisco, they're calling it 'improv-core,' like hardcore improv; there's a lot of press support there for doing improvisation. It's funny, because unlike the rest of my peers, I don't work a lot in Europe, I work mostly in the States, and I'm intrigued by taking this crazy instrument into places that normally wouldn't see this kind of music. For instance, I've done solo improv gigs on my electric harp – which is a fairly hardcore situation to get yourself into – in places like Chattanooga, Tennessee. The organizers, who were musicians themselves, invited a local dance school and rustled up incredible press. They paved the way for people to understand what was going to happen. For the audience, liking or not liking wasn't the issue anymore, because they were all there waiting to have this experience. It was so different than New York, where people would say, 'Oh we've heard this before.'" Parkins sighs. "We are a Nirvana generation after all."

It is the first day of class at Cass Tech, a Detroit institution of higher learning which offers arts *and* vocation; you can major in refrigeration while you minor in theater.[5] Cass Tech's hallowed halls are *alma mater* to a surprising range of musical performers, including Geri Allen and Diana Ross. It is here we first find Zeena Parkins, a pianist with a pretty straight classical background who likes Hendrix and Cream. Since all keyboard players are requires to learn a choral instrument in addition to their 88s, Parkins has been assigned...harp. She recalls her first brush with the music of the spheres with mock horror. "I went to room 101, annex of the music department. I found a small room, seven *huge* harps sitting on the floor, and a really insane woman who was absolutely determined to teach anyone who passed through those doors."

Undaunted, Parkins was soon plucking out '30s pop tunes at Masonic Temple Dances. But somewhere along the line, the glamour went out of it. Parkins knew that she wasn't using the instrument to its full advantage. Not that she could foresee that one day she would be dueting with a man who artistically abuses record albums, but she just knew something was missing. "After the harp indoctrination in school, I was completely fed up with the instrument," she says. "It seemed like the direction I was headed for in the piano world. So I decided not to pursue that path on two instruments. Besides, the Circus beckoned."

Signing on as a dancing bear, costume designer, and director of finance, Parkins joined the Janus Circus, a small, one-ring traveling theater troupe formed by some Detroit friends in 1979. After several successful summers, the show was invited to Europe in 1982, where they based themselves in Rotterdam. On tour overseas, Parkins picked up a cheap used accordion in a flea market outside Amsterdam. "I was getting itchy to play again," she recalls. "Even with the accordion I still felt itchy, and still thought about...harp. It seemed like there were enough keyboard players around, and I thought it would be interesting to extend an instrument no-one had thought of. What really pushed me into pursuing it again was meeting Chris Cutler. For two summers the Circus toured with The Black Sheep, in which I sang and Chris played drums. Chris was saying he'd been looking for a harp player for the last ten years, so I said, 'You're kidding! I play harp. We have to do something together.'"

Two years later, Parkins eventually found herself as the resident harpist for Cutler's News From Babel project.[6] With Lindsay Cooper and Cutler, she helped provide the spartan musical backdrop for the plaintive *dramatis personae* of Dagmar Krause and Robert Wyatt. Working with Cooper was Parkins' introduction to the European Feminist Improvising Group, a collective of women improvisers and activists who would prove to be an oblique inspiration to the budding improviser. "It didn't influence me to start doing something, but I think it set a precedent for making improvisation something a woman could do; something okay and comfortable," explains Parkins.

Owing to impossible schedules, News From Babel only released two LPs, *Work Resumed On The Tower* and *Letters Home*,[7] and never played live. But playing in the Brechtian ensemble offered Parkins the opportunity to rediscover the harp. "I started with traditional technique to get my hands back in shape, and then I just took off in a completely different direction," she remembers. "Thinking about improvisation, it seemed natural on the harp. So I just started playing as much as I could. That coincided with my sudden move to New York in 1984, and all of a sudden being exposed to all this improvisation. It was like, 'Is this *possible*? I can *do* this?' In fact, once I found the scene in New York, I wasn't surprised to find similar scenes in Europe, Montréal and Tokyo. It made sense; this was bigger than just here. I was so excited that it existed at all."

It was in New York she first met Tom Cora, four of the eight limbs of Skeleton Crew. The nimble cellist built her first electric harp; the contraption featured steel guitar strings, one single-coil and five humbucker pickups, and a whammy bar. If that wasn't bizarre enough, since it was plugged into a 120 volt outlet, it could be hooked up to digital delays, harmonizers, and a volume pedal, opening up the noise gates to unheard-of sounds. "That's just not possible in the classical world," says Parkins, "Improvised music allowed this instrument to be taken seriously, and the electric harp was my *entrée* into that world. I was open to try anything on it. For a while there was this great store in New York called the St Mark's Music Exchange which sold used equipment. You could go in and for $35 you could pick up an effects box. I didn't know what anything was at the time; the first thing I bought was a compressor."

Today Parkins displays astonishing control over her effects and instrument live, using the electronics to amplify, skew and fracture the ringing purity of the harp's crystalline tones. Close your eyes and she sounds like Bill Frisell coaxing a calm drone out of taut steel, open them and she's battering the strings and shoving hat pins in between them. In both her playing and approach to her instrument, Parkins recalls another downtown string player and mutant guitar builder, Elliott Sharp. Governed by a queer pinball logic, the sonic textures of their improvisations together on *Psycho Acoustic*[8] shift like mercury as they pick their way through a rich junkyard of harmonics and distortion. It's the most fun to hit improvisation since Eugene Chadbourne discovered the Rake.

Parkins' quick mastery of her new instrument prompted Cora to invite her aboard Skeleton Crew for their second LP, *The Country of Blinds*.[9] This, she explains, was to get around the fact that Cora and Fred Frith were tired of being surrounded by instruments. "Skeleton Crew's whole interest in bringing in a third person began with an interest in exploring *less* improvised stuff; stretching maybe what song structure *is*, but still integrating improvised elements in a live set of songs. Whoever had an idea, we all tried it. This total openness and flexibility was Fred's calling card. Some people are good producers because they have a formula, an easily recognizable sound, and they impart this sound to every project they work on. Well, that's one way to do it, and it isn't Fred's."

Parkins used Frith's studio intuition and her own considerable technique in cutting her debut album, *Something Out There*.[10] A suite of short instrumental vignettes, it pitches Parkins' electric harp against the supermarket muzak of Christian Marclay's whizzing, cascading turntables, the insistent percussion of Samm Bennett, and Wayne Horvitz' fluid keyboard patches. Parkins walks the tightrope between classical structure and the chaos of free playing, drawing on a wide palette of musical influences along the way. "We're really fortunate in that we're a media generation," she reflects. "How valuable has it been for me to have at my fingertips every kind of music that's been recorded! Either it's on my shelf at home, or I can probably dig it up somewhere. That's amazing."

When Skeleton Crew called it quits in 1987, the novelty of the "downtown scene," was on the wane. John Zorn was being courted by the majors, Fred Frith had moved to Europe, the Knitting Factory sported queues along Houston Street. Parkins busied herself by moonlighting in an accordion trio, the BeeZee Squeezies, organizing "Accordion Summits" in cities like New York and Chicago. She also formed No Safety with guitarist Chris Cochrane and ex-members of Curlew and V-Effect. No Safety at first crossed the blunt passion and integrity of the burgeoning hardcore movement with the razor-sharp intuition of improvisation before expanding their horizons on two albums, *This Lost Leg* and *Spill*.[11] "No Safety is a lot of layers," says Parkins. "It started as Chris and I as a duo, and over five years it's transformed with the times. Today we combine drums and drum machines, use tapes, layers of singing, tricky structures. There's not one composer but five; it's not just one person's ideas being played. It's a whole different way of composing music, a very generous way. And I think it's really strong."

While the Knitting Factory flourished and Roulette and The Kitchen hung on, smaller arts spaces shut their doors. Festival bookings became increasingly conservative, NEA grants dried up, Loisaida rents skyrocketed, and the Lower East Side looked to Brooklyn. Yet Parkins managed to stay on her feet. "People can live on this music if they're diverse," she explains. "You're not going to make a living just being an improvisor. You have to be just as creative in finding funding as you are making your music. For myself, being involved in different things has been key to making a living. Don Byron[12] makes a lot of his money playing klezmer music, I make a lot of my music composing for choreographers. In New York, especially for younger composers, the dance world allows you to try out your ideas. First of all, you're not really performing for a musical audience, you're performing for a dance audience, and a lot of new ideas can be covered in a less critical environment. Also, there's more money for a dance commission, as opposed to just getting a commission for composing on your own. If you're able to hook into that, it's one way of developing work as a composer, and it's really worked out for me."

In fact, Parkins' first foray into the thorny world of composition started as a commission from choreographer Jennifer Munsen. *Ursa's Door*[13] explores the sparks that fly when a trio of classical musicians – Parkins and her sisters, cellist Margaret and violinist Sarahjam – met with a trio of improvisors: drummer Ikue Mori, turntable whiz David Shea, and guitarist Chris Cochrane. It shares the complex structures and trigger-happy changes of John Zorn's gaming works and Butch Morris' conductions, yet invests the proceedings with a distinct chamber feel, vacillating between a modernism reminiscent of Bartók and open stage night at Company Week. Opening with mournful, Terezin strings, the melodic line soon gives way to Mori's instinctive rubato drum patterns and shards of vocal samples raining down. Throughout the work, the improvised elements challenge the hegemony of the strings, the skronk of Cochrane's guitar at times reducing them to helpless glissandi and decaying phrases. Other times, the strings lay down middle eastern rhythms before deconstructing them.

"It was an interesting turn for me to all of a sudden take people from really different trainings, and not just work with my usual bunch, who really speak a similar language," Parkins explains. "I wanted to do something with my sisters in a basic way knowing they were classical players, knowing that you have certain flexibilities with people that you can just plop music down in front of. They're extremely open to doing different things, but they're classically trained musicians. I really wanted to explore putting them together with people who didn't read music and have different capabilities. Chris reads a little, Ikue doesn't read at all, but I consider them all sort of the tops at what they do with their instrument in their way. You can describe a sound to Ikue in a narrative way and all of a sudden there it is. With three drum machines and a reverb unit she can make an incredible sound that's very specific. I was really intrigued with this, and wanted to work with it in the context of extended technique. Not in the sense of within an instrument, but within a composition. If you think of your composition as your instrument, then you can extend the range of what the composition can do. You have this really wide variety of what the players are able to do. As a composer I find that exciting."

Downtown may not be the place Petula Clark once sang about, but its denizens continue to mature as artists, and the scene they made, remains a fond memory. "It helped define a community, for one thing," Parkins says. "Certainly one of the ways that I got to know people was playing in John Zorn's *Cobra*.[14] That was a big ensemble, and you had a real sense of people doing things together; even if that wasn't true, you still had that sense. A few years after that, things sort of dispersed."

Judging from her work with Butch Morris,[15] the seeds Parkins helped plant in the hothouse loft atmosphere of the mid-1980s has been assimilated into both the new music vernacular and the vocabularies of many an improv artist. Morris has just completed a week's stand at the Village Vanguard with his 13-piece band. For this grand occasion, Parkins brought her new pride and joy, a Venus pedal harp made for her by a harpsmith formerly from the prestigious Line & Healy Harps of Chicago. "I think it was the first time they had a harp onstage there for years. I played mostly acoustic, which is great because there aren't many places that will use an acoustic harp; it's very inconvenient. But not for Butch. He's one of the few people who still puts together people from different parts of the spectrum. There's J.A. Deane on trombone, using processing and extended techniques on his instrument, and then there are more straight players like Reggie Workman, who are totally intrigued by the extended techniques, and who are more than willing to jump in. It's a real cross-fertilization, and it's really extraordinary. And here we are at the Village Vanguard."

Zeena Parkins: Something Out There (no man's land, 1987), Ursa's Door (Victo, 1992), Nightmare Alley (Table of the Elements, 1993), with **News From Babel**: Work Resumed On The Tower (Ré, 1984), Letters Home (Ré, 1986), with **Skeleton Crew**: The Country Of Blinds (Rift, 1986)
with **No Safety**: This Lost Leg (RecRec, 1990), Spill (Knitting Factory Works, 1992)
with **Butch Morris**: Current Trends In Racism In America (A Work In Progress) (sound aspects, 1985), with **Justine**: Suite (Ambiances Magnétiques, 1990), La Légende de la Pluie (Ambiances Magnétiques, 1993), with **Elliott Sharp**: Psycho-Acoustic (Victo, 1994)

Footnotes:
1. The *Village Voice*, January 23, 1990: p.68, 2. DGC Records, 1991, 3. See *Justine*, p.212
4. A trombonist and one of the co-owners of Roulette, a New York improv "hot spot" in the 1980s
5. Portions of this chapter were originally published as part of "Femmes Vitales: The Festival of Innovative Women In Music," the author, in *Option* Magazine N21, July 1988: pp.60-65
6. See *Chris Cutler, 7*. Ré, 1984 and Ré, 1986, respectively, 8. Victo, 1994, 9. Rift, 1986, 10. no man's land, 1987, 11. RecRec, 1990 and Knitting Factory Works, 1992, respectively
12. A Black jazz clarinetist known for his work with David Murray's Big Band and his traveling klezmer show dedicated to the great Mickey Katz
13. Victo, 1992, 14. See *John Zorn*, p.148 15. See *Radical Brass*, p.62

Tenko

[Japanese] female performers will often present themselves as women who have experienced all there is to life, while they simultaneously smile coquettishly and crinkle their noses like young girls.

> *Judith Ann Herd, "Trends and Taste In Japanese Popular Music: A Case Study of the 1982 Yamaha World Popular Music Festival"*[1]

Among the New York avant garde, it was all so theoretical, it was all just a head trip...They were just so cool, right? There was that very asexual atmosphere in the music. And I wanted to throw blood.

> *Yoko Ono*[2]

Few women throughout history have managed to embody the fleeting magic of the nightingale's song. It can be found, *vox et praeterea nil*, in the syllabic density and 'pataphysical delight of Ella Fitzgerald's sublime scat on "Air Mail Special" and heard in the evil dread festering between the hushed lines of Billie Holliday's mournful "Strange Fruit." It suffuses the diaphanous, finely-poised folk songcraft of Sandy Denny, spices the earthy bottom register and impetuous phrasing of Italian mezzo-soprano Cecilia Bartoli as she sings Cherubino in Mozart's *La Nozze Di Figaro*, and sends chills up our spines during Diamanda

Galás' harrowing descent into hell in her *Plague Mass*. If, like the nightingale, we are voice and nothing else, their voices stand as the purest of song.

We can add to this list the stunning work of Japanese improvisor and vocalist Tenko. For over 15 years Tenko has been extending the technical and emotional compass of the female voice while deconstructing the stereotyped image and characteristics of the Japanese women who make their living with it. Equally at home leading a Willem Breuker-style burlesque or participating with slashing guitars and brutalized turntables in a cathartic, two-minute punk roar, Tenko's voice is a supple thing indeed. Her solo album *At The Top Of Mt. Brocken*[3] treats the listener to over an hour of chameleonic shape-shifting: With Motoharu Yoshizawa's bowed bass, she uses her voice to color "If I..." *à la* Joni Mitchell, a foil to cooking drums and the barely controlled, '60s thing chaos. On "Blue Heat," her urgent breaths and grunts give way to tribal stutters and peyote ceremony shouts over Yoshihide Otomo's industrial soundscape of turntables and processed metal samples. She's a torch singer deep inside the changes to "Someone To Watch Over Me" on "Dressed In Memories," a traditionalist on the vaguely Yiddish sounding folk song "There Play Children In The Flowering Meadow," an overdubbed babel of voices hovering over Yukihiro Issou's plaintive *nho-kan* on "The Sands Just Sigh," and a master of haiku on "Water Hours," the syllables etched against Kazutoki Umezu's harsh, strident reeds and ululating clarinet and Otomo's tape loop of a rushing brook.

As Tenko's voice floats high above the elliptical, ringing harmonics of Hideki Kato's fretless bass on "The Last Angel," her voice literally comes to embody a country whose culture is a pitched battle between tradition and the future. "I've never thought about the Japanese tradition seriously until now," Tenko admits freely. "Every country has its own aesthetic sense. I don't know whether you could call it an individual Japanese aesthetic sense or not, but trying to express something 'subtle' is common to many of us. You have to understand Japan has been closed for more than a thousand years, and our culture has fermented as a result. Today there are still tons of traditional things, but I don't think my work is especially alien to them."

This astonishing subtlety and keenness for the heat of the moment is what places Tenko at the head of a small pack of intrepid women improvisors worldwide that includes England's Maggie Nicols, France's Catherine Jauniaux, Mongolia's Sainkho Namtchylak, and Brooklyn's Shelley Hirsch.[4] Her attention to detail gave her the title of her debut LP, *Slope/Gradual Disappearance:*[5] "Sometimes the world doesn't look too good, it's too full of dramatic change. But it's also full of gradual change, which is trickier to see. I'm interested in gradual change, whether it's events happening in the world or shifts in my creativity. I sometimes feel I am being swallowed up by the world."[6]

Born and raised in Tokyo, Tenko boasts no musical training. The self-taught, fortysomething guitarist and singer first made waves in 1978, when she began to play with a quintet of five women who called themselves Mizutama Shobodan, or "The Polka Dot Fire Brigade." Describing themselves as "Five women who make their own songs and play," the deadpan firefighters went completely against the grain of contemporary Japanese pop. They had three strikes against them: by playing rock instead of pop, they were treading on men's turf; they weren't young and "beautiful" in the coy, fashion model sense of the word, and they were independent, self-producing their own records and releasing them without the help of major record labels.

"Our first album was extremely difficult to produce and distribute," Tenko explains. "People come to me and say, 'Wow, you're from Japan, there's so much new and avant-garde music happening there.' It's not as widespread as you think; it's very fringe-like, and we're very far out on the fringe. The music industry in Japan is a lot like America, dominated by large record labels like CBS and Sony, and you have to be very young and beautiful in order to sell records or get a record contract. Pop stars are ridiculously young in Japan, it's all so image-oriented. Since Mizutama Shobodan were neither young nor beautiful, we had to do it ourselves."[7] To this end, Tenko formed the cheekily-named Kinniku Bijo ["Muscular Women"] Records to release their first LP, *Otome-No-Inori-Wa Da! Da! Da!*[8]

Mizutama Shobodan's deconstructed rock and pop forms offered something qualitatively different from the punk/progressive rock brew of other Japanese underground bands like The Ruins and The Boredoms, something that baffled audiences and critics alike. "We were called an exception," Tenko recalls. "In Japan, people say something is an exception when they can't put it in any category. We stopped performing six years ago, and people still remember the band, not as a women's band, just as one of the good bands of that age. Mizutama Shobodan was quite a strong band, you could compare it to anything men were doing at the time. While the quality of the sounds and the words were quite heavy, I feel we could give people a challenge, some sort of energy more or less special to women. But I don't know what's going on in female Japanese bands these days; it's difficult, because in Japan everything quickly changes all the time, even common sense. Twenty years ago, I had never heard about other female rock singers of my generation in Japan. Women had to get married by the time they were 25. Now some parents say that's too early."

In 1980, Tenko formed The Honeymoons, a duo with bassist, vocalist and percussionist Kamura Atsuko. On albums like *Warau-Shinwa*,[9] The Honeymoons proved even more ferocious and volatile than Mizutama Shobodan; their live shows could be journeys into spontaneous combustion, and often featured surprise guests like mischievous British saxophonist Lol Coxhill. At a 1988 gig at Montreal's Foufounes Electriques as part of Festival de Musiciennes Innovatrices,[10] Kamura busied herself with a table of unlikely percussion – a hubcap, rubber mice, a pie plate, and a sheet of bubble packing – while Tenko mesmerized the audience with a seemingly schizophrenic recital of songs, *recitative*, glossolalia, voices and characters, occasionally pealing off heavy power chords from the strat strapped to her shoulder. The entire concert hinged upon a thrilling, mercurial unpredictability as Kamura thought on her feet to keep up with Tenko's endless *dramatis personæ*. "If you hear some characters in my singing, all I can say is 'Everything is part of myself,'" Tenko says cryptically. "But on the other hand, when I sing I try to be empty, to be part of the world and not myself. Actually on stage I don't know what I am going to do next. I don't have any room to 'act out' or 'play' when I sing, I just concentrate. Sometimes during performance I find I can make a new world which I've never known before. It's thrilling. That's why I love improvisation."

Her work with The Honeymoons revealed Tenko's increasing interest in improvisation, and after she voyaged to New York City for the first time in 1981, she slowly began to make inroads in what has traditionally been a narrow, male-dominated field. "It's besides the point how many improvisors exist in the world," she says. "And I'm not going to go into the popularity of improvised music. It comes down to choosing friends. It really doesn't matter what kind of field they are involved in; it's just exhilarating to discover fine spirits." Tenko's first impression of New York was that it was rich in arts and full of people's creative energies. "It was hot in spite of being wintertime," she recalls. Captivated by the Big Apple, she met many new friends and fine spirits there – Zeena Parkins, Kramer, Ned Rothenberg, Wayne Horvitz, Tom Cora, David Moss, Art Lindsay, and Fred Frith – all denizens of the Lower East Side and all destined for in cameos on Tenko's debut album, *Slope*.

Slope reveals the voice of a woman lost in the big city, yet defiantly maintaining her identity against the polyglot urban landscape. In "Passing By The Night," she's a Japanese Lotte Lenya, moaning and whispering with Parkins' accordion in a dark, Brechtian tango; in "Somewhere, Far Away," she's a grown-up child enraptured in a nightmare lullaby set to Horvitz' steely piano and spluttering DX7 electronics; as "The Sleep Walker," she wails in dreamtime, fragments of music echoing in her memory as fast as turntable whiz Christian Marclay can slip-cue them. In these unusual settings, Tenko's focus is sharp indeed; she can carry a mutant hoedown on "The Time Drawers" against Cora's 'cello and Kramer's Indian banjo, and sing a jazzy trio with herself, vamping with Ned Rothenberg's grainy alto sax on "A Watchdog Of The Labyrinth."

"When we were recording *Slope*, I would listen for other sounds and events first, then would make my sound with my voice and body," she has said. "I consider my entire body to be an instrument, and have no real voice training. When I sing, I think of Butoh, a traditional Japanese meditative dance which requires total concentration and awareness of the body. So I listened to whatever Christian, Fred or Arto were doing and responded based on that."[11] Tenko brought this aleatory approach to both composition and improvisation throughout much of her later work. The writing of "Orage," her Ligeti-with-a-backbeat contribution to Justine's 1990 multimedia performance, *La Légende de la Pluie*,[12] is a good example. "Joane [Hétu] had already decided that my part would be called 'Orage,'" says Tenko. "In Japan, I sat down on a chair, closed my eyes and the storm started in my mind. I imagined the carnival of a Wind Goddess. I then did the main bassline and melody on a keyboard. In effect, it was a score. But of course, I asked the others to add improvised parts after I had let my imagination loose."

Tenko made the cultural exchange between Japan and America a two-way street; in 1985, she brought John Zorn and a coterie of downtown improv musicians – Ned Rothenberg, Elliott Sharp and Christian Marclay – to Japan for a groundbreaking series of concerts. The same year she landed a job with David Moss [perhaps the male vocalist who comes closest to Tenko's surreal, total sense of singing] and toured Europe with his Dense Band, singing both accompaniment and lead on Moss' roulette wheel of polymorphously perverse pop lunacy, which on any given night could include Albert Ayler, Prince, Tom Jones or Cheb Khaled. Yet amongst her new circle of improvising friends and fine spirits, it was Fred Frith and his guitars on the table that left the most lasting influence on Tenko. "When I saw Fred for the very first time, I was surprised that what he was doing could be called music," Tenko says. "And I immediately knew that was the way I would go. Fred gave me a very close feeling about improvisation, despite the fact that we had very opposite backgrounds. His 1981 concert in New York was inspiring to me. It opened lots of opportunities to play throughout the world, and it gave me the chance to work with other musicians. I can say it was the first time I really *heard* improvised music. I thought to myself, 'I can play this music, I can sing it.'"

Tenko met Frith again in 1983, this time on her home turf, when he and Tom Cora toured Japan as part of Skeleton Crew. To her surprise, she discovered that Frith had bought the Mizutama Shobodan and Honeymoons albums, and was astonished that the same singer was fronting two totally different bands. Tenko gigged with Skeleton Crew and Frith produced Mizutama Shobodan's brilliant followup LP, *Manten-Ni Akai-Hanabira*.[13] The bond between Tenko and Frith went beyond their work in the studio and onstage; they had a son together, Yui.

[Frith can be seen playing with him in the film *Step Across The Border*.[14]] Yet soon after a 1989 tour of Europe, Frith and Tenko went their separate ways.

The recording of *At The Top Of Mt. Brocken* in Tokyo's Gok Studios throughout 1990 and 1991 introduced Tenko to many unusual and eccentric Japanese musicians, such as Yoshihide Otomo, whose work on turntables and guitar gave Ground Zero – a cacophonous unit who have collaborated with John Zorn and draw on '60s free jazz, '70s punk, and '90s grunge – its exciting edge, and noise guitarist Tsuneo Imahori, a member of avant-pop ensemble Tipographica. So in 1992, Tenko decided to form an ad hoc band, Dragon Blue, and rounded up some of the *Mt. Brocken* session players. After just one rehearsal, Dragon Blue's first gig was released as a eponymous CD.[15]

Rounding out the quintet of Dragon Blue is the rhythm section of New York-based bassist Hideki Kato [also a member of Ground Zero] and drummer Tatsuya Yoshida, half of the infamous Tokyo underground duo The Ruins, who whipped high opera with hardcore punk and extended, progressive rock structures that wouldn't be out of place in Magma. "This man *breathes* in weird time signatures," says Zorn in the liner notes. "I feel I have something very intense," Tenko says of Dragon Blue. "It's a bit old-fashioned because some of the material was old, but it has a real, indescribable energy. It's different from *Slope*. I feel that *Slope* is quite dreamy, whereas *Dragon Blue*, which was recorded live onstage, is more realistic. When I make an album, I avoid emotional expression consciously. I think it is totally different for an audience, going to a concert and listening to an album. Also, band work and producing a project are quite different. On *Slope* and *Mt Brocken*, I really enjoyed being a producer. On *Dragon Blue*, I took pleasure in being a singer."

As a singer, the duet is perhaps the most challenging and ideal format for Tenko; the sparseness of sonic materials at hand compels her to marshal her energies in concentration, and offers her an exciting setting only surpassed by the highwire act of solo recitals. Recent memorable duets include a spectacular series of gigs in Hong Kong in 1993 alongside turntable whiz Otomo; a unique CD with electronic drummer and percussionist Ikue Mori, *Death Praxis*;[16] and a 1992 tour of Europe with dancer Uzumi Ashikawa from the Butoh dance troupe Hakutobho ["The White Peach Cell"].

Butoh represents perhaps the deepest wellspring of inspiration for Tenko. Pioneered by Japanese dancers Tatsumi Hijikata and Kazuo Ohno in the 1950s, *Ankoku Butoh*, or "The Dance of Utter Darkness," represented a revolt against the domination of Western dance forms as well as the ossified complacency of traditional forms of Japanese theater. In the bleak cultural landscape of postwar Japan, *Noh* and *Kabuki* had become hollow vessels of entertainment: *Kabuki* had long been stripped of its funky and perverse plebian roots, while *Noh* had become the equivalent of Opera at Covent Garden, an ostentatious spectacle for the well-heeled. Juxtaposing the grotesque and the beautiful and freely plundering modern and pre-modern dance techniques, Butoh appealed to the disenfranchised Japanese avant garde. Infamous dances like *Kinjiki* ["Forbidden Colors"] and *Nikutai no Hanran* ["Revolt Of The Flesh"] were performed in complete silence with no interpretive program notes, packed a violent, expressive power rooted in the irrational, and seethed with a raw, sexual energy. But more importantly, Butoh's primitivism brought the body back in tune with nature. Acclaimed Butoh troupes like Sankai Juku – who toured America in the 1980s – set their performances amid prehistoric ruins, basking in the aura of the dead in an attempt to reach a collective unconscious.

"It's not necessarily an influence, but I've really felt a similarity between Butoh and my work," Tenko explains. "Many Japanese want to be Western. So in Japan, traditional things are okay for ordinary people, but to many, Butoh is for the birds. They think it's ugly. But I think Butoh shows us honestly, as our real selves. It affirms anybody, even if they have short legs, long trunks and big heads, to be Japanese. And we *are* Japanese; we are one of the Asian nations. In Japan we are under a lot of influence from foreign countries, and maybe we are losing some of our tradition. But I'm not afraid of that, it's the destiny of tradition in all countries. Butoh is quite a new tradition; it's just over 30 years old, but it's also the furthest you can get from Western dance. It shows we should be building *new* traditions."

Tenko: Slope/Gradual Disappearance (RecRec, 1987), At The Top Of Mt. Brocken (RecRec, 1993), Dragon Blue (Sound Factory, 1993)
with **Mizutama Shobodan**: The Virgin's Prayers Da! Da! Da! (Kinniku-Bijo, 1981), Sky Full Of Red Petals (Kinniku-Bijo, 1985),
with **The Honeymoons**: Laughing Myth (Kinniku-Bijo, 1982)
with **Justine**: La Légende de la Pluie (Ambiances Magnétiques, 1993)
with **Ikue Mori**: Death Praxis (Nonsequitir, 1993)

Footnotes:
1. In *Popular Music*, Volume 4, 1984: pp.77-78
2. In conversation with Mark Kemp, *Option* Magazine N45, July 1992: p.76
3. RecRec, 1993, 4. See *Fleurs Carnivores*, p.95 5. RecRec, 1987
6. As told to the author, "Femmes Vitales," in *Option* Magazine N21, July 1988: p.65
7. Ibid., p.65, 8. "The Virgin's Prayers Da! Da! Da!;" Kinniku Bijo, 1981
9. "Laughing Myth;" Kinniku Bijo, 1982, 10. See *Justine*, p.209
11. "Femmes Vitales," p.65, 12. Ambiances Magnétiques, 1993; see *Justine*, p.212
13. "Sky Full Of Red Petals;" Kinniku Bijo, 1985
14. See *Fred Frith*, p.29, 15. Sound Factory, 1993, 16. Nonsequitir, 1993

Cut And Paste

When French composer Pierre Schaefer began to bulk erase the past at Radio Television Français in 1948 in the name of *musique concrète*, music took a quantum leap forward in both form and content. In past, music was something passed down through the eye and ear, by notation and rote. With the recording studio music could be now recorded, stored, played back, manipulated, even cut and spliced as if one were editing a film. Was it live, or was it Memorex? More than the simple amplification of instruments – which imbued them with a whole new tonal and harmonic palette – the recording studio paved the way for new musics, encompassing everything from Romanian composer Iancu Dumitrescu's hallucinatory electroacoustics to De La Soul's *3 Feet High And Rising*.

What *musique concrète* and the recording process did was throw the creation of music back into the studio, where the organization of sound could be quantified and manipulated electromagnetically. In the 1950s, John Cage was among the first artists to explore the boundaries between sound and music; works such as *Cartridge Music* [1960] and *HPSCHD* [1969] freed music from the mathematical straitjacket of the Serialists and are touchstones which *musique actuelle* musicians like Fred Frith continually return to.[1] Cage embraced the tape recorder, radio and turntable for the same reasons George Maciunas of the notorious New York Fluxus art collective poured water from a french horn in *f/h trace* [1963][2] or their contemporary, the renegade composer Harry Partch built bizarre homemade instruments such as chromolodeons and cloud chamber bowls: to create exotic new timbres and derail traditional, linear compositional thought. By introducing elements of chance to both performance and composition and treating music like William S. Burroughs treated narrative in *Naked Lunch*, Cage became the prototype post-modern cut-and-paste artist.

The cut-and-paste aesthetic broke out of the "serious art" ghetto and into the world of popular music in the late 1960s, led by Jamaican record producer Lee "Scratch" Perry, who pioneered the use of the recording studio as an instrument in remixing "dub" versions of reggae songs in his Black Ark Studios in Kingston. At the same time, British producer Brian Eno availed himself to aleatory and chance techniques on a series of breathtakingly perverse pop records in the 1970s,[3] rewriting the rules of how pop music could be recorded in the studio. Eno always considered himself to be more of a painter than a musician, and it is no accident that the media of painting and modern art play a great role here; the methodologies and vocabularies of the two are strikingly similar: British drummer Charles Hayward, whose use of the tape recorder in This Heat was seminal, acknowledges both Kurt Schwitters and Mark Rothko in his work. Just as Jimi Hendrix once sculpted the air with what was once considered an annoying byproduct of amplification – feedback – groups like America's Biota or England's Zoviet France now create striking sonic oils and watercolors through recording techniques and processes such as looping, overdubbing, tape manipulation and signal processing.

While the introduction of the compact disc by Philips and Sony in 1982 brought a host of new experimental possibilities as a creative medium – notably enhanced programmability – few have been as quick to exploit them as they did the vinyl LP. The exception of course, is sampling, the most popular spinoff of digital technology and the hardware manifestation of our short attention span. With the introduction of digital samplers like the Fairlight CMI and Roland DX7 in the early 1980s, sampling became easier as the "window" or length of sample could be protracted and the sample then played through a keyboard. Thus a single John Paul Jones guitar chord from *Led Zeppelin II* became the driving force of Herbie Hancock's 1980 hit "Rockit;" five years later the voice of Wolfman Jack was borrowed for M/A/R/R/S' dance hit "Pump Up The Volume;" and the James Brown and Parliament rhythm sections [the virtual font of modern funk] are still being plundered by countless hiphop bomb squads.

Of course, sampling need not be merely hip, ironic window-dressing. San Francisco musician and former journalist Bob Ostertag uses the technology in works like *Sooner or Later*[4] to hammer home a scathing indictment of oppression. Negativland, a radical sound collective also hailing from the Bay Area, use a dense collage of samples on their landmark LP *Escape From Noise*[5] as a devastatingly funny and sarcastic comment on noise pollution, suburban culture, the power of the media and our hyperconsumerist society. And Italian ethnomusicologists Roberto Musci and Giovanni Venosta weave field recordings from around the world into a very subtle and sophisticated tapestry indeed.

Yet sampling has opened a Pandora's Box of legal and moral issues, something Negativland and Canadian composer John Oswald discovered the hard way. Negativland's notorious 1991 single "U2"[6] – with samples of the Irish supergroup's hit song "I Still Haven't Found What I'm Looking For" mixed with some savagely funny and profane outtakes of American Radio personality Casey Kasem offended Island Records sufficiently for them to believe that the line between satire and copyright infringement had been crossed, and they successfully brought crippling litigation against the band which bankrupted them and destroyed their relationship with SST Records, who sued them in turn. Also in 1991, Oswald, who coined the term "plunderphonics" and who creates new musical works entirely with reappropriated music, was forced by CBS Records to destroy all copies and the master tapes of a CD that sampled Michael Jackson, even though it was distributed free of charge. Clearly sampling is the new frontier on which the battle for intellectual property is being fought. There is a considerable amount at stake here, and the battle is far from over. Surely parody laws in the United States exist to protect more artists than just Weird Al Yankovic?

Paradoxically, by replacing the LP as the primary form of music consumption, the compact disc has revived interest in old records. Quick to make a buck from master tapes lying in their vaults, record labels have plundered their back catalogues for reissue on CD: everything from Charlie Parker's rarest air shots to obscure opera classics to Martin Denny's *Exotica* LPs of the 1950s. In this infotainment era, we now have access to more information from around the world than at any other time in history, and as we channel surf through the late 20th Century, our attention span is shrinking faster than that of Marshall McLuhan's Global Village. Think of this mercurial cut-and-paste aesthetic played in *real time*, and you have some idea of the celebrated, polystylistic "downtown" scene of 1980s New York, where musicians like John Zorn, George Cartwright, Christian Marclay, Shelley Hirsch, Tom Cora, Zeena Parkins, Jim Staley, Butch Morris, David Weinstein and David Moss all brought their encyclopedic record collections and knowledge of music to recombinant new musical forms.

At the eye of the downtown new music hurricane, John Zorn's work cannons through musical styles like a haberdasher through a flea market: hardcore versions of Ornette Coleman's harmolodics, imaginary *film noir* soundtracks, game pieces where improvisors do battle. It recalls the work of composer Carl Stalling, whose brilliant Looney Toons soundtracks for Warner Brothers in the 1930s and 1940s did more to shape the musical sense of our generation than most modern composers. Not coincidentally, Zorn did his master's dissertation on Stalling. Perhaps it's fitting then, that along with Pierre Schaefer, Bugs Bunny and Foghorn Leghorn have the last laugh.

1. See *Fred Frith*, p.28
2. Rare audio works by Fluxus artists such as Maciunas, Jackson MacLow, Yoko Ono, and La Monte Young can be found on two fascinating compliations: *FluxTellus* [Tellus casette, 1990] and *Fluxus Anthology* [Zona Archives, 1990]
3. *Here Come The Warm Jets*, *Taking Tiger Mountain By Strategy*, *Another Green World* and *Before And After Science*; Editions EG 1973, 1974, 1975 and 1977 respectively
4. Rec Rec, 1991
5. SST Records, 1988
6. For a thorough appraisal of the Negativland/U2 case, see *The Letter U and The Number 2*, published by Negativland in 1992, and pulled from circulation soon after as part of a second lawsuit. Cassette dubs of both Oswald's *Plunderphonic* and Negativland's "U2" can be acquired from the Copyright Violation Squad; see appendix.

John Oswald

An author is entitled to claim authorship and to preserve the integrity of the work by restraining any distortion, mutilation, or other modification that is prejudicial to the author's honor or reputation.

"The Right Of Integrity," Canada Copyright Act[1]

All the sounds are immigrants...None is intent on creating a past.

Paul Haines, "Jubilee"[2]

In the postscript to his *114 Songs* of 1922, composer Charles Ives calls the possessor "the gentle borrower." "Some have written a book for money; I have not. Some for fame; I have not...In fact, I have not written a book at all – I have merely cleaned house. All that is left is out on the clothes line..."[3] Living in an age when public domain was home to more than just folk songs, "O Christmas Tree" and Tin Pan Alley, Ives disdained the creative confines of copyright, privately publishing and distributing his own music free of charge, exhorting listeners and musicians to copy and spread works like "Paracelsus," "In Flanders Fields," and "At The River" as they saw fit. Today, public domain has a legally defined fence surrounding its shrinking boundaries, and Ives' quaint, eccentric ethos would be seen as commercial suicide. Rare is the composer who will give their music to the people and forsake lucrative mechanical royalties. Just ask the man who owns the rights to the Lennon/McCartney canon.

Yet what of pop culture icons who all but exist in a public domain because their music is available everywhere we look or listen, seeping into our consciousness from televisions, elevators, ghetto blasters, walkmen and passing jeeps? Armed with technology as simple as magnetic tape or a multi-speed turntable, or as sophisticated as a digital sampler and pitch-shifting music software, can we use the beats, hooks, basslines, choruses and spirit of pop music in the same way Ives himself dovetailed the popular hymns, parlor songs, and marches of his day into new songs? Can we use their sounds in the way Pierre Schaefer hijacked concordes, birds and waterfalls for his *musique concrète* or the way Dickie Goodman recycled hit parade choruses in his novelty tunes of the '50s like *The Flying Saucer*? At what point does a sound claim ownership? Just ask the hardest working man in show business.

The answer to this conundrum is the elusive top quark John Oswald has long been searching for. A Toronto-based experimental composer and quiet, reclusive pop theoretician, Oswald prefers to speak through the music of the Mystery Tape Laboratory while shrouding his own past in, well, mystery. His creative quest has revealed itself in his Mystery Tapes engaging and exotic exercises in sonic and musical obfuscation – and plunderphonics, pop collages that skirt the boundaries of what is considered legal by radically recombining and retrofitting elements of other people's music. "I'm not afraid to fiddle with music that I like but doesn't quite satisfy me," Oswald once told Mark Hosler of Negativland. "There's a possibility that I can make something better of it."[4] Like Stravinsky, who once opined that "A good composer does not imitate, he steals," Oswald's underlying philosophy toward sonic appropriation is an honest and open one: "Music is information and, as such, is a renewable resource. Intellectual real estate is infinitely divisible. The big difference between the taking of physical property and the taking of intellectual property is that in the latter case the original owner doesn't lose the property. They still have it. Theft only occurs when the owner is deprived of credit."[5]

Many such cogent, informative, and witty points are to be found amongst the prose and fastidious footnotes of Oswald's essays and papers. His crucial treatise "Plunderphonics, or Audio Piracy As A Compositional Prerogative" has been translated into Danish and German, and was reprinted in the *Whole Earth Review* and the *Ré Records Quarterly*. "Plunderphonics" is a term Oswald coined to cover the counter-covert world of converted sound and retrofitted music, where "collective melodic memories of the familiar are mined and rehabilitated to a new life."[6] A plunderphone is an unofficial but recognizable musical quote,[7] be it a James Brown grunt, an old Unesco Philips recording of pygmy chant, the spliced bounce of Count Basie's Orchestra, or a computer playing Glenn Gould. Ever since the invention of the portable cassette deck in the 1950s, each advance in home entertainment technology has made it possible for the home listener to create their *own* music from this multiplicity of existing sources. Add a DAT recorder, a portable mixing board and some computer software, and the future is here. "Now can we, like Charles Ives, borrow merrily and blatantly from all the music in the air?"[8]

"It's somewhat ironic that in visual arts, there's been all sorts of appropriation issues and dialogues going on for a long time. There's people who do much more extreme things than I do, like take a photograph of a photograph and put their name on it and say 'This is my art.' This sort of transformation is old hat, like Marcel Duchamp painting a moustache on the Mona Lisa."

John Oswald is sitting in the kitchen of the Mystery Tape Laboratory. Squirreled away on leafy street somewhere in downtown Toronto, the Mystery Tape Lab is a nondescript enough building overlooking a park, identified only by a small clay plaque stamped with a human ear affixed next to the doorbell. With thinning, greying hair tied in a ponytail, Oswald is a quiet man, inwardly intense as he talks shop and philosophy in a delightfully byzantine manner over cups of steaming espresso, taking time out occasionally to answer the denuded telephone behind him as its exposed insides ring clangorously. We have just finished listening to the final mix of Oswald's latest composition, *Plexure*, a meta-sampled 20-minute aural bombardment that consists of 1,001 "electro-quoted" pop samples – and 1,001 potential litigants.

"The legal side of copyright entails two issues," Oswald continues, shuffling papers. By the window, a row of plastic birds with vibration-sensitive computer chips quirp at the sudden draft. "The most common one is a financial gain of one party over another. Then there's some sort of moral protection which, most often in the recording industry, is tied into financial gain also: 'We don't want to besmirch our clients' reputation because maybe they'll make less money then.' All of that stuff seems above and beyond morality to me, which is just are you screwing other people around when you're doing something or not. I've noticed that talking to musicians and composers, most often they are not resistant at all to someone reusing their material in an ethical sort of way. There's various approaches: 'Don't mention my name,' or 'It sure would be nice if I got a credit.' It varies, but there's no real great resistance, and very rarely will you run into someone who will say, 'Well, how much do I make out of this?' The only resistance I've run into is management and lawyers representing management. After an initial foray to looking at copyright policy just to find out what might and might not be allowable, I discovered that's quite a confusing question in legal terms. I'm really not that interested in the legal aspects. I am interested in ethical issues about the use of other people's music. I've always felt quite free about using other people's music to create new things."

John Oswald has been using other people's music to create new things since he bought a sixty dollar reel-to-reel tape recorder when he was a kid. "I think everyone has a preferential choice of instruments," Oswald once said. "They'll gravitate to the piano or guitar or whatever. I do that also and, to some extent, I can articulate with those kind of instruments. I'm very much interested in sounds I'm familiar with. And I think my choice to do the sort of thing I do is related to my experiences as a *listener*. My experience with The Beatles goes way back and there's something that seems to resonate more with playing with those actual sounds than with putting my hands on musical instruments."[9]

As a musician, Oswald's roots lie in improvisation – in the late 1970s, he played alto saxophone in a fertile trio with trumpeter Toshinori Kondo and guitarist Henry Kaiser.[10] As a composer, Oswald's first appropriation of another's work as such came in 1981, after spending long sleepy hours listening to the voice of William S. Burroughs. After Burroughs gave his blessing to the project, Oswald released *Spoors*, an intriguing mix of taxonomy and linguistics that applied Burroughs' cut-up technique to two-track tape and field recordings of animals. The juxtaposition of sound was something that reminded Oswald of the "mystery" tapes Canadian poet Paul Haines regularly sent him; a typical tape could feature anything from retrograde pygmy chants to British vocalist Robert Wyatt improvising to the beatific sounds of deep space quasars. Haines, who has lent his gravelly voice to recording projects by Carla Bley and Curlew,[11] writes poetry as surreal as Slim Gaillard's *vout* and as musical as a Jazz Messengers date, and this excerpt from his "Jubilee" goes a long way in describing the psychological methodology behind the mystery tape concept:

> "There is an interesting inventory of sound wisdom based in no tradition and not new, using what is with what hasn't happened yet. Sounds make no noticeable attempt to understand grasp. They believe in no afterlife: our *after*, they hold, still **then**. Soul, of course: theirs the liquid core to all musics, whatever their fettle: glazed, thinned, of clung to like drool, compressed into the hardest chromatic beads, cockatrice or honeyed-jingled arousal."[12]

Thus the Mystery Tape Laboratory was founded in the early 1980s as a very exclusive sonic research center "To ferret & fashion, to appropriate against [dices error] all odds, to place in cahoots a cornucopia of essential & vivacious sounds from everywhere & whenever, to map them into vortexual sequences & overlaps, symphonies & cacaphonies, cartoons & realisms, typically byzantine in format. Pop stars deform & implode, the Classics get what's coming to them...all in 30 minute chunks, 2 to a tape."[13] Thematically, Mystery Tapes range from the Ivesian collage of LX/X^5 to the DJ scratch of "Funky X" on *Kissing Jesus In The*

Dark to the drifting, ambient *XMap*. While it is possible to write the Lab to get the sources of a particular cassette deciphered, many choose to keep them a mystery, instead preferring to contemplate the index of possibilities. "I can't say much about it because it's a mystery," says Oswald with a mischievous twinkle in his eye. "Mystery tapes is the opposite of plunderphonics in a lot of ways, although it can seem like some of the sources in the mystery tapes can seem like acquired sources of existing music. Plunderphonics entails dealing with quotation, where mystery tapes really does deal with obfuscation, hiding all the information. It can seem very mysterious in that way. It becomes this sort of ritual thing, because some of the correspondences are quite amazing."

With works for turntables and radios like *Imaginary Landscape N°4* [1951] and *Cartridge Music* [1960], John Cage blurred the distinction between sound producers and sound reproducers. Twenty years later, young hiphop DJs would use turntables to "scratch" albums into their rap rhymes and disco DJs would use two or more LPs to beat mix and slip cue fragments of several records together into collages. While today these tasks are handled by digital samplers and computer software, for a brief decade the wheels of steel enjoyed a heyday as an instrument of postmodern guerilla warfare. Record scratching was an integral part of hiphop's sound, from Grandmaster Flash through Public Enemy; De La Soul took the concept to new heights on their landmark album *3 Feet High And Rising*,[14] using quotes from Steely Dan, Hall & Oates, and a French instructional record. Record industry bean counters took notice, lawsuits were launched, and sampling soon became a ethical issue, with the ironic result that negotiations for sample clearance now occupy much of the production time of hiphop records; the American release of De La Soul's followup album, *De La Soul Is Dead*,[15] was delayed over a year.

"I like what Steve Stein says," Oswald explains. "He says, 'You want the *thing*. You don't want the almost thing.' You don't want Rich Little doing James Brown, you want James Brown doing James Brown. Sure, you can't make an exact copy of a James Brown snare sound, but anybody with some skill could do the same sort of thing that forgery painters do with the past masters: something that fools almost everybody. I'm sure there's always samples which musicians think are hidden enough or obscure enough in the contents of the music that they don't have to mention them or pay for them, but anything that's obvious they're going to be negotiating the rights for. But I'm really against the idea that 'It's not very obvious, let's not tell anybody about it and maybe we can get away with it.' The lawyers tell me that all the time: 'If nobody's going to notice it, then just do it.' Still, according to the legal system, it's illegal. They're saying it's okay to steal if nobody catches you."

As Oswald has often said, the noun sample in our society is often prefixed by the adjective free.[16] Intrigued to find out just exactly how free, he planned as a not-for-sale CD that would both take advantage of the sequencing possibilities of the digital medium of the compact disc and provide a sampler of music lifted, scrambled, sifted, filtered, and reascembled through a variety of studio techniques. The results on *Plunderphonic* are highly radical yet instantly recognizable portraits of the artists plundered. Thus Michael Jackson's voice is subjected to a massive multi-track overdub worthy of Stockhausen [at one point there's 10,000 tracks] in "Dab," James Brown gets his revenge as all the hiphop artists who boosted his riffs and grunts are themselves sampled in "Black," a computer gamely guesses Glenn Gould's next move as it is fed his *Goldberg Variations* in "Aria," Dolly Parton gets an aural sex change by slowing down the speed of one of her singles in "Pretender," Beethoven's *Symphony N°7 Op.92* is given the minimalist treatment in "Prelude," and the rhythm of Count Basie's big band swing is cut, spliced and given two left feet, as is Metallica's heavy metal thunder in "Net."

According to Oswald, the source material and the appropriate plunderphonic technique is a chicken and egg situation. "Sometimes there is an experimental technique looking for a source, or sometimes the content will dictate the technique," he explains. "It might have ironic levels; there might be something in the lyrics of a song. 'The Great Pretender' is a good example. Although the idea of slowing down Dolly Parton was my idea, two separate Dolly Parton fans told me on two separate occasions that I should listen to Dolly Parton 45s at 33 RPM, because she sounded really great at that speed. And it's true. Whereas the intent of the Metallica piece was to take what I found to be a very satisfying recording of heavy metal and make the drummer's parts interesting. My overall focus was to make this drummer's part *happen*. Two-track editing tack was an obvious technique; dealing with precise rhythmic things without getting into denser orchestrations. And I've always liked doing two-track editing; it's like crocheting or something."

Like Ives' *114 Songs*, *Plunderphonic* was never intended for sale. Oswald included a disclaimer that encouraged dubbing; he also went out of his way to disable the digital copy-protection flag[17] so that the CD can be digitally reproduced, or "cloned." A thousand copies were pressed, and were sent out on Hallowe'en 1989. Oswald sent them to libraries, radio stations, the artists who had been electroquoted, and the press. One week before Christmas, after seven hundred or so copies had been distributed, Oswald got a letter from legal counsel representing the Canadian Recording Industry Association [CRIA]. The letter, which contained amusing double negatives such as "We do not want you to not distribute this" ["I had lawyers telling me that no, you can't use bad grammar as an excuse in court," quips Oswald], stated that Oswald had one week to stop distributing *Plunderphonic* and recall all CDs.

It seems that CRIA and CBS Records, representing Michael Jackson, were upset by the cover graphics of the CD and the fact that the cut "Dab" just *might* contain samples of Michael Jackson's voice. That Jackson was the only electroquoted performer to take legal action brings up something CRIA nor CBS would come straight out and say: Not only was Oswald getting any money from giving away CDs that he encouraged people to copy freely, but *neither was Jackson, The Beatles or any of the others whose copyrights he owns.* "In CRIA's eyes the average consumer, more than half of whom condone home taping, is a pirate," Oswald later explained to Norman Igma of *Musicworks* Magazine. "Their latest solution to this crime wave is to lobby for the instigation of a royalty tax of 50 cents on every blank cassette tape sold to individuals. So even if you're recording baby's first words or yourself playing an improvisation on the bazoozaphone, Michael Jackson...will get money for the record they didn't sell."[18]

Distribution of *Plunderphonic* was stopped as of December 24, 1989, and legal negotiations regarding to what extent Oswald was willing to meet the demands of CRIA, CBS Records and Michael Jackson, continued through January. "We finally agreed on a list which made me quite happy," says Oswald. "It effectively took me out of the *Plunderphonic* CD distribution business; I could no longer send these things around for free. I was ordered to destroy the CDs which I had remaining in my possession, which were about 300. They were delivered to CRIA's lawyers by my lawyers and were subsequently crushed by somebody they hired. This made me quite happy because it put them in a position of being CD crushers, audio book burners and all the things we can associate with those fascist type tactics.

"Their initial demands were that all copies be recalled. I said I wasn't willing to do that, and I got my lawyer to convince them that it was impractical and unnecessary. But to back that up, I had statements from several radio stations, most particularly KPFA in San Francisco, that they weren't willing to give up their copy, and they would welcome a visit from the RCMP trying to take it back. We also had an agreement that if I fulfilled those requirements I could talk all I wanted about the thing. Silence was entailed during settlement negotiations, and it was very difficult for me, as I'm not used to having to obfuscate about anything." Ultimately, Oswald wasn't concerned about the destruction of the master; because of the disabled copy-protection flag, any of the existing CDs could be recorded digitally, and after all, it could be listened to in libraries and radio stations across the country. Distribution was then taken up by radio stations and organizations like the Copyright Violation Squad of Iowa, who will dub copies free of charge if supplied with a blank cassette.[19]

In a bizarre postscript to the *Plunderphonic* debacle, Oswald soon after received a call from Nonesuch Records president Bob Hurwitz who told him that he and Elektra Records president Bob Krasnow were excited about the *Plunderphonic* CD and wanted him to do a plunderphonic EP version of their 40th Anniversary CD *Rubyait*. A collection of today's Elektra artists plundering the music of yesterday's roster, *Rubyait* was a high concept dud that no amount of post-modern irony could save. Needless to say, Oswald agreed. "Because I was working for Elektra, I could have had access to multi-track master tapes," says Oswald. "But I said, 'No, let's do it the same way we did the previous *Plunderphonic* CD.' I have access to commercial recordings the same as everybody else. Part of the edge to this idea is that anybody is in a position to do this kind of thing; you don't have to be in tight with the record company to do it."

The first cut Elektra received was The Doors, a fairly simple Plunderphonics-style cut with a burst of quotes from various Doors songs. Elektra saw some commercial potential in the track until they talked to The Doors' lawyers, who wanted a full royalty on each of the 13 songs quoted in the cut. Elektra switched it to a radio-only release, refused to talk about it publicly, pressed 4000 copies, and it promptly sank from sight.

Down the hall from the kitchen is the nerve center of the Mystery Tape Lab, a hermetic room packed with a benign tangle of tube equipment, softly glowing computers, percussion instruments, and stacks of DAT tapes and floppy disks. A corkboard ahead of the mixing station and above the Apple computer monitor has a breakdown of current projects and notes posted beneath signs like "feels good." A ball of magnetic recording tape sits like a Duchamp statement on a drafting board. It was here that the final stage in the Plunderphonics project, *Plexure*,[20] was born.

Plexure had its origins in Oswald's fascination with what he called "the threshold of recognizability," or just how little sonic material we need to hear to identify a song. "I've discovered that if I'm familiar with a piece, I can hear 20 milliseconds of a sound, or a 50th of a second, discretely in space and recognize it," explains Oswald. "Potentially, you can pack together 50 different sounds together in a second, which, if you're able to isolate them, would have the character and the signature of the source they came from. Mostly I'm dealing with samples over a third of a second in duration. Although that seems like a fairly quick piece of time, it can incorporate a couple of words of a phrase, or a whole measure of a piece of music. In parts of this project, I'm dealing with samples below that threshold. There are events that are five milliseconds long. At that point, other things start happening."

No stranger to short attention spans, composer John Zorn gave Oswald a commission with no strings attached to create a work of sampling under the aegis of his Japanese record label, Avant. "Zorn pointed out that it would be great to hear something that had to do with sampling although I tend not to call it that because there's very little use of samplers in therethat isn't some way nostalgic," recalls Oswald. "A lot of hiphop samples today are used to quote from previous eras. That's partly practical; it's more difficult to win a court case in the U.S. trying to protect recordings done before 1976, when their copyright law changed.[21] We wanted very much a 'pop now' feeling.

"Second, the past 10 years since the introduction of the CD I see as an epoch of change. It represented a change in sound, packaging, marketing, and the number of versions you could get for any particular recording. An album release today is much more of a diffuse entity than it used to be. Something like *Sgt Peppers'* sticks in your mind as a very distinct release that has two sides like movements of a classical piece that are most often listened to in their entirety. Now everybody's putting out records that exploit the CD maximum of 70 to 80 minutes. These things are quite often not listened to in their entirety. When the album was really important, people tended to have some sort of big climax number at the end of the record, and put a lot of thought into the two sides. There's a tendency now to place the weirder stuff towards the end of a CD, so it won't drive away customers."

Oswald then began to gather pop music sources from the decade spanning 1982 to 1992. Six months later, he had several thousand sources indexed according to tempo, from the slowest – 40 beats per minuteto the fastest – 284 beats per minute. With the aid of ProTools Digidesign software, Oswald then assembled a suite exactly 20 minutes in length – the traditional side of a record LP – and called it *Plexure*. Webster's Third defines "plexure" as the act or process of weaving together; Oswald has taken as his fabric the music of a decade that saw seismic shifts in musical trends, styles and audiences, and reworked their tacit codes [aesthetic, lyric, production, image] into a breathtaking new pop form. Hard cutting and beat mixing heavy metal, Top 40, bubblegum, new wave, new romantic, hiphop, CHR, AOR and C&W, *Plexure* is a complex mnemonic concordance to a decade of number ones with a bullet that skips across the radio waves like a K-Tel album gone insane, channel surfing with a toddler's sense of wonder and an architect's sense of structure. Public Enemy, Chicago, Peter Gabriel, Genesis, Tears For Fears, Kate Bush, The Jam, U2, Negativland and Huey Lewis are compressed into a relentlessly physical mix that packs the most dynamic punch since Phil Spector's revolutionary wall-of-noise.

"That's pop music," Oswald says later with smile. "It's a bit difficult, but you can tap your foot through the whole thing. There's a dependable beat. It's square all the way through. If you find a place to start tapping your foot after the overture, more or less, you can follow it through all the way. It just gets faster and faster. The thing that makes it undependable is the amount of variety going on. That's the thing missing from pop music: the redundancy."

Oswald's dictum has long been "If you sample, give the credit due. If you have been sampled, consider the credit you have been given."[22] Yet because of the exceedingly large number of sources in *Plexure*, it became somewhat unrealistic for him to give credit for the sources as he had fastidiously done before. "It's always a legal impracticality to blatantly list your sources," Oswald admits. "I'm no expert in this, but I suspect that it's more difficult and expensive to credit your sampleeven if you've done the behind-the-scenes negotiations to use itunless you're bigger than the guy you're sampling. It was obviously impractical to negotiate the royalties for several thousand songs, for all the obvious reasons. So, rather than credit the artist, we took a tack from the recording. There's quite a bit of overlap in the piece, and the results are quite similar to visual morphing in a lot of ways. So we made a bunch of morph names, like Jello Belafonte, Sinéad O'Connick Jr, Marianne Faith No Morrisey, and R.E.M.T.V.Hammercamp." The lyric sheet for *Plexure* gleefully follows the same approach, the spliced lyrics reading like the dada phonetics of Kurt Schwitters' *Ursonate*.[23] *Wow! Chaka's back splat [plum de umbre, um]* segues into *do it like that/do it like that/can you hear me on earth?/whiddit squid pyjama*, while not forgetting *Ghandi as a young yeti/eats Verdi...ow!* Because there is currently no minimum duration below which copyright of a sound lapses, Oswald is once again testing the waters of legality with *Plexure*. "This being a commercial release, it's a whole new ballgame," he says. "The density and scope of sources will turn the issues upside down if anybody cares to pursue it. The sources are so short in most cases that no-one will likely come after me; but there are also potentially 1000 litigants rather than 12."

Oswald's status as an outlaw composer has overshadowed his work in other fields. Not many know, for instance, that Oswald is a dancer and has done soundtracks for cutting-edge Canadian choreographers James Kudelka, Denise Fujiwara, and Holly Small. A compendium of his dance works, *Discosphere*,[24] explores these "psycho-ballets", whether they be the musical possibilities of artificial voice generation, a Paul Haines mystery spliced together from cut-up phrases, or brilliant plunderphonia Americana where *Rocky* literally meets *Rawhide*. He has also returned to the unplugged, organic pleasure of free saxophone playing, recording acoustic duos, trios and quartets with violinist Mari Kimura and guitarists Henry Kaiser and Jim O'Rourke. On the sessions for *Acoustics*,[25] Oswald's Albert Ayler wail, along with Kaiser's sympathetic deep blues playing, is a welcome foil to Rourke's dry, prepared guitar percussion and Kimura's synapse-tight classical fretwork.

Yet it his plunderphonics that has made Oswald fans far and wide – including The Kronos Quartet, who have recorded his "Spectre,"[26] where pizzicato, bowing, and other physical sounds of string quartet are subjected to Oswald's "swarm" technique of massive overdubbing used on "Dab." Oswald has more work in the cards for Kronos – notably the fourth movement of Beethoven's B-Flat Major Quartet Op.130 – as well as more soundtracks for choreographers Kudelka and Small. And Jerry Garcia has invited Oswald to sift through the Grateful Dead's vaults of live material and assemble a plunderphonic historical overview of the Dead from 1969 to the present. Oswald chose to build the project, mystically entitled *Grayfolded*,[27] from 51 concert performances of the Dead's live psychedelic juggernaut, "Dark Star," and dryly describes it as a "Grateful Dead acid album. Guitar solos begin in 1969 and end in 1993."

Like the fluxus of the ever malleable mystery tapes, there are also plans of taking *Plexure* to a Eurocentric perspective, including classical and even world music. "Hell, somebody could play it on shuffle play and get an experience I haven't had with it yet," muses Oswald. "All this stuff is always eligible for someone to fiddle around with it. I would be the last person to retain any credibility by saying 'don't screw around with my music.'"

John Oswald: Alto Sax (Mystery Tapes cassette, 1980), Salmonmoose (Mystery Tapes cassette, 1980), Spoors (Mystery Tapes cassette, 1983), Plunderphonics EP (1986), Plunderphonic CD (1989), Rubyait (Elektra, 1990), Discosphere (ReR Megacorp, 1992), Plexure (Avant, 1993), Grayfolded (Swell/Artifact, 1995)
with **Henry Kaiser, Mari Kimura & Jim O'Rourke**: Acoustics (Victo, 1994)
Mystery Tapes: X^1/X^2, LX/X^5, MX/X^3, GX/EX, Kissing Jesus In The Dark, XMap

Footnotes:
1. Reprinted in Oswald, "Plunderphonics, or Audio Piracy As A Compositional Prerogative;" *Musicworks* Magazine N34, Spring 1986: pp.5-8
2. "Jubilee," published in *Musicworks* Magazine N34, Spring 1986: pp.12-13
3. Quoted in Henry Cowell, *Charles Ives And His Music*, Oxford University Press: New York, 1955: p.77
4. Interview with Mark Hosler, for *Mondo 2000* Magazine, date, 1992
5. Oswald, "Creatigality," an essay revised and printed as a guest editorial in *Keyboard* Magazine, March 1988: pp.12-13, 6. ibid.
7. Just how recognizable depends which side of the copyright fence you stand on. In 1990, under threat of litigation, The Canadian Recording Industry Association forced Oswald to destroy 300 copies and the master tapes of his 1989 *Plunderphonic* CD. This was done at the behest of CBS

Records and Michael Jackson, who appeared on the CD radically remixed [and rejuvenated], and on the CD cover from the neck down as a naked woman underneath his trademark leather jacket, a string of pearls about his/her waist

8. "Plunderphonics, or Audio Piracy As A Compositional Prerogative," *Musicworks* Magazine N34, Spring 1986

9. Interview with Mark Hosler

10. Their work can be heard on *Salmonmoose*, Mystery Tapes

11. Bley's *Tropic Appetites* [Watt, 1972] and *Escalator Over The Hill* [JCOA, 1974]; Curlew's *A Beautiful Western Saddle*; [Cuneiform, 1992]

12. In *Musicworks* N34: p.12, 13. Mystery Tape Pamphlet, 14. Tommy Boy, 1989, 15. Tommy Boy, 1992, 16. "Plunderphonics," p.5

17. Standard issue on all CDs to prevent digital copying

18. Norman Igma, "Taking Sampling 50 Times Beyond The Expected: An Interview With John Oswald," published in *Musicworks* Magazine N48, Autumn 1990: pp.16-21

19. They also distribute Negativland's banned SST release *U2*; see *Cut And Paste*, p.129

20. Avant, 1993

21. In 1976, the United States revised the U.S. Copyright Act to include sound recordings in that country for the first time

22. Oswald, "Creatigality"

23. Schwitters' infamous 1932 classical sonata of nonsense syllables inspired by Raoul Hausmann's 1918 dada poem "fmsbwtözäu," The *Ursonate* has influenced artists as diverse as composer Brian Eno and British performance artist George Melly; Eberhard Blum gives a rousing, definitive reading of the work on a 1992 Hat ART recording of the same name

24. ReR Megacorp, 1992, 25. Victo, 1994, 26. Released on Kronos' *Short Stories*, Elektra, 1993

27. Swell/Artifact, 1995

John Zorn

"It is as if Stravinsky had discovered in certain rhythmic units a latent energy, just as it has been claimed that the day is near when the scientists will discover and release enough energy now contained in every atom to blow a battleship from its harbor to a mountain top...But there is that in this music which repulses as well as attracts. It is an orgy, and an explosion of force, but very brutal and perhaps perverse. It is easy to believe it is the expression of one who is fundamentally a barbarian and a primitive, tinctured with, and educated in, the utmost sophistications and satieties of a worn-out civilization."

1924 review of a performance of Stravinsky's The Rite Of Spring[1]

[*fade in*] Like Jean Genet or William S. Burroughs before him, John Zorn has a little image problem.

Alto saxophonist, composer, improviser, arranger and gamesman, Zorn is perhaps the most successful figure to emerge from the New York "downtown" improv scene of the 1980s. He was a lightning rod for new music talent in New York; his game pieces regularly employed a who's who of new music talent and revealed him to be one of America's most intriguing new musical thinkers. His solo saxophone work rewrote the book on improvisation, proving there was life after circular breathing. He has been instrumental in creating an ongoing new music dialogue with Japan, through setting up a label there and bringing Japanese groups such as The Boredoms to America. And his chaotic, cartoon-inspired compositional style popularized the cut-and-paste aesthetic and in the process changed the way we hear music.

He may have never done hard time or played William Tell with a loaded shotgun, yet infamy has dogged him like a reucurring nightmare. It could be the sordid subject matter his music is ofter steeped in, such as film noir, Jean Genet or Kristallnacht. Or his affinity for hardcore, grindcore, speed metal and death metal, music whose brutal soliloquies he is unafraid to meet head on. Zorn has always been cast as the *bête noire* of the downtown scene, a musical magpie and smart-aleck who blew his saxophone into a water tank and soloed on a table of duck calls, and for this Zorn has been mercilessly caricatured in the mainstream press as a rude, obnoxious and pretentious provocateur, an art school brat who spends too much time in pursuit of adolescent hobbies such as cartoons, hardcore music and detective movies. His blunt, no-nonsense conversational style, often peppered with the vernacular [At a 1988 press conference for Naked City in Victoriaville, Zorn let into Werner Uehlingher of Hat Art, limning his contractual difficulties with the Swiss new music label using colorful anatomical language] only added fuel to the media fire.

Zorn has seen this bad boy archetype highlighted time after time in interviews and features about his work. So in 1993, after nearly twenty years at the helm of the avant garde in New York, after letting his contract with Elektra Nonesuch lapse and moving his base of operations to Japan, Zorn severed his ties with the mainstream media and decided that it was time to be quiet. "I have a deep mistrust in verbal communication and a justified cynicism of intentions and surfaces," he declared. "Until I can hone my skills a bit I prefer not to do any interviews." Two years later, Zorn is in no hurry to break this silence. Unlike The Residents, who use their flimsy "anonymity" as a slick marketing tool to peddle their back catalogue, Zorn's silence is genuine, and speaks volumes about his commitment to music. [*dissolve*]

[*flashback*] Born in 1953 and raised in New York City, Zorn has always had an omnivorous love of music. A fanatic record collector, he amassed a staggering collection and a deep, encyclopædic knowledge of music, particularly jazz, classical, and Asian pop and traditional idioms. East Village denizens often catch him at local emporiums for the musically rare and exotic such as Finyl Vinyl, Bleecker Bob's or Lunch For Your Ears – that is, when he's not listening to the city. As he once told Howard Mandel, "You can't get a more mixed city than this. Any hour of the day or night you can walk a block in Manhattan and see different types of people – Asian, black, white, Hispanic. It's something I'm used to, something I need, something that was bred in me. And I think it's an important element in the *sound* of this city. That kind of mix comes through in my music."[2]

The overriding characteristic of Zorn's music is without a doubt its short attention span. Whether the frenetic, quicksilver purity of *The Classic Guide To Strategy*,[3] his solo improv cycle for alto and soprano saxophone, Eb and Bb clarinet and bird calls, or the hairpin turns and schizophrenic playlist of Naked City's channel-surfing *Radio*[4] [which namechecks Bob Demmon & The Astronauts, Bernard Hermann, Orchestre Baobab, Sammy Cahn, SPK, Charles Mingus on Candid, Morton Feldman and Corrosion of Conformity *inter alia* as "Inspirations/Refer"], Zorn doesn't hover over a musical note or thought for very long before it's discarded like a split Rico reed. Indeed, many of Zorn's records sound like the product of sophisticated studio collage and hours spent at the editing block, yet the ripstart changes in tempo and dynamics and seamless segueing are done in real time.

It surprises many to discover, then, that Zorn was schooled as a composer squarely in what he likes to call the American maverick tradition: Charles Ives, Harry Partch, Elliott Carter. Yet even while studying composition and heavy into counterpoint with Argentine-born composer Leonardo Balada at the UN School in Manhattan in the late 1960s, the music of fast changes was embedded in his head. Bored with the laborious tasks of rewriting and rescoring, Zorn began to consider other ways of notating music. While attending Webster College in St Louis during 1971-1972, he found it in the form of a 1969 double LP on Delmark by reed player Anthony Braxton, *For Alto*.

The improvisations of *For Alto* bristled with an unbridled free energy that startled Zorn, yet Braxton also had a cool, intellectual way with structures that intrigued him; a way of instantly applying conceptual ideas to a piece. Saxophonist Oliver Lake was also teaching at Webster, and suggested Zorn check out the activities of the Black Artists' Group, as well as concerts by alumni from Chicago's Association for Advancement of Creative Musicians [AACM]. The music of Braxton, Lake, Roscoe Mitchell and Leo Smith pointed a way out for Zorn. In the 18 months he spent in St Louis before dropping out and heading to the West Coast to play solo saxophone gigs, Zorn picked up the alto saxophone and steeped himself in the American improvising tradition, a deep collaboration that was at the other end of the jazz continuum from the ivory tower world of composition.

Originally a piano student, Zorn chose the alto because of its superlative vocal qualities and the fact that the instrument's gamut was being radically rewritten by Albert Ayler, John Coltrane and Pharoah Sanders. "I think the main reason I picked up the sax as a possible instrument was that I looked at it as a sound-maker more than anything else," he told Bill Milkowski in 1984. "There was something about the breathy quality that I was attracted to. So right away I began doing tonguing experiments on the sax – flutter-tonguing, double-tonguing, triple-tonguing, trying to get as many squeaks and sounds and chords as I could out of it."[5]

Zorn's style was to become even more unorthodox: He would play his horn submerged in a fish tank, stuff footballs into its bell, and blow through duck and bird calls [Olt and Weems brands, thank you] rather than the usual reeds. Zorn picked up on the bird and duck calls partly because of the AACM's fascination with the tone color provided by little instruments [for one European tour the Art Ensemble of Chicago took over 500 instruments with them], and partly because they offered him an even faster conduit to convey the musical collages in his mind. As he would later display in his improvisations with trombonists George Lewis and Jim Staley, Zorn was driving at a new way of improvising, strikingly different from the classic European model exemplified by Derek Bailey or Evan Parker. Rather than developing ideas through extended blowing, layering and building up a head of steam in the traditional solo manner, Zorn worked with an internal structure and communicated the parameters of this structure to his players by eye or cue. Fragmented, Zorn's crying saxophone echoed the human sound of Ornette Coleman, Lennie Tristano and Jimmy Giuffre, asethetic outlaws all.

Zorn's interest in structured improvisation took him back to one of his earliest loves: cartoon music. Like the film medium itself, cartoon music works in a unique, suspended universe: it is very linear yet illogical; a sort of musical shorthand that emphasizes, underscores, or counterpoints the action. At Webster, Zorn did his master's thesis on Carl W. Stalling [1888-1974], the man behind the brilliant, wacky music of the Looney Tunes.[6] In his heyday of the 1940s, Stalling piloted a 50-piece orchestra through madcap quotations, mickey-mousing to Bugs Bunny, Foghorn Leghorn and Yosemite Sam in classic Warner Brothers cartoons by Chuck Jones, Friz Freleng and Tex Avery. Zorn saw in Stalling a clear line back to composers such as Stravinsky. "The guy is really a genius. When you just listen to his music, abstract it from the visuals of the cartoons, it's really incredible. There are a lot of abrupt changes in his music. And you can see how Stalling's work related to Stravinsky's and to Webern's experiments in the early part of this century. Stravinsky's whole thing was working with blocks of sound and reordering them, which is also very important for me. His *Rite of Spring* is a typical example of this. Throughout the whole piece, basically, all that's happening is boom-boom-boom, these quick changes."[7]

[*jump cut*] John Zorn moved back to New York City in 1974. Settling in the bohemian, low-rent neighborhood of Loisaida on Manhattan's Lower East Side, he discovered a pool of avant-garde talent open to improvisation, including guitarist Eugene Chadbourne, violinist Polly Bradfield, pianist Wayne Horvitz, cellist Tom Cora, vocalist David Moss and sound manipulator Bob Ostertag. Zorn decided to apply what he learned while at Webster, scoring structured improvisation contexts for groups ranging from trios to large ensembles. Each of these game pieces, including *Lacrosse* [1977], *Hockey* [1978], *Pool* [1979], *Archery* [1979], *Jai Alai* [1980] and *Cobra* [1986], follow complex sets of rules and/or systems. For example, run through at random all of the permutations of duets or trios in a 12-ensemble group. [*Archery*, a piece for 12 players, yields over 208 possible combinations of duo and trio.] As the prompter, Zorn flashes cues to the musicians, yet the participants are allowed to influence how the piece develops, cueing and signaling the changes to Zorn.

It's no accident that all his game pieces have combative titles; even the title of *Cobra* does not refer to snakes; it was taken from a war game.[8] Each is a pitched, collective battle of musical reflexes and wits, with Zorn is playing general or coach, marshalling and deploying his troops for the swiftest possible attack. As he explained to Gene Santoro in 1988:

"[The game pieces] are like a sport – it's an exciting thing to see, it's very visual when all the musicians are making signs at each other, trying to get each other's attention. With this system, you can give a downbeat and have no idea what's going to happen – you might be playing with no one or one person or 10 people – or you might give a downbeat and you'll have a pretty clear idea *who* you'll be playing with but no idea of what kind of music is going to happen, or you can give a downbeat and have a clear idea of what's going to happen musically by using different modifiers like fast or loud. My role there was to set up rules so that the people in the band have to make decisions, have to communicate. All I'm concerned with is that people make the most possible decisions in the smallest amount of time, so that everything is jam-packed and the music changes incredibly fast."[9]

According to Zorn, the game scores evolved both from his increasing involvment with structured improvisation as well as his desire to create orchestrations for individuals and musicians who have developed their own personal system of notation; a sort of esperanto for improv:

"When I first started working with improvisers, my first thought was: 'Here are a series of individuals; each has their own personal music.' Each worked on their instruments on their own, to develop a highly personal language that's often unnotable. It's often the kind of music Pierre Boulez would say can't be written down on a staff. So my problem was: how can I involve these musicians in a composition that's valid and stands on its own without being *performed*, and yet inspires these musicians to play their best? And, at the same time, realize the musical vision I have in my head? What I came up with was the decision, which I think was the most important, NEVER TO TALK ABOUT LANGUAGE OR SOUND AT ALL."[10]

In their organization of musical material, Zorn's game pieces began to resemble composer Earle Brown's mobile form of the 1950s, whose graphic scores featured floating sections that could be played in any order, each with lines representing specified pitch relationships. What Zorn did was suspend the time element: There is no specified time in a work like *Cobra*. It's more like the game theory of its namesake, a set of rules and parameters meant to spark relationships between players. Zorn thus has a general idea of how a game piece works, in the same way we know there will be nine innings in a baseball game. Yet what happens in between and how long the game lasts can never be predicted. As an example, *Archery*[11] has a two-page score, one of 208 possible duo-trio combinations, the other of 12 divisis [trading events by cue or free groupings of indeterminate length]. The piece moves through a series of overlapping, ad lib duo-trio combinations until someone calls a divisi and the musical focus shifts until a player cues a return to the duo-trio combinations. Any player can call a divisi or a duo-trio combination. All of the music is improvised, none notated.

As time went on, the players in Zorn's gaming works became became more intuitive, and the works themselves became more sophisticated and more accessible. *Locus Solus*[12] took his game theory and applied it to the foundation of the three-minute rock idiom – rhythm, vocals, electricity and volume – in four different stripped-down groups, including a trio with lyricist Peter Blegvad and turntable player Christian Marclay. The result was one of Zorn's freshest and most satisfying improv rock LPs. On *Cobra*, Zorn drew on a loft full of hot improv talent: harpists Zeena Parkins and Carol Emanuel, guitarists Bill Frisell and Arto Lindsay, drummer Bobby Previte, keyboardists David Weinstein and Horvitz, accordionist Guy Klusevcek and trombonist Jim Staley were among the 14-strong ensemble. *Cobra*'s kaleidoscope of richocheting quotations – Cecil Taylor-like free jazz piano, a muzak take on *The Sound of Music* and Japanese pop – made it one of Zorn's most popular and enduring gaming works.[13] It was also the last, and the *ne plus ultra* of one of the most fertile periods in his growth as a composer. It was to be the furthest he would take his cut-and-paste improvising systems live before he brought them into the hermetic atmosphere of the recording studio.

[*wide angle: montage sequence*] In 1987, when asked by The Brooklyn Academy of Music to do a project for their annual Next Wave Festival, John Zorn decided to pay homage to the film music of Italian composer Ennio Morricone. Zorn had always admired Morricone, a veteran of over 300 film scores and the man behind the innovative music of the subversive, revisionist spaghetti westerns of Sergio Leone, such as *Once Upon A Time In America*, *A Fistful of Dollars* and *The Good, The Bad And The Ugly*. Like Zorn, Morricone was mercurial and impossibly catholic [he would think nothing of scoring a Bible picture after finishing a horror flick or a comedy]. He was also profoundly interested in collage and studio technique, and found immense satisfaction in upending the rules of orchestration. Morricone was among the first commercial film composers to use found sound as soundtrack material [dripping water and buzzing flies were favorites], and among the first to to treat film music as psychologically suggestive material instead of using it to merely amplify the action. Like Carl Stalling, his scores often carried a cheeky or disquieting subtext, playfully cluing in the audience to something not evident in the narrative.

Zorn took these suggestions and ran with them, placing explicit or subliminal elements of the movies in his arrangements of the music. For example, for the war movie *Battle Of Algiers*, Zorn double-times the martial drumming and uses Christian Marclay's turntables to drop staccato gunfire and screams. For the deadpan western *Giu La Testa*, he employs Michihiro Sato's tsugaru shamisen to evoke the preeminent influence of Japanese director Akira Kurosawa over the spaghetti western genre. For *Once Upon The Time In The West*, one of the first soundtracks to really exploit the harmonic possibilities of the electric guitar, Zorn teams up guitarists Robert Quine and Jody Harris in a psychedelic take drenched in gorgeous feedback. In playfully and deftly translating Morricone into his own language, Zorn's take on Morricone eschews imitation and approaches the wit and imagination of the film master himself. "They're still arrangements [Morricone] could have thought of, if he lived here on the Lower East Side and had access to these musicians. That's where the connection to Morricone is really strong: not in the melodies or harmonies, which are there, of course, but it's beyond the black and white music on the page. It's the feeling and the essence of what he tried to accomplish with this musical piece."[14]

With Zorn's BAM show in the autumn of 1987, cheekily entitled "Once Upon A Time In The East Village," his fortunes changed overnight. It was a hip success and netted him a six-album deal with Elektra Nonesuch, who released the project on LP as *The Big Gundown*. For someone who had been toiling away in the performance spaces and lofts of the Lower East Side for close to 14 years and had been critically lampooned for his unorthodox improv work, the change was like suddenly switching from grainy, 16mm art-house stock to cinemascope. More importantly, *The Big Gundown* was Zorn's first chance to exploit the recording studio, a stretch of canvas as big as one of Sergio Leone's unrivalled close-ups to work with. He also had a budget to afford session talent to augment his downtown posse, talent that had previously been beyond his reach, such as harmonica player Toots Thielmans and organist Big John Patton.

Applying his compositional block method to recording in studio, Zorn would place musical ideas on a set of flash cards, shuffle them and sight read the results. Some of these musical ideas were notated, others were simple verbal instructions, like "play cheesy cocktail piano" or "Quote *à la* Lizst's *Hungarian Rhapsody.*" Zorn's follow up project, *Spillane*,[15] had little more than a 60 flashcards in 25-odd minutes and a mood to go on when he assembled his crew in studio. *Spillane* grew out of many of Zorn's obsessions: hardboiled detective fictionparticularly the Mike Hammer novels of Mickey Spillane – sleazy soundtracks, 1950s jazz, film noir, the work of crime photographers like Weegee and the dank underbelly of Gotham City in general. Establishing musical leitmotifs for the characters and plundering the hackneyed vocabulary of film music, Zorn weaves a evocative musical narrative to a movie that doesn't exist on celluloid, in much the same way the Morricone wrote and recorded the score for *Once Upon A Time In The West* before any footage had been shot.

Zorn would go on to try his hands at film scoring for Lower East Side independent filmmakers like Rob Schwebber, Raul Ruiz and Sheila McLaughlin. What these soundtracks[16] revealed was Zorn's skills as a superlative arranger, keenly aware of musicians' styles, strengths and weaknesses. Each soundtrack was radically different from the other, scored and cut to fit the film style and recorded with a different lineup of musicians. Drawing on a wide textural palette – Brazilian percussion, celeste, turntables, harp, oboe, DX7, and his vast knowledge of film and music, Zorn proved he had a head for innovative orchestration in the post-modern rock age. As he explained to Josef Woodard in 1987:

> "Modern orchestration is different from Berlioz, from Rimsky-Korsakov. Their books are still valid, to a certain degree, to people like us and to a large degree, to the people in a very different worldthe world of string quartets, symphonies. For people like us, orchestration is a matter of putting instruments together in intelligent, fresh ways. Instruments now include all those sounds. So you can't teach instrumentation anymore without including all these new electronic devicesthe electric guitar, the electric organ, all these instruments that are available now...You've got to make music that's right for the medium that we're dealing with today."[17]

[*split screen*] By the late 1980s, John Zorn's taste for speed was growing, and his fascination with the aesthetics of violence, rebellion, alienation and pain was drawing him into darker and darker corners of the human psyche. He was increasingly interested in hardcore punk, and was gigging in a death metal trio – Painkiller, with bassist Bill Laswell and drummer Mick Harris – and a grindcore trio, Slan, with drummer Ted Epstein and guitarist Elliott Sharp. Paradoxically, this love of thrash was first heard in two retro jazz hommages, *News For Lulu* and *Spy Vs Spy*. On the former, a 1988 Hat Art trio date with guitarist Bill Frisell and trombonist George Lewis, Zorn paid tribute to hard bop giants like Sonny Clarke, Kenny Dorham and Hank Mobley in the classic, austere trio format of Jimmy Giuffre's Atlantic recordings. Yet rather than paying respect by playing bebop under glass *à la* Wynton Marsalis, Zorn, Frisell and Lewis reinvented the tradition by soloing atop each other. "Bebop is not just running changes the way Sonny Stitt or Bird did; there's no point in copying that, you can take the record out and play it if that's what you want to hear. It's tunes and changes and a certain tradition that needs to be updated to keep it alive."[18] By shoehorning the traditional head-solos-trade fours-head of bebop into the dynamics of a hardcore gig ["Special thanks to Agnostic Front and Hüsker Dü," read the liner notes], Zorn managed to swing tradition without riding the irony rocket.

On *Spy Vs Spy*,[19] Zorn and fellow altoist Tim Berne tear like road runners through the Ornette Coleman book, infusing the raucous R&B element in Coleman's music with chaotic, on the edge collective free improvisation. The rhythm section of this all-out assault on harmolodics – Mark Dresser on bass, and the team of Joey Baron and Michael Vatcher on drums – bristle with punk attitude. Zorn has said that he wanted to make a record that caught the outrage of people, the controversy that Ornette met when he first started playing. "It took a long time for people to get used to it," Zorn told Graham Lock in 1989. "In 1973 someone described a record of [Coleman's] to me as 'one long squeak.' ... There was a real *shock* value to his music when it first came out and I wanted that kind of edge, that shock, to be there on my record, too, like a punch in the face."[20]

This undertow of violence is never far beneath the surface of Naked City, an ersatz sleaze combo that Zorn formed with Fred Frith, Joey Baron, Bill Frisell and Wayne Horvitz in 1988. Like any borough in their home town, Naked City has eight million stories to tell, and they careen from style to style with all the gusto of a grindhouse double-bill: greasy organ numbers, hardcore, bossa nova, N'Awlins R&B, surf rock, country twang, Webern Bagatelles, Japanese pop, grunge, famous movie themes. The parody and precisionnot to mention whiplash temposin Naked City recalls the work of both Spike Jones and Frank Zappa, yet by now Zorn's experience in soundtrack and studio work gave his music an added dimension that his earlier music didn't have: the power to evoke a time and place using older, referential music, then bloodletting the nostalgia with the violent composition and improv techniques of today.

Yet Elektra Nonesuch were reluctant to follow Zorn down into musical equivalent of the Bowery, Alphabet City and Tompkins Square Park all rolled into one. Fully half of Naked City's sets could be given over to blistering hardcore numbers that clocked in under a minute with titles like "Jazz Snob Eat

Shit," sometimes with guest vocals by Yamatsuka Eye of the intense and seminal Japanese hardcore outfit The Boredoms. And Zorn's ideas for cover design leaned toward the shocking: erotic photography by Man Ray, stomach-turning pictures of dismembered bodies. This atrocity exhibition led to disputes over the cover art of Naked City's eponymous debut CD in 1990. Elektra finally conceded to using the sordid, graphic "Corpse With Revolver" by Weegee as the cover image, and left Maruo Suehiro's strangely beautiful, violent Japanese comic book imagery on the insert. After licensing *Film Works* for North American release to fulfill his contract, Zorn left Elektra and looked East to Japan.

John Zorn has long been a follower of Japanese pop music and culture ever since his college days, and has traveled and gigged there widely. He boasts one of the most comprehensive collections of Japanese pop in the States; indeed he is somewhat of an authority on Okinawan pop.[21] His first Japanese forays brought him into contact with tsugaru shamisen player Michihiro Sato, with whom he worked on the 1985 Yukon LP *Ganryu Island* and eventually brought him to New York for *Rodan*, a 1988 Hat Art CD of trios and duets with New York musicians. He has long championed the exilarating, noisy Japanese underground: bands like The Boredoms, Ruins, YBO^2, and brought some to New York when he curated "The Hidden Fortress" at The Kitchen in 1987. According to Zorn, Japan's culture can be rather aloof and insular and their social dynamics complex and mysterious, yet the truly adventurous and stubborn can eventually become accepted. As he told Ben Chant in 1989:

> "Everyone has an attitude that you go there for the first time and you're treated like a king. You have got to realize that's the first time you went and they wanted your total experience. They get the John Zorn experience or the Ned Rothenberg experience and then they chuck you the hell out, and you go back again and you don't get the same treatment and that's not necessarily a bad thing, that's just the way it is...I'm very fortunate to be able to tap into really great players right away because there is an exotic element of someone coming from the States who can speak Japanese, who lives there a lot, who enjoys meeting other musicians and playing...They're willing to try anything. I mean could you imagine me doing a duo concert with Bob Dylan? Forget it. It couldn't happen. But the equivalent of Bob Dylan over there I *have* done a concert with. So it's a very open place. A place where things can happen."[22]

Things are happening for John Zorn. In Japan, he has found a keen receptivity to his work unlike anything in mainstream America, where he has largely been forgotten, yet continues to work outside of the incestuous and fickle culture/media loop that once hailed his work as visionary and cutting edge before bailing out when the vision got a little dark. Zorn's two most recent studio projects, *Elegy* and *Kristallnacht*,[23] are a case in point. The former is an oblique and forbidden homage to French author Jean Genet that is remarkable for its unorthodox arrangement and cast: turntable guerilla David Shea and hardcore guitarist Scummy play alongside new music percussionist William Winant and viola/bass flute player Barbara Chaffee in an impressionistic tone poem that sets Genet's *journal de voleur* to 20th Century chamber music. The latter is a devastating and intensely personal take on the inhuman Nazi pogrom of October 20, 1938, spiking haunting klezmer and Terezin styles with frequencies so loud they are designed to invoke nausea, headaches, and tintinnabulation. Neither project would have stood a chance on an American label. It took Masanori Akashi of Eva Records in Tokyo, who had long been impressed with Zorn's work, to release them.

It was natural, then, that Zorn would choose Tokyo as the home for his new label, Avant. Although formed in 1991 as a label for Naked City, Zorn intends Avant to be home to an important repertory of recordings with complete artistic freedom by composers he respects, composers whose work he feels is undervalued and ignored elsewhere. The catalogue thus far spans an electic range of styles: from John Oswald's plunderphonics to Buckethead's P-Funk-style jazz/metal guitar freak-outs; from Richard Teitelbaum's thought-provoking work with computers and artificial intelligence to David Soldier's rescoring the earthy Carmina Burana for String Quartet; from Peter Garland's new music peyote ceremonies to Keiji Haino's dark prepared guitar atmospheres.

Judging by the Avant catalgoue and the maturoty and power of his more recent solo work, it is clear that John Zorn can no longer to be ignored.[24] At 41 years of age, Zorn has lost none of his power to shock. He is a necessary irritant to the musical process, the proverbial fly in the ointment. His sharp sense of humor and love of mischief takes the piss out of uptight new and experimental music. The parodic surface of his cut-and-paste music belies the meticulous and sophisticated intelligence of the musical architecture underneath. Even when the parody is intentional, as in Naked City, it is heartfelt. Sometime in the future ethnomusicologists will unearth and listen to *Spy Vs Spy* or *Spillane* and realize that there is a real composer underneath the post-modern slapstick. After all, it took Stravinsky half the century.

[*blackout*]

John Zorn: School (Parachute, 1979), Pool (Parachute, 1980), Archery (Parachute, 1981), The Classic Guide To Strategy Volumes 1 and 2 (Lumina, 1983), Locus Solus (Rift, 1984), Ganryu Island (Yukon, 1985), Cobra (Hat ART, 1986), The Big Gundown (Elektra Nonesuch, 1986), Spillane (Elektra Nonesuch, 1987), News For Lulu (Hat Art, 1988), Spy Vs Spy (Elektra Nonesuch, 1988), Film Works 1986-1990 (Eva, 1990), More News For Lulu (Hat Art, 1991), Elegy (Eva, 1992), Kristallnacht (Eva, 1993), Cobra (Knitting Factory Works, 1994), Masada I (DIW, 1994)

Naked City: Naked City (Elektra Nonesuch, 1990), Torture Garden (Toys' Factory, 1990), Leng T'che (Toys' Factory, 1991), Grand Guignol (Avant, 1992), Heretic (Avant, 1993), Radio (Avant, 1994), Absinthe (Avant, 1994)
with **Painkiller**: Guts of A Virgin (Earache, 1991), Buried Secrets (Earache, 1992)
with **Sonny Clark Memorial Quartet**: Voodoo (Black Saint, 1987)

Footnotes:

1. Olin Downes, The *New York Times*, March 16, 1924; reprinted in Slonimsky, Nicolas, *The Lexicon Of Musical Invective: Critical Assaults On Composers Since Beethoven's Time*, Seattle: University Of Washington Press, 1953: p.201

2. Howard Mandel, "I Have A Lot Of Little Tricks," in *Ear* Magazine, October 1986: p.17

3. Lumina, 1983

4. Avant, 1994

5. Bill Milkowski, "John Zorn," in *downbeat* Magazine, February 1984: p.45

6. Stalling's music has been collected by producers Greeg Ford and Hal Willner and issued as *The Carl Stalling Project*; Warner Brothers, 1990

7. Milkowski, "John Zorn:" p.45

8. Another of Zorn's obsessions. The jacket of *The Classic Guide To Strategy* depicts schematics of famous war battles; the liner notes to *Cobra* acknowledge gaming masters like John Butterfield who designed war games for Avalon Hill

9. Gene Santoro, "John Zorn: Quick Change Artist Makes Good," in *downbeat* Magazine, April 1988: pp.24

10. Mandel, "I Have A Lot Of Little Tricks:" p.17

11. Parachute, 1982

12. Rift, 1983

13. It has been staged on a regular basis at The Knitting Factory ever since 1986 and was recorded twice: for Hat Art in 1986 and Knitting Factory Works in 1994

14. Santoro, "John Zorn: Quick Change Artist Makes Good:" p.25

15. Elektra Nonesuch, 1988

16. Collected on on *Film Works 1986-1990*; Eva, 1990

17. Josef Woodard, "Zornography," *Option* Magazine, July 1987: pp.32-36

18. Santoro, "John Zorn: Quick Change Artist Makes Good:" p.25

19. Elektra Nonesuch, 1989

20. Graham Lock, "Hard Core Zorn," in *Wire* N61, March 1989: p.32

21. See *After Dinner*, p.242

22. Ben Chant, "Game Plan: In Conversation with John Zorn," in *Coda* Magazine, N221, August 1988: p.25

23. Eva; 1992 and 1993, respectively

24. Even Naked City's latest release, *Absinthe* [Avant, 1994] is a stunning departure for the group, informed more by electracoustics and the classical contemporary music of Messiaen and Varèse than pop radio

Charles Hayward

"The word Merz denotes essentially the combination of all conceivable materials for artistic purposes, and technically the principle of equal evaluation of the individual materials. Merzmalerei makes use of not only paint and canvas, brush and palette, but of all materials perceptible to the eye...Moreover, it is unimportant whether or not the material used was already formed for some purpose or another. A perambulator wheel, wire-netting, string and cotton wool are factors having equal rights with paint."

Kurt Schwitters, "Die Merzmalerei"[1]

Just a stone's throw from the center of the world, Charles Hayward's flat lies the aquatic shadow of the River Thames, on the third floor of a block of apartments bathed in the soft hum of electrical power plants that dot the South London community of Deptford Creek.[2] No matter how you look at it, the ebb and flow of the meandering giant has an undeniable pull on the quintessentially British drummer, once the tricky timekeeper and propulsive force behind This Heat and leader of now-defunct Camberwell Now. The massive West India Docks lie just across the river; one of the most famous trading ships of the last century, the Cutty Sark, is in drydock just down Creekside Road; and the National Maritime

Museum, Royal Naval College, Royal Observatory, and the prime meridian are all about half a mile down the road at Greenwich.

Hayward's life-long fascination with water can be heard rippling throughout his 30-odd years of percussion and kit work, from This Heat's call for "A New Kind Of Water" through the retrograde sea shanties of the Camberwell Now's debut to the liquid drones of his stunning solo composition "Thames Water Authority." "I have this big thing with water, yes," Charles Hayward says as the teapot whistles furiously, signaling tea time on a brisk sunny June afternoon in Deptford Creek. "Water has always been a big source of connection between people. The first Camberwell Now effort was called *Meridians*. That was all about the sea, sailing, empire, people diving for pearls and getting very little recompense while the pearls ended up around the neck of this very rich woman in the west. When you look at it, the boat itself is a very small political microcosm. Plus three-quarters of us are water—it's a big, big reality."

Hayward waded in the deep political realities of water while recording "Thames Water Authority" at Silent Music studios down by the Thames in July of 1989. "When I wrote 'Thames Water Authority,' Thames Water and all the other water boards in England were being sold off into private hands," Hayward explains. "Down in Castleford in Devon, all this aluminum was somehow dumped into the water supply, and people were turning yellow and developing memory problems; children were being born deformed. If water is privatized and run by companies, there's bound to be cost-cutting exercises, and in the future water is going to be very expensive. Water is a very political thing." Going out every ten minutes or so during the sessions to stare at the Thames, Hayward recorded an electricity power plant down by the shore, capturing the drone of the electricity being generated, the sussurus of the river, and the clatter and shriek of hovering birds. The resulting atmospheric work—heard on his 1990 tribute to Mark Rothko, *Skew-whiff*[3] – represents the pinnacle of years Hayward has spent honing two of his most powerful musical tools: the drum and the drone.

"There's ways of suspending disbelief, of getting the audience in, that if you can bring them into the music will make lots of other things possible," Hayward says, adjusting his lanky frame into a comfy chair and precariously perching his teacup on the arm. "One is strongly played rhythm. Not necessarily quartz rhythm, immaculate tempo, but this idea of always knowing where you are in this sort of cycle, and the other thing is the drone. You can really hook people on a drone. You can listen to some band who are completely all over the place, and if they didn't have a great drummer at the center, then it would be a load of noise, and it wouldn't sustain people's interest. But if this band has a really good drummer, who's making all the events quiver and dance on this pulse, then people get into it, even if it's incredible noise. You can take these things that work in an orthodox way and make them work in an unorthodox way. To try and speak to people."

Charles Hayward always felt he was musically inclined to speak to people. His father had turned him on at an early age to the sublime phrasing of Ella Fitzgerald and the orchestral genius of Duke Ellington, but it really wasn't until he was 12 years old that he discovered his mother tongue. Listening to the radio under the bed when he should have been asleep, Hayward heard The Who sing "Anyway Anyhow Anywhere." "There's certain things in my life that were switches, and hearing The Who playing 'Anyway Anyhow Anywhere' was a bloody big switch," says Hayward. "It opened my head right up. Within a year I was into Albert Ayler and Archie Shepp."

Spurred on by Keith Moon's gonzo pyrotechnics and Ayler's monster sense of swing, Hayward taught himself drums for a year and a half before his father eventually intervened. "Great bloke, my Dad. 'You're just bashing away at that,' he said. 'I'm going to get you some lessons.' So he did. So I did lessons for a year and half, then taught myself for another three years. Then I went to see Ella Fitzgerald with my Dad when I was about 15, and at the time Ella's drummer was Ed Thigpen. I sat behind Ed Thigpen in the choir seats at the Royal Victoria Hall. I thought he was the bees' knees. I went to see him backstage after, and he was a real gent. He invited me to this drum clinic he was holding the next night, and he told me he was going to see Max Abrams, his teacher. His *teacher*? Ed Thigpen had to see a *teacher* to get his left hand sorted out?"

Abrams' rhythmic wisdom proved to be pricey, and Hayward only took three sessions with him. "But they sorted me right out. At the time I thought he was a right crusty old bastard, but there are things he'd taught me that I'd forgot, and even after all that, they come back." With one eye on technique and the other on style Hayward studied Sly Dunbar, Christian Vander, Han Bennink, and Ringo Starr as closely as he did Ed Thigpen Hayward gigged through an odd assortment of middling to obscure British pop groups, most notably The Amazing Band, Daevid Allen's Gong, and Phil Manzanera's Quiet Sun.

By placing ads in the *Melody Maker*, Hayward happened to meet Liverpudlian guitarist Charles Bullen in early 1973, and the two hit it off immediately, gigging in a succession of groups with names like Radar Favourites, Dolphin Logic and Friendly Rifles. Three years later, after a failed attempt to recast Quiet Sun with bassist Bill MacCormick, the trio of Hayward, Bullen, and Gareth Williams started recording, and within three weeks, on Friday the 13th of February, This Heat were doing their first gig.

There were a few problems, though. "Gareth couldn't play a note, and we only had two songs, both written by me," recalls Hayward. "I sang one and the three of us sang the other one. Gareth had to do something, so he played organ in a sort of Jackson Pollock style." Hayward breaks into a smile and chuckles at the memory. "Gareth is fantastic, he has this really strange, amazing energy. We would have very strict compositions, but with someone who couldn't play a note, a lot of the composition would be areas of sound, or clusters of notes. Meanwhile, I was always interested in writing songs, and Charles was always interested in recording techniques, miking rooms, and was quite happy with the results you could get from a cassette machine."

Besides a beautiful old Ludwig drum kit, a bag of kazoos, ocarinas, and whistles people had passed on to him, and a few simple laptop keyboards, Hayward's basic repertoire of instruments now included the tool that would define This Heat's aesthetic approach and revolutionize their sound – a portable cassette recorder. "It was a particularly hot summer in July of 1976, and I woke up one morning and I thought what if I placed a piece of tin foil over the erase head of my cassette machine? It *won't erase*, that's what. It means I could superimpose sounds. So I went to a park and I recorded 45 minutes of the park. And I stuck this tin foil over the erase head, and walked around for the rest of the morning, just recording the summer.

"Then we went to rehearsal, at that time we were rehearsing at my parents' house. It was extremely hot, and we had to play very quiet, because we had the windows wide open. I played the cassette I had made this morning, and we came up with this whole piece. Because we were living our lives like this all the time, the accidents weren't considered accidents, they were just all part of what we were doing. So we built up this aesthetic, which was specifically recorded sound, songs of mine I kept bringing to the group, and the bomb, which was a big big shadow over our heads. We really had this thing about Armageddon, and because of that our pieces became more and more lyrical. The music changed from being sort of 20th century avant garde towards being some sort of a recreation of a nonexistent folk music. Or something."

Presided over by a series of hip engineers like David Cunningham, Adam Kidron, and Anthony Moore, This Heat spent two years recording and honing their debut LP of this "non-existent folk music" at Cold Storage, a reconverted deep freeze in Brixton. Opening with 48 seconds of inaudible frequencies and closing with a locked groove, *This Heat*[4] is a brilliant collage of improvised songs shattered by recorded snippets of the playground and the factory; its stark beauty and hypnotic grooves sound refreshingly shocking 15 years later. Its drones, particularly those of the album's stunning exercise in dub, "24 Track Loop," betray the work of Mario Boyer Diekuuroh, a Ghanian percussionist, xylophonist, *griot*, and delayed pioneer to London who was a regular guest at This Heat gigs and whose influence was immense.[5]

In his review of *This Heat* published in the May 1979 issue of *Sound International*, Chris Cutler quoted Edgar Varèse in his analysis of the band's aesthetic approach: "The music of the future lies in the procession of organized sounds, for it is those which are the sounds of human experience." This prescient observation was one explored even further on This Heat's follow-up, *Deceit*[7] Here the full-blown manipulation and treatment of the topology of everyday sounds captured on magnetic tape goes beyond *musique concrète* and suggests an eerie parallel in the world of modern art: that of German dada artist Kurt Schwitters. Just as Schwitters discarded nothing, collaging bus tickets, cancelled stamps, cigar packages, burlap, netting, gauze, and bits of newspaper into his *Merzmalerei* ["Art paintings"], This Heat's "composed" their works from found sonic materials using studio treatments such as filtering, varispeed tape playback, gating, compression, and dynamic inversion. Even *Deceit*'s cover invokes Schwitters: a horrifying collage of Cold War atomic bomb paraphernalia and song lyrics, projected onto a screaming face.

Ultimately, the trio found their creative process to be a consuming and exhausting one. "You've got to understand it wasn't like going to rehearsal where there's a score, sheets of paper, three or four staves with lines of music, and a few instructions or suggestions," Hayward stresses. "This Heat was much more like a process of living. It was a very extreme experience. It involved getting up in the morning, eating a bowl of porridge, cycling to Brixton, rehearsing eight or nine hours a day, getting back on the bicycle, coming back here and cooking some food, listening to what we'd done that day, and going to sleep. Waking up, and doing it all over again. Now I've got a little boy, and I don't know whether I could sustain the same level of energy in the same way. At the time, it was a completely extreme way of living."

After This Heat imploded and went their separate ways – Williams to India to study dance and Bullen to become an engineer at Cold Storage – Hayward went through his first heavy drone period. "If you have drones, or very simple chords, drums soak up that harmonic information, and they seem to imply much more melody," he says excitedly. "It's like you're lighting a stage set. If you take the drums as the object and the chords as your lighting, then you can sound these harmonic shadows and things off the drum kit. That's interesting for me as a drummer, but it's also very interesting for me as a musician in terms of communicating with people, because it meant a lot of the work is done by the audience. I'm still interested in this, giving as little information as possible that implies a larger amount of information. Not only can you have multiple readings of it, you can involve the audience creatively. There will be phenomena that exist so strongly in an audience that's it's a unifying factor, even though it's a mystery, even though it's not actually there. Yet everyone's heard it – sort of."

The key that enabled Hayward to unlock the tumblers of this collective unconscious and open the door to a new compositional process was the tape switchboard. Built by Steve Rickard [This Heat's sound engineer] in the sampling stone age of the early 1980s, it consisted of four varispeed tape decks, the eight discrete outputs of which were fed into a stereo mixer. The crude piano keys for each channel allowed the operator to tap into – yet not start nor stop – the cassette tapes, which were stacked with everything from voice loops, sustained chords, a Sunday afternoon in Hyde Park, or old This Heat jams.[8]

"The tape switchboard was based on this idea that Steve and I had, which was a way of taking some elements of the everyday and being able to assimilate them with things that weren't to do with being in a room with electric guitars and drums. It was a way of making the everyday more symphonic." The tape switchboard soon became the heart of Hayward's new trio, The Camberwell Now, and its accidental alchemy is heard throughout their second and final LP, *The Ghost Trade*.[9] A series of spliced voices in "Speculative Fiction" utter nonsense phrases like "used-needle data litters endless corridors," while splinters of feedback play havoc with the time of "Sitcom" as Rickard plays the switchboard like Glenn Gould tackling a Bach fugue. Bassist/guitarist Trefor Goronwy's discreet funk and Hayward's airtight drumming may be way up in the mix, yet *The Ghost Trade* has no bottom end in the conventional sense, and the palpable feeling of dislocation is matched only by late Joy Division records. It is also a deeply downbeat work – it reeks of boiled cabbage, industrial decay and rising damp, warmed only by the flickering of old tube TV sets. "We are only building on thin air," Hayward laments near the end of the title cut.

The Ghost Trade profits from one of the recurring motifs of Hayward's music – the alienness of words, and the subsequent bankruptcy of emotional communication in the age of the fax and cellular phone. Its harrowing cover art – tangled, disembodied talking heads on either side of the TV screen – underscores the music as a powerful and pointed metaphor for communication breakdown. Hayward has always treated the spoken word as glyphs, random constructions of phonetics; a jumble of meanings in search of a syntax. Witness This Heat's lyrical catalogue, which includes elementary latin conjugation ["Amo amas amat" from "Triumph of The Will,"] dada [the "rhubarb rhubarb rhubarb" of "Makeshift Swahili"] and lyrics lifted from a history book ["Independence"].[10]

"I'm very interested in lyrics, because lyrics deal in a very codified world of 'the chair is a chair,' and music is this world that is completely abstract and imaginative," says Hayward. "You can make the two relate, or give one set of meanings to one world and the other set of meanings to the other. Then you're really multiplying the two worlds, and all the music goes on inside the listener's head. As far as I'm concerned, everything else is crap and irrelevant. Whether it's politically right-on in the way it was made or using new techniques or old techniques or whether it was made by some billionaire pop star who has a completely dissolute lifestyle doesn't matter to me. What matters to me is what goes in my ears and what it does to my imaginative world.

"So the lyric thing relates to all these other elements because it poses a problem. Drum rhythm has its own inevitable movement forward, and you've got this other set of lyrics about how nobody sort of talks to each other, really, we're all sort of talking makeshift swahili, and stuff like this. So we're trying to communicate on a physiological level, and we're communicating on a verbal level, but what we're communicating on a verbal level isthis isn't working. This has been a big attraction to me: you have this attempt that admits its own failure on a different sort of level."

After The Camberwell Now dissolved, Hayward entered the studio to record what he thought would be a simple, stark album laced with lots of silence. Instead, a whole album of songs, *Survive The Gesture,*[11] poured out. Not just songs with quirky shifts in time and upside-down arrangements, but verse-and-chorus *tunes* like "This Misunderstanding," "Australia," and "You and Me," are among the warmest and emotionally straight-forward music Hayward has written. He puts the sudden case of reckoning down to the intense upheaval that then marked his life. Camberwell had split, two of his friends had committed suicide as he began recording, another friend was hooked on heroin, and his wife Lesley was pregnant and getting bigger and bigger. "I'm very, very proud of that record," he says. "It's not as wild as This Heat, it's not as conceptually tight as some of the Camberwell Now, but it's got this quality I really like about it. Everything was up in the air at that time. In a way it's my favorite record."

Yet Hayward was still looking for a way to fuse verse and chorus, automatic writing and improvisation. He was having fantastic arguments about the place of lyrics in music with Heiner Goebbels as they flew across the Atlantic, bringing Goebbels' *Der Mann Im Farhstül* to New Music America in 1989.[12] Yet unknown to Goebbels, Hayward had an ace up his sleeve. In his head he called them "English Raps." "I was sick and tired of hearing American speech rhythms and stuff," he says. "I had always disliked the spoken word in music. But I had adopted a strong position, and the minute I adopt a strong position, the thing to do is to defy it. So I decided to make a record with the spoken word on it. I also have a big love for Mark Rothko, and I wanted to let people know that this guy existed. Some areas of my audience probably didn't know he existed, and I can use his world as a meditation for music. So I posed this record to Sub Rosa, and they said fine, lovely, let's do it. "And I did it very quickly. It's very improvised. I would go in with the words and the rhythms and the backing would evolve from that, or I would go in with a pile of cassette tapes from 1971 up to two months ago, lay down a drum track and try to build up these Rothkoesque ideas – you know, you focus on one place, and there's really another place behind it. After awhile, you find you're really listening to something else. It's like wandering around in sound."

While hiphop beats introduce *Skew-whiff – A Tribute to Mark Rothko*, Hayward's "rhymes" are sheared of their obligatory rhythmical thrust, thus being free to act as sonic ciphers for a deeper reading of the shifting planes of sound and the slippery time of the piece. The sideways orchestrations of "The actor merges with the crowd" are built as the lyric says: *Every move goes down like magnetic tape/to be played back to us at some later date*. The prismatic, fractured voices raised and lowered in pitch against the drums in "Cold blue sun" recall the jazz swing and playful, freeform vocalisms that Robert Wyatt sung with Soft Machine. Elsewhere, Rothko's clarity and deep evocative power are invoked in the unfurling metallic drones of "Lopside" and the elliptical pools and currents of "Thames Water Authority."

Hayward's latest project actually came as quite a shock; the drummer was unprepared for the force of the muse that hit him when the smart bombs of the prime time Gulf War riveted the world to their TV screens just under a year ago. "I was doing the washing up, Lesley and Lewis were late, and I was worried," he recalls. "I opened the door and a really ambiguous moment happened. Train went past on the railway, man was shouting at his girlfriend, girlfriend was shouting at her dog, baby was crying. All presented to me as this little sliver of sound by the door. It was like: what's going on? So I had this notion for a detective story, I phoned up Sub Rosa, and said, I have this idea. Then the [Gulf] War happened. I phoned them up and said, forget the detective story, put that on the back burner. The war's happening. Let's make a war record."

Fueled by the Gulf War, Hayward first took his ideas in January of 1991 to Club Integral, a low-key, itinerant London performance space with a wide-open booking policy. One fierce, improvised solo gig later, he had himself a record. "It *is* the most extreme record I've ever made," he confesses of *Switch On War*,[13] which was recorded in a morgue and is stamped with the maxim "Overload sometimes enhances." Juxtaposing the CNN logo with a quote from Donne ["They also serve who only sit and wait"] on its jacket, *Switch On War* plunders military buzzphrases and wartime argot as the anguished lyrics for a tableaux of uncompromising and brutal noise that rivals the work of Merzbow in its morbid fascination and intensity.

"It was recorded in what used to be a coroner's court, with tiled walls and very high vaulted ceilings," Hayward explains. "Completely unusable acoustically, unless you really design the music for it. So I designed this piece, with huge slabs of chords. It's a very extreme record. People will listen to it very very rarely. I will probably listen to it very rarely. It has to be listened to extremely loud."

Apart from plotting his detective yarn, Hayward has been sitting behind the traps recently for Fred Frith's Keep The Dog on their acclaimed tours of Europe.[14] He is currently adapting the poetry of Canadian author Michael Ondaatje for a South London theater troupe with ex-Pinski Zoo bassist Nick Doyne-Ditmas;[15] and working with bassist Bill Gilonis, vocalist Catherine Jauniaux and cellist Tom Cora in a quirky pop ensemble called The Hat Shoes. That is, when he's not arguing with the Heiner Goebbelses of the world about the current state of pop music. "You know, it's a weird old scene," he says, fired up as the afternoon draws to a close. "It's like we've lost the physiological element of music. Especially if you watch hiphop stuff. You see Betty Boop, Masai warriors, and a high speed aeroplane, assembled together at random. All we have left is the cultural iconography. If you like these shoes, this sort of coat, and you wear lots of gold, then you will listen to *this* kind of music. If on the other hand you think of yourself as a far more cultured person who listens to Bartók and the like, then you will wear *these* kinds of clothes. We've all been reduced to signs. Well, there's too many signs, too much music, too much information, and post-modernism is only window-shopping. It's the demonstration of a culture that's totally bankrupt. It's serving the function of rapid eye movement, it's cultural dreamstate, and it's high time we get rid of a load of it."

Charles Hayward: Survive The Gesture (Ink, 1987) Skew-whiff (Sub Rosa, 1990), Switch On War (Sub Rosa, 1991), with **This Heat**: This Heat (Piano, 1979), Health and Efficiency EP (Piano/Rough Trade, 1980), Deceit (Piano/Rough Trade, 1981), Repeat (These, 1993), with **The Camberwell Now**: Meridians (Duplicate, 1985), The Ghost Trade (RecRec, 1986), Greenfingers EP (RecRec, 1987), with **The Hat Shoes**: Differently Desperate (RecRec, 1993), with **Nick Doyne-Ditmas**: My Secret Alphabet (Sub Rosa, 1994), with **Quiet Sun**: Mainstream (Island, 1975)

Footnotes:
1. In *Der Sturm*, Vol.10 N4, July 1919; reprinted in John Elderfield, *Kurt Schwitters*, Thames & Hudson: London, 1985: pp.50-51, 2. An earlier version of this chapter was originally published as "A New Kind Of Water," the author, in *Option* Magazine N42, January 1992: pp.32-35
3. Sub Rosa, 1990, 4. Piano, 1979, 5. Diekuuroh's presence can also be felt strongly throughout the 12" EP *Health and Efficiency* [Piano/Rough Trade, 1980] and the three pieces on the posthumous studio release *Repeat* [These, 1993], 6. Translated by Alessandro Achilli and reprinted in "This Heat: Materiali," in *Musiche* N13, Estate/Inverno 1992: pp.46-51, 7. Piano/Rough Trade, 1981
8. For a detailed description, see Rickard's "The Tape Switchboard," in The *Ré Records Quarterly* Vol.2 N2, 1987: pp.45-47, 9. Rec Rec, 1986, 10. All from *Deceit*, 11. Ink, 1987, 12 See *Heiner Goebbels*, p.57 13. Sub Rosa, 1991, 14. See *Fred Frith*, p.36 15. The results can be heard on *My Secret Alphabet*; Sub Rosa, 1994

Roberto Musci & Giovanni Venosta

The decision to use [found] voices arose from a disenchantment with conventional song formats and from an excitement generated both by the intrinsic qualities of the voices and by the peculiar new meanings that resulted from placing them in unfamiliar musical contexts.

Brian Eno and David Byrne[1]

Algerian Muslims chant the Koran over Frippertronics. A New Orleans preacher fires up his congregation with fire and brimstone ["He's so high you can't get over him, he's so wide you can't get around him, and he's so low you can't get under him!"] over timbales and congas. An exorcist rids a New York tenement resident of evil spirits ["She was intended by God to be a virtuous woman. You have no right there. Out, Jezebel! Out in the name of Jesus!"]. An agitated caller ["I'm sorry, I committed a sin, I made a mistake, and I ask my spiritual mother for forgiveness; please forgive me, and he said 'Mea culpa!'"] and an unctuous radio host are stuck in time over a dusty tribal drum pattern and droning bass. And a Lebanese mountain singer soars atop Busta Jones' bass in a loping, Material-style white funk workout.

While the appropriation and manipulation of found ethnic musical sources and the grafting of radio broadcasts onto studio funk grooves seems a bit old hat and even quaint by today's standards,[2] *My Life In The Bush Of Ghosts*[3] was a true oddity in 1981. A collaboration between Talking Heads vocalist David Byrne and producer Brian Eno, *My Life In The Bush Of Ghosts* came near the tail end of Eno's work with the acclaimed New York post-punk quartet, presaging the breathtaking release *Remain In Light*[4] the year before. The recording techniques used on that LP – extended jam sessions produced mesmerizing, elliptical African grooves that were laid them as musical beds; lyrics were written and recorded later – were drawn from *Bush Of Ghosts*, where new music was created for recordings of obscure folk artists from other countries, like Lebanon's Dunya Yusin and Egypt's Samira Tewfik, as well as bizarre broadcast ephemera they had both been taping off the air onto cassettes.

Of course, *My Life In The Bush Of Ghosts* did nothing new; Byrne and Eno were merely the latest armchair ethnomusicologists to juxtapose the familiar with the alien, stitching umbrellas to sewing machines. The German progressive rock group Can, who gleefully let exotic world music rhythms, melodies and tonalities percolate through their psychedelic jams as early as the late 1960s [bassist Holger Czukay was a longtime shortwave buff] even suggested a tongue-in-cheek term for the concept: ethnological forgery. Until Can, this musical jet-setting was rare in the pop musician. Yet progressive rock ensembles had been doing this sort of fakery since the 1960s, and classical composers since the turn of the century, when Bela Bartók recorded wax phonograph discs of Hungarian, Romanian, Turkish, and Slovak folk music and wove their earthy purity into the pungent writing of works like *Bluebeard's Castle* [1918] and *The Miraculous Mandarin* [1926].

What's important to remember about *My Life In The Bush Of Ghosts*, however, was that it was released a full five years before the levee broke wide open with Paul Simon's runaway hit LP *Graceland*,[5] and the "world beat" boom began. As Simon spread the word about Johannesburg and the township jive of Soweto, interest in other traditional ethnic and pop music from other cultures grew chic. David Byrne started a label, Luaka Bop, devoted to Brazilian, Cuban and Asian music; Peter Gabriel, who had been recording with musicians like Senegalese pop sensation Youssou N'Dour and Pakistani Qawwali singer Nusrat Fateh Ali Khan for several years, and built a label and recording studio, RealWorld, devoted to multikulti without borders. Yet the reason *My Life In The Bush Of Ghosts* has come to be one of the most influential albums in the Eno and Byrne canons has to do with its use of source material: The sources are used as chance sound, rife with historical and psychological suggestion, not just a novelty vocal on a skewed funk bed. [Naming the record after Nigerian author Amos Tutuola's famous fable of African magic and culture shock was a hint at the methodology at work.[6]] There was an eerie congruence to the musics Byrne and Eno mixed together, musics separated by gulfs of geography and time, a synchronicity that demanded a new way of listening to music.

Enter Roberto Musci & Giovanni Venosta, two Italian ethnomusicologists who have been musically stamping their way through dozens of passports for over 10 years. Choosing a sound source – say, the pitch of an Ethiopian cow-seller, a pygmy mushroom gathering chant or a Burundi storyteller the same way one would choose a 'cello, clarinet or fretless bass – Musci and Venosta build up works from field recordings, juxtaposing synthesized and natural sound in much the same way Ennio Morricone built up soundtracks from buzzing flies. If Eno and Byrne's work was the tip of the iceberg, the real beauty and elegance of Musci and Venosta's music is revealed beneath its playful surface: theirs is a true hybrid that transcends the mere mosaic and seizes on the potential of recorded sound as an overwhelmingly charged material, its timbre and evocative power outstripping the resonance of traditional acoustic instruments.

Three examples: In "Technowaltz," from the Grammy-nominated *Water Messages on Desert Sands*,[7] percussive tree trunks are rhythmically and electronically treated to form a loop beneath a waltz piano figure; samples of Ethiopian male chorus and a Mongolian Tuvan singer engage in a call-and-response celebration. In between the two a British voice gently reminds us that "this is a blank formatted diskette." "El Lamento De Los Ayatollah," from *Urban And Tribal Portraits*,[8] is a piano-based minimalist work featuring a french horn singing with taped voices from Bahrain, Tunisia, and Oman. A looped kora and pizzicato and glissandi fragments of the Lutoslawski string quartet sampled and shuffled provide the counterpoint. In "The Umbrella's Angle, 2nd Variation," from *A Noise, A Sound*,[9] a loop of slick American hiphop triggers samples of pygmy women imitating animals and Pakistani pop music.

Both Musci and Venosta are aware of the potential pitfalls of enrolling as popular musicians in Ethnomusicology 101. Despite exposing the music of other cultures to larger and larger audiences, Byrne, Gabriel and Simon have paradoxically come under fire in recent years for shellacking it with Western pop forms and production values: Putting this sort of pop gloss on an indigenous folk form such as Senegalese *mbalax*, goes the argument, is like painting a fiddleback maple violin metallic red white or blue. Yet context is the all-important rub. It *is* possible to judiciously fiddle with a found source and still stay true to its roots. "Our good faith and respect for the cultures in question pays its dues, even if they are somewhat distorted and decontextualized," Venosta says. True, no matter how quixotic Musci and Venosta's folk-tinged, RIO-styled songs get, they always retain the character of their sources: "The Ups & Downs Of A Chewing Gum"[10] draws its circular structure from Korean, Indian and Pygmy ritual song; "The Well-Tempered Inuit"[11] rivals The

Residents' *Eskimo*[12] for its radical yet faithful take on the rhythmic throat singing of the Canadian Inuit. Never stooping to blatant mimicry, their music is closer to Fred Frith's *Gravity*[13] in tone and concept, a meeting of cultures rather than a clash. "No, the real danger in this music lies in the risk that this commercialization of ethnic music will fulfill itself only as passing fad," Musci adds. "A momentary and superficial trend, something not conscious on a cultural level.

Roberto Musci and Giovanni Venosta met in the winter of 1983. Both in their late thirties, the two discovered they shared a passion for ethnic music. A surgeon with a deep knowledge of ethnic music and *musique concrète*, Musci has produced books and cassettes of field recorded ethnic musics, and is a collector of traditional musical instruments from around the world. He broadcasts infrequently at Radio Popolare and gives seminars at University of Milan. A lover of the "minimalist experience," the musically omnivorous Venosta is an ethnomusicologist and pianist who graduated in 1981 with a pianoforte diploma from the Milan Conservatory. Having done soundtracks for numerous documentaries and art installations, Venosta was fascinated by creating music out of parts drawn from a multiplicity of sources. When they met, Musci was working on fusing electronic sounds, acoustics and treated ethnic sources. He called it *The Loa of Music*[14] and intended to put out on his own label, Raw Material, of which he was President, Vice-President, Artistic Director, Administrator, Head of Distribution and rack-jobber. When Musci heard Venosta's *Olympic Signals*,[15] a subversively funny parody of the minimalists, he offered to release it, and a kinship was born.

Where ethnomusicology and field recordings were once the domain of academics and Folkways field operatives armed with Nagras, in the late 20th century the "world music" section of any record store is packed with a cornucopia of ethnic music for enjoyment and easy reference: Algerian *rai*, Nigerian juju, Jewish klezmer, Indian *bhangra*, Celtic reels, Brazilian *forró*, Indonesian jaipongin. This proliferation of available musics is revealed in our intrepid travelers' scrupulously annotated sources, which are extraordinary in their exotic scope: Lullabies from the Solomon Islands, Inuit chants from the Canadian North, sacred Balinesian chants from the magic ceremony of Sanghyang, sung in Ketjak. Rhythms of Mexican copper workers, Armenian duduk, Jews' harp from Kirghiz Republic, Japanese Buddhist chant, and a talking Dogon mask from Burkina Faso. "Tracking down sources is infinitely easier today," says Venosta. "The fast and efficient control which we now have through new digital technologies has also created an explosion of creativity. The quantity outweighs the quality at times, but a greater number of people now have the opportunity to make new music from old."

Musci and Venosta's studio methodology appears to be a yet another subtle variant on the old *musique concrète* saw. "Our composition process does appear to be a repossession and simplification of *musique concrète*, minus the high culture and the abnegation of the composers of that time," says Musci. Yet the duo remain resolutely open to chance in their work. Venosta in particular strongly believes in indeterminacy's credo of honoring thy error as hidden intention. Musically, Venosta is the wild card to Musci's poker face, and his anarchy often changes the course of arranging or recording a piece. "The rule is to avoid having any," says Venosta cheerfully. "Even if our compositions seem to have been rigidly structured with written parts – many are improvised from the samples at the time of recording. *A Noise...A Sound* is not only the title of our second CD, but also a way of composing and hearing music."

"Following our rule that there are no rules, our process is compositional and in fact, rather simplistic and intuitive," Musci elaborates. "Often I prepare some bed – usually an ethnic piece transposed to a guitar – while Giovanni rearranges it and turns it upside down." Musci laughs. "But it's not a rule of thumb, since at times, the opposite occurs. The ethnic sources are surgically sectioned off, sampled, looped and filtered through effects. Often we also use the pure sound source to be used as a solo." Musci is an associate at Milan's FX Recording Studio, where he has access to sophisticated digital technology. FX is also where Marco "Bill" Vecchi – Musci and Venosta's silent partner and the man whom Musci calls the "Grand Vizier of digital mixing" – works. "In this process of composition, improvisation has a great importance just as much as a harmonic and melodic structures have great importance in music played from ethnic sources. In some tracks my mystical and meditative side predominates while in others, the rhythmic and 'congested' side of Giovanni surfaces. Nevertheless, each piece is always a common project and is signed by both of us."

From the opening cut, which has bass-heavy samples of jaguars and monkeys underpinning a blues harmonica and gospel riff, *A Noise, A Sound* is the most complex and radical example of Musci and Venosta's eccentric, remixed aural world. Elsewhere the metallic clanking of Mexican copper workers, outdoor ambiances of a Japanese market, and deep whalesong are folded into music. Timbre is held in high esteem here, no matter what produces the note – a DX7, Oberheim or Prophet sampling keyboard, classical guitars, horns, spinet, harmonium, or bass clarinet. There is an impish playfulness in the arrangements and hairpin turns the music takes, and delightfully Musci and Venosta do not spare the white musician from being sampled: David Moss and Maurice Ravel are grist for the sampling mill too. A noise, a sound, a music.

Given the degree to which Musci and Venosta are wired to the studio, playing their sonic tapestries live would require dexterities that even the most accomplished DJs are incapable of. "To paraphrase [Frank] Zappa, We're Only In It For The Record!" says Musci, roaring with laughter. "It is unthinkable, especially in Italy, of a group that plays live music like ours. The strength of our music comes from the juxtaposition of the instruments; the real acoustic timbre with the electronic and sampled. To recreate a live concert with the same ambiance we so diligently create in studio would require an enormous effort, an incredible amount of rehearsals and a small fortune. When one depends on machines, you know, the risks are even higher. We also do not have the kind of money to ask musicians who collaborate with us to put their lives on hold to follow us in our projects, and we don't believe it would be any less interesting to rearrange our material for a lesser group. We would miss varying the instrumentation on a whim, which happens quite often on our records between one piece and another." Pause. "Or even in the middle of the same piece!"

Even if they did want to tour, Musci and Venosta would likely face the same stony wall of indifference that earlier Italian progressive/alternative groups like LA 1919 met 10 years ago and Stormy Six nearly two decades ago.[16] Now, as then, there is a paucity of *lire* to fund and promote new music. "A fierce individualism bullies and drives out the few musically valid voices," says Musci. "We could, therefore, talk about making a new musical community in Italy and perhaps in Europe. But then again, we could also talk about hoping for the birth of a non-consumerist society, multi-ethnic and other-utopist." Musci's cynicism has a valid point. Musci and Venosta's music, like much *musique actuelle*, is too young to be codified, and simultaneously rooted in the past and so far ahead of its time that it cannot be easily defined; something that Franco Fabbri, guitarist for Stormy Six, lamented in an 1982 essay entitled "What Kind Of Music?":

"This question has been put to me by hundreds of people, always for different reasons: by fellow train passengers who want to know what I do; by hi-fi dealers anxious to advise on the right type of speakers...by theater managers when I ask to hire their premises for a concert; by a young spectator while I am tuning up my '63 Stratocaster; by civil servants responding to my application for a state grant; by the RAI...when I am engaged as a guitarist and they want to determine how much I should be paid; by frontier guards throughout Europe when I go through customs with my identity card, on which is: 'Profession: Musician.'"[17]

"It has always been difficult for us to analyze any contemporary phenomenon with objectivity and exactitude, be it musical or artistic," says Musci, rather grandiloquently. "Or, on a larger scale, whether its context is historical, political or social. We believe that in order to be able to talk precisely about a particular musical event or musical aesthetics and trends it is absolutely necessary to have a certain temporal and personal detachment. Only future generations will understand if the game pieces of John Zorn,[18] the linguistic and guitaristic [*sic*] research of René Lussier,[19] or our own music, when considered with the music of all the cultures of the world, has any artistic value or is simply fashionably post-modern, and the result of temporal and cultural forces."

"To claim ahead of time that our music or the current artistic milieu in general that we belong in can be considered the classical music of tomorrow seems to us a little conceited," Venosta offers in translation. "We think it would be more fun if our music could be considered as barroom music for the future colonies of earthlings on Mars or dance music in the rainforests of Gabon."

Roberto Musci & Giovanni Venosta: Water Messages On Desert Sands (Recommended, 1987), Urban And Tribal Portraits (Recommended, 1989), A Noise...A Sound (ReR Megacorp, 1993)
Roberto Musci: The Loa Of Music (Raw Material, 1984)
Giovanni Venosta: Olympic Signals (Raw Material, 1984)

Footnotes:
1. 1981 Sire press release for *My Life In The Bush Of Ghosts*
2. Indeed it was to become a staple in most techno and industrial dance music
3. Sire, 1981
4. Sire, 1980
5. Warner Brothers, 1986
6. See *Tom Zé*, p.251
7. Recommended, 1987
8. Recommended, 1988
9. ReR Megacorp, 1992
10. From *Urban & Tribal Portraits*
11. From *A Noise, A Sound*
12. See *The Residents*, p.222
13. See *Fred Frith*, p.30
14. Raw Material, 1984
15. Raw Material, 1984,
16. See *Rock In Opposition*, p.12
17. In *Popular Music* Volume 2, 1982
18. See *John Zorn*, p.146
19. See *René Lussier*, p.176

Vive Le Québec Libre

Great Canadian artists have always been loners and visionaries.[1] Deeply influenced by the sheer geographical expanse of their country, they have felt oddly at home in the wilderness, be it a real one with tundra or windswept prairie, or a barren media landscape coded with the token fragments of a solitary population's culture. Media prophets like Marshall McLuhan, pianists like Glenn Gould, poets like Irving Layton, painters like A.Y. Jackson, filmmakers like Atom Egoyan, even metal hackers like Voivod [who spawned an inverted cyberpunk sound in an aluminum factory town sprouting from the frozen ground in the middle of the Canadian Shield] none can escape the pull of a nation whose past was essentially defined by radio and a railroad.

Yet Québec is different. Where electroacoustics dominate new music in Vancouver on Canada's west coast and artistic tendencies in Upper Canada have been shaped by the trendy media philosophies of McLuhan, the conceptual art of Michael Snow[2] and the weekly improvised total music meetings of the Canadian Creative Music Collective [CCMC] at Toronto's Music Gallery, Québec has long been isolated musically. This province of seven million people [roughly one-quarter of the country's population], mainly francophone, is a linguistic and cultural microcosm within Canada. Because of this, Québec has evolved a unique music: loose, quixotic and vernacular, it's a style rooted in folklore, contemporary music, the avant garde and progressive rock. This thirst for new sounds is seen in bands like Fat, a young Montréal power trio who have traveled the globe, remixing Czechoslovakian heavy metal bands and jamming with Berber pop musicians in Morocco. Québec is a case study of how a small network of dedicated musicians, promoters, critics and fans can foster the growth of a new musical genre: A distinct music for a distinct society.

Québec's stubborn musical distinctness can be traced back to a single tract: Réfus Global, perhaps the most vital art manifesto to ever emerge from Canada. In 1948, painter Paul-Emile Borduas and composer Pierre Mercure exhorted artists to renounce Québec's oppressively conservative and religious society. A charter member of Fluxus, Mercure organized The Semaine Internationale de Musique Actuelle in Montréal in 1961, inviting John Cage, Yoko Ono, Edgar Varèse, Merce Cunningham and Milton Babbitt. It was at this landmark event that the term *musique actuelle* meaning "new music" or "music of the moment" was coined. As Cage performed *Atlas Eclipticalis* on August 3, 1961, it was clear that Mercure's musical vision for Québec was light years from the accepted gospel of Pierre Boulez, and that the European hegemony of new music there was coming to an end.

Through The Quiet Revolution during the 1960s, Québecers awoke from their cultural slumber. In 1962, Sun Ra parked his Arkestra at the El Mocambo club in Montréal, exposing Québecers to free jazz. At jazz *boîtes* like The Barrel, one could drink in the heady brew of Sunny Murray and Albert Ayler. In the late 1960s, the province was rocked by the music of two ensembles which began to reclaim aesthetic ground lost to America and Europe: Le Quatuor Jazz Libre du Québec and L'Infonie. The former was a blistering free jazz outfit whose comet-like streak through the underground came to a fiery end in 1970 during the political violence at the height of the October Crisis: The RCMP, suspecting Jazz Libre of collaborating with the insurrectionist Front de Libération du Québec [FLQ] and The Black Panthers, burned down their artists' barn in Ste-Anne-des-Monts. L'Infonie was an "orchestra of the infinite" founded during Expo 67 by two tripping composers, Raoul Duguay and Walter Boudreault. Fueled by hallucinogenics, L'Infonie's notorious multimedia "happenings" were scandalous to some but extraordinarily influential for their potent and prescient blend of jazz, classical and rock structures.

Three decades after the Semaine Internationale de Musique Actuelle, Québec has blazed a trail unparalleled in Canadian new music circles. In 1982, the *musique actuelle* torch was passed to The Festival Internationale de Musique Actuelle de Victoriaville. Founded by Michel Levasseur and modeled after small, intimate European fests like MIMI,[3] FIMAV has built an international reputation as one of the world's best new music festivals, bringing Sun Ra, Evan Parker, Iva Bittovà, After Dinner, John Zorn and Albert Marcœur [to name six at random] every autumn to a sleepy town in Québec's *bois francs*. In North America, all new music roads lead to Victoryville. Back in Montréal, the Société Musique Contemporaine du Québec [SMCQ], formed in 1966 after the tragic death of Pierre Mercure, remains the province's flagship new music ensemble, commissioning works from Québec composers. Le Nouvelle Ensemble Moderne are a peerless young new music chamber group in residence at L'Université de Montréal, and have brought composers Mauricio Kagel and Franco Donatoni to town for thought-provoking symposia.[4] Electroacoustic music also flourishes here; Montreal is home to think tanks like The Canadian Electroacoustic Center and L'Association pour la creation et la recherche electroacoustiques du Quebec [ACREQ], as well as a full-time electroacoustic label, empreintes DIGITALes. New Music America even came to Montreal in 1990.[5]

But it was the seeds planted by Jazz Libre and L'Infonie that would bring *musique actuelle* to full flower during the late 1970s, when guitarist René Lussier of Les Granules began fusing Québecois folk music with progressive rock. The music of Lussier and his contemporaries – guitarist André Duchesne, saxophonist Joane Hétu, reed player Jean Derome, poet Geneviève Letarte – is that of a generation reared on folklore and prog rock [*passé* everywhere else but still hugely popular in Québec], as well as post-modern lit ['pataphysics, Beckett] and modern art [dada, *art brut*]. It is improvised, grassroots, polystylistic, irreverent, and speaks passionately of their culture and politics.[6] In 1983, eight of these musicians formed Ambiances Magnétiques as a non-profit collective; today they have a catalogue of over 30 releases that are sold worldwide.

In a country as large as Canada, it comes as no surprise that radio – or, as veteran CBC announcer Allan McFee was fond of calling it, "vacuumland" – has played an important part in Canadians' artistic identity as a whole. It is also key to the success of *musique actuelle* in Québec, through programs like *Musique Actuelle* and *Les Chants Magnétiques*. Works like *Muss Muss Hic* by Bruire – an open band headed by broadcaster and percussionist Michel F. Côté – clearly follow in the radio footsteps of Glenn Gould's experimental works for the CBC like *The Idea Of North*: they try to capture the quintessence of being a Canadian through a common, everyday medium.

Ultimately, new music and new arts thrive best where there is a well-developed infrastructure of sympathetic media and government arts funding agencies. Québec is embarrassingly rich in this area, yet the patronage of culture always becomes a hot potato whenever the constitutional wrangling that has occupied Québec's political and cultural agenda on and off since the October Crisis heats up. On the eve of an acrimonious 1995 referendum which could split Canada and finally give the province's *séparatistes* a country of their own, artists are understandably apprehensive. The heady late 1960s freedom of Le Quatuor Jazz Libre du Québec may sound quaint these days, but *musique actuelle* sounds more urgent and liberating than ever.

1. Part of this essay was previously published as "New Music North America 1990: Musique Actuelle Comes to Montreal," the author, *Option* Magazine N37, March 1991: pp.74-80

2. Artist, jazz pianist, filmmaker, composer and holographer, Michael Snow is the Joseph Beuys of Canada. His work was given a major retrospective at the Royal Ontario Museum in 1994. Several excellent books were published in conjunction with the exhibit; *The Michael Snow Project: Music/Sound 1948-1993* [Power Plant/Alfred A. Knopf, 1994] provides a good overview

3. See *Ferdinard Richard*, p.47

4. U de M is also the publisher of the new music journal *Circuit*, and its curriculum is typical of the highly developed music departments at Québec universities

5. What is sorely needed, however, is a club or performance space like The Knitting Factory in New York. And Montréal audiences are notoriously apathetic when it comes to supporting jazz and new music staged at any other time than during yearly festivals. Paradoxically, many *musique actuelle* artists like Justine find more receptive audiences outside the province

6. In this regard it has clear ties with the Recommended/RIO movement in Europe; see *Rock In Opposition*, p.11

Les Granules

To see the World in a Grain of Sand/ And Heaven in a Wild Flower/ Hold
Infinity in the palm of your hand/ And Eternity in an hour

William Blake, Auguries of Innocence, 1863

For William Blake, nothing in the universe was too small to stop and roll
between his fingertips. Centuries later, his bold, unchained spirit and affinity for
the tiny things in life lives on in the music of Montréal musicians René Lussier
and Jean Derome. Les Granules ["The Kernels"], as Lussier and Derome have
nicknamed themselves, excel in playing the sounds of life around us. They
traffic in the music of small change and falling dust, of splintered radio
frequencies and jammed cassettes, of digital splices and hand-cranked
phonographs, stitched together with painstaking care and executed with the
slapstick timing of a Harold Lloyd silent.

"In everyday life, there's a lot happening," says Lussier. "Politics, humor,
strife, learning, love, eating, contemplation, tension, all sorts of things. Music
can also be aggressive, funny, quiet, loud. There's no reason why we shouldn't
touch on all these layers. So in our music there's memories, power chords, funny
rhythms, folk songs. It's like city life." Listening to a Granules record can trigger

long-forgotten, deeply embedded memories. Among their mnemonic fragments one can discover an homage to Alfred Hitchcock, an ode to the belly button, a recipe for blood pudding, a reworking of the traditional "P'tit Pain" [Québec's "national" anthem], a suite dedicated to Steve Lacy, text-driven pieces where the spoken word is used as a thematic and melodic generator, humorous ditties about matters religious, and a satirical transcription of the Canadian unemployment insurance card.[1] "Wine calls for cheese," Jean Derome once wrote of Les Granules' stylistic smorgasbord. "I could never resolve to eat only one food to the exclusion of all the rest and the same is true for musical styles."[2]

Both Lussier and Derome have roots in progressive Québécois folklore ensembles of the 1970s Lussier with Conventum, Derome with Nébu. Since 1978, the duo have forged an intuitive working relationship and a brilliant cut-and-splice compositional method over years spent in Montréal screening rooms, recording soundtracks for over 50 documentaries, films with subjects as diverse as the closing of an iron mine in Schefferville[3] to the bizarre synchronicity of the Pope *and* Michael Jackson visiting Montréal the same week.[4] Onstage or in the studio, Derome and Lussier show a high degree of finely-honed, intuitive interplay, chops and technique in spades, and plenty of vaudevillian tomfoolery. Their intriguing solo projects – such as Derome's music for stage adaptions of Samuel Beckett and Alfred Jarry to Lussier's examination of the musical possibilities of the French language – betray a more sober, though no less zealous, approach to their individual interests.

Derome and Lussier also share a passion for both the absurdity and the seriousness of improvised music. "There's an unwritten pact," Lussier says. "If one of us proposes something, no matter how outrageous it sounds, we will try it before saying no." This blithe musical spirit extends to their choice of instruments, none of which are at the cutting edge of digital technology. In addition to flutes, saxophone, homemade percussion and birdcalls, Derome is a maestro of the "battered synthesizer," while guitarist Lussier believes in the musical possibilities inherent in a boiling kettle, a broken harp, or amplified feet. Live, they play this plethora of instruments [packed into four small suitcases, mind] simultaneously with the aid of tapes; the dexterity of their eight limbs quickly gained them their *other* nickname, *les hommes-orchestres*.[5]

The sleeve of their second album, *Le Retour des Granules Vol.2*,[6] contains a meditation on sand by French writer Jacques Brosse. Indeed, Lussier and Derome can be seen as a living homage to sand, dust, chaff, powder, pollen and crumbs; their official motto is "We may be small, but we infiltrate everywhere." "Jean and I were in studio," Lussier recalls, "and we took to calling incidental bits of music, leftover notes and such, granules. And like kernels or snowflakes, no two granules are exactly alike."

René Lussier

Winter, 1988. Bitter March winds howl outside the Montréal Spectrum on a cold Sunday night while inside, the semi-finals of the Jeu d'Improvisation Musicale are underfoot.[7] The JIM is a wickedly funny spectacle that places improvised music in the context of a hockey game, complete with three periods, a penalty structure, play-by-play, and cheesy organ fills between periods. Each team of four "players" wield instruments instead of sticks, and pass improv ideas back and forth in place of a puck. The audience determines the winner by holding colored flash-cards aloft after the play. Imagine John Zorn's *Cobra*[8] in an ice rink and you'll have some idea of how wonderfully demented all this is.

Tonight, the Reds fight it out with the Blacks to determine who plays the Whites in the series final next week. The referee calls out the first improvisation. "Mixed improvisation. Title: 'Walking on Eggs.' Number of players: one per team. Length: three minutes. Character: with grace." The two teams have 30 seconds to decide how to approach the challenge; a difficult one as the two opposing players must play at the same time. The Blacks' captain, guitarist René Lussier [number 12/8], decides to send out his star player, reedist Jean Derome, out against the Reds' contrabassist Michel Donato. Derome's flute is indeed graceful, and he carefully and amusingly sidesteps Donato, who is clearly having trouble. The referee hears this, and signals a penalty when Donato strays from the theme. After the three minutes are up, the audience holds high a virtual black wave. René Lussier smiles, satisfied. Another point for *l'equipe noir*.

To Lussier, the improvisational music game is a very serious one. "I make my living with improvised music," Lussier explains over coffee, orange juice and a chain of cigarettes the following morning. He surveys the living room of his Plateau duplex with his hand. Besides the disarray of musical instrumentsguitars, a harp, some keyboards and assorted effects devicesthere are plenty of records of every kind of music imaginable and shelves of reel-to-reel tapes marked with cryptic labels like "Grand Bruit." On the wall, gazing serenely down, there is a poster for *Zero de Conduite*, Jean Vigo's gentle, surrealistic 1932 parable about a revolution at a French boys' school. "In last night's game, there were a few people pulling clichés and *cabotinage*[9] in order to win," Lussier continues. "I think they need to be a bit more serious about the game."

Lussier's singular style could hardly be called frivolous. Found somewhere between the cultural straitjacket of the Arpin Report[10] and the cultural eclecticism of the late 20th Century, René Lussier's guitar holds the keys to a music where everyday sound, folklore, free jazz and social protest meet at the crossroads Quebec has dubbed *musique actuelle*. The 36-year-old guitarist, improvisor and composer got his start honing the folkloric traditions of Quebec during the Me decade in Conventum. Yet he was hooked on a progressive musical revolution across the Atlantic in European acts like Henry Cow, Albert Marcœur, Stormy Six, and Faust. An unusual Québécois folk quintet [three guitars, violin and bass], Conventum successfully fused traditional folk structures to progressive rock. Québécois culture during the mid-1970s provided the touchpaper for Conventum's fire; it was a time when French struggle for identity in a largely English-speaking Canada was manifesting itself in both traditional and radical movements.

Conventum only lasted for four years in the late '70s,[11] but folk music is a touchstone to which Lussier still compares his work. "One of the strongest periods in Quebec history, from the '30s to the '50s, might not have been musical in nature, but music played a very important part," he says. "When nationalism and traditional music were everywhere, music was a very *social* thing. People lived further apart then, and when they got together, they played music. Sometimes without any instrumentsthey used their hands, their feet, their bodies." Lussier sets down his coffee and provides an animated little example of a reel. "Now I'm no specialist in folklore, and I love 'free' music, but I always tap my feet when I play. I've even amplified it. I like the quality of electric feet."

After the breakup of Conventum, Lussier participated in numerous improvisational ensembles like Le Grande Urchestre de Montréal for little or no money. He busied himself with film work to pay the rent, and with his sidekick Jean Derome scored many a documentary for the National Film Board of Canada. Lussier's international big break came in 1986, when Michel Levasseur of the Festival International de Musique Actuelle de Victoriaville asked him if he would like to perform a concert with guitar luminary Fred Frith. Lussier had already mailed a cassette of his first solo album, *Fin du Travail [Version 1]*[12] to Frith and was a big fan of Skeleton Crew. "I saw Skeleton Crew when they came to Montréal," remembers Lussier, "Boy, were they loud. I got quite a headache. But I did enjoy them." Enthusiastically, he agreed to play with Fred. The concert showcased some of Frith's most inspired, plugged-in playing in years, with Lussier's electric feet setting the pace for guitarscapes that are by turns ethereal, industrial, traditional, heavy, pristine, and improvisational.[13]

Lussier kept in touch with Frith, and in 1988 Frith invited him and Jean Derome to The Kitchen in New York to partake in a retrospective of Frith's work, from Henry Cow through his solo projects. The sextet – Lussier, Derome, Zeena Parkins, Bob Ostertag, Charles Hayward and Frith – became Keep The Dog, Frith's most fertile ensemble in years; their European tour during the summer of 1991 was an unqualified success. In the beginning, Keep The Dog was fairly straightforward, but Frith soon got bored with playing his greatest hits. With the lineup of talent he had at his disposal, he tinkered with the idea of introducing improvisation into the mix.[14] "I would say that Fred when he works with musicians, he always takes risks," says Lussier. "No risks, no tension, no fun. He liked to introduce improvisation into songs on the spot. So although Fred composed everything, by the end of the tour, a third of the concert would be improvised. Every night we were doing a different concert, every set list was a new composition. In this sense, it became something much more solid than what it was, and it gave more freedom to the band."

Although they weren't the rhythm section, Lussier and Derome were the powerhouse heart of Keep The Dog. They can be seen rehearsing with Frith in *Step Across The Border*, a 1989 "celluloid improvisation" by filmmakers Nicolas Humbert and Werner Penzel. Ostensibly about Frith, *Step Across The Border* encompasses within its technique and content a fresh way of hearing and viewing the world around us, recalling the alien spontaneity of the Hans Richter's dada films of the 1930s and Chris Marker's juxtaposition of hallucinatory images. "It's a film on music, on life, on philosophy, it's not only on Fred," says Lussier. "He's just the *lietmotif*."

For Lussier, the vocabulary and techniques of cinema were the *lietmotif* in unlocking the process of the recording studio. "Movies helped me a lot, particularly in mixing," says Lussier, who has always had a fascination with film music, citing a love for Bernard Hermann, Nino Rota, Ennio Morricone, and the way Woody Allen scores his films. "I liked the idea of superimposing different layers, using straight cuts, crossfades, montage, and using speech and real sounds. Since I started working in cinema, I've used live tapes of found sound in my work. For me, found sound comes from cinema, it doesn't come from Pierre Schaefer or *musique concrète*. But I don't try and go for the easy effect; I want to find a stronger, underlying meaning. In the 1950s, you'd see a guy getting out of a car and walking 20 feet away and what you'd hear would be what was going on in his head, through the music. It was much more suggestive and psychological than today. Today you'll hear his footsteps amplified and the sound of his clothes. With all these effects, there's no space for the listener. Sometimes you don't need to hear the door slamming to know it's shut."

The twin engines of the spoken word and folklore form the chassis for Lussier's masterpiece, 1990's *La Trésor de la Langue*.[15] A painstakingly assembled road movie inspired by the way we talk, *La Trésor* follows Lussier and his sidekick, sound technician Claude Beaugrand, as they drive up Le Chemin du Roy to Québec City, armed with a Nagra and a stack of tapes. The recorded results – everything from a stuttering Anglo negotiating the directions to the National Archives at Université de Laval to some impromptu homespun wisdom in thick French dialects – were later transposed to instruments by Lussier, and reveal just how musical speech can be. Early inspirations for the project included a work by composer André Duchesne on hockey, Hermeto

Pascoal's album *In Grupo* [where the Brazilian composer musically interprets a soccer match], and Zappa's *Man From Utopia*, pieces all that celebrated the sing-song timbres of everyday speech that Lussier wanted to capture.

"There's always something melodic in everyday talk," Lussier says three years later, relaxing in the kitchen of his renovated turn-of-the-century house by the shores of the Richelieu in bucolic Mont-Saint-Hilaire. "So much music around us. In talking, there's very complex rhythms and melodies, often all in the same breath. Sometimes more complex than contemporary music. My original idea was to do a compendium of different accents in French in Quebec. I was listening to one woman's tale, and I didn't understand a word. I was just writing it phonetically. And it was *French*, it wasn't a dialect like Catalan. It was not so far from here. There's some people who have very strong accents. At a point, I decided not to become a monk, I left that to the linguists."

Lussier and Beaugrand certainly had it easier than the first archivists in the 1950s, who ran a long wire and microphone from their running cars [to provide the current for the tape recorder] into storyteller's shacks in the countryside, capturing the legend of Ti-Jean or the Crooked Man for posterity. "At the beginning we were so shy," recalls Lussier. "I didn't have much experience interviewing people, like you do. You've got a purpose, you have a subject, a list of questions. We didn't. Even Claude, who had done a lot of documentaries, didn't have a camera to hide behind. One of the reasons we are asking directions on the record was because we didn't know what to ask at first." The question they wound up asking most – Is it important to speak French in Quebec? – came from songwriter Richard Desjardins. "I met him four years ago, just talking about show business, the music scene in Montréal, the world of producing records, do you know a cheap studio, should I go to the cutting, and things like that," says Lussier. "He called me up and asked me how to produce a record. We talked about life and record production. I told him I wanted to go on the street and ask people a question about language, and he said, 'Well, you just have to ask a simple question. Is it important to speak French, and why?'"

Needless to say, many of the interview subjects responded in the positive. Add to this excerpts from famous speeches by Charles de Gaulle and an broadcast extract from the FLQ Manifesto, and *La Trésor* appears to resonate with nationalistic vibes, at least on the surface, sort of like *Enfin Oui René*[16] set to music. "I was excited about those speeches, probably more about the FLQ than De Gaulle, but my initial idea was not to provoke," Lussier claims. "It was me learning my own history. When I went to get those archives through the CBC or other sources, I was acquiring pieces of my history that I wasn't aware of when they had happened. Some people of course saw it as a nationalistic statement. I didn't consciously write it that way, I see it more as a historical work, while others might say it's a linguistic work, or a musical work. I didn't think it would freak out a lot of the people at the state radio. Some people at Radio Canada really liked it, while others said it's really interesting, but we're gonna have a problem with the FLQ stuff."

This double-edged use of recorded history is part and parcel of *La Trésor*'s study in contradiction: It's an archival document that lives and breathes, an award-winning work[17] that's *souvrainiste* in principle, yet not political in intention. As to whether the province's political climate played any part in the release of the album, Lussier takes the fifth. "Personally, I'm not so interested in nationalistic politics. I think they're a laugh," he says. "In Quebec, we do have some problems we'd like to take care of ourselves. I can understand that. But when they want to build a cultural bureaucracy that will judge if a book, a record, an art work, a play is worthy of being produced or not, that's dangerous. That's going to be a big problem for all of us."

La Trésor and its live show were a project that took up a good three years of Lussier's life, but he believes as a composer that such work shouldn't be hurried. "In new music there's a lot of records that are half-baked," he says firmly. "My idea is that you do a record, you take the time you need to do the best record possible. I work on my records for a long time, and when it's over, it's over. I don't go back to it. That's the reason a project like the one with Chris[18] takes so long. I'm not in a hurry to release a record every six months to prove I'm productive. I'd rather take two, three years to do a record. And when it comes out, it's strong, will age well, and stand on its own."

So no major project is on Lussier's drawing board; rather he is busying himself with studying the daxophone[19] and corresponding with kindred spirit and French progressive rock wit Albert Marcœur about a proposed project that will map out the wine routes of France's Rhone, Bourgogne and Medoc in much the same way Lussier mapped out Quebec's linguistic diaspora for *La Trésor*. He's also mulling over commissioned works, more of which have been pouring in since his works for Lise Daoust and Tim Brady. The former, *Zone Grise*, is a haunting electroacoustic piece for flute and magnetic tape, while the latter, *Roche Noire*, is a whimsical fable about Irish immigration and displaced folklore that samples Brian Mulroney and Ronald Reagan singing "When Irish Eyes Are Smiling." "I'm interested in all sorts of folklore," Lussier says. "Recently Jean and I did a soundtrack on a Newfoundland fishing village, and I played mandolin and acoustic guitar. I was really happy to be able do that. But I also think Bela Bartók is a folkloric composer. Or group like After Dinner, from Japan. I think there's a difference between traditional music and folkloric music. They're certainly not unconnected, but I think folklore is just a way to know what you're made of. It means you're open to touch all those histories."

Jean Derome

For Jean Derome, the way to musical enlightenment is through the stomach. "I like the fact that some people call their compositions *compotes*," he once wrote. "And that to improvise can, in English, be rendered as to *jam*."[20] Derome has long been fond of combining the pleasures of eating and music. The 38-year-old musician wrote the above epistle in 1988 as part of "Matter/Manner," a series of 100 opinions, proverbs, and ruminations that draw such savory comparisons between gastronomy and music appreciation as *Brown bread, white bread/Music is made of noise/and it would be a mistake to mill the flour too fine.*[21] His first solo album, *Confitures de Gagaku*,[22] is an elegant suite based on Japanese court music that depicts the Tao calendar; its title also plays on the double meaning of the word "jam."

"What I like about food is that everybody has to eat," says Derome over baklawa and coffee at a Lebanese *patisserie* on Rue St-Denis, taking a break from busy summer that sees him off to Europe with René Lussier's *La Trésor de la Langue* and Lars Hollmer's Looping Home Orchestra, then back home, touring the Canadian jazz festival circuit with his large ensemble Les Dangereux Zhoms. [If that wasn't enough, by summer's end he hopes to commit his one-man show *Le Magasin de Tissus* to record.] "When you start talking about food, there are some things that if you apply them to music they open a lot of possibilities in the minds of people. Like if something tastes strange to you at first, you can get accustomed to it. People will do that with food, but when it comes to music they say, 'There's a lot of music I like, I don't want to learn anything new; I just want to listen to my old Genesis records.' Yet more and more would become pleasurable to them if they just opened their taste buds. If culture is always presented like a remedy, it will never work."

Listening to Jean Derome talk is like peeling back the layers of an onion. Underneath his calm demeanor lies the heart of a clown, then the soul of a poet, and then the technique of a virtuoso. Since his days of teaching flute and musical theory at CEGEP St-Laurent and Conservatoire du musique de Québec, he has added the hats of improvisor, composer, producer to his menu. Derome is the literary half of Les Granules, the poetry to Lussier's passion. His lyrics, texts, and poems all explore the morphology of words. To Derome, words can be codes, synonyms, antennas, pedal points, tools, raw material for the possibilities of syntax. Indeed, the deft wordplay of "Matter/Manner" recalls the 'pataphysical *jeux des mots* advanced by the French Oulipo group of writers during the 1950s. Its inner logic and playfulness in particular evokes the work of Raymond Queneau, who was fond of elegance and permutation in works like his landmark 1949 *Exercises de Style*.

Derome draws on many vocabularies in his work. With his sidekick Lussier, the language of the cinema provides the impetus for his compositional approach as Les Granules, an approach that reached its apotheosis with their third album, *Au Royaume du Silencieux*.[23] As Derome explains it, the duo initially wanted to record an album that was closer to their *les hommes-orchestre* stage shows, eschewing the fussy, 24-track cinematic overdubbing that earmarked their first two discs. "We got into real problems because our records were lush and then we have only two of us live," he says. "So we started playing in a way where we could change very quickly from one instrument to another. In some parts of the record, it's hard to tell there's only two guys playing, it sounds so orchestral."

So Derome and Lussier went into studio and recorded three of their "live" shows directly to DAT, segueing the eight or nine tunes per show as they typically do in concert. "The original idea was to edit the tapes like a film," says Derome. "Since we had over nine hours and there were four or five versions of many tunes, we tried to pick up our favorite parts of each version and try to edit them together. We knew at the beginning this would be difficult, because the dynamics, choice of instruments, tempo, and tuning was never the same. On one song I'd play the flute, in another version I'd play the saxophone. It took us a week in the studio to record it, then two years to edit it. I think there's about 400 edits in it. At a few points it became hopeless; we were ready to throw it in the trash. We were working with diagrams, this tune had Part A and Part B, and we had six versions of Part A, but we couldn't connect them, then we get lost in our tapes, and parts were inserted backwards. The ironic thing is that the live parts, where there are no edits or cuts, sound choppy, while the edits are smooth."

In his solo work, Derome conspicuously shifts away from frenetic cutting and *mise-en-scene* to more classic, abstract and modern styles. For the past four years, he has been involved in scoring the incidental music for a series of productions by the Montréal theater group Théâtre UBU. Led by Denis Marleau, Théâtre UBU excels in staging the work of 20th Century surrealists, writers, filmmakers and artists like Yukio Mishima, Raymond Queneau, Pier Paolo Pasolini, Kurt Schwitters, Alfred Jarry and Samuel Beckett. To date, Derome has worked on *Cantate Grise*, a protracted existential Beckett gag, *Les UBS*, a compendium of the absurdist UBU plays by Jarry, and *Luna Park 1913*, a work devoted to the Russian futurists. All three can be found edited into suites and collected onto a double CD.[24]

"Theater is quite different from film because when you start working you've only got text," Derome explains. "When you score a film, the film is almost finished: you have visuals, the editing is complete, you've got the mood, you've got the timings you need. With theater you never know if you're writing exactly to length. What you have to do to inspire yourself is to do basic research on all the texts. For *Cantate Grise*, I read all of Beckett. Really. I really read everything. For Les UBS, I did the same with Alfred Jarry. *Luna Park* was a bit harder 'cause it was about the Russian futurists. It was very hard to find musical examples of what we were looking for, because most of them ended up in the Gulag or were killed in the war. It was a very strange project, and the results are quite different from the others." Like Hector Zazou's work in the halcyon days of ZNR, Derome's theater scores play like pensive miniature improvisations drawn from an unusual, delicate instrumental palette – celeste, violin, bassoon, euphonium, jews' harp – only subjected to the ruthless taxonomic eye of an experimental filmmaker like Peter Greenaway. Indeed, the serial counterpoints and geometric progressions of his score for *Cantate Grise* recall the systems soundtracks of Michael Nyman, cut with the dry, laconic wit of Nino Rota.

Whether it's the silver screen or the stage, Derome's choice of instrumentation and thematic approach to composition varies from project to project. "What are you looking at in terms of texture? Is it rough, is it soft, is it a reference to a musical style or not? If it's not, what is it? Is there a percussion instrument? You have to choose a number of colors. In film music, there's a lot of music that is under dialogue. So you have to be careful that the music is not too layered because when they bring the level of the mix down underneath the dialogue, all the subtleties will be lost. Theater music is generally more transitional, between scenes, because you cannot bring the dialogue higher than the music, like in the movies. And also, you don't have a lot of money to do these projects. You can't hire lots of musicians and go into the studio and fool around. You have to budget your talent and time. If you choose a violin and hire a violinist and then don't use it in a project, you've got a problem. So you pick up instruments very carefully.

"In the end, you try to do something that is totally focussed on the subject; that's what's the hardest. You get to compose music for subjects you don't normally think about or know about. I just did a documentary soundtrack for a film about prospectors. Old prospectors, 60, 70 years old going with their canoes in the north of Québec and stopping somewhere and just breaking rocks. At first I couldn't figure out what I was going to compose for that. You look at the film, you read about the subject, you think about it and you just walk in the house, back and forth. After a while, something comes and you start writing sketches, and sometimes there's links between the sketches that you don't realize until after you've written it. It's strange, because I feel that I am doing nothing; I'm just waiting. When the deadlines become close, and then it's there. It's been there for three weeks."

When he's not in the screening room or looking through the microscope with René Lussier, Jean Derome can be found at the local coffeehouse playing bebop.

Along with bassist Pierre Cartier and drummer Pierre Tanguay, Derome's saxophone propels the trio Evidence through takes of tunes like "Hackensack," "Criss Cross" and "Well, You Needn't"[25] that remain faithful to Monk's spiky, unerring sense of tonality and swing. "When I started playing Monk's music about 20 years ago, I would learn by jazz fakebooks," Derome explains. "But I learned after a while that they were full of errors. The tunes were 'normalized,' if I could say that. If Monk used maybe a six-bar bridge instead of a normal eight-bar bridge, then they'd add two bars to make it fit into a more traditional bebop framework. If a tune had a strange intro or a little finale he'd always play, they wouldn't keep it. There's even errors in notes. If chords are strange, if they're not on the first beat of the bar, they'll put it there. When I realized that, I started copying the records. We try to play very faithfully, almost like musicologists, but improvise at the same time. We're like three parallel lines that interact. I think this is the greatest strength of the group."

A common thread throughout all of Derome's work is the notion of folklore as the logical end of innovation, or, as he himself once put it, "From bebop to Ti-Jean Carignan, all styles eventually become folklore."[26] "I think styles are a bit of a game," Derome explains. "When there's enough novelty in something, we call it a new kind of style. After a while, listening to it, you start incorporating all the information and the way of thinking that is implied, because each style of music is like a set of references or rules, like playing chess or cards. But you can change the rules using the same cards. Then the ace may be worth more while the king becomes less. But it's always the same card. A classical violin player will work on his tone, and he will talk about his tone and describe it, but there are many other things in the sound of the violin that he doesn't even listen to anymore. He doesn't hear the sound of the bow rubbing the strings. In another style, this sound could be moved into the foreground. Then the tone isn't as important as the violin as a generator of noise.

"I think it's the same for styles. In music, the basic elements are always there: time, melody, rhythm, a sense of form, but the way they are perceived is the matter of the style. The more you become aware of a style, the more you understand its components, what references they're making. And eventually, it becomes folklore. It becomes part of you and you don't even know when you learned it and how you learned it. At first a style looks like an explosion, it's totally new, totally free, you can do what you want, but then it becomes very articulated, it almost becomes a language. Nowadays there's some free music that you can call 'traditional' free music. Derek Bailey is a good example. He says that his type of playing is 'traditional free improvisation.' Now that's funny."

Les Granules: Soyez Vigilants, Restez Vivants! Vol.1 (Ambiances Magnétiques, 1986), Le Retour des Granules Vol.2 (Ambiances Magnétiques, 1987), Aux Royaume du Silencieux (Ambiances Magnétiques, 1992)

René Lussier: Fin du Travail [Version 1] (Ambiances Magnétiques, 1983), La Trésor de la Langue (Ambiances Magnétiques, 1990), Le Corps de L'Oeuvrage (Ambiances Magnétiques, 1994)

with **Conventum**: Réédition 1977-1979+ (Ambiances Magnétiques, 1985)

with **Robert Lepage**: Chants et Danses du Monde Inanimée (Ambiances Magnétiques, 1984)

with **Fred Frith**: Nous Autres (Victo, 1987)

Jean Derome: Confitures de Gagaku (Victo, 1987), 3 Musiques Pour UBU (Ambiances Magnétiques, 1995)

with **Les Dangereux Zhoms**: Carnets De Voyage (Victo, 1994)

with **Evidence**: Evidence (Ambiances Magnétiques, 1993)

with **Lars Hollmer**: Looping Home Orchestra (Victo, 1994)

Footnotes:

1. "Avez-vous travaillée?", written for Quebec filmmaker Jacques Leduc's documentary about the fortysomething lives of aging political activists, *Charade Chinoise*, and a popular number at Granules gigs

2. Derome, "Matter/Manner," published in *Ré Records Quarterly* Vol.2 N4, 1989: pp.30-34

3. *Le Dernier Glacier*, Roger Frappier and Jacques Leduc

4. *Passiflora*, Fernand Bélanger and Dagmar Teufel, 5. "The one-man band[s]"

6. "The Return of the Kernels," Ambiances Magnétiques, 1987

7. Portions of this section were originally published as "New and Improvised," the author, *Option* Magazine N21, September 1988: pp.78-80

8. Zorn's gaming piece where a large ensemble of improvisors spar with each other, controlled by a sophisticated series of musical parameters and hand signals; see *John Zorn*, p.148

9. The musical equivalent of mugging for the audience

10. A 1991 provincial task force on culture headed by Cultural Minister Liza Fruller-Hebert which recommended that the purse-strings of arts funding in Québec be given over to the provincial government and that the majority of funding go to projects promoting Québécois culture

11. Their two albums, *A L'Affut D'Un Complot* and *Le Bureau Centrale Des Utopies*, were reissued as *Réédition 1977-1979+*, Ambiances Magnétiques, 1985, 12. Ambiances Magnétiques, 1983

13. Luckily Levasseur had the tapes rolling, and the evening can be enjoyed again and again on *Nous Autres*; Victo, 1987

14. See *Fred Frith*, p.37 15. Ambiances Magnétiques, 1990

16. The slogan printed on buttons, T-shirts and posters by the separatist Parti Québécois during the 1980 referendum on sovereignty in Quebec

17. The Prix Paul Gilson, awarded for excellence in radiophonic work

18. A trio recording with Chris Cutler, Derome and Lussier, still mired at the mixing stage

19. German guitarist Hans Reichel's wooden idiophone crafted from exotic timber and played with a bow; Lussier plays the unique instrument in two trios: Hickory, with Reichel and percussionist Ikue Mori, and Le Bœuf Qui Rit, with bassist Normand Guilbeault and drummer Pierre Tanguay

20. "Matter/Manner," *Ré Records Quarterly* Vol.2 N4: 1989, pp.30-34 21. ibid., 22. Victo, 1987

23. "The Kingdom Of The Silents," Ambiances Magnétiques, 1992; the title comes from the motto of a muffler dealer in the Saguenay-Lac St-Jean region of Québec

24. Ambiances Magnétiques, 1994, 25. see *Evidence*, Ambiances Magnétiques, 1993

26. "Matter/Manner", p.32

Fat

After the rivers of milk too accustomed to the uproar of the fisherwomen, the estuary's small bells beneath discoloured banners and in these pearls lustre themselves with so many past adventures that it's pleasant. Born of the casual embraces of spun-out worlds, that god growing up for the welfare of the generations to come, understanding that the time was up, disappeared into the distance of the thousand similarly directed electricities.

Sweating vertebrate superior cathedrals.

André Breton & Philippe Soupault, Les Champs Magnétiques[1]

The cellular phone rings insistently at the next table of a dim sum palace on the edge of Montreal's Chinatown, its shrill whine piercing the early afternoon silence. Drummer Phil Giborski winces and puts down his chopsticks. "Cancer of the ear," he retorts, as a tray of stuffed eggplant and curried calmars is wheeled by. This cracks up his bandmates, Eric Rosenzveig and Jeff Noble. It's a succinct absurdism, and an appropriate one, coming as it does in the middle of a conversation about technologically perverting a "rebellious" Czechoslovakian heavy metal band: Giborski had been explaining how the SMPTE time code[2] had been brought up in the mix as a lead instrument of one ballad, its irritating timbre a deadpan foil to the hollow, arena rock pyrotechnics.

Such is the tao of Fat, an improv trio of no fixed address who delight in the art of absurdism. What else could possibly explain a band who name-checks Raymond Queneau, André Breton, Groucho Marx, *and* Lee "Scratch" Perry? A band who used a 1963 Charles Tyler ESP dust jacket as the "cover" of their debut album [and pasted up random, banal bank circulars as the "liner notes"]? This is a band whose idea of fun is to do a tour of mining towns in Slovakia; three guys whose names would look great on a law firm's door yet are famous for unleashing ferocious, shredding free improvisation decked out in 1960s jazz suits and skinny ties.

An electric power trio who flunked the free school, Fat works the 'pataphysical edge of new improvised music. In front of the test-crash dummy epics of 16mm *auteur* Mark Nugent, Fat explodes the traditional bass/drums/guitar lineup, jamming together buckled splinters of raw noise, rock'n'roll, free jazz, ambient and third world musics. The result is heavily treated live by the trio, who deftly wield found tools like vibrators, magnets, clothespins, digital delays, hijacked cassette voices, rubber balls, radios and feedback with all the precision of a neurosurgeon backing a dumptruck into infinity. Eleven years of living and collaborating together have allowed Fat to stop on a dime while navigating complex pieces that shatter the musical compass with astonishing strength, power and fluidity.

"I was talking to a jazz journalist earlier this year about groups and soloists, and his point was that the group wasn't as important as the soloist," explains guitarist Rosenzveig, who, along with Giborski and Noble, is fortifying himself with fried yams, shrimp toast, sticky rice and chinese tea on this bitter November day. "I said, 'Name your favourite ten records of any style in jazz and then tell me the group is not important.' Charles Mingus kept his group together for many years; Cecil Taylor played with Jimmy Lyons and Andrew Cyrille for over a decade. Some of the best work of Derek Bailey and Evan Parker to name two of improvised jazz' most distinctive soloists was done together. I remember reading Coltrane saying that they would never play a tune live until they had played it together a year, a year and a half. That's really important to us; it's an essential part of Fat. In our first summer together, we rarely spoke; we just jammed six hours a day for four months. When we went home, it was to a bedroom down the hall in a shared house. We went on to live and work together in Europe for four and a half years. That's the difference between Fat and most other improvising groups: we have a group dynamic that's much greater than the sum of its parts."

In the recording sessions for his 1975 album *Another Green World*,[3] Brian Eno asked guitarist Robert Fripp to improvise a lightning-fast guitar solo for "St Elmo's Fire" that would imitate the electrical charge flowing between two poles of a Wimshurst high-voltage generator; "like a sled shooting over snow."[4] It was a visual affinity for music not unlike this that inspired Rosenzveig, Giborski and Noble to rent a house together in 1982 and embark on an Enoesque studio project with a newly-minted four-track tape recorder. "We always saw music in pictures, or in images," says Giborski. "That's how we still tend to compose. 'Bring that wooden slice down here, and then I want some black holes punched in.' I'm always reminded of the time when Eno was onstage mixing Roxy Music as an instrument."

Not content to merely emulate Eno's painterly, oblique pop aesthetic, Fat wanted to pin the needles with a wicked dub of them live in the mad tradition of Jamaican studio master Lee "Scratch" Perry. "Perry is a master of timbre and production, and he does it *live*, which is very, very appealing," says Rosenzveig. "The music is up and happening, and he deals with that music as up and happening. It's not as if the music is *constructed*, which I find very unappealing about a lot of people who use technology to make records, early Eno excepted." The use of live digital delays give Fat's debut album, *Plays For You*,[5] a loose, spacey feel; the swamp of sustained bass fuzz, looped guitar textures and fake muezzin vocals bounce along a wacky, Perryesque groove, although the quirky heads and interplay on cuts like "A Man Is His Dog" and "ESP" hint at free jazz, Five Spot style.

"A decided difference between us and some of the other improvising groups is that our approach comes out of Black improvised music rather than a progressive rock one," Rosenzveig says. "We don't come from a jazz background *per se* of *playing* jazz, but an influence or a reason to play music for us was the free music of the early 1960s. Archie Shepp's asymmetrical lines, especially his early work when he had those really strong quintets on Impulse in the early '60s, Cecil Taylor, a lot of the ESP catalogue. I'm not saying we're free jazz players – we're definitely rock'n'rollers – but that energy, that vibe..." Rosenzveig drifts off. "Funny thing is, we started playing free music before we knew much about it. Then we discovered a body of work that we later aspired to. It was as if we were working in a similar vein, although perhaps an untutored or naive one. When I heard Sonny Sharrock playing, it wasn't so much 'That's the style I want to copy,' but 'That's how I play!' Derek Bailey has come to be one of my favourite musicians, but again it was sort of reaffirming something that I already knew."

The key to Fat's unique tumble through the topology of borrowed sounds is their quixotic insistence on eschewing digital effects and treatments for a more primitive, hands-on approach. The swirling, scraped guitars, doppler-shifted bass and liquid beats of "Jangled" and the deep dub grooves of "Le Père Du Scrap" – both from their chaotically funky follow-up LP *Hit*[6] – are good examples. "I think there's been some misconceptions about how we do our work," says

Rosenzveig. "People think it's heavily treated, and there's many overdubs. We use very very few effects, and often we use quite simple means to process things. Jeff and Phil have used a digital delay since the beginning. I play a Fender Mustang through a Fender Twin amp with no effects except an overdrive pedal, and occasionally a wah-wah. Because we traveled without a soundman our first few years, we were forced to play our own effects from our instruments. On *Hit*, more than half the tunes have no overdubs and no studio treatments; all the processing was done as we were playing. A lot of things that people think are heavily processed or multi-tracked are just manual, digital techniques." Rosenzveig flexes his fingers and smiles.

Fat honed their "digital" techniques to razor-sharp precision on the fully improvised *Magnetizer*,[7] but did so with a subtle ear for sound more common to groups like Biota, Zoviet France and The Hafler Trio. "One thing that's really bothered me about Fat is the lack of recognition of the research we've done in terms of timbre," Rosenzveig regrets. "It's curious that some death metal groups are more keen on how they sound than some improvised players; The Swans were very careful about how their sound was used. It's unfortunate that more care is not taken with sound. All too often it's a case of 'make everything sound good, compress everything, get it all up there.' With Fat, the whole thing has been the sound of the music *is* the music."

In addition to sharing an improvised life together, Rosenzveig, Giborski and Noble shared something more important; a restlessness that would ultimately be their passport to new influences. "Our lifestyle is extremely important to our music," Rosenzveig agrees. "We've always chosen to have that all-consuming curiosity in interesting places, whether we're sitting in Brno or Budapest, Essouaira or Barcelona, London or Prague." So between 1987 and 1992, Fat spent four-and-a-half years on the road in Europe, living on East German deodorant, toothpaste and Russian tins of herring and sardines as they zigzagged through gigs and festivals across Poland, Russia, Hungary, Switzerland, Spain, England and Austria. Home base was split between Barcelona, London, and Montreal, with the occasional trip to Morocco and New York.

During 1990, Fat accepted an invitation from a Czechoslovakian agent, Borek Holecek, to play a handful of gigs there. Clinching the deal was the fact that Holecek, a former dissident and coal stoker [a career given most dissidents in the former Communist regime] had arranged accomodations for the band. He was also prepared to pay the penniless Fat handsomely by Czech standards, about $70 per gig. "It became apparent that we could stay if we wanted, even though we had no money," Rosenzveig recalls. "We could live there just by performing. We thought, 'It's an interesting time, just eight months after the Revolution, why don't we hang out and see what happens?' So we hung out."

Yet Borek had more on his mind than stoking coal. "He was setting up a new record label, Rachot Records, and his influences were exactly what we were doing," Giborski says. "And here he was with very little money, offering to put out a record for us. We would be the first Western band to record in Czechoslovakia. It just so happened that in his basement where he stoked coal, he had a small practise space that he let us jam in. We took the opportunity. Everything thing just seemed to fit into place."

Despite the short time they had before studio – just five weeks – Fat weren't keen on cutting another improvised record. They began improvising, but whenever they chanced upon something that intrigued them – a passage, a drum riff, a duo, a single sound – they would stop and dub it on cassette. They compiled all of these cassette vignettes, assigned each a number, and indexed their notes, chords, finger positions and effects settings in little black books. The result of these sketches, *Automat Hi-Life*,[8] is a complex, deceiving carnet of sounds. Averaging between 38 seconds and two minutes in length, the 31 cuts atomize music at the source, creating new and interesting shapes and timbres, and let them roam. The music then filters back, origins unrecognizable. Although pressed on vinyl in Czechoslovakia, the album is better suited to the CD medium; shuffle play reveals a kaleidoscope every time it's played.

When Fat were scouting for studios to record *Automat Hi-Life* in, they soon discovered the only ones available were the studios of the former Czech pop stars. Under the Communist regime, the state-controlled music industry allowed [read tolerated] a pop star for each genre, such as easy listening, country and western, and heavy metal; each of these "officially" sanctioned pop stars had their own 24-track studio. While visiting Ostrava, a stone's throw from the Polish border, Fat settled on the studios owned by the state heavy metal band, who went by the name of Citron. When they returned to Citron's studios after a month-long, slash-and-burn European tour to cut the phenomenal, full-on *Magnetizer*, a curious Rosenzveig asked the engineer if he had any Citron around. The engineer produced the 24-track tapes of the group's latest LP, *Vypste Psy!*,[9] and threaded them on the reel-to-reels. "We all looked at each other," Rosenzveig recalls, breaking into a broad grin, "and we suggested he head home a little early this evening. So on the last three days, after we sent the engineer home early, we took out the 24-track tapes and remixed the whole record in three nights."

Fat calls *Citron* their homage to Lee "Scratch" Perry, and it's not hard to see why; the unreleased remix brings to mind the glory days of the Black Ark prophet circa *Super Ape*,[10] as well as the most radical work of Adrian Sherwood's On-U-Sound dub. It even echoes the recombinant pop [if not the runaway commercial success] that Brian Eno and U2 achieved on *Zooropa*,[11] only infinitely more twisted. By playing the mixing board and its outboard gear – filters, compression, noise gates, spring echo, EQ, tape speed – like Perry, Fat transformed the pretentious minor-key bombast, lockstep martial drumming and ridiculous Russian basso of a middling, pompous heavy metal band into an unearthly, electroacoustic mutation of Laibach: disembodied and heavily processed heavy metal vocals are screamed in Czech over quicksilver feedback flitting from one speaker to another; songs shift gears, gradually increasing from Killdozer tempos to speed-metal velocities; cracking, high-pitched background vocals are brought up while lead vocals are erased; vapid air-guitar solos are stripped of their lower frequencies; a 15-piece drum kit is heard through the hi-hat mike only; cheesy, canned emulator strings evoke the kind of music one hears at an ice-skating championship.

Yet an astonishing subtext courses beneath the dub anarchy. Despite being a "serious" statement by Citron on the recent political changes in Czechoslovakia, *Vypste Psy!* rang hollow in a free music industry deregulated after the Revolution. "It's about appropriation, the East and the West, and the East dying to be the West," Rosenzveig says. "The humor in it is incredible, starting with the fact that it's called 'Sic The Dogs!' Citron were the state heavy metal band under the Communists, so in terms of their political orientation, they were obviously in opposition to the sort people we were hanging with, the dissidents involved in the Revolution. Yet we get out to their studios and the lead singer has a Mercedes, a swimming pool and a 24-track studio! And this was their attempt to tell people how the former Communists mistreated the people over 40 years. Citron used to sell 200,000 copies under the Communists; they've died since then, no-one touches their stuff. When we were punching the vocals in and out in the mix, we had no idea what the singer was saying; we didn't understand Czech. But our friends who did were hysterical with laughter when they heard it. It turns out we would be highlighting words like 'Hopeless!'"

After spending almost two years living in Barcelona, Fat first travelled to Morocco in the winter of 1989. Like The Rolling Stones, Mickey Hart and Ornette Coleman before them, Fat had been hearing a primordial, timeless groove wafting over the Strait of Gibraltar. They followed it to its epicenter to Essaouira, a coastal crossroads originally settled by the Portuguese. The Living Theatre, Jimi Hendrix and the Art Ensemble of Chicago had all been drawn to this bustling, cosmopolitan city, seduced by the intoxicating power of the trance. "Moroccan music is like most music in the world, incredibly propulsive and intense," says Rosenzveig. "Only when we get a single record of a given style or genre, it's watered-down. A little snatch or example of a style of music may be three minutes long on an ethnomusicological recording; what they may not tell you is that that song might have lasted for two days." Giborski concurs. "Most

Moroccan indigenous music is based on some form of trance or ceremony or ritual that necessitates some way of getting outside of normal," he says. "It really is a pleasure to pick up the rhythms and let them take you."

It was in Essaouira that Fat first encountered the Gnaoua, a religious sect descended from West African slaves whose rituals revolve around deep trances that could last for days. In time they met Mahmoud Guinia, the foremost trance musician in Morocco. While Fat were fascinated with the Gnaoua, they felt the sublime ecstasy of their trance was absolute. "We spent a lot of time with the Gnaoua, became familiar with their music and studied them, but we decided that we didn't feel we had anything to offer to a collaboration," says Rosenzveig. "Our two styles of music weren't suited. While we were spending a lot of time listening to the Gnaoua, we started listening to Berber pop music."

The long, hypnotic elliptical lines of the instrumental music Fat were entranced with turned out to be *ahouad*, a regional pop genre exclusive to the Tachelhit-speaking Berbers from an agrarian area of south-western Morocco known as Ihahane or HaHa. Heard at local weddings thoroughout the summer and at weekly market festivities in villages where traders and farmers hawk fruit, olives, goat meat and *argane* nuts, *ahouad* is named for the small wooden recorder or flute which is its melodic instrument, a flute which is now more likely to be cut from ABS plastic pipe. In *ahouad*, two flute players will play unison melodies with Swiss precision, while two or more small *bendir* frame-drums will accompany the flutes. A steel tire rim called an *n'kous* keeps a strict bell-like rhythm. Depending on the size of an *ahouad* gathering, a number of dancers, or *ahwach*, also provide foot-stamping rhythms and handclaps under the lead of a single conductor, who directs the moods or the rhythms with bird-like call. While the melodies are often drawn from old folk songs, new melodic lines are spontaneously added; one *ahouad* group was famous for improvising on a piece commissioned by the Moroccan government to commemorate a World Cup soccer match. The offhand way that flawless melodies are strung together on the rhythmic line, like black pearls on a string, imbues them with a dynamic, improvised feel.

"We wanted to work with the Berbers almost from the moment we met them because we found their music was similar to our own," explains Rosenzveig. "It was repetitive, quite complex rhythmically, simple melodically, it worked with interesting frequencies, and the stuff just burns." Determined to work with the Berbers on their return to Morocco in the winter of 1990, Fat trekked deep into the interior of the HaHa with just a bootleg cassette in search of a group named Ahouad Mia; a task that proved more difficult than the proverbial camel and the eye of the needle. Eventually they came across someone carrying a *bendir*. Asked if he knew the musicians on the cassette, the man grinned and pointed at himself. In broken Tachelhit Berber, Fat inquired if his group would like to perform with them. The whole group turned up in full costume fully prepared to jam that afternoon.

In the summer of 1991, Rosenzveig, Giborski and Noble arrived for their third time in Morocco to rehearse and record with Ahouad Mia. Moving to Smimou, the closest town to the group's home with electricity, Fat rented a house and began rehearsal with the ensemble. As the roots of *ahouad* lie in improvisation, any attempt to structure the sessions proved futile; rather the two groups spent five weeks recording daily rehearsals and listening back to them. From the outset, the Berbers were excited about the project's unconventionality and Fat's western technology, particularly when it came to Giborski's drumming. Giborski was playing an Alessis HR-16 drum machine from an octapad, with samples contoured to sound like *bendir* hits. "That's what I was playing, but what I was recording to the computer was a series of digital sample triggers in Cubase Audio," Giborski explains. "When we got home, we substituted samples for the MIDI triggers at the volume and position that I played them live. Nothing was hidden from the musicians; they understood the process and were intrigued. But to groove it was much easier to play like they did. It really brought us together." Giborski also constructed plywood boards for the *ahwach* with contacts underneath that would trigger samples as they stomped. "It made for a nice mix of technology and ritual," he says.

The searing intensity of the sessions between Fat and Ahouad Mia can be heard on the unreleased *Fat And The Masters of HaHa*. Cuts like "Zig Zag," "Y'taf Tit" ["He Has The Eye"] and "Issmdaden N'dounit" ["The Pegs Of The World"] crackle with the smouldering heat and electricity in the air. The forward, physical and incredibly hard *bendir* drumming is the first thing one notices; it underpins the mix of keening flutes, ringing *n'kous* and guitar skronk, which change when the *ahwach* leader calls out new clavés with whoops and handclaps. "North African hand drummers are the fucking heaviest drummers around, with the exception of Cubans," Rosenzveig says with admiration in his voice. Noble's astonishingly fluid fretless bass work anchors the finely incised melodies and bizarre urban samples triggered by the *ahwach*, who pounce like cats. Despite the 41° heat and a charcoal barbecue present in the room to heat and tune the skins on the *bendir* drums, they didn't dare stop playing, even while recording, for fear of losing the groove; a cross between traditional Berber rhythms and Sonic Youth noise, it could go on for hours. "As soon as the first note hits, it's like you're on this train and you just keep chugging," Giborski explains. "It was very very satisfying. There was a sense of satisfaction I had never had before. We were working with world musicians on our their level, and they were working with us on our level. It was complete unity. We were into a

John Coltrane, one-side-of-a-record-groove thing; *A Love Supreme*. It has that drive, that intensity, that just goes on and on."

Collaborating with other players has finally convinced Fat to take a sabbatical after 11 years of playing as a trio. "We didn't feel it was necessary to live together anymore, and we wanted to return to recording having made quantum leaps," Rosenzveig says. "The band's a long-term thing. We always saw Fat as school. When we learned how to play music properly, we sort of stopped Fat. Now that we've learned how to play music, we're quite anxious to get back together and make another dozen records."

Giborski and Rosenzveig have been amassing frequent flyer points with dizzying speed in one of the projects they're currently immersed in, a world music jam that had its genesis with a festival of indigenous musics Rosenzveig curated in Montreal during the summer of 1992. "To simplify things, the closest analogy would be something like one of Kip Hanrahan's projects," he explains. "Players from a lot of different styles or schools, trying to create a music that doesn't exist but nonetheless would sound very natural. I hear no difference between a Cuban *batà* drummer and a Laotian *khan* player, and a New York city guitarist and a free jazz bassist from Germany. It's all music, if the quality's happening and the dynamic is happening, it can be put together." Despite the impressive roster of global talent – Adelqui Reve, one of the top *batà* players in Cuba; Mahmoud Guinia, ace *gimbri* player and trance technician from Morocco; Indian slide guitarist Mowan Vishwa Bhatt – Rosenzveig is quick to point out that this is not a Peter Gabriel-style ethnological forgery. "*Citron* to the contrary, I don't like the idea of treating people's performances," he says. "If someone's going to give something, his timbre, his sound is quite important. Someone's sound is what they're about; I don't want to tamper with that. I think out-and-out rip-off stealing is *great*, but if you invite a French Guianan tribesman to contribute a drum track, well, you should treat that track with a certain respect."

Giborski, meanwhile, is planning to relocate to Indonesia for several months in 1994 to study *jaipong* in Bandung. "It's indigenous music, but it's a pop music form," he explains. "The two most important elements are percussion and the dance. The percussion sounds like a solo instrument but it's the most important, driving force in the whole music. It's quite fractured, but has very very beautiful motifs." There's also a duo record in the can by Rosenzveig and Noble, a stripped-down improv duet with little more than distortion pedals. "I think it's almost the best thing I've done," Rosenzveig confesses. "It's very singular, very focused. It's comparable to Frith's *Guitar Solos* record; a very unique approach to guitar, a distillation."

Rosenzveig has also been hacking at video manipulation software for the past year. Fat is no stranger to visuals; they have always made graphics an important element of their work. For many of their gigs during the 1980s, Montréal filmmaker Mark Nugent rescued NASA test footage, '50s psychiatric films and other industrial arcana from cold storage, alchemized them through an optical printer and projected them onto a hallucinogenic silver screen behind the band. When spliced with Fat's onstage performance, Nugent's imagery magnified the ordinary and shed light on richly textured worlds of freedom, imagination, and intensity. Yet Fat found they had to tailor their performance to fit the cloth of the visuals. "The problem with film is that it's inflexible," says Rosenzveig. "If the film has an eight-second passage, you have to switch at the end of eight seconds. There's not the freedom you have when you improvise. I've been looking for ways of controlling the image, so that the image is tied to the music, and can be improvised in real time as well."

Enter Screen, a new trio with Rosenzveig, Giborski, and filmmaker Willy LeMaître. Where most multi-media or virtual reality events are merely buzzwords for two-dimensional performances with discrete soundtracks, Screen makes live inter-media improvisation possible: LeMaître improvises images on a videocamera and feeds them to Rosenzveig, who manipulates them with David Rokeby's Very Nervous system, a motion analysis progam that translates body movements into MIDI data. The images can also be stored and Giborski can trigger them from his octapad. Upping the absurdist ante, Rosenzveig envisions taking Screen to Asia and playing in front of massive video screens in village markets in India, or floating the trio down the Mississippi, sending LeMaître ahead to videotape the next town like a tourist, and plugging in every night to recharge. The fact that Rosenzveig is playing software instead of hardware in Screen fazes him not a bit; and herein lies the essence of the Fat aesthetic. "I never really considered myself to be a guitar player," Rosenzveig confesses. "I had to use the guitar to play the music that was in my head."

Fat: Plays For You (Amok, 1988), Hit (These, 1989), Automat Hi-Life (ReR Megacorp, 1991), Magnetizer (Megaphone, 1992), Fat And The Masters of HaHa [unreleased], Citron [unreleased]

Footnotes:
1. *The Magnetic Fields*, translated by David Gascoyne; Atlas Press: London, 1985: p.42
2. The normally inaudible digital click track that synchronizes everything in multi-track recordings
3. Editions EG, 1975
4. Quoted in Poyntor, Andrew & Mills, Russell, *More Dark Than Shark*; Faber & Faber: New York, 1986: p.98
5. Amok, 1988, 6. These, 1989, 7. Megaphone Records, 1992, 8. ReR Megacorp, 1991
9. "Sic the Dogs!", 10. Island, 1976, 11. Island, 1993

Bruire

"A recording in which the sounds are very clear and distinct, giving the impression that their source is very close, is considered to be good. Yet the everyday world of our ears does not consist in only the latter sounds; it is also comprised, and indeed to a far greater extent, of confused and muddled, very impure, distant and more or less misheard sounds. The decision to ignore the latter leads to a specious art, dedicated to only a certain category of sounds which, all things considered, is pretty rare in everyday life...recordings thus obtained, however much clearer they may be to the ear, however much freer from flaws and minor mishaps, do not speak any louder to the spirit as a result."

Jean Dubuffet[1]

Sitting behind a low set of acoustic traps and percussion and nursing a Black Label, Michel F. Côté is telling me excitedly about a news item he had heard this morning on the radio. "For a year the United States has been developing a project listening into deep space," Côté says, his cigarette smouldering and sending smoke curling upward into the sepulchral basement air. "NASA has invested 100 million dollars in it. It's a big, big interstellar listening project. After one year of operation, the radiotelescopes have just received 12 minutes of a signal they think may have come from intelligent life."

Whether the signal source is a beacon from intelligent life, the last cry of a dying sun, or just the fax machine of the Gods matters little to Côté; it's merely another source of found sound for the percussionist, *bruitiste*, poet, treasurer of Ambiances Magnétiques, and founder of Bruire. Alongside turntable savant Martin Tétreault and reedist Robert Lepage, Côté spins sonnets from the steelyard, media debris, the synapses and sinews of flesh-and-blood improvisation, and the fluxus of the recording studio, collaging and sculpting it into a dreamlike musical universe somewhere left of the dial, half-composed, half-improvised and imbued with rock's primal energy.

Bruire takes its name from the French word for noise, and Tétreault, Côté and Lepage all have grounding in one sort of racket or another: Tétreault in vinyl flotsam and jetsam, Côté in the aether of radio waves, Lepage in the emotional tightrope of free improvisation. Bruire's 1989 debut, *La Barman A Tort de Sourire*,[2] is a grab-bag album of sonic textures and readymade instruments – you can find shortwave broadcasts, cheap samplers, steel drums, a little frenetic accordion, drums, a mandolin, phonograph records, a talking Captain America doll, a black & white TV set, sandpaper, and a few astronauts coloring short vignettes that range from the whimsical to the politically cold. "Recycling is a touchstone of our times," says Côté. "All of our musical material is what society throws out. Out of this junk, we create music."

Côté, Tétreault, and Lepage have come together in Bruire's practise studio on an early June evening to talk about junk culture. The studio is hidden in a maze of split level rooms with mismatched wallpaper and moldings in the bowels of a reconverted school in Montréal's east end. The haphazard interior decoration betrays Bruire's percussive foundation: drumsticks and percussion mallets are scattered about, some gathered in olive cans on the shelf; the octapads of an electric drum kit lie unfinished in one corner; *tuyeaux* made from copper tubes are hung suspended from the ceiling; a tuned series of ABS pipes are arranged on the wall. At the rear of the studio lies Tétreault's turntables and record collection, next to Lepage's lone clarinet, perched beside a music stand. Patch cords and posters dot the walls. A radio blares outside, the tinny disco of Lipps Inc's "Funkytown" cutting through the muggy haze of twilight just as NASA's mysterious signal cut across the galactic gulf. "In decades of listening to deep space and hundreds of noises they have received, they have never heard anything so articulated," Côté continues. "It has a definable sequence and a complex form." "Can we make a piece with it?" asks Tétreault innocently. "It would be real *musique actuelle*."

Among other things, Michel F. Côté is a billiards fanatic. The game that made Minnesota Fats famous calls for a precise aim and a mastery of the thousands of random combinations that result when the cue scatters the balls across the felt-covered slate with a sharp crack, and it is precisely the confluence of these elements – chance and structure – that deeply fascinate the 35-year-old percussionist. A quick glance at his primary influences confirms this: John Cage, Holger Czukay, Duke Ellington and Jean Dubuffet were all artists intrigued by hidden intentions and happy accidents.

As a drummer and percussionist, Côté's first serious influences were John Bonham ["that heavy backbeat"] and Bill Bruford. "I love to listen to Led Zeppelin. At the heart of my generation, we are children of rock'n'roll," he says. "My formative reference has always rested there. It hasn't kept me from listening to other things, but I return always to that spot. The instrument I play can't help but take me back there; drums are typical of my generation. Snare, bass drum, hi-hat all say rock'n'roll. At the same time, rhythm is also a universe that one can exploit in a superb way. Look at how contemporary composition utilizes percussion. These two sides of the same coin can be found in a single performer, like David Moss, or Paul Lovens of the Globe Unity Orchestra." Indeed, his recent moonlighting with Montréal theater ensembles shows that Côté can balance timbral detail with the backbeat, and that he is adept on both acoustic and electric traps. For Carbone 14's *Krieg* he played a hard rock score on a traditional acoustic set, while for Brouhaha Danse's *Le Galerie des Horribles*, he played a collection of sampled metals and *tuyeaux*. "I tried to mix the two together, but it wasn't obvious, nor easy. They are two completely different ways of approaching the materials. The more I play, the more I realize that it has to be one or the other."

Yet more than the drums, it was a Christmas gift of one of the first Sony Walkmans when he was 11 that shaped Michel F. Côté's eventual aural perception of the world around him. Côté played radio announcer with his new portable tape recorder, and later in life he went on to volunteer at CIBL, Montréal's flagship community radio station, and since 1985 he has been working for Société Radio Canada, the French arm of the CBC, as a researcher and host of *Musique Actuelle*. The zenith of Côté's interest in radio surfaced in Bruire's stunning *hommage* to vacuumland, *Muss Muss Hic*,[3] commissioned by the CBC and Hörspiel Studio at Germany's WDR Köln and premièred at Chapelle Historique du Bon Pasteur for The Acustica 90 Festival in May of 1990. "Like music, radio broadcasting is an art of the times," Côté proclaims in his best mellifluous announcer's voice, guiding us through this dense thicket of radiophonic history, an archaeological dig into the strata of past popular musics, radio soaps, news bulletins and adverts. Like ghostly transmissions received on a shortwave radio with crashing batteries, Côté's shamanistic percussion and Lepage's mournful clarinets establish blocks of music between the sound bites, while Tétreault's skipping disks imitate channel surfing.

The wireless is a hobby Côté shares with many great composers of the modern age, from Italian futurists like Luigi Rossolo to *musique concrète* guru Pierre Schaefer, pioneers whose work drew on the techniques and vocabulary of visual arts. "Visual arts is probably the universe closest to my own sense of aesthetics and music," Côté admits. "People in visual arts have always fascinated me because they characterize music as something abstract. Now, I admit there's no meaning behind that. When Cage said 'My mother said I made a music extraordinarily sad, but when I played it in concert everyone laughed,' I understood then that music is extremely relative, probably meaningless in a way, and can be compared to a game of semantics. So I have always drawn more inspiration from the writings of artists than the writings of musicians. Outside of a few enlightened composers – Varèse had interesting things to say, so did Messiaen at times, Derek Bailey is an interesting exception – the great tradition of Western music has very few theoreticians. People in visual arts have explored the universe of abstraction and creation longer than those in music, and the impacts are political and cultural as well."

Chief among Côté's visual arts influences is French Art Brut sculptor Jean Dubuffet. Indeed, with its primitive *bricolage* and use of varied textural surfaces, *La Barman A Tort de Sourire* is an aural analogue to Dubuffet's famous 1954 sculpture installation made from cast-off material and cultural ephemera, *Little Statues of Precarious Life*. To his delight, Côté discovered that Dubuffet also tried his hand at music; just after Christmas of 1960, Dubuffet brought a Grundig TK 35 tape recorder to the house of his friend, Danish painter Asger Jorn, and recorded the two improvising on piano, violin, cello, and trumpet. Over the next few weeks, the sessions took on an even freer character and the instrumentation veered toward the exotic: hurdy-gurdy, tsigane, Auvergnat bagpipes, and bombarde were provided by Alain Vian, the proprietor of a shop in Rue Grégoire-de-Tours that sold rare instruments. Vian soon sat in on the sessions, which were eventually released as a limited edition 6 LP box set.

"It's the most radical, *out* music I think I've ever heard," says Côté. "As well, Dubuffet wrote interesting discourses on music and *création sonore* which was closely tied to his work in visual arts. He talked a lot about objects and materials, and applied his ideas to music and many art works besides his own. His books *Les Bâtons Rompus* and *Fixations de Culture*[4] are extraordinarily articulate discourses on art in general, and have a spirit which I think characterizes *musique actuelle*."

Côté formed Bruire in 1989 as an open band dedicated to a Dubuffetian exploration of organized sound with a core trio of himself, Tétreault, and Lepage. "At first Bruire was my home project," says Côté. "In the beginning I never thought of the group as fixed." Thus *La Barman A Tort de Sourire* featured a 13-piece ensemble with cameos from many of the Ambiances Magnétiques collective playing pieces that hopscotched across the vast terrain of postmodern pop styles. "A willingness to be eclectic is natural," Côté explains, "So we listen to jajouka, then some Japanese *noh* chants, after that Elvis Presley. Inevitably, when you are a music buff, you spend years building up an immense collection of records."

In the studio, the modus operandi for Côté has always been a 50-50 mix between improvisation and composition. "It's an ideal way of composing," Côté says. "It's not as radical as Derek Bailey, for example, who does not compose at all. He improvises. Bailey says that music is the most perfect when musicians meet and improvise for the first time together, not knowing each other, and also when they improvise for last time, like the absolute climax. It's ridiculous to limit your musical experience to just that. I like direct improvisations in the studio, but I also like to compose and manipulate music after it has been recorded. It's like Pollock painting with magnetic tape, reworking certain elements of a recording and creating something new. So, afraid of improvisation, I compose, afraid of composing, I'll deconstruct things. I want it both ways."

Quebec conceptual artist Raymond Gervais once christened the 20th Century gramophone "a small, visual theater of sound."[5] If so, Martin Tétreault is perhaps the the mechanical dervish's most skilled interpreter and irreverent visionary. Like Lazlo Moholy-Nagy, Joseph Beuys, and Milan Knízák before him, Tétreault prizes the long-playing LP as an *objét d'art*, and the record player as a touchstone of the modern age, an invention of leisure that has profoundly shaped our modern artistic sensibilities. Like Christian Marclay, he scratches, cuts, glues, bends, heats, and warps records and improvises with the results; spinning a favorable surface for a new rhythmic, percussive and melodic language of pops, skips, locked grooves, pitch wobble and surface noise.

A visual artist by trade, Tétreault started listening to records because of his older brother, a Bach fiend. "At our house in the country, there were only two albums to listen to. *Power Biggs Plays Bach* and Felix Leclerc. It was truly fucked up. After that, my other brother arrived one day with an album that started with an organ. I said, 'Oh no, not more Bach,' and then the drums kicked in. It was Led Zeppelin. My ears began to open after that."

As it happened, vinyl would point the way out of the conceptual cul-de-sac in plastic arts that Tétreault found himself in during the early '80s. "I couldn't go any further; I had run out of language and emotion with the materials at hand," he says. "I didn't know what to do; I was contemplating writing books." In July of 1984, Tétreault had a brainstorm. Since he had been cutting and arranging various materials like paper and plastic, he decided to subject a phonograph album to the same process. "I took a knife, cut a record, changed side A for side

B and glued them back together. I put it on a record player, and *wow*. It had the conceptual side of the work I was doing up to then, but it also had a narrative aspect, for a record ultimately is an endless narrative tale." Cassettes like *Snippettes*[6] are brilliant examples of the fantastic extended improvisations Tétreault can spin with just two turntables and a stack of flea-market records.

The improbable thing about Tétreault's musical discovery was that, like Dubuffet knowing nothing of any modern music, Tétreault new absolutely nothing about *musique actuelle*. One day, Tétreault's neighbor, who happened to be Conventum guitarist André Duchesne, heard the bizarre goings-on and came over. "As neighbors I didn't know he played music either," says Tétreault. "When he told me so, I said, 'Here, listen to this. I make records, too.' He was curious. He listened to it, and said, '*C'est capotée ton affaire-la.*[7] You have to meet René Lussier.'" Lussier quickly rang up Côté and told him there was someone in their backyards who was doing the same sort of things with turntables and records that Christian Marclay was doing in New York. "I called Martin and asked him if he had ever heard of Marclay," says Côté. "He told me he had never even heard of this musical universe. We met in the studio here and started to talk about music, then we began to play. I was knocked out. In working with records as raw materials, Martin had a bank of musical information unheard-of in the history of music. I called Robert Lepage and said 'You've gotta hear this; it's been six or seven years since I've heard anything this radical.' I mean, he was mixing Wagner and Oum Kalsoum."

Tétreault's two favorite PVC abuse techniques are scratching and cutting. The former is no stranger to anyone who has heard a hiphop record, but the latter is truly warped – take three albums [say *The New Sound America Loves Best*, *An Evening With the Corps At Carnegie Hall*, and *The North Sea Soviet Army Choir*], cut them into wedges, glue them together in different combinations, and put the needle to the record. "Hours of amusement," he promises. Both methods show up on Tétreault's debut album *Des Pas Et Des Mois*.[8] At a time when most major record labels were shutting down their record cutting and pressing plants, Tétreault cheekily packaged his new CD in old record sleeves; mine came in *Sammy Kaye Swings and Sways Popular American Waltzes* [Columbia Stereophonic 1018]. Half of the CD is a brilliant deconstruction of a unique pop culture artifact – the instructional dance record – the other half an impressionistic appreciation of the months of the year, to which Côté contributed seasonal *ambiances sonores*. "It's also two aspects of the world in which I work musically," says Tétreault. "There's music with precise thematic material, then there is music that is more poetic. I liked all the rhythmic possibilities of social dancing; this dancing is based in reality, these are the footsteps of history. The months of the year, on the other hand, are full of aleatory images."

Like most DJs worth their BPMs, Tétreault uses Sony turntables, but his pride and joy are his four Califone 1420Cs, indestructible school turntables that go from 0 to 78 RPM, with settings of 16, 33 and 45 in between. "Super powerful, the jeep of turntables," Tétreault says, checking the stylus and flipping a disc entitled *100 Great Motorcycle Sounds* on one of the tables. Thunderous, flatulent biker exhaust spews out of the speakers. "Really great disc, that." Behind the turntables, stacked in shelves on the wall, are Tétreault's working records, sorted according to music type: horns, percussion, piano, organ, disco, "Happy Moog," contemporary music, and instructional records. [A thousand or so more reside at home.] Most have 99¢ stickers still attached to the shrinkwrap. "Ils sont pas neufs, ils sont neuf-neufs,"[9] Tétreault quips. For his needles, Tétreault relies on the same source that supplied his Califones: a friend inside the school commission, where the equipment sits gathering dust on the shelf.

"I have to avoid records that are too strong instrumentally or have a lot of orchestrations, instead I go for specific albums of piano, horns, percussion," Tétreault explains. "It's like building an inventory of an orchestral instruments or putting together a band. It sounds crazy, but I get these ideas in a record store. I'll see a record of bebop piano and a record of Indian music, and I imagine on the stage a bebop pianist with someone playing a sitar. I go home and assemble them together, and I get a meeting of people and cultures that's fantastic."

On November 14, 1990, Tétreault got to meet his New York colleague Christian Marclay for an impromptu session of dueling turntables as part of the exhibition *Broken Music*.[10] The two gramophone *bêtes noires* were right at home amidst the installations, which included Nam June Paik's *Random Access*, an interactive stack of records with tone arms on loose wires; Cage's *33 1/3*, 12 listening posts with a selection of 100 records that could be played at random; Robert Rauschenberg's cover for the Talking Heads *Speaking In Tongues*, Joseph Beuys' Fluxus nickel master plate for his *Schottische Symphonie*, Raymond Gervais' collection of hand-cranked gramophones, RCA's Nipper, and Marclay's *Footsteps*, where gallery-goers could walk over dozens of records such as *Jack Costanzo's Bongo Fever*, *Chopin in HiFi*, *The Grand Illusion* and *The Chambers Brothers Now!* that were laid across the floor.

At their performance, entitled *Les Derniers des Vinyles*,[11] Tétreault and Marclay paid bizarre homage to Thomas Edison, then cut up their mentor with a vengeance. Wound tighter than clockwork, the two hovered over four tables and assorted volume pedals, doing things to records at a blinding speed that would give an audiophile a heart attack. Tétreault's right hand started a skipping rhythm with a hot disco 45 while his left bounced the stylus off another record, blasting snippets of Fauré out of the speakers. Marclay then dragged an album under the fang in his tone-arm cobra before running *I Pagliacci* backwards.

Without missing a beat, Tétreault gamely followed by shoving a pencil under a spinning '40s weepie soundtrack and faded in a burping ragtime march, achieving not only polyphony, polytonality, but post-modern epiphany while he was at it. After the gig, Tétreault compared records with Marclay and was surprised to find that they had pretty similar collections, were interested in the same musical sequences on records, and even look for the same bargains in record stores. "The great buys these days is jazz," says Tétreault. "You'd be surprised what's in the cutout bins everywhere, great stuff like Anthony Braxton, and free jazz going for 99 cents. Either everyone's bought the CD reissue or no-one cares anymore."

With Columbia's introduction of the 33 RPM long-player in 1948, vinyl replaced shellac, extending its playing life. Now that the compact disc has effectively ended the playing life of records for good, Tétreault is for all intents and purposes working in a dying art – and one that forces him to constantly create new work. "If I do a piece with a record that is very used, I won't be able to do that piece for very long before the raw material is gone," he explains. "I can't use it over and over; I have to restart every time. But it's easier to find a record now than it is to find a needle. You'd better stock up on your needles."

Robert M. Lepage's latest work-in-progress is about a musician who travels around the world with a clarinet to relearn his art. A character out of Jules Verne, or perhaps Paul Bowles, our protagonist drifts from village to village, unpacking his Dubuffet, listening to the music of the locals, and transposing it for his rich, melancholy instrument. It's a fitting allegory of the 44-year-old reedist's career; Lepage is a quick-witted improvisor with a dry sense of humor – he calls himself a "mechanical urban folkie" – fond of mixing music from around the world. Today's composer is a privileged chef, says Lepage, with the spices of the world's musics – Gregorian chant, *musique concrète*, dub reggae, flamenco, opera, zouk – all ingredients in the cake of *musique actuelle*.

"It's a question of portions," he elaborates. "Take Pierre Cartier, Jean Derome, René Lussier and me. Cartier has more Baroque music in his mix, Derome has more Steve Lacy in his, Lussier more rock. Me, I like New Orleans and fanfare marches. I think it's really the music of your own personal experience. And it's not always attributable to your surroundings; René is deeply influenced by Québécois folklore, but Pierre and Jean? Not at all. Their styles come more from the music they studied in the conservatory, and their personal tastes for jazz and Renaissance music. We all have access to all these folk traditions, musical styles, and we pick selectively. Everyone has a similar eclectic mix, but the ingredients within that mix change from person to person."

Lepage taught himself the clarinet, fusing improvisation with other media throughout the 1970s; between 1973 and 1975, he was part of Montréal's watershed Atelier de Musique Experimentale. His liquid, quicksilver phrasing on soundtracks like *Les Métamorphoses Clandestines*[12] is reminiscent of the pawky humor of silent movies. Indeed, Lepage's fondness for lyric irony and nostalgia lent itself extremely well to film music, for which he has scored everything from historical documentaries to animation. He made his mark in 1985 with his soundtracks for experimental filmmaker Pierre Hébert – collected on *Chants Et Danses Du Monde Inanimée*[13] – and two years later, with a beautifully realized suite of mnemonic memories for clarinet, *La Traversée De La Memoire Mort.*[14]

While Lepage feels the process, technique, and form of the cinematic medium does not exert an influence him as a composer, he admits the subject matter often provides an engaging stimulus and a starting point for musical research. In 1987 he collaborated with Pierre Hébert for an exhibition at Montréal's Musée de Beaux Arts on Leonardo Da Vinci.[15] The results, collected on *Adieu Leonardo!*[16] are a catalog of imaginary, gentle music for perpetuum mobiles, birdsong, water organ, and sun dials, music spun from the beauty of mathematics and invested with a childlike innocence: *Si j'augmente la vitesse de/trente-trois tours et un tiers/Quel sons vais-je entendre?*[17] "Most people don't know that Da Vinci was better known as a musician and composer than an inventor in his time," says Lepage. "He wrote a lot of music and music theory, and designed these wonderful imaginary instruments that played music. That's what I wanted to capture on *Adieu Leonardo*, the music of an inventor with the soul of a poet."

Lepage is often more felt than heard in Bruire, exerting a mysterious and invisible influence. A musician of few words, impish, precise, and endlessly lyrical, the warmth of his clarinet is often the anchor to Tétreault playing Jackson Pollock on the wheels of steel and Côté's Zen aesthetics. His 'pataphysical sense of humor is never far from the surface; the clarinet contest in *Muss Muss Hic* – where Lepage's instrument imitates a range of voices on a radio call-in show – recalls the delightful absurdity of a Marx Brothers routine. His phrasing also pays tribute to the entire clarinet timeline, from Pee Wee Herman through Jimmy Giuffre [He pines to do a straight-ahead New Orleans dixieland jazz album]. In fact, when the chips are down, Lepage is more influenced by two soprano saxophonists who have pushed the improvisation to new timbral planes – Steve Lacy and Evan Parker – than the bebop tradition and its young disciples. "I'm fascinated by improvisation," he confesses. "It's a creative force with me. But as much as I like improvisation, I don't like spreading myself too thin. I don't like people who scatter their ideas all over the place when they play. When I listen to improvisation, I like very clear and very concise things, not great solos that never finish as they go through the changes. I like people who can create spontaneous melody and not just arpeggiate or play scales inside a head like they're filling a little box. That doesn't interest me at all. Economy of means interests me. Everything that came after Coltrane sought to use as many notes as possible in the same chord. I have a lot of admiration for Coltrane but the worship, that whole academic mentality that followed him, I find a total disappointment."

The closest Michel F. Côté has come to a quantum fusion of visual and musical influences is Bruire's *Les Fleurs de Léo*.[18] It covers a very large stylistic compass indeed. The opening cut, "Tout Rompre", suggests what the Viennese Cool School might sound like fed through an interactive computer program for big-band, "Pierres Précieuses" bristles with knife edge-improvisation, particularly the Hendrixian 'cello of Claude Lamothe, "Cette Cloche" is a zen electroacoustic piece built up from field recordings in Japan and China, and the lyrical "Sphères Unies" crosses Satie with the Soft Machine.

"Right after we cut *La Barman*, I started writing *Les Fleurs de Léo*," says Côté. "I love to write; every piece of music I make is accompanied by a text. I wanted to do a poetic piece; a record that spoke of emotion. I wrote about a man who travels across the century, who was born at the turn and sees the end. I got the inspiration from my grandparents. They've crossed a special time in our history. I worked on this for about two years. Alongside the writing I was fortunate enough to have very precise sessions with musicians like Ikue Mori and Diane Labrosse, duos and trios which were entirely improvised. If you listen closely to Ambiances Magnétiques records closely, you'll find that they have very little to do with improvisation as such, and a lot to more do with the studio. I had the idea to bring musicians into the studio and have them play spontaneously, *à la* Dubuffet.

"Also, after *La Barman*, I wanted to exercise restraint. I wanted to do pieces that were more abstract and less eclectic than *La Barman*. I had really wanted to do a European record. European in composition, structure, and arrangements, but also 'free' but in the spirit of FMP and as far from the New York style of free. Finally, I wanted to deal with the textures of electroacoustic music, and place the whole thing in a *univers bruitiste*, because that's what characterizes Bruire."

Les Fleurs de Léo is dedicated to Simon Dupire, a bass player who was friends with the Ambiances Magnétiques gang and who shuffled off his mortal coil when he committed suicide in 1990. "Simon could turn all the clichés on their head: samba, cha cha, metal, speed jazz," says Côté. "He could play with session musicians and TV professionals and also mix it up with René, Martin and myself. I dedicated the whole project to him as an *hommage*. Perhaps this is why it is as dark as it is, or as nostalgic. I admit it *is* difficult to get into. If he were alive today, *Les Fleurs de Léo* would probably sound a lot different."

Next up for Bruire is a project entitled *L'Âme de L'Objét*,[19] an idea inspired by Dubuffet, Cage, and a disembodied voice on Martin Tétreault's *Snippettes* that intones "Objéts inanimées, avez-vous donc un âme?" ["Inanimate objects, have you a soul?"] Bruire's lineup for this project will be augmented by Jean Derome on reeds, Joane Hétu on saxophones, Diane Labrosse on keyboards, Claude Fredette on bass, and Jerry Snell on vocals. "There are no poetic overtones to this project, it's more straightforward," says Côté. "We'll approach the materials as raw sounds," Côté hits a cymbal. "Sound is probably the closest we can get to the soul of an object. Now, I'm not an animist; I don't think inanimate objects have souls. But if they ever were to have one, it would be sound."

Ultimately, this is the passion of Michel F. Côté: divining the eternal song of the inanimate and creating what Alexander Von Schlippenbach once called the living music. "One of the things I like most about *musique actuelle* is that it is a live music, made by living musicians. While I admire the music that has come before me, I do not choose to mimic it. I could do hommages to my mentors like many others do and steal all their ideas, but I am not a necrophile. I prefer the music of living souls because I am one. That's what characterizes *musique actuelle* for me; it's an eminently living music."

Bruire: La Barman A Tort de Sourire (Ambiances Magnétiques, 1989), Muss Muss Hic (Ambiances Magnétiques cassette, 1992), Les Fleurs de Léo (Ambiances Magnétiques, 1992), L'Âme de L'Objét (Ambiances Magnétiques, 1995),
Michel F. Côté & Diane Labrosse: Duo Déconstructiviste (Ambiances Magnétiques, 1994)
Martin Tétreault: Des Pas et des Mois (Ambiances Magnétiques, 1990), Snippettes (Ambiances Magnétiques cassette, 1992)
Robert M. Lepage: Chants et Danses du Monde Inanimée (Ambiances Magnétiques, 1985), La Traversée de la Mémoire Mort (Ambiances Magnétiques, 1988), Les Métamorphoses Clandestines (Ambiances Magnétiques cassette, 1992), Adieu Leonardo! (Ambiances Magnétiques, 1992), Les Choses Dernières (Ambiances Magnétiques, 1995)

Footnotes:
1. Liner notes to *Expériences Musicales*, 6LP box set, Galleria del Cavallino, April 1961
2. "The Bartender Shouldn't Smile," Ambiances Magnétiques, 1989
3. Ambiances Magnétiques cassette, 1992, 4. Editions Minuit: Paris, 1966
5. Introduction to *Travaux Récents: Disques et Tourne-disques*, an exhibition at the Montréal Musée D'Art Contemporain, November 1990-February 1991, 6. Ambiances Magnétiques cassette, 1992, 7. Roughly, "That's pretty far out", 8. "The Steps and The Months," Ambiances Magnétiques, 1990
9. "They're not new, they're 'nine-nines'", 10. November 1990-February 1991, Montréal Musée D'Art Contemporain, 11. "The Last of the Records", 12. "Secret Changes," Ambiances Magnétiques cassette, 1992, 13. "Songs and Dances of the Inanimate World," Ambiances Magnétiques, 1985
14. "The Crossing of Dead Memory," Ambiances Magnétiques, 1987
15. *Leonardo Da Vinci, Ingénieur et Architecte*, October 1987, 16. Ambiances Magnétiques, 1992
17. "If I increase the speed from 33 1/3, what sounds will I hear?" from the liner notes to *Adieu Leonardo!*
18. Ambiances Magnétiques, 1993, 19. "The Soul of the Object," Ambiances Magnétiques, 1995

Justine

"For Franz music was the art that comes closest to Dionysian beauty in the sense of intoxication. No one can get really drunk on a novel or a painting, but who can help getting drunk on Beethoven's Ninth, Bartók's Sonata for Two Pianos and Percussion, or the Beatles' White Album? Franz made no distinction between 'classical' music and 'pop.' He found the distinction old-fashioned and hypocritical. He loved rock as much as Mozart."

Milan Kundera, The Unbearable Lightness of Being[1]

Never let it be said that the members of Justine aren't prepared to improvise at the drop of a hat. When it seemed impossible to tape our chat because the erase lug on the cassette of awful corporate rock we were taping over had been punched out, keyboardist Diane Labrosse came to the rescue. She produced a band-aid. The four members of Justine – Labrosse, saxophonist and keyboardist Joane Hétu, bassist Marie Trudeau, and percussionist Danielle Palardy Roger – have never been reticent to try something new, either in studio or onstage. During their ten-year stint as Wondeur Brass [and its hipper more impulsive sister, Les Poules], their brazen, fresh collages of time, mood, and style revealed an intuitive grasp of both formal structure and passionate improvisation, and established them as a provocative, uncompromising, and *out* ensemble, even for

Québec's intrepid *musique actuelle* community. As Justine, the quartet have been shaking the tree since 1990, bearing musical blossoms closer in spirit to venus flytraps than posies. Justine are finely balanced: Hétu and Labrosse are the impulsive sprites orbiting the *gravitas* of the aloof Roger and Trudeau, the strong, silent type. In creating dense and multi-layered works like the fractured classicism of *Suite* and the mythic tableaux of *La Légende de la Pluie*, Justine have accomplished more than merely casting off the albatross of being a "women's group." They have forged a *langage fantastique* limned with breathtaking new musical possibilities in a brave new genre whose absence of borders can be as problematic as they are liberating.

After fourteen years of hard work, Justine may have seen their original definitions of musical feminism tempered by the years and watched their audience undergo a demographic and gender shift, but their sense of purpose has remained resolute. "Within the music we're playing a dead serious game," says Labrosse. "Our music is still a political, social and artistic commitment. There are a lot of choices offered, and people have to make some kind of investment when they listen to us. We can sometimes be a little harsh, a little cruel."

Drummer Danielle Roger once said that if Justine were a book, it would be *The Unbearable Lightness Of Being*. Certainly the quartet have an *esprit de corps* that recalls the impulsiveness of Tereza and Sabina in Kundera's modern parable of ordinary mortals caught up in a maelstrom of geopolitical, social and sexual change. Fittingly, Wondeur Brass was born in a city in flux, a bustling, cosmopolitan center enjoying a free street movement in the grand old tradition of New Orleans brass bands and European marching bands. Montréal was a *ville ouvert*, the sense of freedom in taking an unfamiliar instrument and trumpeting it in the street was exhilarating, and that's just what Wondeur Brass did.

From the outset, Hétu, Labrosse, Roger, trombonist Louise Bédard, saxophonist Judith Gruber-Stitzer, and bassist Ginette Bergeron formed Wondeur Brass as a feminist musical collective with a political agenda, and not surprisingly their music was perceived as stubborn and abrasive. They also turned a lot of heads as the one instrument closely associated with rock music, the electric guitar, was conspicuously absent from their lineup. "In Québécois pop it's hard to find group who have fewer than two guitars," says saxophonist Hétu. We're sitting in a *casse-croute* around the corner from Justine's east-end practise space, a cramped basement studio shared with reedist Jean Derome, drummer Pierre Tanguay, and "Serge L'Accordeoniste," a mysterious figure no-one ever sees. Outside, Masson street serves as a drag strip for idle motorcycle gangs. "Even in avant-garde American music, there are a ton of guitars. It's so heavy. For us, there was something about creating that strength without guitars. I don't even know any chords anyway, and I compose music."

"It's also symbolic at the same time," adds Labrosse, "It shows that music can be strong without macho guitars. You obviously wouldn't think it's a group of guys playing when you listen to us, but we can be just as powerful."

Wondeur Brass released two brilliant albums, *Ravir* and *Simoneda, Reine des Esclaves*,[2] the latter of which captured the diamond-hard performances and risky volatility of the band members in fertile arrangements, and featured impeccable research into the life of Simoneda, a 14th Century Serbian queen who ended her life in Turkish captivity. Yet despite the critical acclaim, Wondeur Brass found little support from either the feminist or Québécois new music communities; ironically, their take on urban dissonance and emotional chaos was too weird, too European, a Prague Spring for those who expected a Quiet Revolution. Indeed, it took a trip to Paris in 1984 to play at The Fourth Congrès International Femmes & Musique for Wondeur Brass to realize that they were not alone.

"The way we were perceived in Europe was completely new to us," says Labrosse. "People there had no preconceptions. We were scared and unsure before we went overseas; we thought people might not understand what we were doing. But at The Fourth Congrès, we found a lot of people who did." Those people included members of the Feminist Improvising Group, the Recommended Records gang, who had been listening to Wondeur Brass and the Ambiances Magnétiques circle with growing interest, and Nikad Robom, a collective of women improvisors and activists from Ljubljana, Yugoslavia. "Yugoslavia was also a very significant step for us. It was the first time we were in a non-capitalist country. There was an appetite for music or art. The people there weren't blasé. It was enriching to go out of Québec to be a part of this."

Coming back to Québec, Wondeur Brass felt that if there was any place in Canada that could serve as a locus for such an exchange of cultural and musical information between women musicians from around the world, it was Montréal. Now slimmed down to a quartet, Wondeur Brass got down to business, joining the Ambiances Magnétiques collective and forming Les Productions SuperMémé as both their management and an arts promotion agency dedicated to their goals. In 1988 and 1989, SuperMémé presented two new music festivals featuring women, bringing singer Sussan Deihim, pianist Margaret Leng Tan, Japanese duo The Honeymoons, harpist Zeena Parkins, and the European feminist big band Canaille to Montréal. Since then, they have embarked on less ambitious but no less intriguing projects such as *Les Muses Aux Musée*, a project based on the nine muses with improv vocalists Shelley Hirsch, Catherine Jauniaux, and Maggie Nicols, staged in May of 1992.

While they received critical kudos for such events, Wondeur Brass continued to collect its laurel leaves almost exclusively overseas. They didn't exactly find themselves big in Japan, but they did find themselves bigger in Berlin, London,

Lille and New York than they did in Montréal. In 1987, they played The Moers Jazz Festival, a year later they played the Music Action Fest in Nancy and the Frauen Rock Fest in Berlin. 1989 saw a show at The New York International Festival of The Arts, and a brilliant two-night stand at Ronnie Scott's in London; back in Montréal a year would pass between gigs. "People want new things, new groups, new faces," Labrosse lamented. "We do new things, but if they've made their mind up, they can keep it that way. For 10 years."

In 1990, Wondeur Brass decided it was time for a change. "When we started working on this new music, this new project, we knew that we were going to produce it under a new name," says Labrosse. "Musically, we wanted to integrate more electronics; almost a cross between what Wondeur Brass used to do and what Les Poules did. Les Poules turned a big page for us. Where Wondeur Brass went into the studio very much prepared, very much structured, Les Poules did a lot of improvising. We have never had so much freedom. The studio 'cans' the music if you're not careful. We wanted to have a whole new repertoire of fresh air, liberated from the old Wondeur Brass. So we wrote the musicthemes, arrangementsand then we went into the studio. We recorded some material, changed it around, and shaped it more through improvising. It was a bit of a blend, and that's what made our new sound." Shorn of the "brass" – a lone saxophone remained – the quartet called themselves Justine: "A new flavor, a taste of the north, the squirt of an orange, the persistency of a fly caught between two window panes."[3] The mysterious new name didn't come from anywhere in particular, although it is worth noting it was the name of one of De Sade's partners in lust. Roger offers this explanation: "It's a name that's direct, plain, but at the same time reverberates with possible significances."

According to Roger, the initial concept was to do a dance record based on one of the oldest forms of music written for dance, the partita – albeit one that J.S. Bach would probably not recognize. "The idea was to do a suite *à la moderne*," she explains. "The suite is a succession of dance rhythms in the same tonality, moving from fast movement to slow movement to fast movement. We recorded the songs this way, but when we were in the studio, we thought it would be much more interesting to do a suite of the suites, to completely mix them up."

Thus each member of the quartet would bring a composed piece with lyrics, play them, and ask for opinions and suggestions; democratically, the decisions would rest with the individual composers. "There's not one of us who's the boss," says Hétu. "No-one says, 'That bassline is good, keep it.' As a general rule, each of us makes decisions about our material once it has been discussed." Essentially, this compositional approach is a refinement of what the quartet did as Wondeur Brass, where the composition and lyrics were individual but the arrangements and polishing were a collective task. The only difference this time was the presence of the studio itself. "We used the studio and the recording processmontage, cutting, and editingas if it were another musical instrument," says Roger. "We literally transformed our sound in the studio. It was the first time it took close to a whole year to record an album. It gave us the time to reflect, and let the music become much, much more intricate. Not that the other albums aren't as intricate, but *Suite* is more so." Roger admits that dwindling finances curtailed this luxurious fine-tuning. "With four women composers, the combinations are endless. We know of no other way to obtain that rich sound," she says. "Yet the process of composing as a quartet is much longer than if we did it individually. It's always a question of money, and we had to decide that it was finished. In Les Poules, we were always in the process of re-evaluating our music. So, yes, the record is done, but the music is far from finished."

Listening to *Suite*[4] is like getting a free ticket to an old gothic amusement park once run by Carla Bley and rebuilt for speed by John Zorn. Just about every kind of carnival, vaudeville, showboat and broadway music ever made can be found in its grooves, plundered, gutted, rearranged and scored for post-punk classical quartet. The funhouse starts with "Le Monstre", a dynamic, *Noh*-style cabaret piece that began as an improv jam and evolved into an allegory about environmental degradation and their hometown. Hétu offers a simplistic explanation: "It's very trendy now to talk of environmentalism and pollution. I wanted to do a song but have it on a more interesting and complex level than simply saying 'recycle your garbage.'" Labrosse takes a more philosophical approach. "We've always talked a lot about the things that are present in our lives; we've done that throughout all the albums," she explains. "I think we're very close to this city. We live in it; we're part of it, we deal with it constantly. And even if we're traveling, we're reminded of it, because it's where we're from. There's an urban energy in the music."

Some tunes are propelled with a moody, seesaw organ or pulse with herky-jerky calliopes reminiscent of Bley, some groove to arpeggiated '50s surf music, some even swing hard. Most are miniature suites in themselves, containing swift, abrupt changes in tempo and musical style, switching from rippling keyboard runs to free saxophone freakouts to a hail of cascading harp notes. In bizarre, distended rondo form, several themes reoccur periodically, just like a real suite, although some songs, like the double blast of "J'ai Perdu Le Temps" and "J'ai Perdu Le Sommeil," throw away the classicism all together. "It *is* going a step further," admits Labrosse. "We usually switch our music around pretty fast but this time we're pushing it even further. But then again, we've never produced anything that's easy to listen to, something that you can put on and have dinner at the same time."

The sound of the female voice figures prominently in *Suite*. Just as the group sports no soloists, accompanists or rhythm section, Justine shatters the traditional archetype of the chanteuse by deploying its four voices percussively, rhythmically, and melodically. On "L'Intelligence Du Coeur," massed or disembodied radio voices seep through the savage, free jazz keyboard blurts. Elsewhere they shriek, whisper, caress, laugh, and yelp. "We always said that we were not authentic golden voices with a pristine range and technique," says Labrosse. "We've always integrated the voice as another instrument rather than use it in a nice way, a pure way, an effective way. Since the beginning, we've had no lead singer. This is why everyone sings; none of us is more accomplished than the other. Something new is that everybody sings on the same tune. Before Joane would sing cinema, Danielle *les amours*, but now in one song it goes round to everybody. We throw the ball at each other more than we did before."

"When we started playing together, we found that women singers were traditionally limited in the types of voices they could sing in," Roger says, picking up the ball. "There was this double standard that real singers, real poets, real musicians could use their voice freely, but a woman was obliged to sing well. The guys could sing bad, growl, or do strange things with their voice, but the women had to be pristine. We said that was crazy. I listened to these guys pretending to be Jacques Brel, and thought 'I could sing better than that.'"

Hétu considers Justine's lyrics to be *poesie bruitisque* and believes that to subject them to the scrutiny of the pop spotlight would effectively take them out of context. A contemporary pop *vedette* might be at home singing lines like *When your kisses made me blush with bliss/I was timeless/I was sleepless*, they might not have such an easy time with *I am detestable/abominable, friable, taxable/I am sinkable and dismantable/and living in Montréal*. "We're not Céline Dion. It's weird for the public who always think that the lyrics are the most important part of a song, and that the lead singer is always the center of attention. I have trouble with that." "So does the sound man," quips Roger.

For *Suite*, Justine enlisted electric harpist Zeena Parkins and the Japanese Queen of onomatopoeic improvisation, Tenko, finding kindred spirits in both their energy and way of working. "We all seem to have a craft in sounds," says Roger. This fascination with the intimate landscapes of sound prompted the sextet to regroup for *La Légende de la Pluie*, a multi-media theater piece first staged in Montréal as part of New Music America 1990. A collection of modern day fables about the rain in five tableaux set to the poetry of Geneviève Letarte, the choreography of Nathalie Derome, and the photography of Suzanne Girard, *La Légende de la Pluie*[6] is audacious in its stylistic and textural diversity, and crafted with an exquisite ear for electroacoustic detail: Parkins' "Les Pluies Acides" ["Acid Rains"] is an impressionistic, shifting soundtrack soaked with black rain, Hétu's "L'Attente" ["The Waiting"] opens with Western player piano rolls before giving way to stuttering tangos and mutated square dance riffs. Roger's singsong narrative in the minimalist film *noir* "Le Brouillard" ["The Fog"] recalls Laurie Anderson, and Tenko's "Orage" ["Storm"] weds Ligetian, soaring vocal chords with a violent, hard-edged urban beat. "It's nice to find different textures on the same instruments," says Labrosse. "Drums, keyboards, sax and bass... these instruments have been played so much and so well. It's not easy to explore the different possibilities. But we search for other things because we're not great virtuosi or soloists."

The stunning complexity of *Suite* and *La Légende de la Pluie* may free Justine from the limiting labels imposed by a musical culture that emphasizes gender over musicianship. "That's changed primarily in our own minds," says Labrosse. "At some point you stop focusing on gender, and in the last years we focused on the fact that we are musicians. Of course everyone's personality comes into their work. That in itself is a fresh perspective." Roger concurs. "More and more our collaborations, whether within Justine or with others, are approached on a musical level, and everyone has to pull their weight." This is borne out in Justine's eclectic solo projects. Roger is working on an electroacoustic ecological fable,[7] Hétu moonlights with Roger and Jean Derome in the jazzy Aux Pays de Castor, while Diane Labrosse plays with Michel F. Côté's Bruire[8] and is working on a solo CD.[9] Just as Kundera viewed life as an ongoing concerto, there are no codas for Justine. "I think we have to grow, to continue to change our music," says Danielle Roger. "But it's also important to break away from the process of becoming a star. We'll probably all be here in another 10 years, working in the shadows, in our own *metier*, and continuing as long as we can." Or, as they themselves once put it, "We shall never submit, we shall never surrender, we shall walk freely, we shall speak all languages.

Justine: Suite (Ambiances Magnétiques, 1990), La Légende de la Pluie (Ambiances Magnétiques, 1993), Langages Fantastiques (Ambiances Magnétiques, 1995)
Wondeur Brass: Ravir (Ambiances Magnétiques, 1985), Simoneda, Reine des Esclaves (Ambiances Magnétiques, 1987)
Les Poules: Les Contes de L'Amère Loi (Ambiances Magnétiques, 1986)
Danielle P. Roger: L'Oreille Enflée (Ambiances Magnétiques, 1994)
Diane Labrosse: with Michel F. Côté: Duo Déconstructiviste (Ambiances Magnétiques, 1994)
Diane Labrosse: Etats d'Ame (Ambiances Magnétiques, 1995)

Footnotes:
1. Harper & Row, New York, 1991: p.92, 2. Ambiances Magnétiques; 1985 and 1987, respectively, 3. Justine press release, 1990, 4. Ambiances Magnétiques, 1990, 6. "The Story of the Rain," Ambiances Magnétiques, 1993, 7. *L'Oreille Enflée*; Ambiances Magnétiques, 1994, 8. See *Bruire*, p.205, 9. *Etats d'Ame*; Ambiances Magnétiques, 1995

We're Only In It For The Money

Protest music has a long and rich history, from "I've Been Working On The Railroad" to "Free Nelson Mandela." In many ways Bob Dylan wrote its book, but Phil Ochs was its most eloquent champion. Yet the simultaneous release during the summer of love in 1967 of The Beatles' *Sgt. Pepper's Lonely Hearts Club Band* and The Beach Boys' *Pet Sounds* changed the rules of the game forever. Heretofore the long-playing record album was a collection of pop songs; after these two LPs, it became a work of art. The baroque stylings and unorthodox studio techniques on songs like "God Only Knows" and "A Day In The Life" turned the music industry on its ear and pulled popular music into post-modern adulthood. The pop song as a two-and-a-half-minute bite of ear candy was gone, and with it went the traditional protest song: Protest need no longer be spelt out in the lyrics, although songs would continue to tell us to "Take This Job And Shove It." No, the pop song's real message could now be found in the medium that carried it, and its unique morphology is the truest arrow in the quiver of each of the artists and ensembles in this section.

Using your two-and-a-half-minutes of pop fame as a platform for subversive comment not just on pop culture, politics, society, poverty, war, racial inequality, injustice and a myriad of other causes but on *the inherent compromises bound up in the form itself* goes back to Frank Zappa and The Mothers of Invention, hence the title of this section. The Mothers' third LP, *We're Only In It For The Money*[1] was a savage piss-take on flower power and hippiedom in general. Recorded in New York, far from the love-ins and LSD-fueled bustle of Haight-Ashbury, *We're Only In It For The Money* borrowed heavily from musical trends and styles of the period: aural collage, freakout guitar solos, tape-splicing [on "The Chrome-Plated Megaphone of Destiny"], witless, dippy psychedelic ditties and a wicked parody of *Sgt. Peppers'* on the sleeve. By deftly parodying these elements yet remaining true to their form and taking aim at anti-authority figures everywhere, be they cops, parents, politicians or hippies, Zappa managed to reveal exactly how conformist late 1960s counterculture had really become. The only other performer to break such new ground was Zappa's protégé, Don Van Vliet, alias Captain Beefheart. Starting with a musical form that was seemingly as *Safe As Milk,*[2] Beefheart rocketed the blues into deep space on hallucinatory works like *Lick My Decals Off Baby* and *Trout Mask Replica.*[3]

Needless to say, in the moribund years of the early 1970s, musicians who practiced this sort of subversion remained resolutely underground. Beefheart worked within the majors as long as it tolerated him [which wasn't very long], then struck out on a series of independent labels. Zappa was fed up with major label meddling at a very early stage in his career and founded his own labels, Straight and Barking Pumpkin. Meanwhile the lessons and music of Zappa and Beefheart were being idolized and studied very closely by The Residents, a bizarre group of San Francisco recluses. Lapsed filmmakers, The Residents taught themselves the rudiments of pop music and marketing, and went on to build a counterculture empire, The Cryptic Corporation. By maintaining complete and unequivocal anonymity throughout their 20-year career, they have focussed attention on their unique music, which, like Beefheart and Zappa, is frighteningly accurate in its savage indictment of pop's more fascistic tendencies.

Of course, with every mutation that pop music underwent since the late 1960s, major labels have been one step behind with their petri dishes. The majors have co-opted almost every independent music boom since punk rock hit like an air raid in 1976, when, after the success of The Sex Pistols, the majors went down to CBGBs on the Bowery and signed The Clash, Blondie, Television and Talking Heads. In the halcyon days of "indie" college rock during the latter half of the 1980s, R.E.M., Hüsker Dü, Sonic Youth and The Replacements got the nod. In 1988, when the majors realized there was a huge, untapped audience for Grandmaster Flash, Run DMC, Public Enemy, and De La Soul – well beyond the inner city projects and deep into the heart of MTV middle America – Afrocentricity, rapping and hiphop argot became widespread in popular culture. And the majors' reflexes are getting quicker: In 1991 when Nirvana, Pearl Jam, Jane's Addiction and the whole enchilada that is grunge rumbled out of Seattle, the majors had their checkbooks ready. Two years later, the exploitation of perhaps the last outpost of the underground, rave/ambient dub culture, began when The Orb, Moby, and Aphex Twin got lucrative record deals.

Those on the cutting edge, meanwhile, burrowed further underground and bred stronger and more virulent strains of their music: on the streets of Compton in South Central LA, Ice T, NWA and Snoop Doggy Dog unleashed their ultraviolent "gangsta" rap, or hiphop with a body count. American bands like Killdozer, Big Black and The Butthole Surfers spearheaded "pig-fuck" music, a sub-genre of indie-rock which mixed the nihilistic heaviness of Black Sabbath with drug-addled, plodding tempos.[4] And in the nation's capitol, Dischord bands like Fugazi, Beefeater, and Jawbox stubbornly refuse to be bought and are redefining grassroots, hardcore punk in much the same way that San Pedro's legendary Minutemen pushed the traditional guitar-bass-drums lineup and hardcore ethic to jazzy new heights in the '80s.

It should come as no surprise that music industries in other industrialized countries around the world are in the hands of the bean counters as well. The

Japanese pop industry, for example, is as tightly-regulated and image-conscious as its American counterpart. What's more, their popular music is often a bald imitation of current American rock, rap and soul styles. Amidst all this cookie-cutter pop, the subtlety and popcraft of After Dinner is a cool tonic. A truly Japanese ensemble with unparalleled sound design, After Dinner fuse traditional kabuki with modern pop textures, recalling the idiosyncratic playfulness and rigor of the films of Yasujiro Ozu.

In countries with oppressive economic, political and social regimes, the pop song can be even more of a loaded firecracker, akin to the perils of playing free jazz in pre-*glasnost* Russia. Wreck Sony, a/k/a The Kalahari Surfers, has tried to use the pop song as a weapon against the apartheid of segregated radio in censorship-ridden South Africa. A white South African dissident, Sony parlayed his stint in the media as a soundman into a string of critical, documentary-style LPs that carry whiffs of Zappa, protest rock, township jive, Henry Cow, Indian music, and The Residents. Just like Sergei Kuryokhin, Sony has only recently been allowed to sell his LPs in South Africa, and has been banned for reasons of blasphemy. Tom Zé suffered a similar fate. A gifted student of modern classical composition, Zé lived through the dark days of military rule in Brazil during the 1970s, joining forces with the countercultural *tropicalismo* movement, building fantastic instruments out of kitchen appliances, and penning rebellious, willfully odd samba albums. In such situations, the challenge to diffuse the message is even greater, and the resulting fringe of enlightened pop troubadours even more sparsely populated. Yet in their hands, pop is perhaps the best defence, an innocuous yet potent and corrosive form, and the ideal vehicle for subversion. Just ask Unca Frank.

1. Verve, 1968
2. Title of Beefheart's 1967 debut album for Buddah
3. Straight Records, 1969 and 1970 respectively
4. Proof that the system, in its quest to part youth from their money, will quaff even the crudest hooch: The Butthole Surfers, famed for their misanthropy, shock value and gross-out live shows, provided the music for a 1994 Nintendo TV ad

The Residents

"All truly holy objects lose their truth as soon as they are exploited by witless dupes who didn't see the incredible import of their ubersymbolism until it is slapping them in the face. The pure glory of inanity, the Holy Insipidity, the dreamlike trance state induced by random editing serve to FREE US from the stinking MEDIOCRETY of the workaday world, TRANSPORTING US into a dreamlike universe of SHEER UNCONTAMINATED TECHNOFEAR so GAUDY as to actually go BEYOND ART and off into the realms of myth and religion...For when down the Rungs of the Art Ladder we descend to a certain level of shoestring-budget 'Exquisite Badness,' we reach a cut-off point where bulldada begins, an 'edge' where [we] start finding almost religious interpretation of the results of atrocious craftsmanship...'Bad movies' are already reaching a point of recognition which will threaten to DEFUSE their badness and make them once again JUST MEDIOCRE. THIS my friends is what we must avoid so we strongly suggest that you NOW EAT THIS ARTICLE and forget we ever said anything. Thanks."

J.R. "Bob" Dobbs, High Epopt of The Church of The SubGenius[1]

It all started innocently enough with two little 45 rpm singles about a wiener dog dressed in a Santa Claus suit. The gatefold sleeveshand silk-screened, intentionally mis-numbered and sloppily glued togetherwere disguised as a

Christmas card from an insurance company. Four hundred were mailed free in September of 1972 to friends and enemies, including Frank Zappa and Richard Nixon. While it is open to speculation whether Nixon may still have his copy, Zappa returned his, unopened, to the sender, who enigmatically called themselves The Residents.

Like Kafka's Josef K, The Residents have existed in anonymous chiaroscuro ever since. The San Francisco quartet have built up a vast and eclectic body of work that defies easy taxonomy, encompassing a collection of 40 rendered pop hits, several unrealized operas, a hallucinatory 14-hour B-movie starring midget mediums and atomic shopping carts, sinister and deviant nursery rhymes, a futuristic Steinbeckian epic about class war, a psychosexual analysis of Elvis Presley, and a dark meditation on freaks. Like the best celluloid trash, the banality of their *oeuvre* is largely iconic; religion, literature, philosophy, psychology and sexuality were all grist for The Residents' metaphor mill, all cunningly and dramatically deployed utilizing the strategies of nearly every school of modern art. The Residents were "Performance Artists" long before Laurie Anderson's answering machine started taking calls.

Along with Faust, The Residents drew *the* blueprint for the possibilities of studio experimentation, and their filmic aesthetic would have reverberations in popular music for decades to come. While their deconstruction of popular musics plundered from Black sources – such as R&B, rock'n'roll, soul and doo-wop – savagely exposed the inner workings of the music business, it was the wide-eyed naïveté with which they approached the creative process that makes much of their work magical. After all, the sublime analog cheesiness, dime-store production values, and inept chops of early Residents music was bound to appeal a generation weaned on corporate rock'n'roll, post-modernism and commercial television. The fact they subversively employed mass marketing and advertising techniques to successfully promote their Art was the icing on the cake, a shell game that allowed The Residents to bridge uptown and downtown, playing a punk club one night and an opera house the next.

The Residents accomplished all this while remaining distant and aloof from both the media [who of course wanted to know more] and a fantastic cult following [who craved and demanded the obvious, false veneer of anonymity]. Latter-day mummers decked out in shredded newspaper, radiation suits, or elegant eyeball, top hat & tails, The Residents fabricated an elaborate mythology to shroud their origins, established the Theory of Obscurity, and erected an equally fictitious business empire – Ralph Records, Cryptic Corporation, Pore No Graphics, The Uncle Willie Eyeball Club – about them to realize their goals. To this day, theories circulate as to whether any of these are in fact separate entities or merely incorporated masks with powers of attorney. No matter. This is not the place to expose The Residents; after two decades of self-imposed obscurity, ironic detachment is part and parcel of The Residents game.

"They're not really obsessed with obscurity," says Hardy Fox, A&R Manager for The Cryptics. "They consider that more a media obsession about them than their own self-attitude. Their point of view was that they just wanted to be perceived as a group. Any time a group of people establish themselves under a group name, the minute they start being referred to as individuals, then it undermines the group identity and destroys them. It just creates tension. If people are trying to work together, there's no reason why the media should pry them apart and say that this person is this and this person is that. Because then it becomes ego-competitive. They always liked to have a group identity and they like to have a group name and a group look, they don't want to be known as the 'cute one' or 'the short one' like Davey Jones in The Monkees."

According to popular mythology, The Residents hail from Shreveport, Louisiana. Of this fact we can be reasonably sure; Southern accents rarely lie. However, like much else about the group, true facts about the band's origins and early days are as rare as hen's teeth, and often spurious. For instance, we are often told that The Residents met in high school during the 1960s, loved *Catcher In The Rye*, sat glued to the boob tube, listened to scratchy James Brown and Bo Diddley 45s, and were a textbook case of middle-class alienation. So says *The Official W.E.I.R.D. Book Of The Residents*, published in 1980 by the first officially recognized Residents fan club, W.E.I.R.D.[2] Savage Pencil, Chris Cutler and Gary Panter all contributed to the elaborate tissue of lies found herein; then-unknown cartoonist Matt Groening, who would go on to create *The Simpsons* and *Life In Hell*, was the appointed historiographer, and bravely tried to set the record straight:

> "Let your mind drift back to more simpler, more pathetic times...to an age when American teenagers jitterbugged in plastic hula hoops to the savage jungle rhythm of payola'd rock'n'roll, and spent their parents' hard-earned pay on Kookie crumbs and Jughead comics...when Ozzie choked in the basement rumpus room on a piece of Harriet's fudge, and Rick and Dave kicked at each other on the patio, pausing only for a healthful grape drink break...after which they would retreat to their rooms to masturbate with *Tales From The Crypt* while wearing 3-D glasses."[3]

Upon graduation in 1966 and terrified of the grown-up world of draft, college, career and suburbia, our fab four fled Shreveport and started off down the road to San Francisco, where the psychedelic revolution was underway, and the summer of love was just around the corner. Their truck broke down some 25 miles south of their destination in sleepy San Mateo, where they stumbled across a large supply of instruments and recording equipment, including the first four-track and eight-track recorders available on the market. Hooking up with British expatriate guitarist Philip Lithman, whom they would later dub "Snakefinger," and mysterious Bavarian musicologist N. [Nigel] Senada, they cut twisted party tapes and sent them to some friends back in Louisiana, who effusively wrote back offering to manage them. In 1970, after recording two unreleased reel-to-reel tapes, *Rusty Coathangers For The Doctor* and *The Ballad Of Stuffed Trigger*, they submitted a third album of 39 songs to Captain Beefheart's producer Hal Halverstadt at Warner Brothers, reasoning that if anyone in the record industry would understand them, it would be the man who worked with Beefheart. They called their demo *The Warner Brothers Album*, and packaged the tape complete with the famous Looney Tunes logo. It was returned, judged too weird, addressed to The Residents.

Undaunted, The Residents took this sign of non-acceptance as an omen and moved to San Francisco proper. They formed Ralph[4] Records, and released *Santa Dog* a few days before Christmas of 1972. From the desecration of "Jingle Bells" on "Explosion" to the reworking of Amadeo Roldan's 1930 rhumba hit "Ritmico #6: Tiempo de Rhumba" on "Lightning," *Santa Dog*[5] is the seminal Residents recording, revealing a group of studio savants more interested in the actual recording process than songwriting or performing in the traditional sense. This approach was highly curious in the 1970s, even more so considering they were literally non-musicians. True, the symphonic overtones, treated vocals, hammered piano, tape loops, toys, unorthodox tunings, and classical and free jazz plunderings were being explored by Faust. Yet where Faust were avant garde ambassadors of conventional Rock music, The Residents were more interested in the field of popular music *as social criticism*, and seized upon its most basic and mythic unit, the gramophone record, as their textbook.

Nowhere is this seen better than their debut, *Meet The Residents*.[6] "The First Album By North Louisiana's Phenomenal Pop Combo," *Meet The Residents* lampoons just about every musical idiom you can think of, with special attention paid to seminal R&B and the commercialization of the monkeypod, Martin Dennyesque exotica that was rampant in 1950s pop. There's operatic parody mixed with Southern ballads ["Spotted Pinto Bean"], a mutant New Orleans march driven by a *Mother Popcorn* wah-wah guitar ["Infant Tango"], as well as a predilection for bad puns ["Guylum Bardot"] and a devastating, off-key send-up of "These Boots Are Made For Walking." All of this segues with the free association of Surrealist Art and is accomplished with a minimum of instrumentation [voice, guitar, winds, percussion, a few household items, toy pianos and trash] and crude tape manipulation techniques [splicing, overdubbing, varispeed]. Most intriguing, however, was the fact that there were no Residents to meet, only a crustacean distortion of the jacket for The Beatles' American Capitol/EMI debut. The Theory of Obscurity was in full force.

True iconoclasts, The Residents went back into the studio in 1974, not to record a follow-up record, but to shoot a movie. In a small, windowless studio on Sycamore Street in San Francisco, The Residents embarked on a musical/video extravaganza that would tell the tale of Siamese Twins and tag-team wrestlers Arf and Omega, menacing atomic shopping carts, and an eternal love triangle between a schizophrenic outlaw cowboy, Lonesome Jack, and an Eternal Goddess, Weescoosa. It was called *Vileness Fats*. The choice of film as the medium for the project is a telling one, because at its core The Residents' work is imbued with a dramatic character rather than musical one; they approach their songs, albums and projects through characters and archetypes. Chris Cutler expands on this idea in his incisive 1980 essay "Living In The Electric."[7] If architecture, Cutler writes, was once the flower of all the Arts – including philosophy, physics, maths, music, astronomy, sculpture – then film is its modern corollary, including acting, painting and sculpture, music, writing, dramatism, montage, and the technical mastery of electronic and motion picture equipment. It is here that The Residents cut their aesthetic teeth.

With *Vileness Fats*, The Residents did for the cinematic medium what they did for pop music on *Meet The Residents*. For example, their studio was so small The Residents decided that everyone except Arf, Omega and Weescoosa should be one-armed midgets to make the demented, incredibly complex hand-painted sets look larger. Their technical faculties were always two steps behind their imagination, however, and behind schedule and over budget, the film spiraled out of control. It was abandoned in Christmas 1975, with 14 hours of footage shot.[8] After an incident in Chinatown known in Residents apocrypha as "The Great Dim Sum Riot of 1974,"[9] they settled the creative differences that had snarled their work on the film and went to work on another studio record. With its hypnotic mesh of strings, percussion and horns and lyrics that sounded as if they were written in Sanskrit, their new creation carried their unusual juxtaposition of song forms to new heights. Bound by the theory of obscurity, The Residents called it *Not Available*[10] and vowed it would never be released.

This clever cat-and-mouse marketing scheme is a brilliant illustration of the irony The Residents have traditionally deployed to subvert the mechanisms and channels of the pop music media. Throughout the years they have played the corporate music game to the hilt: issuing "official" press releases, shooting bizarre promotional videos, doing anonymous radio interviews, and running an aggressive marketing arm for Ralph that exclusively offered hand-made Residents paraphernalia and "collectors editions"[11] to their cult within a cult, the Uncle Willie Eyeball Club [UWEB], under the slogan "Buy Or Die." "Using manipulative forms and techniques...allows for pointing out how inherently ridiculous and dehumanising they are," Cutler wrote. "One becomes a co-conspirator, a partner in shared pretence."[12]

The next Residents album to be officially released was *The Third Reich'n'Roll*.[13] What The Beatles underwent on *Meet The Residents* was a tea party compared to what 1960s pop music suffered on *Third Reich*. Opening with Adolf Hitler singing "Let's Twist Again," the album features a slew of hideous and unrecognizable cover versions of '60s pop hits ranging from bubblegum to R&B to psychedelia. "Yummy Yummy Yummy, I've Got Love In My Tummy," "Sunshine Of Your Love," "Inna Gadda Da Vida," "Hey Jude," and "Papa's Got A Brand New Bag" all get disemboweled in two side-long suites entitled "Swastikas on Parade" and "Hitler Was A Vegetarian."[14] The surfeit of sonic puns buried in the songsgunfire, airplanes crashing, car horns, and broad, parodic vocalsrecall the biting, satiric genius of Spike Jones and Ernie Kovacs, yet the vaudevillian mugging is used to make a dead serious point: Pop music is more than just the opium of the masses, it's a deeply compromised, global, multimillion dollar corporate behemoth that believes you should sit back, relax, and *buy*. If you got this far and missed the point, there was always the cover, which featured Dick Clark in Nazi drag.

By 1976, the four Louisianans who had expressed an early interest in managing the group moved to San Francisco and formed The Cryptic Corporation. Jay Clem handled the accounting, Homer Flynn took over art and advertising, John Kennedy became production manager, while Hardy Fox fielded interviews for the press and acted as A&R for Ralph. The Cryptics oversaw the production of the next two Residents albums, *Fingerprince* and *Duck Stab/Buster & Glen*, and pragmatically began to rein in the Residents' more excessive tendencies. *Fingerprince*,[15] an important and transitory album between the early, primitive works and the later sophistication of their wacky, sinister pop,[16] was originally intended as a three-sided LP with one side having two concentric grooves *à la* Monty Python's *Matching Tie & Handkerchief* of 1973. The Cryptics pruned it down and truncated a ballet commissioned by the San Francisco Museum of Modern Art, "Six Things To A Cycle."[17]

As the story goes, the Cryptics had big dreams for The Residents. According to another popular bit of Residents mythology, during the recording of the next album, the Residents became frightened of commercial success and absconded with the master tapes to England, where they consulted with drummer Chris Cutler, who had drummed on the sessions. In a financial bind, The Cryptic Corp released *Not Available* to fill the gap, Cutler acted as a go-between, and things were eventually patched up. The album that they held dear to their hearts was *Eskimo*,[18] a patently fake trip to the Arctic concocted in the studio from scratch;

a *Plan 9 From Outer Space* set on the North Pole. The Residents hadn't the slightest idea of what Inuit life was like; of all things, the chilly epic was inspired by a billboard depicting Santa Claus swigging a Coke. As Homer Flynn once told Carle V.P. Groome,

> "I think that *Eskimo*...could have been on Mars as far as they were concerned. It was so far removed from them that it allowed a certain amount of freedom. They were doing their own romanticized version of what Eskimo culture iswhat it should have been. From what I heard, the Eskimos had no musical instruments – they sing and play drums, that's it! When The Residents found that out they thought it would be pretty hard to make an album. So they had to invent the vocabulary of an Eskimo band."[19]

A fart in the tempest of modern Art, *Eskimo* is the quintessential Residents LP, an exercise in ethnological forgery that works precisely because of its tinfoil phoniness. The sonic adventures of Angkakok the Eskimo shaman and his nonsense language invented from English homonyms laid the groundwork for many future Residents projects. It also introduced the most enduring icon we have of the band: the eyeball costume and the image of The Residents as austere, removed observers. Despite the fact they were still shunned in America, *Eskimo* pushed The Residents over the top overseas. As soon as BBC DJ John Peel, and Chris Cutler, writing for *Sounds*, got their hands on *Eskimo*, the jig was up, and they were soon embraced back home – ironically as pioneers of the "new wave."

Functioning like a mutant arm of a major record label, the eyeball wonders – working in tandem with the Cryptic Corporation, of course – adopted long-term marketing strategies, worked on media relations and developed ancillary mail-order merchandising as if they were developing the career of an established pop star who had conquered the arenas and was pondering what to do next. "The Residents feel like you have to plan in order to get anything done," says Hardy Fox on the telephone from the offices of The Cryptic Corporation in San Francisco. Despite his deep Louisiana accent and frequently lapsed pronouns, Fox has consistently denied that he is a Resident. "It's just not very realistic to plan really more than five years in advance, yet they try to work on ten-year plans." The Residents began the Reagan decade in turmoil, not the least of which was a crisis at Ralph Records. Buoyed by the late successes of *Eskimo* and *Duck Stab/Buster and Glen*, The Cryptics also released albums by Snakefinger, Tuxedomoon, Renaldo & The Loaf, Fred Frith, Yello and others. Yet after the new wave boom of the late 1970s and the subsequent indie record fad died out, Ralph soon found themselves in the same dire economic straits as other independents, and Jay Clem and John Kennedy decided to leave the company for greener pastures, leaving Homer Flynn and Hardy Fox to man the sinking ship.

The Cryptics bailed out of the record business, retaining Ralph as The Residents' production company, and started moving The Residents onto other labels.

While The Residents felt that their first ten years were wildly fertile, they felt they had pushed the studio as far as it could go, and that music itself had reached a conceptual *cul-de-sac*. "The Residents' attitude really is that in the world of music there isn't really much worth noting since the '50s," Fox explains. "It's pretty well been rehashed post-modernism, which they've rehashed in post-modern fashion themselves. Their attitude has been that there's more to life than just music. There's got to be something beyond this, a new area that's not so well defined and explored. After the first decade of doing recording, they love music and will always work in music. But they wanted the next decade, which was the 1980s, to start realizing much more of a theatrical direction."

The Residents' newfound theatrical direction was bound up in The Mole saga, a fantastic yarn spun about the ideological culture clash between the Chubs and the Moles. Intended to span six albums – three of music and three of story – the ambitious project dovetailed the sharply contrasting mores of the two cultures through their music. Exuding whiffs of the dust bowl, Africa and Middle East, *Mark of The Mole*[20] introduces us to the primitive and superstitious Moles, or Mohelmot, who live beneath the desert in massive, ant-like colonies. Crossing the desert because of a freak storm, the Moles meet the jolly Chubs on the coast. The warm welcome offered by the Chubs quickly turns into cultural intimidation and a class conflict, and a war breaks out between the two races.

The second album, *The Tunes Of Two Cities*,[21] juxtaposes the music of the Moles and the Chubs. Dark, metallic and tribal, with high fluctuating electronics and bass cadences, the Moles' music serves a deeply ritualistic purpose, and harken back to the wordless, highly stylized and invented language of *Eskimo*. Contrasting the apocalyptic, industrial music of the Moles is the unctuous jazz/pop of the Chubs, although their twisted big band standards, glossy, lurid and hedonistic, have to do with ritual exorcism as well, and as such recall *Third Reich'n'Roll*. Several decades after the Great War, in the "fourth" part of the Mole "trilogy," *The Big Bubble*,[22] The Moles and Chubs live side-by-side in an uneasy peace, although the Moles are forbidden to use their language. Interbreeding has created a new race, The Cross. A pop group of Cross origins, The Big Bubble, shock the Chubs by singing in the forbidden Mohelmot tongue. The singer is jailed and sees himself as a Messiah... The Mole Saga was designed primarily as a stage show, something that would push the visual envelope and allow the Residents to tour for the first time in ten years; they only undertook three actual performances in their first decade.[23] Yet due to the financial crisis at Ralph, plans for a proposed live tour based on *The Mark of The*

Mole were shelved, and a disastrous European tour careened around Europe out of control in 1982.

The Residents never felt comfortable touring because they could never pull off on stage what they had done in studio. That all changed when they bought one of the first available Emulators, a combination digital sampler and synthesizer which allowed them to recreate their scissors and splicing tape aesthetic live. The new technology had already made their impact on The Mole Trilogy – it's all over *The Big Bubble* – and would change the music of The Residents forever. "The studio environment shifting to digital brought a whole new way of thinking about what could be done," says Hardy Fox. "It started affecting compositions and everything. In actuality, most of the '80s was pretty radical for music technically, probably the most radical era that music has gone through. The studio approach to it, the whole MIDI-ization of music and the use of computers to control sound parametersthere's probably nothing in history has happened this radically or certainly this fast in music. I think it's pretty exciting. The whole concept of electronic music, you have a certain kind of nostalgia element that people who think of electronic music as squawks and beeps like the old days. It's all very interesting and very important stuff, but a lot of people do not realize where electronic music has gone, particularly people not involved in music, do not realize that virtually all they listen to now is electronic music. That's pretty radical. Electronic music has almost concealed itself now. It's more electronic than ever, but it masquerades in very interesting ways."

After The Mole Show, The Residents wanted to do something that wasn't crafted from scratch, and they hit upon the idea of a series of records that "Residentified" American composers, with a contrasting pair per release. Only two albums were released in The American Composer Series, a mammoth project originally slated to continue until 2001. The music on *George & James* and *Stars & Hank Forever!*[24] gave critical ammunition to those who insisted that The Residents had run out of conceptual gas. Simply feeding their musical heroes into the Emulator offered a lazy method of work. *George & James* in particular was a step backward, retooling intrinsic elements from Chub and Mole music: "George" was a reworking of Gershwin's jazz milestone *Rhapsody In Blue*, while "James" was J.B.'s 1962 *Live At The Apollo* revisited.[25] Yet their interpretation of Hank Williams burrowed deep into the psycho-sexual subtext of the doomed C&W singer's material on songs like "Jambalaya" and "Kaw-Liga," foreshadowing major works to come, such as *The King & Eye* and *CUBE E.*

With *The King & Eye*,[26] instead of regurgitating the music of the biggest and most pervasive cultural icon America has ever produced, Elvis Aaron Presley, The Residents play up the implicit in his lyrics. As a father tells fables of a long dead "King" to his children, The Residents dismantle and sing sixteen of

Presley's hits in their inimitable deep Southern drawl, offering radical new ways to hear them and opening up deep wells of leering sexuality, gripping drama, and forbidden passion; in short, putting the id of the Memphis Elvis up in the light show of the Las Vegas one. And it is clearly the Las Vegas Elvis that is being lampooned [and cherished] here; The Residents believe that Elvis the musician was nowhere near as important as his legacy, a martyr to his muse. Cryptic Homer Flynn even went as far as casting Elvis as a tragic Greek hero:

> "They were infinitely more interested in the Elvis myth than they were in Elvis himself. It's really the mythology and the cultural phenomenon that they found interesting...He had an incredible myth created around just a couple of years of substantial work. He's an incredibly tragic figure! As they did more research about him, they became more sympathetic to him because naïveté has always been something very close to the heart of The Residents. And they found Elvis to be more and more of an innocent, a very naïve person who was in the right place at the right time – or the wrong place at the wrong time, relative to the way things turned out."[27]

At the rotten heart of *The King & Eye* is The Residents' belief that the 1950s was the decade in which popular American culture had reached its nadir. Arts at the fringes was definitely happening – Jack Kerouac was on the road, Jackson Pollock was making a splash, Sun Ra was mapping the cosmos, Harry Partch was inventing new instruments and harmonies, and Edgar Varèse was bulk erasing history. Yet somewhere along the line, America's two greatest cultural exports – rock'n'roll and bebop – went the way of the Old West, with Elvis and Bird as the last outposts. With their three-part stage show *CUBE E – The History Of American Music in 3 E-Z Pieces*, The Residents completed the left-hand side of the equation they had begun in *The King & Eye*: [White] cowboy music + [black] gospel & blues = [white] rock'n'roll = Elvis.[28]

"The Residents have always been more interested in pop culture than they are in intellectual culture," says Hardy Fox. "Although they enjoy Sun Ra, Partch and Varèse, they don't feel that they were influential as a pervasive culture. *CUBE E* was a lot about the fact that they felt like American culture dead-ended in the '50s, the era of bebop and rock'n'roll. When the rest of the world started reflecting their version of American culture back onto America, instead of forging ahead with their own culture, America started reflecting the reflection back. The English started playing American music, and the Americans started playing the English version of American music, and got into this vicious circle they've been caught in ever since."

A sublime combination of Beckett, cracked *Noh* theater and Mummenschanz, *CUBE E*[29] neatly telescopes a hundred years of American pop into one evening, from music of the plains through the plantation to the plight of American rock'n'roll at the hands of the British Invasion. Set adrift in a stark Road Runner landscape, Part I, "Buckaroo Blues," features alien cowboys under impossible 100 gallon hats sitting in front of electric campfires and singing despairing trail songs like "Bury Me Not On The Lone Prairie." Part II "Black Barry," is introduced by looped gospel samples and pickanniny minstrel dancers who sing 19th Century slave songs and eventually transform death and despair into a voodoo celebration. Part III, "The Baby King," is the 20th century distillation of Buckaroo and Black Barry, concludes with an overweight Elvis imitator being murdered by the music of English pop fans.

Twenty years ago, The Residents couldn't have given their first record away for the price of a Big Mac and fries. By 1992, they were special guests on *Pee Wee's Playhouse*,[30] and MTV was beaming them into millions of households in the teenage wasteland of suburbia. They found it hard to believe themselves, yet The Residents were twenty years old: "Yeah, THE RESIDENTS, that whacko little fart rock combo from the '70s that's STILL AROUND and maybe not quite so whacko and fart rock as you thought."[31] For their 20th anniversary, The Museum Of Modern Art in New York gave The Residents a film and video retrospective, and co-sponsored an installation of performance and video arcana at The Kitchen.[32] The Voyager company underwrote a compilation laserdisc, *Twenty Twisted Questions*, which collected material from the Cryptic video and film archives, and The Residents themselves dissected and reworked their own hits into a "new" random shuffle CD, *Our Finest Flowers*.[33] Sensing that there was a buck to be made ["The Residents are highly collectible," Fox demurs], The Uncle Willie Eyeball Club also commissioned a new version of *The Cryptic Guide To The Residents*, this time called *Uncle Willie's Highly Opinionated Guide To The Residents*.

Yet successfully parading as a dark and deformed limb of American culture had left The Residents as freaks. During the *Mole Show* tours, they would mutter "Everyone comes to the Freak Show" before they hit the stage. The phrase stuck, and it became the inspiration for their most recent release, *Freak Show*.[34] While its music marks little progress from the nadir of *CUBE E* – the sideshow as metaphor for the sensationalist underbelly of the entertainment industry goes back as far as Tod Browning's 1933 documentary *Freaks – Freak Show* nonetheless represents the latest transitional release for the Residents. From the beginning its colorful *dramatis personæ* – Harry The Head, Benny the Bouncing Bump, Wanda The Worm Woman – were intended for new media, the first of which was a "graphic novel"[35] where ten comic book artists, including Matt Howarth and Savage Pencil, fleshed out their pathetic stories. They all worked with video director Jim Ludtke on a CD-ROM version of the novel for the Voyager Company. A new personal computer technology that stores data on a disc similar to a compact disc, CD-ROM allows access to 700 megabytes of digitally encoded information, be it an encyclopedia, a linguistics course, a Sherlock Holmes mystery, a baseball almanac, even the Guinness Disc of World Records. Like its cousin the CD, you cannot store data on a CD-ROM, only read it. Yet you can do so *interactively*, which is what fascinates The Residents, who are approaching the unexplored territory the same way they approached a motion picture camera for *Vileness Fats* – with a toddler's sense of wonder.

"You cannot generate naïveté, you cannot generate innocence; the whole concept is contradictory," says Fox. "The fact that a lot of their early work did have a lot of that sense about it was a very positive thing. They have never been under the illusion that it represented anything other than a reflection of their reality. When you're not so naïve anymore, to pretend you are or try to fake it would not be honest, and would not represent their actual state and what they actually were doing. The music has gotten more sophisticated and technology has taken it in directions that they wouldn't have been able to achieve on their own. It's allowed them to actually achieve some level of craft even though it's mechanically aided. For them, that just became another thing to explore. For The Residents, there is no good and bad in music, just current trends."

This is one of the reasons why, as the turn of the century nears, The Residents are more likely to be found writing software than writing songs, and leaving the stone age of pop music far behind them. "Music is a very powerful medium, but it's just like many art forms now: over-explored and over-exaggerated in our culture as important," says Fox. "There is so much music now and basically people are desensitized to it; it's no longer interesting because it's everywhere. Sometimes they feel guilty for making even more of it because there's so much of it out there. They almost feel that some people should swear to not making any more music as a sign of help for society and our culture.

"So The Residents keep hoping the new baby boom will start something, although they have a sneaky feeling that the new generation will be so busy with their Nintendos that they'll have no interest in music whatsoever. Artistically, video games are probably more interesting for our culture than music. It's sad. Actually, it's not sad because when a medium has been explored and even over-explored, it's good that things shift, because it just becomes decadent if it doesn't. You have to be realistic about things. It's probably a healthy sign."

The Residents: Santa Dog (Ralph, 1972), Meet The Residents (Ralph, 1974), Third Reich'n'Roll (Ralph, 1976), Fingerprince (Ralph, 1977), Duck Stab/Buster & Glen (Ralph, 1978), Not Available (Ralph, 1978), Eskimo (Ralph, 1979), The Commercial Album (Ralph, 1980), The Mark of The Mole (Ralph, 1981), Tunes of Two Cities (Ralph, 1982), Whatever Happened To Vileness Fats? (Ralph, 1984), George & James (Ralph, 1984), The Big Bubble (Ralph, 1985), The Stars & Hank Forever! (Ralph, 1986), 13th Anniversary Show Live in Holland (Torso, 1986), 13th Anniversary Show Live in USA (Ralph, 1986), The Eyeball Show: Live in Japan (Ralph, 1986), God In 3 Persons (Ryko,

1988), The King & Eye (Enigma, 1989), Cube E Live In Holland (Torso, 1990), Our Finest Flowers (Ralph America, 1992), Freak Show (Ralph America, 1992), Gingerbread Man (Ralph America, 1994)

Footnotes:

1. "Creative Truth," From *The Book Of The SubGenius*, Fireside/Simon & Schuster: New York, 1991: pp.72-73

2. The short-lived We Endorse Instant Residents Deification that folded in 1981 and was run by Philip Culp and Mimi King

3. Groening, "The True Story Of The Residents: A brief summary of known facts, top secrets, hazy details, veiled hints and blatant lies," printed in *The Official W.E.I.R.D Book Of The Residents*, The Residents Official Fan Club: San Francisco, 1979: p.3

4. High school lingo for puking, 5. Ralph, 1972, 6. Ralph, 1974

7. Included in *File Under Popular* [First Edition], November Books, London, 1984: pp.81-107. It was considerably revised for the Second Edition in 1992

8. Excerpts were edited together and released as a video and soundtrack, *Whatever Happened To Vileness Fats?*; Ralph, 1984 9. Groening, "The True Story Of The Residents:" p.5, 10. Ralph, 1978

11. For example, a mint-condition *Santa Dog* currently fetches $1275 from the Residents Archives

12. Cutler, "Living In The Electric:" p.90, 13. Ralph, 1976

14. The Residents would eventually take this concept to the extreme in *The Commercial Album* [Ralph, 1980], a sort-of perverted Top 40 consisting of forty one-minute tunes

15. Ralph, 1977, 16. It's important to note that the Partch-like structures of *Fingerprince* also provided the gestation for future long compositions such as *Mark Of The Mole*, and marked the beginning of their fascination with religious themes and control

17. The residue was left as an EP, *Babyfingers*; Ralph, 1977, 18. Ralph, 1979

19. Carle V.P.Groome, "Truth Comes Out Of Fiction," in *Ear* Magazine Vol.15 N2, June 1990: pp.29

20. Ralph, 1981, 21. Ralph, 1982, 22. Ralph, 1985

23. Audition Night at The Boarding House in San Francisco on October 18, 1971; a small gig in Arcata, California on Hallowe'en of the same year, and a performance at Rather Ripped Records, a Berkeley record store, in 1976

24. Ralph, 1984 and 1986; respectively

25. This is not to say The Residents were Luddites unable to adapt to the new technology; their first work designed for compact disc, *God In 3 Persons* [Ryko, 1988], shrewdly exploited the antiseptic, pristine qualities of the medium to underscore the banal drama at hand: a thinly veiled study of the rift between Eastern duality [a pair of androgynous, yin and yang faith-healing Siamese twins] and Western Trinity [a sado-masochistic cowboy infatuated with them]

26. Enigma, 1989, 27. Groome, "Truth Comes Out Of Fiction:" pp.29-31

28. I am indebted to Richard Gehr ["Taking Care Of Business," The *Village Voice*, January 23, 1990] for the new math

29. Available on *Cube E Live In Holland*, Torso, 1990, 30. An anarchic children's television show hosted by Pee Wee Herman, a.k.a. comedian Paul Reubens

31. Ralph America catalogue, 1993, 32. To their credit, MOMA had been hip to the importance of The Residents early on: In 1982, they recognized them as one of the progenitors of the new phenomenon of "music video" and added *One Minute Movies* – four video cuts from *The Commercial Album* – to their permanent collection, 33. Ralph America, 1992, 34. Ralph America, 1993, 35. Dark Horse Publishing, 1992; "graphic novel" is the ten-dollar term for adult comic books

Kalahari Surfers

WARNING/GUARANTEE: The language and concepts contained herein are **GUARANTEED NOT TO CAUSE ETERNAL TORMENT IN THE PLACE WHERE THE GUY WITH THE HORNS AND THE POINTED STICK CONDUCTS HIS BUSINESS**. This guarantee is as real as the threats of the video fundamentalists who use attacks on rock music in their attempt to transform America into a nation of check-mailing nincompoops [in the name of Jesus Christ]. If there is a hell, its fires wait for them, not us.

Frank Zappa[1]

Q: What do Donna Summer's "Love To Love You Baby," Crass' *Christ – The Album*, Peter Tosh's "Legalise It," Pink Floyd's *The Wall*, Prince's "Dirty Mind," George Carlin's *Class Clown*, and Andrew Lloyd Webber's *Jesus Christ Superstar* have in common? A: This incongruous septet of records were all banned for sale, distribution and possession in South Africa by the Direktoraat van Publikasies according to the terms of The Publications Act N°42 of 1974.

It's a question that won't be showing up soon in a future RPM edition of *Trivial Pursuit*, yet it's one that has silenced the career of hundreds of musicians in South Africa since the dawn of apartheid in July of 1950. Since the introduction of The Publications Act in 1974, fines of 500 Rand[2] and jail sentences of six months for first offences have been doled out to scores of musicians, playwrights, authors, artists, and citizens unfortunate enough to be caught with one of the above albums in their possession; to be precise, over 8,000 publications were deemed "undesirable" between 1975 and 1982.[3]

Whether by the State or the marketplace, censorship is part of day-to-day life in South Africa, and the media has historically acted as the go-between for both. Self-censorship has been the solution for many artists who wished to survive in South Africa, and some toned down, soft-pedaled or simply dropped their messages of freedom and revolution to avoid losing their record contracts and being banned, detained or imprisoned. Warric Sony will have none of it. "South African popular artists, in their desire for mainstream success, chose to ignore political content in their music," Sony once wrote. "As a result the archive of resistance songwriting is very thin. Sure the jazz guys came with numerous jams and melodies with titles like 'Song For Winnie.' But I am talking vocal song with penned words like the wealth of political songwriting which blossomed from places like Chile and Nicaragua...where was our Thomas Mapfumo or our Ruben Blades, the songwriters, the balladeers, like the Bluesmen of the American Twenties, like the hundred of radical songwriters in Papa Doc's Haiti? Where were all the soul rebels?"[4]

An underground South African musician and producer, the 36-year old Sony is an outspoken white dissident and the braintrust behind the subversive rock ensemble Kalahari Surfers. After discovering no pressing plant in South Africa would touch his master tapes, Sony found a unique way around the censorship roadblock: he sent his masters out of the country to be pressed by Chris Cutler of Recommended Records in England. Imported back into South Africa, the first three Kalahari Surfers records were ironically lost in the CD revolution and sold so little[5] nobody bothered to submit them to the Direktoraat von Publikasies for "undesirable" status. The fourth Kalahari Surfers LP, *Bigger Than Jesus*,[6] sold the worst of the lot, yet Sony had at least finally figured out how to press it in South Africa. "At the pressing plant, while the guy was cutting it, I talked to him and he turned the volume down and let it run," Sony says incredulously. "He didn't actually hear the album. No-one at EMI has actually heard the album, yet they put it out here. They gave me the copies, because the covers are contracted out and done somewhere else, and it didn't attracted any attention until somehow or other it went to Hillbrow Records, one of the main record shops here. Someone saw the cover, a complaint was lodged, and then it was banned. I appealed the banning, and actually won the appeal."

It wasn't the biting satire of "Plan For Peace" nor the 1966 grave-side eulogy of Dr H.F. Verwoerd, the architect of apartheid, spliced into "Transcending Conviction" that upset the authorities. It wasn't even the "blasphemous" title cut, with its allusions to John Lennon's infamous declaration to Maureen Cleave of London's *Evening Standard* [also made in 1966] that the Beatles were "Bigger than Jesus." No, what blew the fuses of the authorities was a song entitled "Gutted With The Glory." To wit,

> "Exceptionally problematic, however, are the lyrics [the diction is good and everything is heard clearly] of 'Gutted With The Glory'...Here the Lord's Prayer is used, outside any reference framework of theology or worship, for political ends. The Lord's Prayer, for the reasonable and adult Christian, is sacred, especially, as it is regarded as the so-called model prayer. To make of this something that is used for specific political groups will be abhorrent and hurtful towards the reasonable, adult Christian and therefore undesirable in terms of article 47 [2][b] of the Law."[7]

"It's an interesting case," Sony continues. "It took a couple of hours and they had a number of church people there, about 12 what they call Dominees.[8] My lawyer had a very strong argument. Funnily enough, what they objected to on the album – they had to find something to object to – was 'Gutted With The Glory' and the cutup of the Lord's Prayer, which they deemed offensive. Which is very interesting, because their argument was that it was anti-christian, when it was very clearly anti-war. They kind of accepted that in the long run, but the main reason it was unbanned was the fact that I had only sold 200 copies, and on the condition that I change the title to *Beachbomb*. So officially now it's unbanned, but it had to be retitled. The good thing about the whole affair is that there's dialogue now and you can debate things, and I think it was incredibly interesting process. Fuck, it costs money, though."

Growing up white in South Africa means living a bizarre cultural paradox: You are taught by your Christian National education that the land is yours, yet your pop culture teaches you that everything worthwhile comes from overseas. This cultural rootlessness [in Sony's words: *limpet mines/yellow at heart/living in a country that's blowing apart*][9] sparks the urgency of The Kalahari Surfers' albums, where *audio verité* is wedded to a sense of rock doom. It's a state of mind that contrasts sharply with the freedom music of the disenfranchised Black populations of the Zulu, Tswana and !Xhosa tribes, who worship the earth and are part of it. Yet Sony feels an affinity for both roots and pop cultures: his group's name juxtaposes the most famous indigenous inhabitants of the Bush with national pastime of affluent Whites; *Living In The Heart of The Beast*[10] opens with the *mbaqanga* of "Township Beat" and closes with a twisted cover of Creedence Clearwater Revival's "Bad Moon Rising."

South Africans need a psychological safety valve to cope with the cultural schizophrenia and day-to-day inhumanity of their country, and for Port Elizabeth-born Warric Swinney,[11] the coarse black humor of someone like

Frank Zappa neatly fits the bill. "I love his early stuff, *We're Only In It For The Money*[12] particularly," says Sony, on the telephone from Shifty Studios in the Milpark suburb of Johannesburg. "For me, Frank's schizophrenia and sense of humor is the best way to interpret South Africa. It's easy to do African music; the stuff is not difficult to copy, just sit down at the guitar and do what a lot of white guys have done and become quite famous doing. It gives them a special something that the French like. To be honest, being white and South African means you're schizophrenic. You're bombarded by all sorts of contradictions."

Sony grew up in Durban, South Africa's capital of contradiction. For one, the coastal city on the shores of the Indian Ocean boasts the biggest Indian community outside India in the world. Sony was fascinated by the richness of Indian music, history and philosophy, and lived in an Ashram for a year when he was 17, taking lessons in tablas and sanskrit. He studied Carnatic rhythms, Zakir Hussein ragas, and learned to cook a good curry. "Growing up with Indian culture was my biggest eye-opener," says Sony. "What I like about Indian music is that they have no preference to four beats to the bar. They were just as comfortable playing a seven as they were playing a four. If I was going to do a real honest cultural meltdown, I would have ended up playing tablas in a fusion of Indian music and Zappa. To work South Africa into some sort of audio shape was for me Zappa in form, and Beefheart in content. That's my dichotomy. Zappa had the terrific studio techniques and Beefheart had the blues. I love the way Beefheart reflects America with a blues voice without being a blues thief. He has almost the most sensible interpretation of Black-influenced music. If I could have been a millionth as successful at interpreting Black music as Beefheart has been, I'd have loved to been able to do it."

The influence of early Zappa surfaces in the violent, surreal imagery of Surfers songs like "Maid's Day Off" and "Beachbomb", yet it is Sony's innovative, Zappaesque use of the studio that sets the Surfers apart from their contemporaries. Their 1987 album *Sleep Armed*[13] remains the best snapshot we have of South Africa at the time, right down to the jacket photo of rich surfers on Umhlanga Roxx, a posh White beach in Durban on the North Coast of Natal. The album cross-pollinates several indigenous Black South African musical styles with a dollop of Indian tunings and timings, hot-wiring the mix into the newscasts of today.

Take for example, "Golden Rendezvous Part 2," named after a propaganda film of the same name that was part of South Africa's massive image-boosting scheme of the early 1970s. The film was bankrolled by slush funds from the shady Department of Information; the song has Baby Doc, Anastasio Somoza and Ferdinand Marcos collaborating as autocratic *auteurs*. "Rademeyer's Letter To His Wife" is the ballad of a man of phony degrees who rose to the top of the

Electricity Supply Commission and embezzled the government to the tune of four million Rand before fleeing to South America. "This Land" is a truly creepy field recording of Pat Boone singing to a Black-tie crowd in Jo'burg City Hall: atop the sort of nauseating clatter of frequencies and doppler shifts associated with Throbbing Gristle, Pat tells the assembled he *understands*. "We're growing, we're learning how to relate to each other, and I think this song belongs to any mana Canadian, and Israeli, an Arab, an Eskimo, and certainly a South Africanwho will sing with me *This Land Is Mine*. God gave this land to *me*."

Many of the clean samples and timely sound bites that pepper Sony's mulligatawny stew were acquired first hand. Since 1984, Sony has worked in the South African film and television industry as a freelance sound engineer, burning the midnight oil in movie scoring studios lifting snippets from propaganda films and quotes from Pik Botha, Eugene Terre Blank [*sic*], and Mangosuthu Buthulezi, as well as recording the anger, anguish and death that happens daily on the front lines in the townships and provinces. Until he landed his job at Shifty in 1992, Sony spent many grueling overtime hours working with the likes of Ted Koppel when he hired himself out to CBS and ABC to cover the historic release of Nelson Mandela in February of 1990. "I've covered a lot of the heavy violence in this country, and Mandela's release was an incredible moment for our country, a moment of optimism, everything," Sony recalls. "I was there when Mandela was released, one of the first people to corner him with a microphone. It was a very good experience to be a part of. After the Americans pulled out with their cheap shots, we moved to British television, more in-depth documentary stuff. I spent a lot of time doing interesting documentaries. I did one with Donald Woods, with Pik Botha, and people like that. That's incredibly useful as material."

Sony's remarkable field work acquires the cachet of a time capsule on the 1991 cassette release *Free State Music*,[14] released under the name Season Of Violence. We're introduced to Eugene Terreblanche giving a pep talk to AWB stormtroopers in Welkom; we hear the praises of a new, condensed speed-reading New Testament from Brother Sjambok, a Texan radio evangelist broadcasting from Radio Swaziland; we laugh at Zambian president Kenneth Kaunda fumbling through a State welcome for Nelson Mandela ["He seemed to have lost it in that dreamy way that African dictators kind of guess that they're going to be around forever", says Sony]; and we're horrified at a shocking example of basic rifle training involving the shooting of actual civilians, all examples of Sony using his Nagra as a covert weapon to dig out the truth and preserve the lies of history. "I don't give a fuck, I just carry my own machine and I record whatever I'm recording," he says defiantly. "News is such a high turnover thing; they're erasing our history as we speak. In the old days you shot it on film and at least it was archived. These guys they bulk erase the stuff. A lot of the cameramen are people like myself, because we're South African, really have put ourselves out to get the pictures, into dangerous situations, to try and cover the truth. At one stage it was the only way one could try and get some sort of truth. Now you can never get the truth, but you can at least it has often happened that the police have said one thing and there has been video evidence to the contrary. That's all fallen away now, that's just chaos."

Frank Zappa may have had delusions that he was The Mothers of Invention, but Warric Sony *is* The Kalahari Surfers. He plays most of the music on the albums; in fact, besides steady Surfer drummer Ian Herman, many of the guests bear wacko, fictitious names: "Reagan's Polyps" played pennywhistle on *Sleep Armed*, "Umhlanga Roxx" plays bass on *Bigger Than Jesus*. Yet despite this low overhead and relative freedom that Sony enjoys in being able to distribute his albums in South Africa, it remains a Sisyphean task to stay alive doing radical music. "You can't make a living out of music now, or ever, if you aren't Black," he laments. "It's very difficult; there's no audience. I have another album that's ready to go; I don't quite know what to do with it. Even if you're Black, being a musician is fuckin' hard in this country, unless you're a good session player and play commercial music or if you're a star. There is no middle ground. South Africans are not educated into accepting music like ours. The cultural boycott has worked its way to a point where the people see only the commercial success stories." Sony discovered this the hard way, by producing an Afrikaans group from Johannesburg called Koos. "They were possibly one of the most heavy-going, radical groups I had come across. Lyrically, musically, everything," Sony says. "My stuff still has a bit of humor; their stuff was fuckin' dark, you know. It was all in Afrikaans except for a cover of 'Delilah' by Tom Jones. They did a really fantastic version of it, really terrifying. I produced it, and put it out, it also sold about 200 copies on cassette only."

Indeed, from the beginning the only help Sony received was from Recommended Records mogul and drummer Chris Cutler. "I couldn't get my first album, *Own Affairs*, manufactured here," he says. "The guy at the cutting plant objected to it; you might know the story. Now I was a big fan of Henry Cow. While I was in high school I bought a later Henry Cow album and then I bought an Art Bears album, and they had addresses. I was ordering records from Recommended for a while, as I had some queries as to who played what and where in the Cow days, and so Chris wrote to me. I sent him an early cassette called *Gross National Products* that I did in my bedroom on a Porta-studio. He wrote a really good critique of it and he sent it back. So I sent *Own Affairs* over to Chris, and he really liked it and said he'd do it." Yet even Cutler has been choosy with the material Sony sends him, electing to decline releasing certain efforts, as is his wont.[15] "I sent the Koos tape to Chris, but Chris has a bit of a funny thing about sex. I think he didn't put it out because it had one or two tracks that were a bit gross sexually. I tried to translate the lyrics as best I could, but you had to have been South African and been in the Army to kind of understand the gross aspect of that way of thinking."

After he retired his sound equipment and gave in his media pass, Sony poured his efforts and money into Shifty Music, the record label which sprang out of the Milpark studios owned by South African music entrepreneur – and Sony's benefactor – Lloyd Ross. "Shifty made a bit of an effort to make all my records available," Sony explains. "They put out all my records on cassette and imported the ones that hadn't been on cassette. My label is not really an official label. I couldn't get a bank account opened under the name Gross National Products. I then changed the name of the company to Free State Music, which it still is, and I still use it to put things out. It's basically a subsidiary of Shifty; I'm kind of an artist on the Shifty label, you could say."

Over the decades, South Africa's cultural boycott has insinuated itself into the country's radio infrastructure and record labels, fostering a music industry that inhibits freedom of expression and independent music. The segregated network of the South African Broadcasting Corporation [SABC] operates seven "White" stations[16] and six "Black" stations,[17] while the music industry has long been dominated by two major record labels since the 1930s: Gallo and EMI. Given these straitjackets, the salt-and-pepper artists on Shifty's roster – like Black dub poet Mzwakhe Mbuli or Afrikaaner white trash poet Bernoldus Niemand – had about as much hope of getting airplay as Crass or George Carlin. The shock came in 1992, when the Austrian Bertelsmann Music Group [BMG] set up shop in South Africa and approached Shifty with a deal to distribute their releases. What initially seemed like a breakthrough turned out to be a hollow promise; eleven months later, Shifty is busy disengaging themselves from BMG.

"In the end I think they didn't really grasp what we do," reckons Sony. "They were setting up a new operation and needed the political credibility. They wanted one of our artists they were very keen on, and bought the whole label. They meant well; the main guy who runs it, Keith Lister, used to manage the Soul Brothers. He's experienced, fairly well-thought of in the music industry, and he's a nice guy. He had big dreams with Shifty and the stuff we're doing, we haven't yet managed to sell records. That's because their marketing team are a bunch of jerks. They still only see South African music as being high-turnover Black product. They're completely profit-oriented, high-turnover, no real vision for the future. In a strict marketing sense, you'd call them sales-oriented for short term gain. But we don't have anything that will just *sell*. It doesn't fit the mold. Our most commercial record was by Vusi Mahlasela. Beautiful voice, beautiful singer, reminiscent of someone like a Black Phil Ochs, very political lyrics, but a very sweet singer. Do you know Geoffrey Oryema?[18] Very similar to him. That's why BMG bought us, because of this guy's album. Here we had a Black artist who has a good band, has a lot of good musicians, has a really naff video, everything. I think it has sold about 50 copies to date. It's amazing. As for our White artists, they said, 'Why do all this White product, which should go to the international side of BMG?' It's still very much Black and White.

"Still, we've learned a lot. We have a better idea of what it takes to market the stuff. The key, ultimately, lies in radio. Radio is controlled by the state, except for one or two stations, and there's no way of getting any kind of eclectic music station going or anything interesting, unless you're a pirate. There was a time last year when one of the Universities ran a pirate radio station for about a week or so. There's still strict laws regarding broadcasting. There's a big commission going on right now, part of CODESA,[19] and we're hoping for the deregulation of the airwaves and the beginning of community radio."

One voice Sony wants to hear across the South African airwaves is that of dub poet Lesego Rampolokeng, who has produced a debut collection of poetry *Horns For Hondo*,[20] as well as *Endbeginnings*,[21] a collaborative effort with the Kalahari Surfers. As a dub poet, Rempolokeng's closest analogue would be the great Linton Kwesi Johnson, yet his is no parable of cultural dislocation, no "England Is A Bitch." Years of beatings, repression and detentions has taught Rempolokeng's generation to shoot from the hip, and they have pared down their language to bare minimum. With these words as weapons, Rempolokeng's poetry is violent and unforgettable. He displays astonishing fluidity of rhyme and meter, and his imagery frequently approaches the intensity of that original codex of surrealism, The Book Of Revelations: *Dark explode the blues/& God blows his fuse/the God of death has chosen this nation/guns sing lullabies to children*, Rempolokeng recites in "Dark Explode The Blues." His fierce boasting comes with flashes of dark humor, such as *This vulture on my culture has long begun to tamper with my temper.*[22]

After reading *Horns For Hondo*, Sony was knocked out by Rempolokeng's verse and approached him about collaborating on an album. The result lies somewhere between rap, dub reggae and funk with deep, apocalyptic whiffs of classic dub poets like Benjamin Zephaniah and The Last Poets, and a beat that is hard and uncompromising, yet uplifting. Some tunes are little more than stripped-down rhythm tracks with environmental accents or a buzzing mbira, propelled by fat bass and Rempolokeng's thick, rolling tongue. Elsewhere Sony's textures range from the deep-in-the-pocket On-U-Sound dub of the title cut, to the delayed jews' harp and Prince Far I spaciness of "Tapeworms." Even when Rempolokeng rocks the mic and plays MC ["Rapmaster supreme/word-bomber in the extreme"], Sony's bed is closer to Disposable Heroes of Hiphoprisy than Run-DMC.

Horns For Hondo is only one of several collaborations Sony has long wanted to undertake. In the cards for a year or two now has been a planned collaboration with San Francisco media terrorists Negativland. Sony has been following their plight since their 1991 *U2* CD single was destroyed at the behest of Island Records,[23] who launched a lawsuit claiming they lifted samples of U2's "I Still Haven't Found What I'm Looking For" – along with some profane outtakes of Top 40 American radio host Casey Kasem – without permission. "I think what they did was fantastic," he enthuses. "I don't know if they planned it to be as big a publicity stunt as it became, but somebody had to do it. Someone that I know here quite well, a very powerful person in the music industry, probably the top music lawyer in South Africa, asked me about it. He'd read about the case and was very interested in it. He came around and I played it for him, and he said, 'That's fantastic!'" Sony has since sent Negativland plenty of tapes, and at one point Mark Hosler was planning to visit Johannesburg, but the deal fell through. "It was difficult because the planning sort of coincided with the birth of my daughter, but I would have made time. I think it may still happen, but it's very difficult to communicate with him," grumbles Sony. "He doesn't write a lot and you can hardly get him on the phone. I get this fucking irritating answering machine with a laughing bag on it."

With his considerable experience navigating the loopholes of South Africa's Cultural Boycott and the labyrinthine corridors of its music industry, Sony feels he has the skills to produce and promote South Africa's fertile underground movement, and has since left his full-time gig at Shifty. He plans to again immerse himself in freelance work, only this time far from the hell of the front line. "I've gone a naff TV series that I'm doing, a very heavy film that's very much now, a kind of Townships now," he says. "I'm doing the music with Louis Mhlanga, a Zimbabwean who's living here. He's a fantastic guitar player who has played with King Sunny Adé. I'm looking forward to doing an album with him, something that might shoot out of this film. Film is a nice field to use experimental music. I don't want to have to go back into the townships and do news. It's very heavy now. All over the place. There's fifty people being killed a week. It's like living through a civil war that's broken out between forces that seem to be inexplicable; no-one knows who they are; it's like Algeria at the end of the Algerian-French War. Incredible."

In May of 1994, South Africans elected Nelson Mandela's African National Congress to power in the first free, democratic multi-racial elections to be held in that country. Yet the struggle is by no means over. It will be a long time before South Africa is free of the deeply ingrained hatred of apartheid. Just as it will take more than slick PR work by the Chinese to make everyone forget the 1989 massacre at Tianamen Square [in 1993 they lost a desperate bid to bring the 2000 Olympic Games to Beijing], it will be months, perhaps years before Steven Biko and those murdered in the Sharpville and Soweto riots will rest in peace. And we can rest assured that right-wing extremists like Eugene Terreblanche will no doubt throw a limpet mine into the works, just as Islamic fundamentalists will launch a *jihad* to scuttle the landmark 1993 peace accord between Palestinians and Israelis.

"It's a real worry having a daughter now," Sony confesses. "The old forces of the apartheid regime have been locked in. You must remember that with apartheid, the words can fall away, but the style of government can very easily be adopted by Black people. It's an ideological thing; it has nothing to do with color anymore. Buthulezi is probably the chief mover of the old style of government, and the guy is bad news. I've met him a number of times, and interviewed him, at the core of his heart an absolute liar. It's difficult for the forces of good to prevail against the forces of evil, because it's basically just down the middle, the way I see it."

Kalahari Surfers: Own Affairs (Gross National Products, 1985), Living In The Heart of The Beast (Recommended, 1986), Sleep Armed (Recommended, 1987), Bigger Than Jesus (Recommended, 1990). as **Season Of Violence**: Free State Music (Shifty, 1991) with **Lesego Rempolokeng**: Endbeginnings (ReR Megacorp, 1993)

1. Self-penned warning sticker for Zappa's 1984 Barking Pumpkin release *Thing Fish*; reprinted in Frank Zappa & Peter Occhiogrosso, *The Real Frank Zappa Book*, Poseidon Press: New York, 1989: p.279, 2. Roughly $500 U.S., 3. This figure, as well as much of the factual information here regarding censorship in South Africa, is drawn from Ian Kerkhof's illuminating "Music In South Africa: Censorship and Repression," *Ré Records Quarterly* Vol.1 N2, 1985: pp.9-15
4. Warrick Sony, "Strange Business: The Independent Music Culture In South Africa," in *The ReR Quarterly*, Vol. 4 N1, May 1994: pp.62-65, 5. On average, less than 200 copies each, 6. Recommended, 1990, 7. Letter to Swinney from South Africa's Direktoraat van Publikasies dated September 4, 1989; reprinted in *Ré Records Quarterly* Vol.3 N1, 1990: p.29, 8. Ministers of the Dutch Reform Church, 9. "Limpet Mine," from *Bigger Than Jesus*, 10 Recommended, 1986
11. "Sony" comes from his days with Defense force; he chose to name himself after a multi-national electronics giant because he was the only Swinney in the telephone book. His *nom de guerre* is even funnier considering he sometimes goes by "Wreck Sony"
12. Verve, 1968, 13. Recommended, 1987, 14. Shifty, 1991, 15. See *Chris Cutler*, p.21
16. The English Service, The Afrikaans Service, commercial stations Springbok and Radio 5, and regional stations Radio Good Hope, Radio Highveld, and Radio Port Natal; source: Kerkhof, "Music In South Africa: Censorship and Repression," p.14
17. Radio Zulu, Radio Xhosa, Radio South-Sotho, Radio North-Sotho, Radio Tswana, and Radio Venda-Tsonga; source: ibid., 18. A Ugandan singer who records for Peter Gabriel's RealWorld label
19. Committee For A Democratically Elected South Africa, 20. Congress Of South African Writers: Johannesburg, 1993, 21. ReR Megacorp, 1993, 22. "Treason", 23. See *Cut And Paste*, p.129

After Dinner

"Although I may seem the same to other people, to me each thing I produce is a new expression, and I always make each work from a new interest. It's like a painter who always paints the same rose."

Yasujiro Ozu[1]

Welcome to Dreamland.[2] Land of Suntory, karaoke,[3] and DIW, Japan is every inch the surrealistic title given a seminal 1985 Celluloid compilation of alternative Japanese art rock compiled by Fred Frith. Featuring the freshest take on Western pop music forms since The Beach Boys' *Pet Sounds*, largely unknown groups like Fake, Mizutama Shobodan, A-Musik, Luna Park Ensemble, and After Dinner deconstructed their influences – bubblegum, punk, folk, jazz, the avant garde – assembled them with a traditional Zen sensitivity, and gave them equally delightful titles: "Scramble Suite," "The Formula Of Silence," "The Room of Hair Mobiles," "Yatara Chan's Annoying Noise." The exotic results revealed that today's Japan more than ever is a culture founded on and divided over the struggle between ancient and modern.

Nowhere is this temporal and stylistic dichotomy more evident than in the tightly regulated Nipponese music industry. In "Radio In Japan: The Power of Low Power,"[4] renegade Japanese broadcaster Tetsuo Kogawa notes that radio is either state-owned or in the hands of a frighteningly small number of stations[5] run by überconservatives, apart from a few pirates who operate on 15 microvolts from cafés and record stores.[6] *Kayôkyou*, or pop stars, come vacuum-packed in two archetypes: the masculine *enka*, who sing traditional, minor-scale heroic songs of unrequited love, and *kawaiko-chan*, coy modern girls and boys without a hint of irony or ambiguity.[7] And an NHK survey done in 1982 revealed that 93% of all music listened to in Japan was on TV.

"The Japanese pop industry is basically Michael Jackson," quips Yoshihiro Kawasaki. "You know, *Bad*. In Japanese." Kawasaki laughs, relishing the irony. The mixing engineer, splicing whiz, and resident cut-up of After Dinner is holding court with the band's founder, lyricist and vocalist Haco, amidst the zen gardens and *faux* opulence of Le Jardin du Samurai, a Japanese eatery in downtown Victoriaville. In North America for the first time, the Japanese ensemble is here for the ninth Festival International de Musique Actuelle de Victoriaville. "Sometimes interesting groups like Yellow Magic Orchestra will infiltrate record companies, but it's rare," adds Haco. "Most young people in Japan today favor a European beat. For example, Sandi is big right now. She's a singer from Hawaii who sings in Japanese but has a completely Western image."

Haco understands it's a fine line that separates Sandi from Sade. Just as Yoko Ono's uncompromising work and involvement with the performance/concept collective Fluxus in the 1960s ruffled the feathers of the serious "New York school" of Merce Cunningham, Morton Feldman and John Cage, the work of Japanese women like Haco in the last decade have gone a long way to sandblasting the airbrushed, stereotypical image of the Japanese female pop star. Tenko in particular has been an inspirational figure; her stunning pop work in Mizutama Shobodan have been a model for many young Japanese musicians.[8] Today, Japan boasts a fertile pop music underground which continues to draw the curious and adventurous from the West: Fred Frith, who sojourns to Japan on a regular basis, is now joined by saxophonist John Zorn, producer Steve Albini and Shimmy Disc major domo Kramer.

Haco founded After Dinner thirteen years ago in the Honshu industrial capital of Osaka. The ensemble has gone from being a loose aggregate of musicians headed by an inexperienced 18 year-old singer to being a finely honed theatrical sextet and perhaps the Japanese pop outfit most likely to assume the elusive international crossover torch once carried by the late great Yellow Magic Orchestra. As with other upstart groups of their generation, like Mizutama Shobodan, Wha Ha Ha, Haniwa Chan, Les Soeurs des Lilis Noirs, and YBO^2, polymorphous perversion of the pop song is the name of the game with After Dinner. Yet unlike the few Japanese groups to have become cult items in the West – such as Shonen Knife and British *emigrés* Frank Chickens – After

Dinner eschew jaded cynicism in their plunderings of Western pop, and impart a subversive sonic wit. Their albums are austere, painstakingly-crafted toy collages of dub textures, wind-up arrangements, musical in-jokes and complex singing that falls somewhere between haiku and Dagmar Krause.

Judging from the studio work on their two albums released in the Westtheir eponymous debut of 1986 and *Paradise of Replica*,[9] it's obvious that tape manipulation is big element of their style, whether it be physical splicing or fussing with the motor speed. Yet listening further, one hears the locus of After Dinner's sound: a subtle cross between Western pop and rock forms and Eastern traditional scales and instrumentation, a pop music analogue, if you will, to the timeless films of Japanese master filmmaker Yasujiro Ozu. In movies like 1952's *The Flavor of Green Tea Over Rice*, 1953's *Tokyo Story*, and 1962's *An Autumn Afternoon*, Ozu decentered classical Hollywood narration in favor of a fluid set of relationships dovetailing time, space, and narrative logic. On the surface, Ozu's films may seem thematically indistinguishable [almost all are studies of the modernized, urban life of the contemporary Japanese] and unrelentingly static: his camera is always fixed about three feet from the floor, or eye level of someone sitting on a *tatami* mat. Yet listening further and watching more closely as After Dinner and Ozu probe their mediums, one sees that rigorous technique can become the basis of playful deviation. In Ozu we watch objects jump about the frame, like fruitbowls, ashtrays, chopsticks, or a triptych of wandering beer bottles, in After Dinner a fontana mix of surprises await the adventurous listener: watery, Beatlesque piano melodies and wispy clouds of feedback ripple imperceptibly through songs, a babble of children's voices may hover on the periphery, violins flit, phase-shift and reverse musical polarity, delicate kotos play hide and seek in distorted guitar landscapes, telephone busy signals sing along with Haco, and elliptical editing jumbles the beat.

Like Ozu, After Dinner is less indebted to traditional Japanese aesthetics than to a vibrant popular culture and to subtle ideological tensions. After Dinner even carries Ozu's East-West dichotomy one step further, informing their music with the distinct difference between northern and southern pop styles in Japan. If his country's north is more obsessed with western pop artifice, explains Kawasaki, the south is steeped more in tradition, like on the island of Okinawa in the Nánsei archipelago south of Japan.[10] "The musical community there is very strong," he says. "Okinawa music has a strong beat, different scales, and definable roots. I find myself drawn to musical history in the same way. That is, I found Japanese music after rock music. I started playing rock and roll, listening to the Beatles and Led Zeppelin. Then after 24 or 25, I found Japanese music to be very interesting, and I began to listen to gagaku and other styles."

After Dinner's unique musical hybrid is further embellished by innovations in two key areas: instrumentation and the recording process itself. Aside from the usual bass/guitar/drums/keyboards lineup, the instrument credits on an After Dinner disc can be pretty unusual: scissors, plastic flute, rubber bands, hoover, tabla, yang t'chin,[11] volleyball, even glockenspiel. "Our first two albums was where I learned pop music, live performance and recording techniques all at the same time," says Haco. "I wanted a fresh music, an original music, so I played whatever was at hand, and went wherever the muse took me."

"In recording, anything goes!" agrees Kawasaki, perhaps explaining why there have only been two After Dinner albums in four years. "But the tape splicing took forever. We must get a digital editing block for the next one." When Kawasaki joined the group in the late '80s, he had some mighty big shoes to fill. The group's previous engineer, Yashusi Utsonomiya, had pioneered the group's sound, various 'peculiar analogue inventions' and their unusual recording setupwhich, boiled down, is no EQ, just a keen sense of microphones [Neumann KM-56 condensers were favourites] and mike placement. Onstage, he eschewed traditional monitors ["A waste of sound,"[12] Utsonomiya once said], in favor of Eno-style ambient speaker placement and headsets.

Just as Ozu would fuss over the positioning of props in the frame before shooting a foot of film, crafting a cinematic playfulness at a purely graphic level, Utsonomiya could be often seen scurrying around a studio, feeling speakers, scraping floors, and measuring ceilings to deduce the proper microphone placement for the instruments.[13] A track on *After Dinner* provides a delightful example of his skill and playfulness at work: "Shovel and Little Lady" is a "bio-binaural" [*sic*] recording, and a three-dimensional stereo picture of the eccentric marching song can be created by listening with headphones and moving one's head from side to side. "We still use Utsonomiya's big concert set-up, but it can be too cumbersome," Kawasaki confesses. "Sometimes it's difficult to bring all of the things on the road. It's like the lights and the slide shows and the dance numbers. We do that kind of thing a lot in Japan, but we can't afford to in foreign countries. Costumes will have to do."

A few hours later, Kawasaki plays Adrian Sherwood to Haco's Annie Anxiety as After Dinner take the stage at the Grand Café as part of the festival's closing night gala. *Hello, you are welcome to After Dinner/so many faces around together*, sings Haco, kicking off an evening of quixotic kabuki complete with elaborate costumes and whimsical Japanese court music of the future. The concert's highlight, "Glass Tube" from *After Dinner*, is assembled from fragments and stitched together onstage through the mixing board and tape delays, building an Ivesian collage from Haco's splintered, floating vocals before winding down in discrete steps.[14]

According to the demands of the studio and the stage, After Dinner's personnel has shifted constantly over the years, with the core of the group has remained the quartet of Haco, violinist Tadahiko Yokogawa, percussionist and harpist Ichiro Inoue, and drummer Hideaki Yamagata. But the most important addition to the band recently has been Tetsoo Shimura, a traditional Japanese musician whose *sho* and shakuachi flutes imbue the songs with a wizened center of gravity, a pedal point upon which the stark melodies can shift and change. "There have been many, many changes since we started," says Haco after the show. We're in a medical classroom at a Victoriaville High School, complete with a "corpse" listening intently from the hospital bed behind us. "We had tried smaller units for our live performances, just bass, piano and voice, with a few arrangements on top. Then I met Tetsoo Shimura, a musicologist and music teacher who played traditional wind instruments. Shimura studied gagaku, the ancient court music of Japan, at Seoul University. I wanted to play with him, and asked him to join afterwards. We saw that during the 1980s, our live shows changed as a result. It draws more and more on the rock arena and traditional Japanese court at the same time." "Shimura didn't know much about rock'n'roll," echoes Kawasaki. "But when we assembled the material, it was very striking. Suddenly we found a new music in our songs."

Deciphering the intricate wordplay of Haco's lyrics requires nothing short of a yen for the Japanese language. Yet translated into English they can be quite surreal and have sublime kitsch value. "The first time I read Haco's lyrics and heard her sing them, I was struck by how many double meanings there were," says Kawasaki. "Sometimes she would sing a simple syllable like 'Ha!' But because Japanese pronunciation is very important, the lyrics had more than one set of meanings. These minor differences made her lyrics so flexible. That was interesting."

"Japanese pronunciation is more important than the choice of words," Haco agrees. "When I sing, I have to keep in mind that Japanese lyrics have a Japanese rhythm and inner meter, just like English has an English rhythm and an English beat. Because Japanese is so far removed from English, I like to incorporate the two. This is very, very important for me, to make words fit and change their meanings at the same time. It's like a puzzle. For example, I'm fascinated by the way Americans adopt words from European languages and incorporate computer terminology into their vocabulary. I translate that into a very Japanese style. Japanese people have a hard time understanding us sometimes."

Haco's eagerness to embrace the pop culture of the West is reminiscent of the yearning of countless anti-heroines whose lives Ozu illuminated with his films. Haco could easily be pass as one of Ozu's *shitamachi*, or "downtown people," caught between family tradition and the independence of the modern age. "The lyrics themselves are mostly life in modern Japan, about being a modern Japanese girl. [*laughs*] Now, I'm modern girl. But I kind of understand Japanese traditional beliefs, and I like to mix the feelings and get a very interesting form. Japan is always changing. It's traditional yet not rigid, just like Japanese old style lyrics. Even in haiku, you have basically the same freedom in just 5-7-5."

Haco and Kawasaki spent the rest of Thanksgiving weekend taking in the sights of bucolic small-town Victoriaville, resplendent in autumn gold, listening to the music of everyone from Muhal Richard Abrams to The New Music Ensemble of Vilnius, and never getting over the fact that the food here is very American, yet the people speak French. As the festival's highlight, both later chose Bob Ostertag's solo sampler performance, *Sooner or Later*. Haco was torn between whether she admired the painful work – extracted from a single sample of a child burying his murdered father in Nicaraguafor its unforgettable power or its remarkable artistry. For Kawasaki, the matter wasn't nearly so difficult.

"I'd like to get my hands on that machine."

After Dinner: After Dinner (Recommended, 1986), European Concert Tour (ReR Megacorp cassette, 1988), Paradise of Replica (ReR Megacorp, 1990)
Haco: Solo CD (Stupeur et Trumpette, 1995)

Footnotes:
1. Quoted in *Ozu Yasujiro wo yomu* ["Reading Yasujiro Ozu"], and reprinted in David Bordwell, *Ozu And The Poetics Of Cinema*, Princeton University Press: Princeton, 1988: p.109
2. Portions of this chapter were originally published as "After Dinner's Jigsaw Kabuki," the author, *Option* Magazine N43, March 1992: pp.59-64
3. Literally, "empty orchestra"
4. Robert Weisberg & Tetsuo Kogawa, published in *Ear* Magazine Vol. 14 N2, April 1989: pp.16-17
5. As few as eight in Tokyo during 1985; source: ibid.
6. Ironically, a loophole in Japanese radio laws allowing for wireless microphones and remotes, enough to cover a few blocks; source: ibid.
7. Judith Ann Herd, "Trends and Taste In Japanese Popular Music: A Case Study of the 1982 Yamaha World Popular Music Festival," in *Popular Music* Volume 4, 1984: pp.77-80
8. Their album *Sky Full of Red Petals* [Kinniku Bijo Records, 1984] is a fine example; see *Tenko*, p.123
9. Recommended, 1986, and RecRec, 1990; respectively
10. Okinawa's most famous export is the quirky traditionalist Shoukichi Kina, the songwriter behind Japan's 1966 hit "Haisai Ojisan;" see *The Music Power From Okinawa* [Globestyle, 1991] and *Asia Classics 2: Peppermint Tea House* [Luaka Bop/Sire, 1994]
11. A Chinese dulcimer, 12. Utsonomiya, "After Dinner's Concert Sound System," in *Ré Records Quarterly* Vol. 4, 1986: pp.43-44, 13. See *Fred Frith*, p.35
14. A live souvenir cassette from ReR Megacorp [*European Concert Tour*, 1988] takes this aesthetic one step further, combining several source recordings of the same song together, creating a surreal pop collage.

Tom Zé

When it was about 2 o'clock p.m. I saw a ghostess who was crying bitterly and coming to me direct in a hut where I laid down enjoying myself. When she entered I noticed that she held a short mat which was woven with dried weeds. She was not more than three feet high...I noticed carefully that she was almost covered with sores, even there was no single hair on her head, except sores with uncountable maggots which were dashing here and there on her body. Both her arms were not more than one and an half foot, it had uncountable short fingers. She was crying bitterly and repeatedly as if somebody was stabbing her with knives...When she told me to look at her palm and opened it nearly to touch my face, it was exactly as a television, I saw my town, mother, brother, and all my playmates.

Amos Tutuola, My Life In The Bush Of Ghosts[1]

Tom Zé is afraid of the heat. Downtown Montréal is smouldering in the grip of a summer heatwave, and the mercury has reached a punishing 38° Celsius. While a few brave souls are out in the midday sun on Ste-Catherine street, watching a gospel choir drenched in sweat praise the Lord as part of the annual Montréal International Jazz Festival, the bearded Brazilian is taking refuge in the air conditioned oasis of the piano bar inside the Meridien Hotel. In a rumpled yellow cotton shirt, linen pants and sensible shoes, Zé is rubbing sleep from his eyes, stupefied at the sun's power so far from his home.

Zé is a Bahian, hailing from the parched, unforgiving *sertão*, or badlands, of the Brazilian northeast. Heat is a simple fact of life for the Bahians, as is drought, floods, famine, and chronic unemployment. Paradoxically, Bahia has long been a fertile wellspring of innovative culture, known for its modern music, poetry, theater, and literature. "The place that I come from, the northeast, is one of the poorest regions of Brazil," Zé says. "When you go to sleep you don't know if you'll be alive the next day. In this place, rhythm is very present, very important. It's part of everyday life. When the Portuguese came here, they were very poor and had no culture at all; they did not know how to read or write. They've done crazy things to preserve their culture. They used all kinds of things to preserve what they had: music, theater, dance, stories, folklore, all kinds of resources – but above all, rhythm."

Zé patiently waits for the translator to do her work, taking a drag on his cigarette and looking off into space; a gesture that recalls the eccentric mannerisms of Salvador Dali. Then he tells a little tale of how the Bahians see themselves. "There is this little beast who went to look for food, you see, and he traveled very far to find it." Zé traces his spidery fingers across the marble coffee table to the ashtray. Returning across the table, Zé's fingers bump up against a spoon. "On the way back, if anything happened to be in his way, the little beast would refuse to walk around it." Zé taps the spoon frustratedly. "This is the story of all Bahians. We bang our heads against the wall."

Zé should know. Twenty years ago, he was Brazil's most underrated post-modern troubadour, a former *tropicalista* who was gleefully tossing Beefheart into the bossa nova and needed perplexity and quiddities into Brazilian music. A true poet of deconstruction, Zé flirted with modern composition, linguistics, concrete poetry, experimental melody, and political satire while managing to avoid harmony altogether. His ironic and polyphonic songs played with a deep sense of sarcastic humor, while his instrumental palette was more likely to include berimbau, cow bell, bottles, and assorted household appliances than traditional Brazilian instruments. Even the *cavaquinhos*, the small high-pitched guitars that are a dime a dozen throughout the *favelas* [slums] of Brazil, were tuned as far as possible from tonality.

In 1988, at 51, Zé found himself at a crossroads, without a recording contract for more than a decade. To use one of the Americanisms of which he is so fond of using, Zé had been out of the loop since 1973, when his harsh indictment of government censorship, *Todos os Olhos*,[2] made him a pariah in Brazilian music circles. He was busying himself with odd jobs, writing jingles for leftist politicians, and working for an ad agency when he read in a São Paolo paper that

David Byrne was looking for him. It seems that on one of his shopping trips to Rio de Janiero, the Talking Head and Brazilian music buff had mistakenly bought Zé's seminal 1976 disassembly of the samba, *Estudando O Samba*;[3] Byrne was amazed and thrilled to hear sambas and *cancãos* so jaw-droppingly weird, such delicate songs that buzzed and howled under the influence of heat. "It's funny. I had an association with a palm reader who said that my life line went to a certain point and stopped," Zé recalls. "So my career was as good as finished. But I told her, 'Look, my lifeline continues!' So it was very funny when David Byrne called me. I was ready to leave everything and leave music altogether." So Zé packed his wife and belongings into a little car he auspiciously dubbed "Espera Byrne" ["Wait For Byrne"], and left the concrete jungle of São Paolo to drive home, where his second chance awaited him.

Tom Zé was born Antonio José Santana Martins in 1936 in Irará, a small country town in the northeast of Brazil. To this day, the spiritual, musical, and emotional patterns of life in Bahia still provide his deepest and most basic nourishment. Music and poetry have always been sewn together at the hip in this corner of the world, due to the region's rich cultural heritage: Amerigo Vespucci may have discovered the Bay Of Salvador on All Saints' Day, but the Portuguese who founded and settled the port city in 1549 brought with them a language and culture itself riddled with the argot of their slaves, from The Côte d'Ivoire and Lusitania. Add the native Indian languages, and Bahia becomes an impoverished yet vibrant ethnic mix of African and Brazilian religions, art, music, and rhythms.

"We northeasterners have one foot in poverty and another in cultural riches," Zé once wrote.[4] "They were cultured, our grandparents. And when we found ourselves marooned and impoverished in the dry *sertão* of Brasil, we confronted a paradox. We loved our cultural heritage but we became illiterate. The solution was to speak culture, talk culture, dance culture, sing culture. We began to read metaphysics into daily events."

Zé believed that the backbone to these absurdist, Sisyphean cultural efforts was the indigenous rhythm of the northeast, the *forró*. Propelled by accordion, spoons, and other down-home instruments, *forró* is a pungent, hootenanny-style music of celebration derived from 19th century square dances, and bears more than a passing resemblance to the zydeco of the Southern United States. Outlaw *forró* heroes such as Luiz Gonzaga sang songs that celebrated the land and those who worked it, soul food for the Bahians who eked a living on spartan diets of dry manioc and beans. As Zé once quipped, "In the northeast, Rhythm is God dehydrated."[5]

"The *caipira* [country] music of the south is more lyrical, more based on stories and romance," Zé explains. "The music of the northeast cannot be separated from rhythm. Even the lyrics and rhythm are one thing. [*Zé dovetails his fingers.*] In the south, the lyrics are an afterthought." Zé sings a few bars of a *baião quebrado* to illustrate his point. When he sings, it is a grainy and sweet sound, his sandpaper-rough voice sensuously swaying like a shaker. "It reminds me of Thomas Mann's *Magic Mountain*, where the main character, who is a German, goes to a dinner party, and he hears the Russian language for the first time. He leaned in to hear the conversation more carefully, and was really surprised. To him it sounded like Russian was all bones and joints. 'That's it!' I said. Rhythm is the skeleton of our lives."

The biggest *forró* star Bahia produced in the 1950s and 1960s was unquestionably Jackson do Pandiero. With his flamboyant cowboy attire, Pandiero was a consummate entertainer and a rhythmic powder keg, shooting rapid-fire onomatopoeic verse and sere, stripped down rhythms from the hip. Zé considered Pandiero to be a magician of rhythm, because he taught people rhythms without knowing it. "When I was young in Bahia, my friends and I were crazy for Jackson," Zé once told journalist Anna Maria Bahiana. "We had all his records. We thought his music was beautiful. We especially liked the way he divided the melody, the rhythm in his singing, his grace and subtlety in twisting the words around the rhythm. This is the connection between Jackson do Pandiero and Northeastern musicians in generalthey all love to play with rhythm, make the rhythm complex, pleasurable, tasty."[6]

Zé also admits the wacky language and sharpened satire on Pandiero hits like 1958's "Tum-Tum-Tum" or 1960's "Chiclete Com Banana" ["Chewing Gum With Banana"] was a big influence on his songwriting style. The latter even lyrically presages Zé's fascination with dada: *I wanna see Uncle Sam with a frying pan in a Brazilian percussion jam/I'll mix Miami with Copacabana/I'll mix chewing gum with bananas/And my samba will sound like this/Bachee-kee-bachee-kee-bachee.* Zé would eventually pay homage to the northeastern *forró* master by dedicating his 1993 "comeback" album with David Byrne, *The Hips Of Tradition*,[7] to Pandiero.

Because Irará had no secondary schools, Zé went to high school in Salvador, Bahia's capital, where he had a formal musical education and was classically trained on cello. In Salvador, Zé was exposed to classical music by his communist uncles, who would play him scratchy LPs by Tchaikovsky, Beethoven, and Brahms. Homesick, he began composing Dylanesque songs about the idyllic street life of his home town. At The College Of Music at the University of Bahia in the late 1950s, Zé studied with such modernist luminaries as Ernst Widmer, Walter Smetak, and Hans-Joachim Kollreuther; the latter introduced him to the atonal world of Arnold Schoenberg. Zé then became increasingly interested in atonality, recalling that it was a staple of northeastern Brazilian music, where musicians seemed to play *desafinado*, or out of tune.

When Zé first appeared on Brazilian TV in 1960, on a show called "Escada Para O Successo" ["Stairway To Success"], he gleefully sent up proceedings with a tune called "Rampa Para O Fracasso" ["Ramp to Failure"]. Two other budding songwriters, Gilberto Gil and Caetano Veloso, caught the broadcast, and sought Zé out afterwards. The three soon discovered they shared political and musical affinities, and began to put on shows which mixed their traditional Bahian roots with a budding bohemian consciousness. Their cosmopolitan outlook, encompassing film, dance, theater, music, and writing, would eventually bloom into a countercultural movement, *tropicalismo*, that rivaled the psychedelia, free love and seismic social upheavals which were taking the United States by storm in the late 1960s.

Brazilian pop music has always been an omnivorous beast – the samba and *forró* from the *favelas* were quick to pick up on Cuban and African influences, while the sophisticated bossa nova owes much to the cool expressiveness of Miles and Debussy – yet *tropicalismo* delighted in outright cultural cannibalism, devouring North American and European culture that was arriving by boat, over the television, and hit 45s by the Beatles, transforming it and mixing it with indigenous Afro-Brazilian elements.

"It was never planned as a movement," Zé stresses. "I just happened to be in Bahia with Gilberto and Caetano. We did a lot of shows and wanted to express the music of the region. At that time, the bossa nova was picking up influences from around the world, commercials and ads were everywhere, and television had 'Semana de Veinte,' or 'Twenty of the Week,' a variety show that featured music from around the world. There was no way to stop the information, just go with the flow. Then we discovered that our music became a magnifying glass, a way of looking, a lens that we could see our culture around us. It was then that *tropicalismo* was born."

Tropicalismo's juice was squeezed from many fruits. While purists disdained anything that deviated from traditional samba or bossa nova, the *tropicalistas* plugged electric guitars into a heady mixture of rock, bolero, international hit parade kitsch, indigenous folklore, pop art, avant garde music, rhumba, and tango. Zé became one of *tropicalismo's* most iconoclastic architects, cutting three self-titled albums of songs loaded with satire, leftist politics, and dense allegorical content after he forsook his classical career in 1967 and joined Caetano Veloso in moving to São Paolo, where the *tropicalismo* movement was in full swing. The fact that performers like Zé, Veloso and Gil had access to television was crucial. In the late 1960s, Brazil was in a period of intense social foment and massive culture shock. People in the jungle who never had electricity now had TV sets and were hooked on soap operas. Televised music shows like 'Semana de Veinte' became an ideal platform for criticizing the right wing military government, which had taken power overnight in a 1964 coup.

As government censorship intensified in the late 1960s, the songwriter's craft was put to the test. Many had to resort to oblique metaphors and triple entendres to get their messages across. Both Gilberto Gil and Caetano Veloso were jailed and forced into self-imposed exile in England, while Zé was like an eccentric uncle, too strange to be considered a real threat, and stayed behind. "When *tropicalismo* hit, censorship was really big in Brazil," Zé says. "Freedom of thought, of speech and the press was not present. But we had many different ways of putting things in perspective, and what we did ultimately escaped them; it went through their fingers like water. Those who judged what was good and what was dangerous couldn't understand. When they finally did understand, there was nothing they could do, only detain the authors. But the music lives on." Zé's parting shot to the censors was *Todos os Olhos*, a caustic album of *tropicalismo* featuring a jacket depicting a large yellow eye with a twinkling iris. In reality, this knowing wink at the government was a tight close-up of a marble lodged in an anus, photographed in soft focus.

Like Nigerian author and storyteller Amos Tutuola, Tom Zé draws on an vast wealth of folkloric knowledge and homespun wisdom handed down throughout the centuries, weaving it with the poignant memories of a childhood adjusting to the modern age. In the advertising one-sheets for his album *The Hips Of Tradition*, he relates this tale of life in Irará:

> "In the Brazilian Northeast, the markers of advancing civilization were like poems for the people. A spigot, for somebody who used to have to go and get the water in the river or well, bring it and put it in a cistern or some other place to keep it in the house, then take it out of there and put it in a bowl so you could wash your face – to be able to just turn water on was like having a fountain in the house. Turn it off and the fountain disappears. Only the magicians in fairy tales could do these things.
>
> "My mother took me to see my first movie. Everyone sat on these hard benches and then suddenly this thing is happening in front of you. I was ten years old and I didn't sleep for three days afterwards. Having come from a background like this, I found the electric light, the microphone, and the electric guitar all equally strange. Either they made you afraid or you were afraid of them."[8]

Zé also shares with Italian author Italo Calvino a 'pataphysical sense of glee in deconstructing language, sometimes down to the syllabic level. A thesis on linguistics provides the basis for the opening cut of *The Hips Of Tradition*, "Ogodô Ano 2000" ["Ogodô Year 2000"], a song built up from percussive dada syllables. The funky *baião* "Fliperama," from the same album, has a cumulative nonsense rhyme as a refrain, and the memorable lyric *With the lollipop of science/I beseech*. William Faulkner, Arthur C. Clarke, and Cervantes are merely a few of the other eclectic sources of inspiration listed by Zé for the songs on this album: a children's stage play gave birth to "Sem a Letra 'A'" ["Without The Letter 'A'"], Thomas Edison's "notorious ability to sell his ideas" inspired the quick, cheeky "Jingle do Disco," his work at an ad agency was behind "O Pao Nosse de Cada Mês" ["Our Monthly Bread"], while the tender "Amar" was inspired by Dido's love for Aeneas in Vergil's *Aeneid*.

Whether he's driving the corruscating samba "Tatuaramba" [which "exposes the hips of tradition to the burning irons of ads"] or floating through "Taí," a spirited *baiao-marcha de carnival* once sung by Carmen Miranda, the songs on *The Hips Of Tradition* have a rough-hewn feel evoking the experimental albums Zé recorded in the 1970s. *Estudando o Samba, Correio de Estaçao do Brás*,[9] and *Nave Maria*[10] were spiced with avant garde structures, tart, metallic horns, taut guitars, splintered TV fragments, windup percussion, beat poetry, and bossa nova desyncopated to the point of collapse. It was during these dark days without a record contract that Zé remembered his *musique concrète* studies in school and built his own instruments from household appliances. His biggest project was a wall-mounted console that cannibalized elements of a floor polisher, blenders, vacuum cleaners, toasters, and other appliances that Zé played by pressing a keyboard made out of doorbells.

"It all started with the buffer for waxing floors," Zé recalls. "I had one that wasn't working very well. Every time I plugged it in and pressed the button it went *urrrggghhk*." He laughs mirthfully. "I did this a couple of times, and I thought its knocks and pings had a certain tone. I called some sound engineer friends of mine, and said 'Come over, I have something crazy here.' When I looked at the guys, they were emotional. I realized I was making music from sound. The vacuum, the horns, the toaster, they were the link between the technology and the heart. Sadly they do not exist anymore. I still dream to own them again one day."

Zé is tired. This tour is his longest yet outside Brazil, he's fighting the boredom of the road, and wants to go back home. Yet he's quixotically happy about his newfound cult status in North America. "In life, God sometimes gives one opportunity in music for some people. But I have two. It's a privilege, but sometimes it's really heavy. It's a burden to do twice what everybody does once. But since people from Bahia and Brazilians in general are really religious, I feel it is my duty to do my two chances, so I have to make the best of it."

Tom Zé: Tom Zé (self-released, 1968), Tom Zé (RGE, 1970), Tom Zé (Continental Discos, 1972), Todos os Olhos (Continental Discos, 1973), Estudando o Samba (Continental Discos, 1975), Correio da Estaçao do Brás (Continental Discos, 1978), Nave Maria (RGE Discos, 1979), Brazil Classics 4: The Best of Tom Zé (Luaka Bop/Sire, 1990), Brazil Classics 5: The Hips Of Tradition (Luaka Bop/Sire, 1993)

Footnotes:

1. Faber & Faber: London, 1954: p.161ff, 2. "All The Eyes," Continental Discos, 1973
3. "Studying The Samba," Continental Discos, 1975
4. liner notes to The Best Of Tom Zé, Luaka Bop/Sire, 1990 5. ibid.
6. Luaka Bop/Sire press release, 1992, 7. Luaka Bop/Sire, 1993
8. Luaka Bop/Sire advertisement for The Hips Of Tradition, 1993
9. "The Mailman of Brazil," Continental Discos, 1978
10. "Hail Mary," RGE Discos, 1979

Other music titles published by SAF Publishing.

Wrong Movements - A ROBERT WYATT History by Mike King
160 pages – paperback - Over 80 photographs - ISBN 0946719 101
Price: £14.95
A meticulous biography of a highly respected and individual musician. Packed with previously unpublished archive material and rare photographs.
"King's careful chronology and Wyatt's supreme modesty produce a marvellously unhysterical, oddly haunting book." **** Q Magazine
"Low key, likeable and lefty - like the man himself." i-D

Meet THE RESIDENTS - America's Most Eccentric Band! by Ian Shirley
200 pages – paperback – 8 page photo section – ISBN 0946719 128
Price: £11.95
Meet The Residents is a fascinating tale of the musical anarchy and cartoon wackiness that has driven this unque bunch of artistic mavericks forward.
"Few enthusiasts will want to put this book down." Record Collector
"This is the nearest to an official history you're ever likely to get, slyly abetted by the bug-eyed beans from Venus themselves." Vox

KRAFTWERK - Man, Machine and Music by Pascal Bussy
200 pages – paperback – 8 page photo section – ISBN 0946719 098
Price: £11.95
Rock writer Pascal Bussy has written a uniquely definitive account of Kraftwerk's history, delving beyond their publicity shunning exterior.
"Bussy engagingly explains why they're one of the few groups who've actually changed how music sounds." **** Q Magazine
"Bussy's crisp business-like biography purrs along like one of the top-of-the-range Mercs that Hütter and Schneider used to collect." NME

CABARET VOLTAIRE: The Art of the Sixth Sense by Mick Fish & Dave Hallbery
224 pages – paperback - Over 50 photographs - ISBN 0946719 039
Price: £6.95
Now into its second and updated edition, this definitive book is a critical appraisal of the career of an innovative and influential group.
"The book covers everything from video and voodoo to Dada and Doublevision .... an essential and lively read." Sounds
"A fabulous book which really lifts itself above the mire that is the tacky pop music book world. Essential reading." Zipcode Magazine

The CAN Book by Pascal Bussy & Andy Hall
192 pages - paperback - Over 80 photographs - ISBN 0946719 055
Price: £8.95
A complete history Including biographies of all the group members, a chronology & discography, as well as up-to-date commentary from the group.
"If Can's music is a mystery, this book will make you want to investigate." Q
"A book trying to make sense of their myths and weird psyches has never been more welcome." Sounds

TAPE DELAY by Charles Neal
256 pages - paperback - Over 60 photographs - ISBN 0946719 020
Price £11.95
Interviews and exclusive writing featuring: Marc Almond, Cabaret Voltaire,
Nick Cave, Chris & Cosey, Coil, Einstürzende Neubauten, The Fall, Foetus,
Diamanda Galas, The Hafler Trio, Matt Johnson, Laibach, Lydia Lunch, New
Order, Psychic TV, Boyd Rice, Henry Rollins, Sonic Youth, Swans, Test Dept.
*"A virtual Who's Who of people who've done the most in the past decade to
drag music out of commercial confinement."* NME
*By far the most ambitious attempt so far to link together the large number of
noise-orientated bands to have emerged from the indie ghetto."* Sounds

Dark Entries - BAUHAUS and Beyond by Ian Shirley
200 pages – paperback – 8 page photo section – ISBN 0946719 136
Price: £11.95
With candid commentary from the key protagonists, Ian Shirley unravels the
uncompromising story of Bauhaus, Love and Rockets and Peter Murphy.

WIRE... Everybody Loves A History by Kevin Eden
192 pages – paperback – Over 70 photographs - ISBN 0946719 071
Price: £9.95.
Including interviews and commentary about Wire's history & solo projects, this
book successfully unravels the complexities of this multi-faceted group.
*"Eden delivers a sharp portrayal of the punk industry's behaviour, influence
and morality."* **** Q Magazine
"Any band or their fans could feel well served by a book like Eden's." Vox

Ordering/ Mail Order
All titles are available from most good bookshops, or order from your local
bookshop quoting the ISBN number, author, title and publisher.
To order direct by mail order contact SAF at the address/tel/fax below.
Payment can be made by cheque or Access/Visa/Mastercard. All cheques
must be in pounds sterling and drawn on a British Bank.

Distribution:
UK & Europe: Airlift Book Co, 26-28 Eden Grove, London. N7 8EF
Tel: 0171-607 5792 Fax: 0171-607 6714
USA: Last Gasp, 777 Florida Street, San Francisco, CA 94110. USA.
Tel: 415 824 6636 Fax: 415 824 1836
Canada: Marginal Distribution, Unit 103, 277 George Street North,
Peterborough, Ontario, Canada K9J 3G9. Tel/Fax: 705 745 2326

Titles also available through: Virgin Megastores, Tower Records, See Hear
(USA), Wayside Music (USA), These Records (UK), Touch (UK), A&R
Booksearch (UK), Il Megatalogo (Italy), Sordide Sentimental (France).

SAF Publishing Ltd, 12 Conway Gardens, Wembley, Middx. HA9 8TR. UK.   TEL/FAX: 0181 904 6263

RECORD LABELS
ADN: Via Decembrio 26, 20137 Milano, Italia
Ambiances Mangétiques: C.P. 263 Succ. E, Montréal, Québec H2T 3A7, Canada
Avant: 2-13-1 Iidabashi, Chiyoda-ku, Tokyo 102, Japan
AYAA: B.P. 167; 51056 Reims Cédex, France
BVHaast: Prinseneiland 99, 1013LN Amsterdam, The Netherlands
Crammed/Made To Measure: 43, Rue Général Patton, 1050 Brussels, Belgium
Cuneiform: P.O. Box 8427, Silver Spring, Maryland 20907-8427, USA
ECM: Postfach 600 331, 81023 Munich, Germany
Empreintes DIGITALes: 4487 Adam, Montréal, Québec H1V 1T9, Canada
Eva/Wave: 6-2-27 Roppongi, Minato-ku, Tokyo 106, Japan
FMP: Postfach 100 227, 1000 Berlin 10, Germany
FOT: P.O. Box 505, Bloomingdale, Illinois 60108, USA
Hat Art: P.O. Box 641, 4106 Therwil, Switzerland
Intakt: P.O. Box 468, CH8024 Zürich, Switzerland
Japan Overseas: 6-1-21 Ueshio, Tennoji-Ku, Osaka 543, Japan
Knitting Factory Works: 47 East Houston, New York, New York 10012, USA
Leo: The Cottage, 6 Anerly Hill, London SE19 2AA, UK
Mystery Tape Laboratory: Box 727 Station P, Toronto, Ontario M5S 2Z1, Canada
New Albion: 584 Castro #515, San Francisco, California 94114, USA
Ralph America/Negativmailorderland: 109 Minna St #391, San Francisco, California 94105 USA
RecRec Genossenschaft: P.O. Box 717, 8026 Zürich, Switzerland
Recommended/no man's land: Postfach 11 04 49-8700 Würzburg, Germany
ReR Megacorp: 74 Tulse Hill, London SW2 2PT, England
Shifty: P.O. Box 27513, Bertsham 2013, Transvaal, South Africa
Sub Rosa: P.O. Box 808, CM 1000 Brussels, Belgium
Table Of The Elements: P.O. Box 5524, Atlanta, Georgia 30307, USA
Tellus: 596 Broadway #602, New York, New York 10012, USA
Victo: C.P. 460, Victoriaville, Québec G6P 6T3, Canada
Zona Archives: C.P. 1486, Firenze, Italia
FESTIVALS
Company Week: c/o Incus, 14 Downs Road, London E5 8DS, England
Festival Internationale Musique Actuelle de Victoriaville [FIMAV]: c/o Les Productions Plateforme, C.P. 460, Victoriaville, Québec G6P 6T3, Canada
Mouvement International des Musiques Innovatrices [MIMI]: c/o AMI, 41 Rue Jobin, 13003 Marseille, France
Moers Festival: Postfach 30 01 20, 4130 Moers 3, Germany
Total Music Meeting [Free Music Production]: Lübeckerstrasse 19, D1000 Berlin 21, Germany
PUBLICATIONS AND ORGANIZATIONS
Circuit: C.P. 444, Outremont, Québec H2V 4R6, Canada
Cadence Magazine: Cadence Building, Redwood, New York 13679, USA
Coda: P.O. Box 87 Station J, Toronto, Ontario M4J 4X8
Forced Exposure: P.O. Box 9102, Waltham, Massachussetts 02254 USA
Musiche: Piazza Brin 13, 19122 La Spezia, Italia
Musicworks: 1087 Queen Street West, Toronto, Ontario M6J 1H3, Canada
Option: 1522-B Cloverfield Blvd., Santa Monica, California 90404, USA
ReR Records Quarterly: 74 Tulse Hill, London SW2 2PT, England
The Wire: 45-46 Poland Street, London W1V 3DF, England
Canadian Electroacoustic Community [CEC]: C.P. 845, Succ. Place des Armes, Montréal, Québec H2Y 3J2, Canada
Copyright Violation Squad: P.O. Box 227, Iowa City, Iowa 52244, USA